Vienna and the Fall of

Maureen Healy examines the collapse of the Habsburg Empire from the perspective of everyday life in the capital city. She argues that a striking feature of "total war" on the home front was the spread of a war mentality to the mundane sites of everyday life – streets, shops, schools, entertainment venues and apartment buildings. While Habsburg armies waged military campaigns on distant fronts, Viennese civilians (women, children, and "left-at-home" men) waged a protracted, socially devastating war against one another. Vienna's multi-ethnic population lived together in conditions of severe material shortage and faced near starvation by 1917. The city fell into civilian mutiny before the state collapsed in 1918. Based on meticulous archival research, including citizens' letters to state authorities, the study offers a new and penetrating look at Habsburg citizenship by showing how ordinary women, men and children conceived of "Austria" in the Empire's final years.

MAUREEN HEALY is Assistant Professor in the Department of History, Oregon State University. She was the winner of the Fraenkel Prize from the Wiener Library and Institute of Contemporary History, London, 2000.

Studies in the Social and Cultural History of Modern Warfare

General Editor
Jay Winter *Yale University*

Advisory Editors
Omer Bartov *Brown University*
Carol Gluck *Columbia University*
David M. Kennedy *Stanford University*
Paul Kennedy *Yale University*
Antoine Prost *Université de Paris-Sorbonne*
Emmanuel Sivan *Hebrew University of Jerusalem*
Robert Wohl *University of California, Los Angeles*

In recent years the field of modern history has been enriched by the exploration of two parallel histories. These are the social and cultural history of armed conflict, and the impact of military events on social and cultural history.

Studies in the Social and Cultural History of Modern Warfare presents the fruits of this growing area of research, reflecting both the colonization of military history by cultural historians and the reciprocal interest of military historians in social and cultural history, to the benefit of both. The series offers the latest scholarship in European and non-European events from the 1850s to the present day.

For a list of titles in the series, please see end of book.

Vienna and the Fall of the Habsburg Empire

Total War and Everyday Life in World War I

Maureen Healy

Oregon State University

CAMBRIDGE UNIVERSITY PRESS
Cambridge, New York, Melbourne, Madrid, Cape Town, Singapore, São Paulo

Cambridge University Press
The Edinburgh Building, Cambridge CB2 8RU, UK

Published in the United States of America by Cambridge University Press, New York

www.cambridge.org
Information on this title: www.cambridge.org/9780521831246

First published 2004
Reprinted 2006
This digitally printed version 2007

A catalogue record for this publication is available from the British Library

Library of Congress Cataloguing in Publication data

Healy, Maureen.
Vienna and the fall of the Habsburg Empire : total war and everyday life in
World War I / Maureen Healy.
   p.   cm. – (Studies in the social and cultural history of modern warfare ; 17)
Includes bibliographical references and index.
ISBN 0-521-83124-5
1. World War, 1914–1918 – Austria – Vienna.   2. World War, 1914–1918 –
Social aspects – Austria – Vienna.   3. World War, 1914–1918 – Psychological
aspects.   4. War and society – Austria – Vienna.   5. Vienna (Austria) – Social
conditions – 20th century.   6. Vienna (Austria) – Politics and government –
20th century.   I. Title.   II. Series.
D539.7.A9H43   2004
943.6′130442–dc22   2003063548

ISBN 978-0-521-83124-6 hardback
ISBN 978-0-521-04219-2 paperback

For my parents, Ingrid and Jack Lynch.

Contents

Plates

Maps, figures and tables

Acknowledgments

If texts are produced in context, then the context for this book is the history department at the University of Chicago, whose people (and purse) shaped it from its inception. I wish to thank my advisers at Chicago, John Boyer and Michael Geyer, who trained me to think of Central Europe in broad terms. They gave me confidence to ask big questions, and taught me to conduct careful research to find the answers. Sheila Fitzpatrick read the dissertation from which this book grew and offered helpful comments on chapter drafts along the way. Alf Lüdtke taught a seminar on the history of everyday life that first interested me, and many in my graduate cohort, in this approach to the study of history. I was lucky to have these teachers whom I admire so much as historians, and I hope there are glimmers of them in the pages that follow. I am equally grateful for all I learned from my fellow students. This book will argue that communities are fleeting, and this is certainly true of academic communities. Although we are now scattered around the country, I would like to thank collectively the members of the University of Chicago's modern European history workshop, from whom I learned the genuine pleasures of collegial scholarship.

I received financial and research support from a number of institutions. First and foremost, I would like to thank the Dolores Zohrab Liebmann Fellowship for three years of generous research and writing support. The Austrian Fulbright Commission, the Woodrow Wilson International Center for Scholars, the Andrew J. Mellon Foundation, the Council for the Advanced Study of Peace and International Cooperation, a Bernadotte E. Schmitt Grant from the American Historical Association, and the University of Chicago also provided funding, for which I am grateful. A fellowship at the Center for the Humanities at Oregon State University afforded me the space and time to revise the work. The staffs at various institutions in Vienna assisted me in my research. I wish to thank the archivists and librarians at the Österreichisches Staatsarchiv, the Niederösterreichisches Landesarchiv, the Österreichische Nationalbibliothek and the Wiener Stadt- und

Landesbibliothek. Special thanks to Frau Rosa Hock at the Archiv der Bundespolizei-Direktion Wien.

In Vienna, a number of people offered their support and friendship to me. I would especially like to thank Margarete Grandner at the University of Vienna, who, over the course of several years, answered my inquiries, read chapters, corrected my German, and shared her deep knowledge of Vienna with me. Christa Hämmerle, also at the University of Vienna, inspired me with her own work on war and gender and offered valuable suggestions on sources. Lothar Höbelt generously offered advice on how to navigate the archives and put me in touch with archivists. Eve Dvorak and Maureen Stewart made my long days at the archives amusing, and my nights in Vienna most memorable.

During the gestation of this book, which has lasted longer than World War I itself, many people read chapters or sections of my work, and offered useful comments and criticisms. Carolyn Comiskey, Belinda Davis, Andy Donson, Jean Bethke Elshtain, Jeremy King, Tom Kohut, Alf Lüdtke, Eva Perl, Dan Unowsky and Jay Winter read portions of the work along the way and I would like to thank them heartily for the assistance they gave me. My colleagues at Oregon State University have been most generous, and I thank especially Robert Nye, William Husband and Sarah Henderson for their comments on sections of this book, and Paul Farber for all manner of support over the last three years. Thanks to Mary Vaughn for help with the index. At Cambridge University Press, I would like to thank editors Elizabeth Howard and Helen Barton, series editor Jay Winter, copy editor David Watson, and the mysterious "Reader A" and "Reader B" for their excellent suggestions on the manuscript.

At last, my most personal thanks. The ideas and intellectual spirit of Lisa Moses Leff are wound into this work in ways that cannot be cited in the traditional footnote. She has taught me that friendship and history are interrelated; each is enhanced by the other. I am also most grateful to Jill Johnson for her childcare work during the time I was revising this book. My deepest thanks go to Will Pritchard, who has read this work so many times that he can recite entire passages verbatim, and can smell a recycled sentence a mile away. Finally, I dedicate this book to my parents Ingrid and Jack Lynch, who instilled in me a curiosity about distant places and gave me the education that enables me to study them.

Abbreviations

ABGB	Allgemeines bürgerliches Gesetzbuch
AdBDW	Archiv der Bundespolizei-Direktion Wien
AdR	Archiv der Republik
AHR	*American Historical Review*
AOK	Armeeoberkommando
AVA	Allgemeines Verwaltungsarchiv
GZNB	Gemeinsames Zentralnachweisbüro
HHStA	Haus-, Hof-, und Staatsarchiv
JMH	*Journal of Modern History*
KA	Kriegsarchiv
KM	Kriegsministerium
KÜA	Kriegsüberwachungsamt
MdI	Ministerium des Innern
MfKuU	Ministerium für Kultus und Unterricht
Min [u. St.A.] f. soz. Verwaltung	Ministerium [und Staatsamt] für soziale Verwaltung und Volksgesundheit
MK/KM	Ministerialkommission im Kriegsministerium
MKSM	Militärkanzlei Seiner Majestät
Nö	Niederösterreich
NÖLA	Niederösterreichisches Landesarchiv
ÖStA	Österreichisches Staatsarchiv
Pol. Dir.	Polizei-Direktion
Präs.	Präsidialakten
RGBl.	Reichsgesetzblatt
WSLA	Wiener Stadt- und Landesarchiv
WSLB	Wiener Stadt- und Landesbibliothek
ZAS	Zeitungsausschnitt-Sammlung

Introduction

For hundreds of years, residents of Vienna's inner city lived behind stone fortifications meant to keep them safe in times of war. During numerous battles against hostile invaders, the barrier around inner Vienna had repelled enemies, most famously the Ottoman Turks. In later times, military planners conceived of the fortifications as protection for the Habsburg court, state institutions and upper society against the potentially insurgent lower-class rabble in the outlying areas. In both cases, according to the logic of the walled city, the threat to Vienna was perceived as *external*. In the middle of the nineteenth century, the Viennese did away with their walls: the land where they stood was developed as a grand, circular boulevard, the Ringstrasse, and districts beyond the buffer were incorporated into the city. By the early twentieth century, the city had expanded so rapidly, both in population growth and territorial annexation, that remnants of the old city walls appeared quaint reminders of antiquated modes of warfare.[1] But dreams of walling-off Vienna would resurface during the war that finally brought down the Habsburgs and ended Vienna's reign as an imperial capital. In World War I, military leaders again fantasized about a buffer zone, but this time one designed to protect their troops outside the city from the civilian war *within*.[2] Censors worried that news of the home-front reality would "infect" soldiers with poor morale. Letters from the home front that mentioned food shortage and hunger were confiscated, so as not to "endanger the discipline of front troops and negatively affect their spirits."[3] Despair and defeatism, borne of scarcity and fueled by pre-existing ethnic tensions, had turned Vienna into a collection of mini-fronts, staged daily by women, children

---

[1] With immigration and territorial expansion, the population of Vienna grew from approximately 550,000 in 1850 to 2,100,000 in 1910.

[2] For changing perceptions of cities and war in the European cultural imagination, see Bernd Hüppauf, "Die Stadt als imaginierter Kriegsschauplatz," in *Zeitschrift für Germanistik* 5, no. 2 (1995): 317–35.

[3] AdBDW Stimmungsberichte, January–April 1917 (misfiled). Letter from Marie Krbuschek in Vienna, to brother Anton Wolf; and censor's memo, 27 March 1918.

and left-at-home men (*Daheimgebliebenen*). In this war, the "enemy" was not Russia, France or Britain, but one's neighbors and colleagues.

Before the events of 1914–18 became known collectively as World War I, before the phrase the "Great War" had been coined, and before this civilian war in Vienna had begun to alarm state officials, contemporaries had referred to the conflict as the "War of 1914/15." During this first year of war, residents of Vienna had performed symbolic acts meant to "fortify" themselves and their troops in the absence of more concrete fortification such as a wall. By the hundreds of thousands, they pounded nails into a knightly, wooden figure called the *Wehrmann im Eisen*, the "soldier in iron," which sat in the Schwarzenbergplatz off the Ringstrasse. The *Wehrmann* was a site of ritual, participatory fortification: for a small donation, which benefited war widows and orphans, residents purchased nails and pounded them into the vulnerable figure, thereby covering him in iron, enveloping him in the strength of the Austrian *Volkskraft*. Berta Weiskirchner, wife of Vienna's mayor, offered to a crowd in March, 1915, one explanation of the ritual:

> In these seven months of war we have already dried so many tears that if we could transform them all into pearls and create from them a robe, this *Wehrmann* would have the most beautiful, precious robe ever known to man. I bid you, then, hammer this knight with nails![4]

Whether he was dressed in iron or pearls, the *Wehrmann* was symbolic of civilians' participation – and sacrifice – in the War of 1914/15.[5] But as the war dragged on into 1916, 1917 and 1918, and civilians began to perceive their sacrifices not as generous gifts but as bitter injustice, the *Wehrmann* was abandoned. "The number of visitors grew smaller and smaller as the war stretched on, until finally nobody looked after him at all," reported one newspaper. Another noted shortly after the war that golden nails donated to the *Wehrmann* early on by Austria's allies had been stolen. "The last visitor was, then, a thief."[6]

Both the inverted image of a wall that protects troops from civilians and a symbol of sacrifice that is itself sacrificed tell us something significant

---

[4] WSLB ZAS Hilfsaktionen, *Fremdenblatt*, 16 March 1915.
[5] The *Wehrmann* project was modeled on the *Stock im Eisen*, a wooden trunk near the Stephansplatz into which early modern journeymen passing through Vienna had pounded nails. The *Wehrmann* as fundraiser inspired many copy-cat nailing projects around Central Europe during World War I. For the symbolism of the *Wehrmann* during and after the war, see Irene Nierhaus, "Die nationalisierte Heimat: Wehrmann und städtische Öffentlichkeit," in Gisela Ecker (ed.), *Kein Land in Sicht: Heimat–weiblich?* (Munich: Wilhelm Fink Verlag, 1997), 57–79.
[6] WSLB ZAS Hilfsaktionen, *Reichspost*, 1 March 1919; *Neue Freie Presse*, 28 February 1919.

about the Viennese experience of total war. World War I is often described as Europe's first total war for two reasons. The erosion of boundaries during World War I between the realms of war and "not war," of distinct places where soldiers fight and where civilians maintain social norms so that society can eventually return to peace, is one hallmark of conflicts in the twentieth century.[7] This expansion and simultaneous blurring of the parameters of war is evident in the case of the imagined buffer around Vienna: we see an ambiguity about who needed to be protected from whom in wartime, and a confusion over who or what constituted the enemy. A second feature of total war is the mobilization of vast resources and civilian populations; all members of society, regardless of age or gender, are engaged in war-making in some capacity. In the case of the *Wehrmann*, whose patrons included schoolchildren, housewives and the elderly, we see that groups not traditionally counted as "warriors" were nonetheless engaged in an aspect of war-making and came to play key roles in the discourse of sacrifice.

A third feature of total war, not much noticed by historians but striking in the case of Vienna, is what could be called the refraction of the everyday. Refraction, the distorting of an image by viewing it through a medium, worked in the following way: everyday matters previously considered private or sub-political were refracted through the medium, or lens, of war and, like a ray of light, came out "bent" on the other side. The power of this particular lens was that nearly everything passed through it: food, fashion, shopping, child-rearing, leisure and neighbor relations were just some of the everyday matters reinterpreted through war. Total war, then, became a war in which no action or deed was too small or insignificant to be considered a matter of state.

As a case study of total war, this work interprets the social disintegration of the Habsburg Empire from the perspective of everyday life in the capital city. It reflects my view that the city fell before the state collapsed in a military and diplomatic sense in the autumn of 1918. This "falling" was not a single event, but a process of decline characterized by hunger, violence and a deterioration of social norms that left Vienna nearly ungovernable. At the outset of war, contemporaries had applied the military term "mobilization" – the calling-up and putting into service of troops and machinery – to civilians, who, like soldiers, would be called

---

[7] See Arthur Marwick (ed.), *Total War and Social Change* (New York: St. Martin's Press, 1988); also John Horne, "Introduction: Mobilizing for 'Total War', 1914–1918," in Horne (ed.), *State, Society and Mobilization in Europe During the First World War* (Cambridge: Cambridge University Press, 1997), 1–17, for historical development of the term "total war."

to work in unison for the good of the state. But the term was not really apt; there were no mechanisms by which to call up "society," no institutions (such as the military) to impose order and discipline on the process, no established, hierarchical means of resolving conflicts that arose when an ethnically, religiously, and socio-economically heterogeneous population was asked to cooperate in a cause larger than itself. The outcome of the so-called mobilization of Vienna was communal disintegration. Personal tensions partially dormant in peacetime sprang to life under the material stress of war. War offered a rich vocabulary for understanding the hatred, jealousy, contempt or suspicion one felt for others, but had never put into words: he or she was a traitor, an enemy. Plots, intrigues and conspiracy theories were hatched over questions of "privilege" and access to basic foodstuffs. Contrary to expectations that this society would or could be mobilized, the experience of war in Vienna was not a coming together, but a falling apart.

Geography of the home front

That residents were able to imagine so many enemies in their midst was due in part to Vienna's diverse population. The largest urban center in Habsburg Central Europe, the city was predominantly German-speaking but drew immigrants from around the Habsburg domains. Before the war, German-speakers had reacted to population growth by attempting to preserve legally the "German character" of Vienna.[8] The 1910 census revealed that Vienna's population of just over two million resembled a Central European mosaic. Only 56 percent of residents had legal domicile (*Heimatberechtigung*) – a category that often indicated where a person was born or had "come from" – in Vienna. The other 44 percent of residents had legal domicile in places other than Vienna, most frequently Lower and Upper Austria, Bohemia, Moravia, Hungary, Galicia, Silesia and the German Empire.[9] These figures suggest that Vienna was a city of recent arrivals, people whose families had not been in the city long and who may or may not have intended to settle there permanently. Added to this mix came a host of wartime refugees and transient military personnel of various nationalities. In the fall of 1914, 50–70,000 Polish- and Yiddish-speaking refugees arrived from the Galician front, and refugees

[8] Gerald Stourzh, *Die Gleichberechtigung der Nationalitäten in der Verfassung und Verwaltung Österreichs, 1848–1918* (Vienna: Verlag der österreichischen Akademie der Wissenschaften, 1985), 113.
[9] "Ergebnisse der Volkszählung vom 31. Dezember 1910," in *Statistisches Jahrbuch der Stadt Wien* (Vienna: Verlag des Wiener Magistrates, 1912), 890, 900–902.

evacuated from areas behind the Italian front followed the next year.[10] Some residents imagined themselves besieged by Jews, Czechs, Hungarians and Poles, who conspired to keep bread, milk, meat and potatoes from their "rightful" German recipients. The vocabulary of their neighborhood arguments and street skirmishes was a war vocabulary.

The incivility and low-level violence that thread through the following chapters bring into focus the multivalent meanings of the term "home front." Three terms circulating in wartime Vienna – *Heimat*, *Hinterland* and *Hinterlandsfront* – bear relation to the English term home front.[11] The first, *Heimat*, meant home, but it also connoted a geographic space different from the space of war. Those who lived in Vienna lived "at home" (*in der Heimat*), and soldiers arriving in the city from battle referred to it as the *Heimat*, even if they were not from Vienna. *Hinterland* was a technical military designation for territory behind the front lines and behind the army staging area, but, like *Heimat*, also connoted more generally the civilian, non-combatant realm. As Christoph Führ's map of the Habsburg war geography shows, Vienna was officially part of the Hinterland (see map 1).

The terms *Hinterländer* or *Hinterlandsheld* (hero of the hinterland) were derogatory names for men who did not leave "home," and point to the gendered division of war into masculine and feminine realms. Popular split-images depicted a neatly gendered war with men on one side and women on the other (see plate 1).

Finally, *Hinterlandsfront* equated the war-making activities of civilians with those of soldiers: the work of civilians constituted a front (albeit a secondary one) that supported or complemented *the* front. Common to all of these terms was an assumption that the violence of war was located someplace other than "home." Susan Grayzel writes of Britain and France, "While the First World War created the concept of 'home front,' it never stabilized the boundaries separating war from home."[12] This was true of Vienna, where violence was part of the fabric of life "at home," and

---

[10] The number of war refugees fluctuated as territory in Galicia and Bukowina was captured, lost and recaptured. On refugees in Vienna, see Beatrix Hoffmann-Holter, *'Abreisendmachung.' Jüdische Kriegsflüchtlinge in Wien, 1914–1923* (Vienna: Böhlau, 1995); and David Rechter, "Galicia in Vienna: Jewish Refugees in the First World War," *Austrian History Yearbook* 28 (1997), 113–30.

[11] Richard G. Plaschka, Horst Haselsteiner and Arnold Suppan's brilliant study of military disintegration in the hinterland uses the term "inner front" to describe battles the military waged against its own forces. *Innere Front: Militärassistenz, Widerstand und Umsturz in der Donaumonarchie 1918*, 2 vols. (Munich: R. Oldenburg, 1974).

[12] Susan R. Grayzel, *Women's Identities at War: Gender, Motherhood, and Politics in Britain and France during the First World War* (Chapel Hill: University of North Carolina Press, 1999), 7.

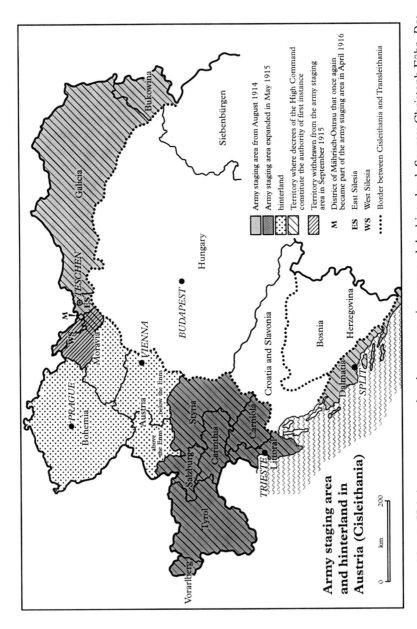

**Army staging area
and hinterland in
Austria (Cisleithania)**

Map 1. Habsburg war geography: the army staging area and the hinterland. Source: Christoph Führ, *Das k.u.k. Armeeoberkommando und die Innenpolitik in Österreich, 1914–1917* (Graz: Böhlau, 1968), 23.

Legend:

- Army staging area from August 1914
- Army staging area expanded in May 1915
- hinterland
- Territory where decrees of the High Command constitute the authority of first instance
- Territory withdrawn from the army staging area in September 1915
- **M** District of Mährisch-Ostrau that once again became part of the army staging area in April 1916
- **ES** East Silesia
- **WS** West Silesia
- ······ Border between Cisleithania and Transleithania

Plate 1. "Front" and "home" – the ideal gender division. Source: Postcard in author's possession.

neighborhood animosities were explained in war terms: battles (*Kämpfe*) over scarce resources were waged against "enemies" and "traitors."

Although Vienna was geographically distant from the three Habsburg battle fronts, residents did not feel physically or psychologically secure. The line between front and home did not exist in reality, but people imagined its existence and feared its permeability. The city was not physically attacked, as it was during the Second World War, but Viennese nonetheless felt vulnerable to invaders: fellow Austrians carrying diseases. Diseases, associated with "the east," and carried on the bodies of returning soldiers and Galician refugees, threatened the local (*einheimische*) population. Even before large transports of refugees arrived in the fall of 1914, disease and east had become linked in the popular imagination and in the minds of city doctors. In August, a police doctor warned that transports from Galicia posed "an imminent danger of infection for Vienna as well as for the regions [the refugees will travel to] after they leave Vienna." Subsequent memos warned that "all of Vienna" would be infected unless the transports of "political unreliables" from Galicia and Bukowina were routed elsewhere.[13] Fears about external contagions were not unwarranted, but the language in which they were expressed created or reinforced divisions among Vienna's constantly fluctuating population. On November 30, 1914, the leading city physician reported 366 cases of cholera in the city. Of these, 349 were military personnel and only seventeen were civilian, most of them *ortsfremd* rather than *einheimisch*. Over the next two years, bi-weekly municipal reports on contagious diseases distinguished between "refugees" and "the population."[14] This official bias also found expression in everyday interactions among the population. Police reported "altercations" among shoppers at markets because "these refugees...touch the merchandise, put it back, haggle over the price and then don't buy it in the end." Residents of Vienna's II. District, where many of the refugees were housed, spoke of a Galician "invasion" of their neighborhood.[15]

As people interpreted social relationships through the prism of war, they were simultaneously defining their political relation to Austria. The state came to serve as a convenient benchmark for measuring one's own heroism, sacrifice or unjust victimization against the perfidy of others. Of course, Herr Prochaska was hoarding milk; he was a *bad Austrian*.

[13] NÖLA Präs. "P" 1914 9/77. Report from Polizei-Oberbezirksarzt, 23 August 1914; 384 1155/366 Pol. Dir. to Statthaltereipräs., 4 November 1914.
[14] WSLA B23/73. Protokoll Obmänner-Konferenz, 1 December 1914; B23/74, 28 December 1916.
[15] AdBDW Stimmungsberichte, 11 November 1914; 1 October 1914.

Of course, the market stall of Frau Steiner had to be destroyed; *hungry patriots* had a duty to punish *traitors*. We find frequent reference to a concept crucial to discussion of citizenship or national belonging in Central Europe: *Gesinnung*, which referred to one's disposition, attitude or political proclivities. Assessing another's *Gesinnung* towards Austria in its time of need was a subjective, and nearly always self-referential exercise in which the righteous assessor interpreted social discord in state terms.

The study focuses on everyday sites of politics where civilians and state officials fought over resources, responsibility and the power to define the meanings of the war. These everyday sites (shops, street corners, schools, pubs, apartment buildings) were more important than traditional political bodies (parliament, political parties, organized interest groups) for determining the course of the war in Vienna, in part because the latter were shut down or restricted, creating a political vacuum. The Vienna city council did not meet until 1916, and then met only occasionally, the Austrian parliament had been dissolved in the spring of 1914 and did not convene until May, 1917, and political parties and their publications were heavily censored. John W. Boyer describes a privatization of traditional politics in wartime, whereby "small groups of conspirators" worked behind the scenes marshaling prewar contacts.[16] During the war, politics slipped temporarily out of the hands of politicians and into the hands of previously "unpolitical" women and children. With greater urgency than male party leaders, and with more room to maneuver in unorthodox political venues, women and children strongly influenced public discourse in wartime Vienna and constituted its newest, fiercest political actors.

With the layer of traditional politics peeled away, the state intervened, through wartime decree, in the everyday lives of Viennese residents in unprecedented ways.[17] Prime Minster Karl Stürgkh, pleased to be governing without the interference of parliament, announced his government's intention at the outset of war to "orient all energies of the state towards the secure, speedy and complete fulfillment of war aims."[18] Civilians were considered "energies of the state," and consequently, authorities attempted to regulate where people worked, what they produced, their

---

[16] John W. Boyer, *Culture and Political Crisis in Vienna: Christian Socialism in Power, 1897–1918* (Chicago: University of Chicago Press, 1995), 379.

[17] See Josef Redlich, *Österreichische Regierung und Verwaltung im Weltkriege* (New Haven: Yale University Press, 1925).

[18] Cited in Gustav Spann, "Zensur in Österreich" (Ph.D. diss., University of Vienna, 1972), 39.

modes of transportation, the content of news and entertainment, the heating of homes, the kinds of fabrics used for clothing, the methods of food preparation, and finally, the number of calories consumed per day. People who had not had much occasion to *think* about the state were now working for it, receiving payments from it, being monitored by it, sacrificing for it, praying for it and cursing it. In wartime, many citizens and proto-citizens developed a *consciousness* of the state that had not existed previously. (The term "proto-citizen" is used here to signal that Austrian citizenship was not an absolute status, but a spectrum, on which age and gender determined one's place.) Some blamed the state for its failure to provide enough food and other essential resources for the maintenance of life. Others appealed to it for assistance in battles against fellow residents, expressing a solidarity or alliance with the state (manifested, for example, in the practice of denunciation) that they did not feel within their local communities. Whether citizens and proto-citizens welcomed state intervention, found it menacing, or experienced a mixture of both, they contended with the Habsburg state in their everyday lives far more after 1914 than they had previously.

In turn, governing Vienna in wartime became nearly impossible if we understand governance as the ability to make and enforce laws. For municipal, regional and imperial officials, who had competing and often contradictory agendas, the largest obstacle to effective governance was their inability to provision the city with food. Other resources – coal, wood, leather, cloth, paper, metal and medicines – were also in critical short supply, but none was as basic to survival, or as central to the process of social unraveling, as food. The provisioning crisis resembled a dance in which the rule-making authorities, unable to secure adequate supplies, lagged one step behind the rule-breaking population, which resorted to illegal means to find them. As this dance sped up, and previously law-abiding residents grew increasingly willing to break laws in order to satisfy needs, "governing" became an exercise in wringing hands and issuing empty decrees. A similar pattern of rule-making and rule-breaking characterized relations between state and population in matters such as the spread of news and information, the control of youth delinquency and civilian interactions with enemy prisoners of war. The astounding number of wartime decrees (those from the imperial level fill four volumes alone)[19] carried with it no guarantee of compliance. Law-breaking and law-making stood in a dialectic relation: behavior produced laws that then defined this behavior as in violation of the law.

---

[19] See the compilation of wartime decrees, *Denkschrift über die von der k.k. Regierung aus Anlaß des Krieges getroffenen Maßnahmen*, 4 vols. (Vienna, 1918).

Administrative road map

In the chapters that follow, we shall see Viennese residents interacting with government authorities on a number of levels. The municipal government of Vienna was headed by Mayor Richard Weiskirchner, whose Christian Social party had been in power for nearly two decades. Weiskirchner governed by decree for the first half of the war, issuing over 1,300 directives before the city council reconvened in 1916.[20] The council met only sporadically thereafter. The mayor did consult a group called the *Obmänner-Konferenz*, made up of representatives from the Christian Social, Social Democratic and Liberal German parties. Minutes of the *Obmänner* conferences show that the overwhelming concern of the mayor and other party representatives during the war was providing Vienna with food, heating materials and other basic supplies.

For a Viennese resident, the city government had two faces: its official face was Mayor Weiskirchner and the civil servants working out of the *Rathaus* in the city center. But for everyday matters, the city government was represented by the faces of lower civil servants in the city's twenty-one district offices (*Bezirksämter*). These offices handled immediate inquiries about food, housing, employment and other wartime concerns. By the early twentieth century, the city government employed more than 30,000 people, which made it the second largest employer in Austria after the state itself.[21] The war brought a staffing crisis in the municipal government, with as many as a third of its employees being conscripted into military service.

Like the city government, the police force maintained a central office, the *Polizei-Direktion*, in the city center, and neighborhood offices in each district. The force, employing nearly 6,000 men, ultimately reported not to the municipal government, but to the governor of Lower Austria (the *Statthalter*) and the Austrian Ministry of the Interior. Lower Austria, which included Vienna, was one of several "crownlands" that comprised the Austrian half of the Habsburg state. The Lower Austrian government (sometimes called the "provincial" government) reported to the crown. It had a diet, but this body did not meet during the war. During wartime, this layer of government figured in the lives of Viennese residents in two important ways: it was in charge of the school system, and it mediated food disputes between city dwellers and farmers in the surrounding countryside.

---

[20] Arthur J. May, *The Passing of the Hapsburg Monarchy, 1914–1918*, 2 vols. (Philadelphia: University of Pennsylvania Press, 1966), I, 310.
[21] Boyer, *Culture and Political Crisis in Vienna*, 28.

The next layer of state authority was the Austrian government itself. Austria had a parliament, a prime minister and a ministerial cabinet. The parliament had been suspended prior to the outbreak of the war and did not convene again until 1917. In its absence, the prime minister and his cabinet ruled by decree, using an emergency clause in the Austrian constitution to give their decrees the weight of law. During the war, three state-level ministries figured most prominently in the lives of Viennese residents. The first was the Ministry of the Interior, which handled matters of internal security and cases passed up from local police districts. Second was the War Ministry, which ran both a massive system of subsidies for families of conscripted men, and a hybrid governmental organization called the War Surveillance Office, which censored civilian news, information and mail. Third, the Food Office, a quasi-ministerial state-level office, was created in late 1916 to coordinate food supply, distribution and pricing. Thousands of Viennese residents appealed to this office for help in procuring foodstuffs. Despite its cabinet-level status, however, the Food Office never succeeded in "nationalizing" food procurement; rather, a haphazard collection of cartels (*Zentralen*) run by private interests continued to manage Vienna's food supply throughout the war.

Like the men in city hall, Austria's state government was preoccupied throughout the war with securing provisions. Austria's wartime prime ministers jockeyed with their Hungarian counterparts and the Army High Command for power and access to scarce resources. A fierce competition was waged at the very top echelons of the state, with each of the three powers – the Austrian and Hungarian civilian governments and the military – appealing frequently to the Emperor for support against the others.[22] These tensions "unquestionably impaired the machinery of the state to a disastrous degree."[23] Atop the layers of municipal, provincial and state authority sat the Habsburg Emperor himself. Assisted by imperial advisers, he ruled the fifty-two million subjects of Austria-Hungary as the "father of his peoples," and based his authority on traditional dynastic paternalism. He was the figure of last resort for anyone from a widow seeking assistance with a pension to a prime minister challenging the claims of the Army High Command.

---

[22] For the Army High Command and Austrian domestic policy, see Manfried Rauchensteiner, *Der Tod des Doppeladlers: Österreich-Ungarn und der Erste Weltkrieg* (Graz: Verlag Styria, 1993), 267–74; for politics in Hungary, see József Galántai, *Hungary in the First World War*, translated by Éva Grusz and Judit Pokoly (Budapest: Akadémiai Kiadó, 1989).

[23] May, *The Passing of the Hapsburg Monarchy*, I, 292.

As this brief outline suggests, "the state" in Vienna was a tangle of neighborhood, municipal, provincial, state and imperial institutions. Readers looking for a tidy flow chart of how a particular case might weave its way through these layers of government will look in vain. As we will see in the chapters that follow, coordination among them was anything but smooth; the deep cleavages that developed during wartime made for non-"user-friendly" governance. For residents trying to navigate the state from below, administrative oversight, duplication and competition proved frustrating. A resident initiating contact with the state might choose as an entry point any of the layers described above. The case would then be handled, forwarded or ignored by any number of administrative offices, rarely in a predictable or linear way. The bureaucratic paper trail that comprises the archival backbone of this study suggests that wartime governance was a four-year game of administrative ping-pong. The war "discredit[ed] profoundly the administrative state which before 1914 had been a fundamental source of political order and cultural rules."[24] Sketching a course for future research on late imperial Austria, Gary B. Cohen has suggested that historians ought to give fuller treatment to "popular political cultures and the relationships between citizens and government."[25] This book attempts to answer this call, in part, by examining state–citizen encounters "from below" in Vienna during the final years of Habsburg rule.

Austria in comparative context

Over the last fifteen years, historians of Britain, France and Germany have rewritten the history of World War I from the "bottom up," demonstrating the significance of the war in fields as diverse as class and gender roles, welfare policy, psychiatry and entertainment.[26] A number of recent works explicate how the state became manifest in people's everyday lives in wartime. As Susan Pedersen, Reinhard Sieder, Ute Daniel and Elisabeth Domansky have splendidly demonstrated using different methodologies, family was a key mediating institution between state and

---

[24] Boyer, *Culture and Political Crisis in Vienna*, 369.
[25] Gary B. Cohen, "Neither Absolutism nor Anarchy: New Narratives on Society and Government in Late Imperial Austria," *Austrian History Yearbook* 29 (1998), 37–61, 38.
[26] Recent approaches to the study of war and society are found in three rich volumes: Margaret Randolph Higonnet *et al.* (eds.), *Behind the Lines: Gender and the Two World Wars* (New Haven: Yale University Press, 1987); Richard Wall and Jay Winter (eds.), *The Upheaval of War: Family, Work and Welfare in Europe, 1914–1918* (Cambridge: Cambridge University Press, 1988); and Gerhard Hirschfeld, Gerd Krumreich and Irina Renz (eds.), *"… keiner fühlt sich hier als Mensch." Erlebnis und Wirkung des Ersten Weltkriegs* (Essen: Klartext Verlag, 1993).

civilians in wartime.[27] So too were schools and volunteer organizations.[28] Drawing on this work, and tracing the collapse of social relations in the capital city, rather than of the state in a military-diplomatic sense, the present study seeks to reinvigorate the older discussion of the Austrian *Staatsidee*, "idea of state."

The choice of *falling* as a motif for this study of Vienna will be familiar to readers of late Habsburg history, which is by and large organized around the theme of "decline and fall."[29] Whether the state was doomed, when it became doomed and the specific contours of this doom are questions that have occupied historians for a nearly a century. Although they approach the weaknesses of this state from different angles – emphasizing, for example, national tensions, the imperial political structure or the state's non-existent program of civic education – historians are in near-unanimous agreement on one thing: Austria lacked a coherent *Staatsidee* – a unifying idea of state – that would emotionally bind disparate peoples to the multi-national, dynastic polity. But few have investigated how this state or government was perceived from the perspective of the governed. The governed here include not just the enfranchised, but also the politically unaccounted for – the millions of women and children who were called to sacrifice for the state in wartime.[30] This is a critical perspective if we consider the explosion of state-oriented discourse that shaped everyday life in the capital.

[27] Susan Pedersen, *Family, Dependence and the Origins of the Welfare State in Britain and France, 1914–1945* (Cambridge: Cambridge University Press, 1993); Reinhard Sieder, "Behind the Lines: Working-Class Family Life in Wartime Vienna," in Winter and Wall (eds.), *The Upheaval of War*; Ute Daniel, *The War from Within: German Working-Class Women in the First World War*, transl. Margaret Ries (Oxford: Berg, 1997); Elisabeth Domansky, "Militarization and Reproduction in World War I Germany," in Geoff Eley (ed.), *Society, Culture and the State in Germany, 1870–1930* (Ann Arbor: University of Michigan Press, 1996), 427–63.

[28] See Stéphane Audoin-Rouzeau, *La Guerre des enfants, 1914–1918: Essai d'histoire culturelle* (Paris: A. Colin, 1993); Andrea Fava, "War, 'National Education' and the Italian Primary School, 1915–1918," in Horne (ed.), *State, Society and Mobilization*, 53–69; and Christa Hämmerle, ed. *Kindheit im Ersten Weltkrieg* (Vienna: Böhlau, 1993).

[29] See Solomon Wank, "The Habsburg Empire," in Karen Barkey and Mark von Hagen (eds.), *After Empire: Multiethnic Societies and Nation-Building. The Soviet Union and the Russian, Ottoman, and Habsburg Empires* (Boulder, CO: Westview Press, 1997), 45–57; and Alan Sked, *The Decline and Fall of the Habsburg Empire, 1815–1918* (London: Longman, 1989), 1–7.

[30] Christa Hämmerle has brought the study of gender to World War I Austria in "'Zur Liebesarbeit sind wir hier, Soldatenstrümpfe stricken wir...' Zu Formen weiblicher Kriegsfürsorge im Ersten Weltkrieg" (Ph.D. diss., University of Vienna, 1996); and "'Wir strickten und nähten Wäsche für Soldaten...' Von der Militarisierung des Handarbeitens im Ersten Weltkrieg," *L'Homme: Zeitschrift für Geschichte* 3, no.1 (1992), 89–128. See also Sigrid Augeneder, *Arbeiterinnen im Ersten Weltkrieg: Lebens- und Arbeitsbedingungen proletarischer Frauen in Österreich* (Vienna: Europaverlag, 1987).

We know certain things about this crisis of *Staatsidee*. First, the idea of a supra-national state was increasingly difficult to sustain in an era of nationalist awakening and political mobilization. Second, this was a state whose very name was in question. Officially "the Kingdoms and Lands Represented by the *Reichsrat*" (the parliament that met in Vienna), Austria belonged to a dual state that went by a handful of names, some more technically accurate than others. They included Austria-Hungary, the Dual Monarchy, the Habsburg Monarchy, the Habsburg Empire, and the Austro-Hungarian Empire.[31] Shifting to the perspective of the governed, paying specific attention to the language ordinary people used to describe their state, their government and their fellow "countrymen" (a term that somehow rings false for the collective of Habsburg subjects), the essence of this state appears even less self-evident. Residents of Vienna spoke and wrote of a state (*Staat*), a fatherland (*Vaterland*) and of constituting half of an empire (*Reichshälfte*), but they did not consider refugees from the eastern part of this half to be Austrians (*Österreicher*). Conceptions of government were equally fluid. The men with power running this state were referred to as the government (*Regierung*), the statesmen (*Staatsherrn*), the singular authority (*Herrschaft*) or plural authorities (*Herrschaften*), as well as a number of derogatory names, including scoundrels, rogues and swindlers, but these terms might be applied to men at any or all of the five levels of government – neighborhood, municipal, regional, state and imperial. Sometimes ordinary people grouped all "government" together, but often they played levels of government against each other, complaining to the Emperor about the mayor, or denouncing one bureaucrat to another. During World War I, the imprecise definition and fluctuating popular understanding of the state in Austria became an acute problem because millions of civilians were expected to sacrifice and "hold out" for this state.

The consequences of the nominal and conceptual weakness of "Austria" for home-front mobilization are striking by way of comparison. If we look at other belligerent countries we see that the nation-state had advantages over the multi-national state when it came to sustaining civilian commitment. France is a case in point. In his study of life on the French home front in World War I, historian Jean-Jacques Becker concludes that what ultimately compelled French civilians to hold out was *France*. He writes:

In the final analysis, despite the weariness, the grumbles and even the anger, the national fabric was too firm and had been knotted together for too long to

[31] István Deák, *Beyond Nationalism: A Social and Political History of the Habsburg Officer Corps, 1848–1918* (New York: Oxford University Press, 1990), 11.

tear part. . . [The French people] accepted the war because they were part of one nation and they tolerated it for the same reason . . . That is why France, a part of her territory occupied or devastated, her youth cut down just at a time when her birth rate was falling, more cruelly tried than the United Kingdom, less rich in resources and men than Germany, despite everything, never gave in.[32]

France, in other words, was not suffering from a crisis of *Staatsidee*.

That Becker compares France to Britain and Germany but does not include Austria (or Russia, for that matter) is characteristic of much recent scholarship on the social and cultural history of World War I.[33] This book aims to bring Austria, one of the five major powers, into the comparative dialogue. When it comes to explaining how civilians were mobilized for war, historians of France, Britain and Germany have documented women and children's value as laborers, consumers and as powerful symbols of the nation and its future. In all three of these cases the *nation* was the essential link between civilians and war. Because Austria was a state, not a nation, it does not fit easily into the paradigm Becker and others have used for comparing the civilian experiences of war.

Recently, however, Jay Winter, Jean-Louis Robert and a collective of World War I historians have shifted our focus from the national to the community level, suggesting that the concrete steps of war-making are taken not by the nation in the abstract but by people embedded in their communities.[34] They propose the capital city as a place where different conceptions of community – the local and the national – meet and can be fruitfully studied. Inspired by this approach, but substituting state for nation, this study explores where and how the idea of state was conceived

[32] Jean-Jacques Becker, *The Great War and the French People*, transl. Arnold Pomerans (New York: St. Martin's Press, 1986), 327.
[33] The Western-oriented scholarship on the cultural legacy of World War I has become its own subfield. Seminal works in English in this field include Paul Fussell, *The Great War and Modern Memory* (New York: Oxford University Press, 1975); Eric Leed, *No Man's Land: Combat and Identity in World War I* (Cambridge: Cambridge University Press, 1979); Modris Eksteins, *Rites of Spring: The Great War and the Birth of the Modern Age* (New York: Doubleday, 1989); Jay Winter, *The Experience of World War I* (New York: Oxford University Press, 1988); Winter, *Sites of Memory, Sites of Mourning: The Great War in European Cultural History* (Cambridge: Cambridge University Press, 1995); and George L. Mosse, *Fallen Soldiers: Reshaping the Memory of the World Wars* (New York: Oxford University Press, 1990). Two recent works that shift attention to the east are Vejas Liulevicius, *War Land on the Eastern Front: Culture, National Identity, and German Occupation in World War I* (Cambridge: Cambridge University Press, 2000), and Aviel Roshwald and Richard Stites (eds.), *European Culture in the Great War: The Arts, Entertainment, and Propaganda, 1914–1918* (Cambridge: Cambridge University Press, 1999). Before the "big three" became the standard comparison, an older project of the Carnegie Endowment for International Peace in the late 1920s attempted to compile social and economic data on all the belligerent countries. Much of the statistical information in the present study is drawn from these volumes.
[34] Jay Winter and Jean-Louis Robert (eds.), *Capital Cities at War: Paris, London, Berlin 1914–1919* (Cambridge: Cambridge University Press, 1997).

in the local Viennese context. Local here encompasses everyday events and experiences in the district, the neighborhood, and within communal buildings and homes. Michael John describes how the Viennese inhabited their city geographically, and how their spatial identity was created: the large unit of spatial segregation was the district (*Bezirk*), see map 2, and the most important small unit in the lifeworld was the Quartier, made up of streets, squares and several apartment buildings.[35]

Vienna was not the undisputed capital city of the Habsburg Empire in the sense that Paris, London or Berlin were for their countries. Vienna was the capital for German-speaking interests, but vied for political and cultural authority with regional capitals such as Budapest, Prague and Cracow. The "idea of state" generated from a study of another Habsburg city might look quite different from the one that emerges from Vienna.[36] As Jeremy King points out, no city in the Habsburg lands is representative of another, but each is representative of the heterogeneity of the region.[37] Typical of "big city provincials" elsewhere, the Viennese often wrote and spoke for all Austria. But the picture of "Austria" generated from their experiences is, at heart, a picture of German-Austria.

State, politics and everyday life

Examining war from the perspective of home-front civilians yields results significantly different from those found in the classic works of Austrian history. Older studies view World War I as a last chapter in a process of decline whereby a supranational state was gradually dismembered by, among other things, the forces of national self-determination. War, which accelerated this process, or produced an international climate favorable to the dismemberment, is seen as the domain of statesmen and military men, waged "from above" and not as an experience of all members of society. "Domestic" politics in this literature refers to the actions of statesmen and politicians within Austria-Hungary as opposed to the international realm, and home front is a synonym for domestic policy.[38] Women, children and "left-at-home" men, if mentioned at all, are objects of state policy.

[35] Michael John, "'Kultur der Armut' in Wien, 1890–1923: Zur Bedeutung von Solidarstrukturen, Nachbarschaft und Protest," in *Zeitgeschichte* 20, no. 5/6 (May/June 1993), 158–86, 162.

[36] See William D. Bowman, "Regional History and the Austrian Nation," *JMH* 67 (December 1995), 873–97, for the relationship of Vienna to the rest of Austria.

[37] Jeremy King, "Loyalty and Polity, Nation and State: A Town in Habsburg Central Europe, 1848–1948 (Ph.D. diss., Columbia University, 1998), Introduction.

[38] See, for example, Oskar Jászi, *The Dissolution of the Habsburg Monarchy* (Chicago: University of Chicago Press, 1929); Robert A. Kann, *The Multinational Empire: Nationalism and National Reform in the Habsburg Monarchy, 1848–1918*, 2 vols. (New York: Columbia, 1950); Kann, *A History of the Habsburg Empire, 1526–1918* (Berkeley: University of California Press, 1974), 468–520.

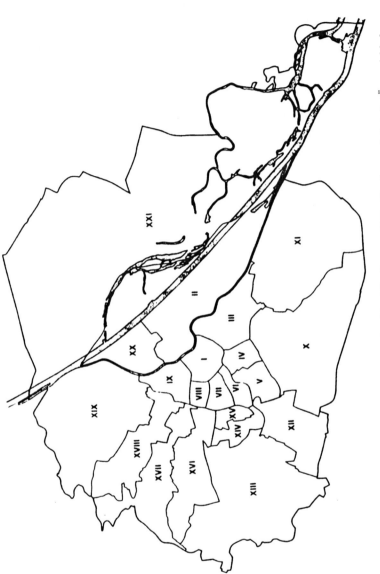

Map 2. City map of Vienna by district (*Bezirk*). Source: Felix Czeike *et al.* (eds.), *Österreichischer Städteatlas* (Vienna: Wiener Stadt- u. Landesarchiv, 1982).

Arthur J. May wrote nearly forty years ago that almost universal economic distress and social misery characterized civilian experiences of Austria-Hungary's final war. Recently, military historians have shown renewed interest in home-front economic and social conditions, and have accorded them significance in the war's outcome. Manfried Rauchensteiner acknowledges, for example, that the "factory war" and the home front "belong to the most important theaters of this war."[39] Enemy military propagandists recognized this too, and played on national tensions, war-weariness and food shortages on the home front to undermine morale among front soldiers. In a study of front propaganda, Mark Cornwall convincingly argues that domestic problems were the "primary reason" the Habsburg Monarchy collapsed in 1918; enemy-front propaganda sought to exploit the poor situation on the Habsburg home front to undermine troop morale.[40] The present study builds on these conclusions, adding a much more textured understanding of the home front by taking us into the truly "domestic" realms of war: the vegetable stalls, apartments, restaurants and schoolyards of the imperial capital.

As Robert Musil recognized, there is a gap between state policy and lived lives. He wrote of the imaginary land "Kakania":

On paper it was called the Austro-Hungarian Monarchy, but in conversation it was called Austria, a name solemnly abjured officially while stubbornly retained emotionally, just to show that feelings are quite as important as constitutional law and that regulations are one thing but real life is something else entirely.[41]

My approach to the study of Austrian politics centers on the feelings and emotions (and actions) of newly mobilized sectors of the population. The space between what Musil calls "regulations" and "real life" has become the territory of historians of everyday life.[42] Focusing on everyday life significantly broadens our understanding of politics in late imperial Austria. For example, if party newspapers are censored; and the parliament is shut down; and no elections take place; and the associational life is

[39] May, *The Passing of the Hapsburg Monarchy*, II, 818; Rauchensteiner, *Der Tod des Doppeladlers*, 257; see also Holger Herwig, *The First World War: Germany and Austria-Hungary, 1914–1918* (London: Arnold, 1997), chs. 6–7 on social and economic factors on the home front.

[40] Mark Cornwall, *The Undermining of Austria-Hungary: The Battle for Hearts and Minds* (New York: St. Martin's Press, 2000), 443.

[41] Robert Musil, *The Man Without Qualities*, translated by Sophie Wilkins (New York: Knopf, 1994), 29.

[42] See Winfried Schulze (ed.), *Sozialgeschichte, Alltagsgeschichte, Mikro-Historie* (Göttingen: Vandenhoeck & Ruprecht, 1994); Alf Lüdtke (ed.), *Alltagsgeschichte: Zur Rekonstruktion historischer Erfahrungen und Lebensweisen* (Frankfurt: Campus Verlag, 1984); Alice Kaplan and Kristin Ross (eds.), *Yale French Studies*, "Everyday Life," (1987), 73 introduction; Michael Gardiner, *Critiques of Everyday Life* (New York: Routledge, 2000).

disrupted by mass conscription, then politics as usual – politics in formal venues – seems to *disappear*. But what if we borrow a wider (and perhaps more interesting) definition of politics offered by historians of the French Revolution and apply it to Austria? Keith Baker suggests that in its essence, politics is about "making claims." Politics is "the activity through which individuals and groups in any society articulate, negotiate, implement and enforce the competing claims they make upon one another and upon the whole."[43] The appeal of Baker's definition lies in its inclusiveness – the "individuals and groups" need not be male and they need not be working through formal institutions. War offered a wonderful vocabulary (patriot/traitor) to Viennese residents of all sorts who were very busy making claims about themselves and others in relation to the whole.

But how to delimit the vast terrain of the everyday for the purposes of study? In her study of Russia in the 1930s, Sheila Fitzpatrick sets the parameters of everyday as "everyday interactions that in some way involved the state."[44] Such a definition only works in situations where the state has a pervasive presence in the lives of its citizens and subjects, and such interactions can only be interpreted by the historian if they leave traces in the historical record. Both conditions were met in World War I Vienna, where the state loomed large in everyday matters, and where residents and state authorities wrote their experiences down. Vienna in those times was an epistolary culture; the Viennese wrote to each other, to relatives at the front and to every imaginable government agency, discussing many aspects of the war experience. These letters – including letters of advice suggesting how an aspect of war policy might be better implemented, threatening letters (*Drohbriefe*) to various officials, letters of denunciation against fellow citizens, letters of petition written to the two Emperors (Franz Joseph and his successor, Karl) and the Empress Zita, and letters written between front and home front containing family news and assessments of the war – form the core source materials for this study.[45] While historians have already found in letters from the front a rich source for the social and cultural history of World War I, this study widens the scope to include a variety of texts from the letter-writing

---

[43] Keith Baker, *Inventing the French Revolution: Essays in French Political Culture in the Eighteenth Century* (Cambridge: Cambridge University Press, 1990), 4.

[44] Sheila Fitzpatrick, *Everyday Stalinism: Ordinary Life in Extraordinary Times. Soviet Russia in the 1930's* (New York: Oxford University Press, 1999), 3.

[45] For methodological consideration of letter-writers' modes of self-presentation in light of a dominant and/or restrictive political language, see Sheila Fitzpatrick, "Supplicants and Citizens: Public Letter-Writing in Soviet Russia in the 1930's," *Slavic Review* 55, no. 1 (Spring 1996): 78–105.

population.[46] Read together with newspapers, police reports on the "mood of the people," and other administrative accounts of the words and actions of the populace, they provide a rich picture of how residents of Vienna conceived of their political identities, the identities of fellow citizens and of state authority.

Vienna in the following pages does not much resemble the Vienna of Carl Schorske's enormously influential work, *Fin-de-Siècle Vienna: Politics and Culture*, which introduces us to society and politics through the prism of high culture. A different approach will be taken here, not because Schorske's conclusions are wrong, but because they have shaped too strongly in one direction our understanding of late imperial Vienna. The characters of his study – Sigmund Freud, Arthur Schnitzler, Hugo von Hofmannsthal, Gustav Klimt and others – have since become canonical, defined as *the* important figures of late imperial Vienna.[47] But Vienna was a city of two million residents, the vast majority of whom did not read Hofmannsthal and were not patients of Freud. This study introduces a different cross-section of Viennese society, in which the key to understanding politics is not art, but food.

We will see that the identities people claimed for themselves were not nearly as stable as the party-political "camps" (*Lager*) that historians have used to demarcate Viennese politics. From the *Lager* perspective, the political landscape of the city consisted of mutually antagonistic blocks of Social Democrats, Christian Socials and German nationalists, each with its own leaders and political subculture.[48] But if we turn again to Musil, we find a composite sketch of Austrian "identity" (what he calls "characters") richer than the narrow party-political model: "[T]he inhabitant of a country has at least nine characters: a professional, a national, a civic, a class, a geographic, a sexual, a conscious, an unconscious, and possibly even a private character to boot."[49] If we add a tenth character,

[46] See Bernd Ulrich, *Die Augenzeugen: Deutsche Feldpostbriefe in Kriegs- und Nachkriegszeit, 1914–1933* (Essen: Klartext, 1997). For a critical study of gender in front/home-front correspondence, see Christa Hämmerle, "'. . . wirf ihnen alles hin und schau, daß du fort kommst'. Die Feldpost eines Paares in der Geschlechter(un)ordnung des Ersten Weltkrieges," *Historische Anthropologie* 6, no. 3 (1998), 431–58.

[47] Carl E. Schorske, *Fin-de-Siècle Vienna: Politics and Culture* (New York: Vintage, 1981). Two works that extend beyond the *fin de siècle* paradigm, which present politics also as the turf of ordinary people, are John W. Boyer, *Political Radicalism in Late Imperial Vienna: Origins of the Christian Social Movement, 1848–1897* (Chicago: University of Chicago Press, 1981) and Brigitte Hamann, *Hitler's Vienna. A Dictator's Apprenticeship*, transl. Thomas Thornton (Oxford: Oxford University Press, 1999).

[48] The *Lager* view of Austrian history is replicated within the Austrian historical profession, where historians affiliate much more strongly with party-political camps than do their American counterparts.

[49] Musil, *The Man Without Qualities*, 30. See also Ernst Bruckmüller, *Sozialgeschichte Österreichs* (Munich: Herold Verlag, 1985), 363–8.

one's access to or distance from food, we have a picture that resembles more closely than the *Lager* approach the social dynamic of daily life in wartime Vienna. The alliances that emerge from the study of letters from ordinary people and from police reports on neighborhood arguments and street skirmishes are fluid and situational: they show people moving in and out of fleeting communities of interest defined not by rigid class or party affiliation, but by the two concepts that ordered home-front social relations: sacrifice and privilege. Contemporaries used terms such as the "suffering people," the "rich," the "people in line," the "people not in line," the "unsatisfieds," the privileged, the scoundrels and the profiteers. Following historian Belinda Davis, I have tried to stay loyal to the actual terms in circulation on the streets, in order to illuminate the new, often ephemeral wartime political constellations.[50] The language used by ordinary people is the starting point for my analysis of politics.[51]

Lager-histories have traditionally ordered the Habsburg political landscape in structural terms. In the study of class, for example, individuals are assumed to have a set "class interest," and shifting relations among the classes are charted through study of the parties or organization that represent those interests. Thus, the "working class" (*Arbeiterklasse*) or the "middle class" (*Mittelstand*) become historical agents in their own right. The general understanding of wartime class relations generated by this structural approach is that the working classes suffered extreme deprivation, offset somewhat by state concessions to the industrial labor force, and inflation and scarcity damaged the economic security and "status" of the middle classes. What this approach misses, however, are the nuances of peoples' multiple interests and loyalties. Although food protests arose most frequently in working-class districts, national and ethnic tensions in these same districts served to deflect some of the force of lower-class consumer protest. Whereas poorer German-speaking and Christian consumers directed some of their rage at the state, we see that they also spent considerable energy targeting Slavic immigrants and Jewish refugees in their midst. In the marketplace, not all of Vienna's poor recognized a shared "class interest."

As a lived category, class encompassed far more than economic measurements. New historical studies of consumption in Europe and the

---

[50] In her study of everyday life in World War I Berlin, Davis traces the emergence of new collective protagonists, such as the "women of lesser means," and the home-front nemesis, the "soldier's wife." Belinda J. Davis, *Home Fires Burning: Food, Politics, and Everyday Life in World War I Berlin* (Chapel Hill: University of North Carolina Press, 2000) chs. 2 and 3.

[51] See Joan W. Scott, "On Language, Gender and Working-Class History," in Scott, *Gender and the Politics of History* (New York: Columbia University Press, 1988), 53–67, for language-conscious techniques of reading historical sources.

United States have shown that varying incomes and occupations acquire social significance and are "embodied, measurable, lived" through consumption.[52] Viewed through consumption (buying, stealing, hoarding, distributing) rather than production, Viennese individuals' identification with a stable "class interest" was notably less clear than older social histories would have us believe. If we take class to mean one's place in society's hierarchy of wealth, privileges and access to resources, Viennese consumers, primarily women and children, measured class, their own and others, by *appearances*. They paid attention to what clothes others bought and wore, and most especially to the quantity and quality of the food others were able to obtain. The art of watching and reporting on others' consumption was a class-building exercise only in a negative sense; it did not lead to sustained solidarity among consumers of any particular income level, but pitted shoppers suspiciously against each other. Importantly, those who were labeled "rich" or who were accused of having unfair privilege were often simultaneously accused of being of a different nationality or ethnicity from the accuser. Determining "richness" in Vienna could be a highly subjective affair.

Inflation (measured both by currency in circulation and prices of goods) had turned traditional measures of wealth and status upside down. In this economy, "connections" (the building blocks of wartime conspiracy theories) were valued more highly than money. For many Viennese not used to being "poor," war had disrupted the sense of one's rightful place in the social hierarchy. For those who *were* accustomed to being poor, conspicuous consumption by others called the bluff of shared sacrifice that ostensibly bound civilians in total war.

Expressions of privilege found in citizens' letters give a subjective, less stable picture of how class was lived than do structural social histories. But are these letters to state authorities representative of opinion in Vienna? After all, isn't it often the squeaky wheel who bothers to write a letter of complaint or threat? Or the truly desperate soul who writes to the Emperor for money? Cataloged randomly in archives, the letters that survive are those that one civil servant or another saw fit to preserve because he thought they somehow "pertained." The letters, then, are an imperfect way to measure public sentiment, but they usefully complement

[52] Judith Coffin, "A 'Standard' of Living? European Perspectives on Class and Consumption in the Early Twentieth Century," *International Labor and Working-Class History* 55 (1999), 6–26, 11. Citing the French sociologist Maurice Halbwachs, Coffin shows that consumption lies at the heart of the "social representation of class." See also Matthew Hilton, "The Female Consumer and the Politics of Consumption in Twentieth-Century Britain," *Historical Journal* 45, 1 (2002), 103–28; Martin Daunton and Matthew Hilton (eds.), *The Politics of Consumption: Material Culture and Citizenship in Europe and America* (New York: Oxford University Press, 2001).

sources traditionally used to assess politics (election results and party records, for example) in that they include the opinions of women and children. Women and minors in imperial Austria could not vote, and in fact were legally banned from joining "political" organizations, so their letters to state agencies offer an otherwise missing perspective. A full *73 percent* of the Viennese population did not represent itself in electoral politics, but anyone who could write could participate in epistolary politics.[53] Every letter, whether a formal petition or an anonymous, scribbled denunciation, was an act of self-representation.

What can be gained by expanding the definition of politics to include everyday life, and by studying war from this perspective? The social disintegration of Vienna provides new clues for understanding the relationship of state and society in the late Habsburg period. The state here was not a static abstraction, a structure that existed "above" everyday life with no apparent connection to it, but was rather a vibrant entity whose meaning, effectiveness and viability were determined by those who lived within it. The Habsburg state, which is sometimes depicted as a soulless polity, a shell consisting of an imperial/royal family, its court, the military and a civil service, and which, to use an organic metaphor, was dying or breathing its last breath, was in fact never more alive in the lives of its citizens and subjects than during World War I.

War chronology

Chronological accounts of domestic politics in Austria during World War I divide the war into two halves: the first phase, from August 1914 to late 1916, was the era of the aged Emperor Franz Joseph, the dictatorial Prime Minister Stürgkh, and an aggressive Army High Command that intervened in many aspects of civilian rule. Joseph Redlich characterized this period as a "war dictatorship" in which the government ruled by decree, civilians in many of the Habsburg territories (although not Vienna) fell under the jurisdiction of military courts and "unceasing tensions" plagued relations between government and military leaders.[54]

Stürgkh and Franz Joseph both died in late 1916, the former by assassination and the latter of old age, making way for the second phase of war

---

[53] The 1907 Austrian electoral reform created "universal" suffrage for men aged twenty-four and older. Based on figures from the 1910 census, this included only 26.6 percent of the population. Women and those of both sexes younger than twenty-four made up 73.4 percent of the population. "Ergebnisse der Volkszählung vom 31. Dezember 1910," in *Statistisches Jahrbuch der Stadt Wien* (1912), 914.

[54] See Redlich, *Österreichische Regierung*, 113–46 and 242–83 for chronological outline of the two phases of war government.

government described by Mark Cornwall as "laxer politically but grimmer economically."[55] Emperor Karl reconvened the Austrian parliament in the spring of 1917 and enacted a number of amnesties for political prisoners in 1917 and 1918. The war government became "politicized," according to Redlich, as politicians resumed their parliamentary posts and ministerial decrees from the period of war dictatorship fell under parliamentary scrutiny. Press censorship was relaxed. During this second phase, military and civilian leaders competed directly for the same dwindling resources, and while military leaders "never tired of complaining about the poisonous effect of the hinterland" upon military operations, they usually retained privileged access to these supplies because soldiers trumped civilians in the hierarchy of total war.[56]

A chronological account of everyday politics is more difficult to construct because the number of actors is much larger and the source base more diverse. There is no Stürgkh of the marketplace, no one woman whose pronouncements over time allow us to gauge significant changes. There are no comprehensive protocols of street conversations like the ones we have for parliamentary conversations. The chapters that follow are arranged thematically into two sections – "Politics and representation" and "State and family" – which together tell the story of the social disintegration of the Viennese home front. They show that the material resources, institutional structures and discursive possibilities of "Austria" were inadequate to mobilize society and sustain this mobilization for four and a half years. Within this thematic framework, however, the rough division of the war into two phases is preserved. Within each of the chapters, we see a general chronological pattern repeat itself. Between 1914 and 1916, citizens and state authorities attempted to sustain early-war optimism in the face of creeping deterioration of material conditions. 1917 was the turning point. The Viennese faced a marked increase in hunger, social discord and low-level violence, and their rampant law-breaking became a protracted civilian mutiny against ineffective government. Around 1917, we also see the defeat of language as a tool to construct "positive" representations of the war. The growing gap between rhetoric and reality, ideology and experience became unbridgeable. During the first half of the war, official, optimistic representations of war had existed alongside the population's more ambivalent attitudes, but after 1917, efforts to portray

---

[55] Mark Cornwall, "Morale and Patriotism in the Austro-Hungarian Army, 1914–1918," in Horne (ed.), *State, Society and Mobilization*, 173–91, 174.

[56] *Ibid.*, 174. In 1917, for example, the War Ministry issued the startling order that the food situation in the army was so bleak that "all available flour supplies in the hinterland will be shipped to the army in the field, without regard to the needs of the hinterland." KM memo, 19 December 1917, cited in Plaschka *et al.*, *Innere Front*, I, 209.

the Viennese as anything other than utterly defeated were left only to the most cynical propagandists.

I.   Politics and representation

The first half of the book charts the radical expansion of the political turf in Vienna. Chapters 1 through 3 attribute the social disintegration in Vienna to shortage of two key commodities: food and reliable information.[57] These were the commodities through which citizen–state relations and relations among citizens were mediated. While food was a physical necessity, and access to reliable or "true" information a psychological one, these scarcities produced similarly destabilizing effects in the form of fantasies and conspiracy theories. The conspiratorial political discourse among ordinary people atomized residents and erased any semblance of community cohesion that had been an implicit ingredient for successful mobilization of society.

II.   State and family

The second half of the book examines the central role of the family in mobilizing civilians for total war. As noted above, there was no ready-made institution such as the military available to state authorities for the purpose of "enlisting" civilians; lacking such an institution, authorities tried to mobilize society via the family. One of the striking features of World War I was the realignment of familial roles for the making of war. When the state needed the cooperation and labor of women and young people, it identified them by familial category (mothers and children) and called them to make war in these respective capacities. As the family was turned "inside out" for the purposes of war-making, motherhood and childhood played central roles in home-front discourse. For men, this realignment of family roles for war had a different effect. Unlike mothers and children, who appeared so visibly in new public capacities, fathers seemed to have disappeared, creating a perceived crisis of paternal authority within both the private family and the "state family" headed by the Emperor.

While the study traces the fall of Vienna in the war years, the conclusion spells out several postwar legacies of the home-front disintegration. First, the experiences of extreme scarcity and continued fears of being cut off from food supplies were reflected in the pessimistic discourse on the

---

[57] Earlier versions of chapters 2 and 4 appeared in the *Austrian History Yearbook* 31 (2000), 57–85, and *Central European History* 35, no. 1 (2002), 1–35, respectively.

Lebensfähigkeit (viability) of the postwar republic Second, while women, children and men had been mobilized for war in their familial capacities, Austrians immediately identified the family as the institution that would restore the social and moral order destroyed by war. This restoration involved putting women and men back in their "natural" places as nurturing mothers and providing fathers. However, desperate postwar economic conditions made these ideal gender roles difficult to fulfill.

Finally, Viennese preoccupation with the "enemy within" continued after 1918. The same groups that had been accused of poor *Gesinnung* during the war were targeted for exclusion afterwards. Anti-Slavic and anti-Semitic groups sought to secure the German, Christian character of Vienna in much more violent ways than they had prior to 1914. In the periodization of Austrian history, the war years provide the bookend to the imperial era, but they also mark a starting point for the violence and disorder of the interwar years.

Politics and representation

1   Food and the politics of sacrifice

Der Morgen, a newspaper affiliated with the Imperial Organization of Austrian Housewives, wrote in 1917, "Completely altered conditions make for completely altered people."[1] In the context of World War I, this statement could have applied to any number of scenarios: to soldiers' life-altering encounters with the machines of modern warfare; to the geographic upheaval of millions of war refugees; or to the pain of a single family dealing with the death of a father or son. But in 1917 Vienna, the "altered conditions" referred to a catastrophic food shortage, and the "altered people" to distressing new modes of social interaction brought on by hunger. In this wealthy imperial capital, residents were theoretically allotted only 830 calories of nourishment per day, and in practice could not obtain even this small amount.[2] By the end of the war, a medical study found that 91 percent of Viennese schoolchildren were mildly to severely undernourished.[3] A journalist noted how food had come to dominate the collective psyche of wartime Vienna: "Every conversation we have is merely pretense and circles back to the question of the supply room. It appears we think only with our stomachs. We talk of menus. We dream of cookbooks."[4] The food shortage soured personal relations among the Viennese; it called the bluff of the Vienna War Exhibition, which depicted the home front as a community of shared interest;[5] and by destroying an implicit wartime contract between civilians and the state, the food crisis created another front in the Habsburg war effort.[6]

---

[1] *Der Morgen*, 20 January 1917, 6.
[2] Hans Loewenfeld-Russ, *Die Regelung der Volksernährung im Kriege*, Carnegie Endowment for International Peace (Vienna: Hölder-Pichler-Tempsky, 1926), 335. This figure is for a regular worker; a hard laborer (*Schwerarbeiter*) was entitled to 1,292 calories.
[3] Clemens von Pirquet, "Ernährungszustand der Kinder in Österreich während des Krieges und der Nachkriegszeit," in Clemens von Pirquet (ed.), *Volksgesundheit im Kriege*, 2 vols., Carnegie Endowment for International Peace (Vienna: Hölder-Pichler-Tempsky, 1926), I, 158.
[4] "Das tägliche Brot," *Neue Freie Presse*, 1 August 1916, 1.   [5] See chapter 2, below.
[6] See the ground-breaking work of Richard Plaschka *et al.* (eds.), *Innere Front: Militärassistenz, Widerstand und Umsturz in der Donaumonarchie 1918*, 2 vols. (Munich:

Food figured prominently in reports of even the most dramatic high political events of the Viennese home front. In October, 1916, the wildly unpopular Austrian prime minister Karl Stürgkh was assassinated while eating lunch at the hotel restaurant Meissel und Schadn. While news reports focused immediately on the sensational identity of the assassin, radical socialist Fritz Adler, son of Viktor Adler, one of the party's most venerable members, the second angle of interest on the story was Stürgkh's lunch itself. Widely blamed for Austria's wartime food crisis, the prime minster had been dining on a bowl of mushroom soup, boiled beef with mashed turnips, pudding and a wine spritzer. No one could prove that Stürgkh's last meal had been in violation of rationing laws, but he had eaten a better lunch that day than most Viennese, and his death evoked little public sympathy.

World War I historians have been particularly drawn to food because of the ways that food figured in the rhetoric of sacrifice in total war in the different belligerent countries.[7] In Russia, the connections between scarcity and large-scale political change have long been recognized. Barbara Alpern Engel writes, "It is virtually an axiom that wartime scarcity and inflation contributed decisively to the downfall of the tsar."[8] While historians of other European countries have not accorded scarcity as prominent a place in their political narratives of the period, several have noted that food crises most often played out in streets and marketplaces, beyond the bounds of traditional political institutions, and that food riots involving "non-political" actors such as women and children require an expanded definition of politics.[9] Lynne Taylor concludes that food riots of the early

R. Oldenbourg Verlag, 1974) for another interpretation of an "inner front" in the Habsburg war effort. The volumes recount in great detail the nationalities conflicts within the Habsburg military and efforts to combat them.

[7] For Germany, see Belinda Davis, *Home Fires Burning: Food, Politics, and Everyday Life in World War I Berlin* (Chapel Hill: University of North Carolina Press, 2000). For Russia, see Barbara Alpern Engel, "Not by Bread Alone: Subsistence Riots in Russia during World War I," *JMH* 69 (December 1997), 696–721; Lars T. Lih, *Bread and Authority in Russia, 1914–1921* (Berkeley: University of California Press, 1990). For Britain, see J. M. Winter, *The Great War and the British People* (Basingstoke, 1986), ch. 7. Thierry Bonzon and Belinda Davis, "Feeding the Cities," in Jay Winter and Jean-Louis Robert (eds.), *Capital Cities at War: London, Paris, Berlin 1914–1919* (Cambridge: Cambridge University Press, 1997), 305–41, offers a comparison of food conditions in three European capitals. For the continuing relationship of food and politics in Austria after World War II, see Irene Bandhauer-Schöffmann and Ela Hornung, "War and Gender Identity: The Experience of Austrian Women, 1945–1950," in David F. Good *et al.* (eds.), *Austrian Women in the Nineteenth and Twentieth Centuries* (Providence/Oxford: Berghahn Books, 1996), 213–33.
[8] Engel, "Not by Bread Alone," 697.
[9] See Davis, *Home Fires Burning*, for rejection of the thesis that food demands are essentially "economic," not "political"; Berthold Unfried, in "Arbeiterproteste und Arbeiterbewegung in Österreich während des Ersten Weltkrieges" (Ph.D. diss., University of Vienna, 1990), undermines much of his own otherwise sound analysis when he concludes, after spelling out the many similarities and parallel developments of food

twentieth century are examples of "politics happening outside of the political arena."[10] But in wartime Vienna, food *was* the political arena. At all levels of Viennese society – from women vegetable sellers at Vienna's Naschmarkt, to the mayor and his advisers, to the paper trail of memos of the War Ministry, Ministry of the Interior and the Police Department – food dwarfed other matters of public concern. Traditional political institutions such as parties (and their affiliated newspapers), the city council and the parliament were restricted or shut down by the dictates of war, leaving a vacuum where "politics" had once taken place. Food, because it directly affected the mental and physical functions of the human body, quickly filled this vacuum. Markets, streets, restaurants, private and public "war kitchens" and any other site of food distribution or consumption formed Vienna's new arena of politics. World War I introduced a novel and important variable into the tangled web of Viennese social identities: one's access to or distance from food.

A study of food provides clues for understanding the relationship of the state and an emergent citizenry that included women and children.[11] Historical literature on modern citizenship has focused on an implicit contract between the state and male citizens, whereby soldiering conferred citizenship; by fighting and offering their lives, men were granted this exclusive status. As had been argued at various junctures in European history, women could not be citizens of the first order because they did not serve and sacrifice for the state as soldiers.[12] Nor, for that matter, could minors of either sex. This assumption about the logic of citizenship was current in World War I Vienna, as recounted by Emmy Freundlich, a socialist activist:

When women approached the state before the war to demand their political rights, they were always told they couldn't ask for the same voting rights as men because

demonstrations and workers' strikes, "Sicher waren die Lebensmittelunruhen weder in ihren Formen noch in ihrer politischen Bedeutung den großen Streiks 1917/18 vergleichbar," 79. For the street as a site of politics, see Thomas Lindenberger, *Strassenpolitik: Zur Sozialgeschichte der öffentlichen Ordnung in Berlin, 1900–1914* (Bonn: J. H. W. Dietz Nachf., 1995).

[10] Lynne Taylor, "Food Riots Revisited," *Journal of Social History* 30, no. 2 (Winter, 1996): 483–96, 493.

[11] Much historiography on modern European citizenship (especially France and Germany) examines the relationship of individual to collective, whereas the focus in Habsburg historiography has been the relationship of the collective (nation) to the state. The Western European individual approach has produced significant work on women and citizenship, while the collective-state approach of Habsburg historians has all but ignored the place of women as citizens. One recent exception to the collective-state approach is Hannelore Burger, "Zum Begriff der österreichischen Staatsbürgerschaft: Vom Josephinischen Gesetzbuch zum Staatsgrundgesetz über die allgemeinen Rechte der Staatsbürger," in Thomas Angerer et al. (eds.), *Geschichte und Recht: Festschrift für Gerald Stourzh zum 70. Geburtstag* (Vienna: Böhlau, 1999), 207–23.

[12] Jean Bethke Elshtain, *Women and War* (New York: Basic Books, 1987).

their claim to these rights was not based on the universal military service of men. On account of being women (*durch ihres Frauentum*) they were hindered from performing the highest act of citizen duty: to give one's life for the well-being of the state.[13]

But debates about food show that women and children – those we might think of as "second order" citizens – were entering into a new exchange with the state during World War I. If the exchange – blood for citizenship – could not be contracted with women and children, how was the state to secure their cooperation and support? Civilians were clearly "involved" in the war, but what were the terms of their involvement? Food would play a significant part in the answers to these questions.

Two key terms – the duty of *Durchhalten* and virtue of *Opferwilligkeit* – framed civilian participation in the war. *Durchhalten*, "holding out" or "endurance," was an essentially *passive* duty. Unlike the soldier, who performed duty actively – fighting, defending or displaying acts of bravery – the civilian's duty was to wait and perhaps suffer, but to do so quietly. Holding out was a means of honoring the more celebrated sacrifice of soldiers.[14] The highest home-front virtue was *Opferwilligkeit*, the willingness to sacrifice resources and especially comfort. The increasingly dire food shortage, and the state's inability to remedy it, disrupted this rather one-sided arrangement. Hungry home-front residents began asking what they were holding out *for*, and what they might expect in return for their sacrifice. They had expected, and were ready to accommodate, inconvenience and burden, but they were not willing to passively endure hunger, illness and even death. As the food crisis wore on, and makeshift distribution schemes broke down, those on the home front who had been called on by the state to sacrifice articulated a powerful new identity for themselves: war victims. The German word *Opfer* – which means both sacrifice *and* victim – provides the semantic underpinning for the trajectory traced in this chapter, the story of how chronic food shortage destroyed assumptions about the role of the civilian in war.

As we shall see, the war precipitated urgent calls for "holding out" and public trumpeting of the "willingness to sacrifice." When the state failed to provide food to the capital city, civilians abandoned the assigned role of heroic helpers of their even more heroic soldiers, and began to see themselves as war victims.[15] This raises the question of just who or what

[13] WSLB ZAS Staatliche Unterstützungen II, "Die Mütter und der Staat," *Arbeiterzeitung*, 24 November 1916.
[14] "Holding out" was a common way of characterizing civilian duty in other European countries. See Charles Rearick, *The French in Love and War: Popular Culture in the Era of the World Wars* (New Haven: Yale University Press, 1997), ch. 1.
[15] For recent work on the exchange between the state and those who claim victim status, see Joseph A. Amato, *Victims and Values: A History and Theory of Suffering* (New York:

was doing the victimizing. The Viennese identified three sources of their victimization: (1) They felt themselves to be victims of the Habsburg imperial structure itself. Not only had other territories (Hungary, in particular) cut off food supplies to Vienna, but the capital was also expected to absorb hundreds of thousands of refugees (read: mouths to feed) from outlying imperial provinces. From the Viennese perspective, even the farmers in the Lower Austrian lands around Vienna had betrayed the capital by withholding food. (2) They considered themselves victims of state and municipal leaders who failed to secure food imports, whose myriad distribution and rationing schemes broke down, and who were utterly incapable of combating inflation and the tactics of war profiteers. (3) The final and perhaps most socially disruptive element of the "victim complex" was the Viennese belief that they were being victimized by fellow citizens. Outrage at Hungary or at municipal authorities paled in comparison to the ire provoked by the figure of the profiteer, who could be lurking anywhere, any time, as the great monster of wartime injustice.

Finally, we shall examine the practice of *Anstellen* – lining up – in front of shops and at markets. This seemingly innocuous practice was the flash point for regular, sustained civilian violence and rioting. In return for their sacrifices, the women and children of the lower and middle classes who participated in the food riots had a specific demand of the state: fair and equal distribution of the food supply. In concrete terms, they did not achieve their goals. The food shortage in Vienna never abated and in fact worsened in the immediate postwar period. But the food crisis – culminating in "lining up" and rioting – had serious consequences for the Habsburg war effort. The result was a dissolution of community – of relations between neighbors, between customers and shopkeepers and between residents and local authorities. By 1917, the persistent refusal to perform duties and the frequent rebellions against authorities amounted to civilian mutiny. In waging World War I, state and military officials needed a stable, productive, *passive* home front. When the capital city became a front in its own right, statesmen found they had lost the realm of "not war" upon which the project of war depended.[16] In certain respects,

Praeger, 1990). Greg Eghigian, "The Politics of Victimization: Social Pensioners and the German Social State in the Inflation of 1914–1924," *Central European History* 26, no. 4 (1993), 375–403; Robert Weldon Whalen, *Bitter Wounds: German Victims of the Great War, 1914–1939* (Ithaca: Cornell University Press, 1984); Deborah Cohen, *The War Come Home: Disabled Veterans in Britain and Germany, 1914–1939* (Berkeley: University of California Press, 2001).

[16] For the dissolution of the boundaries between front and home front in total war, see Elisabeth Domansky's provocative and meticulously argued "Militarization and Reproduction in World War I Germany," in Geoff Eley (ed.), *Society, Culture and the State in Germany 1870–1930* (Ann Arbor: University of Michigan Press, 1996), 427–63.

the victims of the home front were more dangerous to the state than the victims on the battlefields: the latter were killed and could be memorialized as heroes, but the former stuck around as hungry, noisy reminders that states have obligations to those from whom they demand sacrifice.

Civilian duties: *Durchhalten* and *Opferwilligkeit*

The following declaration from Lower Austrian Governor Bienerth, posted in the streets of Vienna, contains three key elements in the wartime discourse of sacrifice on the home front:

> Notice!
>
> Our enemies have openly declared that in order to achieve victory, they want to starve us...
>
> A recent review shows that we have sufficient provisions to last until the next harvest – assuming we practice strict frugality when using the abundant resources of our fatherland, and that we sacrifice not our health but our pleasures and comfort. But these are hardly sacrifices when compared to those made to the fatherland by our brothers in the field![17]

First, by drawing attention to the blockade imposed on the Central Powers by the Allied Powers, the governor cast the food shortage as a consequence of enemy actions against civilians. He stressed that the food question was rooted in the *external* politics of war. Second, he proposed that the solution to the shortage lay in civilian willingness to sacrifice all but the essential foods and resources. With frugality and discipline, civilians themselves had the means to foil enemy intentions. These sacrifices would not be *so* great, however, that civilian health would be jeopardized. Finally, he juxtaposed civilian sacrifices to those made by soldiers, suggesting, as was common in wartime discourse, that the former would be minor in comparison.

When the Allies (led by Britain) began to implement their blockade of the Central Powers in 1914, Vienna newspapers relayed the scandal: "Starvation War!", "Enemies Instigate Economic War!", "They Want to Starve Us Out!"[18] The terrifying prospect of a starvation war (*Aushungerungskrieg*) was cast as an act of enemy cowardliness: "What they could not do by summoning their mass armies, they want to achieve by cutting off our imports of foodstuffs and placing our population in

---

[17] Österreichische Nationalbibliothek, Flugblätter-Sammlung 5/102.
[18] For the series of measures that cumulatively constituted "the blockade," see C. Paul Vincent, *The Politics of Hunger: The Allied Blockade of Germany* (Athens, OH: Ohio University Press, 1985), ch. 2.

danger of starvation."[19] The Allied action was not specifically a blockade of foodstuffs, but the Austrian government portrayed it as such because of the resonance that hunger had with civilians. An "iron blockade" or a "steel blockade" would not have had the same emotional pull with residents on the home front. In fact, Austria-Hungary was, for the most part, *self-sufficient in food production* before the war, so a food blockade should not have had drastic consequences.[20] But as a strategy for mobilizing civilians, "starvation war" was an effective tool; every woman and child in Vienna could imagine herself or himself targeted by the external enemy in a very immediate way, via the aches and pains of hunger.

With a personal, bodily stake in surviving a starvation war, Viennese women discussed their management of food in new, state-oriented terms. The scarcity of food demanded flexible, creative preparation. One columnist noted, "Ever since [the enemy] has wanted to starve us out, it has become a matter of honor to carry out a wise cooking regimen." Cooking had become a more "exalted task" which, when performed efficiently and conscientiously, could "help defeat the enemy."[21] Publishers advertised a new crop of war cookbooks that would help the thrifty housewife to stretch her limited resources. To reinforce women's duty to save, these cookbooks drew on the rhetoric of the starvation war being carried out by a ruthless, external enemy. One explained, "Our enemies want to starve us ... This devilish plan is the work of the English government ... Conserve all foodstuffs ... Squandering foodstuffs is equivalent to squandering munitions."[22] At the beginning of the war, many women responded enthusiastically to the novel idea that they had a *duty* to the state, and were pleased that their management of food had become the focus of discussion among important ministers and men of state. Women's magazines stressed this duty, and urged women to think beyond their personal households when making food decisions. They advised women to put the needs of the general public above their private needs: "We must no longer live in the way

[19] *Volksernährung in Kriegszeiten*, Merkblatt, herausgegeben vom k.k. Ministerium des Innern (Vienna, January 1915).

[20] A 1910 geography textbook boasted, "Wie wenig andere europäische Staaten, kommt Österreich-Ungarn dem Ideal einer sich selbst befriedigenden wirtschaftlichen Existenz nahe; es vermag seinen Bedarf an Nahrungsmittel noch großteils selbst zu decken..." Heidrich, Grunzel and Zeehe, *Österreichische Vaterlandskunde für die oberste Klasse der Mittelschulen* (Laibach, 1910), 8. Hans Loewenfeld-Russ gives a more precise picture of Austria-Hungary's prewar trade balance in food, and concludes that with the exception of a few products, the Monarchy "could generally feed itself from its own production and was less dependent on imports than Germany or England," *Die Regelung*, 28.

[21] "Küchengespräch im Salon," *Neue Freie Presse*, 20 June 1915, 17.

[22] Gisela Urban, *Österreichisches Kriegs-Kochbuch vom k.k. Ministerium des Inneren überprüft und genehmigt* (Vienna, 1915), 3.

that is pleasant for us, but rather in the way that is useful to the state."[23]
In short, the rhetoric of a starvation war allowed civilians to identify personally with a state under siege; they too felt besieged. As one Viennese
writer explained, "[Women] are stocking supplies as if every house were
a besieged fortress, or could become one any day."[24]

Yet, if we return to the language of the governor's notice, we see that
beneath exaltations of women's new public duties and praise for their
efforts was a second message: sacrifice on the home front was relative –
subordinated to the greater sacrifices on the front. Calls for civilian sacrifice frequently contained an "it's the least you can do" clause, intended
to remind the Viennese that theirs was a sacrifice of a secondary order. In
optimistic texts from 1914 and 1915, sacrifice meant giving up inessential
ingredients, accommodating to new tastes, and could even have health
benefits for those from higher circles who had had rich, fattening prewar diets.[25] Civilian sacrifice initially constituted a series of small, almost
inconsequential measures. A typical guide for women recommended:

- "while cleaning [vegetables], only the woody, spoiled and truly unusable
  parts should be trimmed"
- vigorous chewing is thought to release more nutrients; "for this reason, bread should never be eaten fresh, but rather several days after its
  production..."
- gathering and drying tea leaves from local forests (blackberry and linden
  blossom) makes for tea that is not only tasty, "but without a doubt has
  better health benefits than the so-called Russian tea."[26]

Home front sacrifice did not entail *hunger*. The same guide reassured
readers, "Certainly no one should suffer hunger." By this standard, it
was easy to elevate the sacrifices of the front. "However large the sacrifices imposed on individuals may be, they stand in no relation to those
sacrifices our fathers and brothers must offer in the field."[27] In light of
soldiers' battle-front heroics, how could civilians complain of stale bread
or strange-tasting tea?

The discursive elevation of front sacrifice over home front sacrifice,
made repeatedly by government officials, male writers and women themselves, was not unique to Vienna. Rather, it was part of the gendered
structure of the war itself. Margaret and Patrice Higonnet have likened the

[23] *Mein Haushalt: Offizielles Organ des Ersten Wiener Consum-Vereines* 10 (1914), 1.
[24] Adam Müller-Guttenbrunn, *Kriegstagebuch eines Daheimgebliebenen: Eindrücke und Stimmungen aus Österreich-Ungarn* (Graz, 1916), 206.
[25] Johann Joachim, *Österreichs Volksernährung im Kriege* (Vienna: Manzsche k.u.k.
Hof-Verlags- und Universitäts-Buchhandlung, 1915), 40.
[26] *Ibid.*, 33, 40, 37.   [27] *Ibid.*, 43.

front-home front relationship in World War I to a double helix: although the objective situation of women may have changed (new opportunities) and although they enjoyed increased status (new public duties), they remained in an unchanged position *vis-à-vis* men. Men's opportunities and status shifted outward and war provided a new frontier for heroics off-limits to women.[28] While the Higonnets were concerned primarily with work and social activities performed in wartime, their model corresponds equally well to the concept of sacrifice.

If we juxtapose early civilian proclamations about sacrifice with personal letters sent from home front to front later in the war, the *Opfer* trajectory – from willing helper to war victim – becomes clearer. At the outset of war, women from around Austria sent submissions to a publication entitled *The 1914–15 War Almanac of the Patriotic Women of Austria*, in which they spelled out their commitment to sacrifice. The work contains seventy-two entries, laden with proclamations of duty, submission and reverent homage to men in the field. Sophie von Rhuenberg from Linz submitted a poem called "The Shawl," in which an expectant mother on the home front knits for an unknown soldier a scarf that will keep him warm and protect him from bullets because she has "dreamed her love" into the woolen fabric. From Vienna, Anna Friedl-Eichenthal, who ran an organization for midwives, wrote of women, "We are all helpers – important, even indispensable helpers – but still just helpers..." Hermine Cloeter, also from Vienna, described the profound change the war brought to her life. She and other women were no longer satisfied with the minor, petty intrigues of their prewar lives. Full of enthusiasm for a cause that transcended their personal interests, thousands of women and girls offered their services, eager to "help, help, help."[29] Contributors to the *Almanac* were enthralled by their new public duties, but they conceived of these duties very much within the framework of the Higonnet double helix. Soldierly sacrifice overshadowed their own important, but secondary, contributions. The only mention of food in the *Almanac* is a humorous piece on a soldier in a trench who is licking his lips in anticipation of eating a delicious omelet, when a grenade buries the pot it is cooking in. "The omelet – the cursed Russians shot away his omelet!"[30]

[28] Margaret R. Higonnet and Patrice L.-R. Higonnet, "The Double Helix," in Margaret Randolph Higonnet *et al.* (eds.), *Behind the Lines: Gender and the Two World Wars* (New Haven: Yale University Press, 1987).

[29] *Almanach des Kriegsjahres 1914–15 der patriotischen Frauen Österreichs*, Herausgegeben zu Gunsten des Witwen- und Waisenhilfsfond für die gesamte bewaffnete Macht (Vienna, n.d.), 74, 26, 18.

[30] *Ibid.*, 65.

By 1915, notable shortages of basic foodstuffs were evident in Vienna. Police charted the first appearance of market lines for particular items:[31]

Flour and bread. . . . . Autumn 1914
Milk. . . . . Early 1915
Potatoes. Early 1915
Oil. . . . . Autumn 1915
Coffee. . . . . March 1916
Sugar. . . . . April 1916
Eggs. . . . . May 1916
Soap. . . . . .July 1916
Beer, Tobacco, Cigarettes,
Plums, Cabbage. . . . . September 1916

Already by 1915, the warnings about properly trimming the vegetables or baking with less butter were outdated and replaced by acute difficulties in obtaining supplies. Many of the shoppers in market lines were turned away empty-handed, and with little for sale at the markets, civilians began to question the meaning and limits of home-front sacrifice. When the state failed to secure an adequate supply of basic foodstuffs, civilians rejected the initial portrayal of their sacrifices as praiseworthy but secondary, token acts honoring the real sacrifices of soldiers. For example, the thirty women and children who hijacked a bread wagon in Vienna's working-class XVI district in March, 1917, placed their sacrifices on a par with those of their men. Denied potatoes at a nearby market, they attacked the wagon, pounded on the doors and shouted slogans foreign to the language of the *Almanac*: "We want bread! We are hungry! Our men are bleeding to death in the battlefields and we are starving!"[32] This incident, typical of street scenes from the second half of the war, shows how civilian perceptions of sacrifice had changed. Gone were eager statements from thrifty housewives who felt "honored" to be taking part in matters of grave public importance. Gone too was the "it's the least we can do" clause of civilian sacrifice; here, civilians angry at a failed food distribution system placed their sacrifices *alongside* those of the soldiers.

Because subsequent volumes of the almanac were not published, it is impossible to trace changes in attitude of the specific women who contributed to it, and to measure how these women's conceptions of sacrifice changed over the course of the war. But a different set of women's writings from later in the war conveys a very different interpretation of the term *Opfer*. By 1917, state censors had become alarmed at the despairing tone of private letters sent from the home front to soldiers in the field.

---

[31] AdBDW, Stimmungsbericht, 4 November 1916.   [32] AdBDW 1917 V/9 #5386.

Censors compiled a report, stating that in this correspondence, "Comments such as 'When you all return home, you won't find us alive' were not uncommon." Civilians wrote to soldiers, "Be happy that you're over there," and "Don't trouble yourselves – if you starve here or over there, it doesn't make a difference."[33] From these remarks, we see that some women on the home front no longer felt themselves to be on the fortunate side of war; they no longer elevated the suffering of soldiers above their own. Just as battle produced war victims, so too did hunger.

Civilian commentary on food ranged from anger, to despair, to outright surrender. The state found itself with a population that no longer *cared* about the war, as defined by militarists and statesmen. These civilians envisioned their own war in which they and soldiers alike were victims of a state with an utterly failed food policy. Censors noted that numerous women letter-writers threatened "that the womenfolk (*Weiber*) were going to fetch their men, and if they couldn't immediately retrieve them, then the women's war (*Weiberkrieg*) would begin."[34] Others were more passive. Frau Lauer, an Austrian woman whose husband was in a Russian POW camp, wrote him in March, 1917, "I have lost all hope that I and your only child will ever see you again, because we are going to die of starvation. I'm so weakened from the pains of hunger and still, we receive no food."[35] A year later, when Viennese officials met to discuss the latest crisis (an unexpected overnight reduction in flour rations) they noted a mood of resignation among the city's hungry residents. "The people are said to have grown weary of this matter long ago. They are undernourished and exhausted – every day people have to be carted away by ambulance. They explain, if there's no change, [they'd] rather lie down at home than waste [their] last muscle strength getting these measly rations."[36]

Were the Viennese actually *dying* of starvation, as some of these women's comments seem to suggest? In early 1919, city physicians reported inanition (starvation) to be the *direct* cause of between 7 and 11 percent of Viennese deaths during wartime. In 20–30 percent of cases in which post mortems were conducted, starvation was a *contributing* cause of death, helping along some other disease.[37] Many who did not

---

[33] ÖStA, KA, AOK GZNB 1917, carton 3751, #4647, "Stimmung und wirtschaftliche Lage der österr. Bevölkerung im Hinterland," May 1917. Whether these letters are from Vienna or from other areas of the *Hinterland* is not specified.

[34] *Ibid.*

[35] ÖStA, KA, AOK GZNB 1917, carton 4574, "Bemerkenswerte Nachrichten zur Verpflegungsfrage in der Monarchie," 22 March–7 April 1917.

[36] WLSA B23/75 Gemeinderat, Gem. Rat Skaret in Protokoll Obmänner-Konferenz, 17 June 1918.

[37] Hoover Institution Archives, Dr. Böhm, "Sanitary statistic [sic] and mortality of the population of Vienna during the War, 1914–1919," 19 March 1919.

Table 1.1 *Deaths of Viennese women during World War I*

1912	15,355
1913	15,390
1914	15,310
1915	16,305
1916	17,029
1917	20,816
1918	23,898
1919	21,223

Source: Siegfried Rosenfeld, *Die Wirkung des Krieges auf die Sterblichkeit in Wien* (Vienna: Volksgesundheitsamt, 1920), 27.

starve nevertheless suffered acute hunger, which encompassed a number of physical and psychological ailments. Hunger made people irritable, influenced their perceptions and weakened the body to diseases. Civilian deaths did climb during the war, as the above table demonstrates:

Because we do not have accurate statistics on population fluctuation during the war, it is not possible to assess the increase in the death *rate*. But hunger, combined with fatigue from long hours spent working or standing in lines, likely contributed to women's deaths by making them more susceptible to diseases. The psychological effects of urban hunger were twofold: the incivility that came to characterize wartime social relations can be understood, in part, if we imagine a population of two million people, some of whom were experiencing frequent hunger-induced irritability; and hunger may have contributed to the delirium and paranoia that led to "food fantasies," to be discussed shortly.

Despair about food scarcity was not confined to the lower classes. Police reports noted that women of the middle classes also took part in food "excesses." That police specifically mentioned this might indicate that they were surprised or concerned to see *bürgerliche* women behaving in ways not befitting their class. Censors similarly detected food despair in letters from wide segments of the population: "In all manner of speaking, regardless of temperament, education level or political disposition of the writer, whether in truly serious, concerned, ironic or threatening language, this mood of dejection comes through."[38] Of course, to say that

[38] AdBDW 1917 V/9 #W/1-555/17. Runderlaß from k.k. Nö. Statthalterei to k.k. Pol. Dir. Wien, 20 January 1917.

Viennese of various classes expressed similar despair over food shortage does not mean that they shared the same diet. Diversity in diet and in methods of food preparation had been markers of prewar class distinction; accordingly, Viennese were measuring their wartime food sacrifices against the prewar standards to which they had been accustomed.

By early 1917, when censors recorded this pervasive dejection, the state had lost the ability to define the parameters of civilian sacrifice. Whereas women had earlier considered "holding out" a challenge and had responded with enthusiasm, trumpeting creative solutions for stretching supplies, they reached a point where there was nothing left to stretch. The contributors to the almanac had once considered it an honor to be asked to participate in the "world historical event" of war, the "Lehrmeister" that had taught them to place the interests of the whole above their own private concerns. But lack of food changed civilian understandings of "the war" altogether. Censors concluded from home front letters, "In low spirits... any and all interest in the big events has disappeared. Enthusiasm for the grand affair has disappeared along with a belief in *Durchhalten*." For widespread segments of the population, "the question of what one would eat today and how one would feed the family over the next 24 hours" was the defining feature of war.[39]

The three discursive pillars of civilian sacrifice, as outlined in Governor Bienerth's notice, had all crumbled by 1917. The "starvation war" was indeed underway, but the Viennese rarely spoke of the external enemy; the food blockade from without lost its potency as a symbol for unifying individuals on the home front. In addition, frugality and conscientious meal preparation were no longer viable solutions to the food crisis; the shortages were too severe to be combated by recycling, "stretching" and other tricks of careful housewives. Finally, many Viennese ceased to believe in the maxim that sacrifice at the front was greater than sacrifice at home. Instead, they counted themselves among the war's victims and set out to identify the source of their victimization.

War victims and victimizers

Food scarcity was more severe in Vienna than in other European capitals. The rationing schemes began sooner there than in Paris or London, and allotted residents an ever shrinking number of calories. The first ration cards were issued in Vienna in April, 1915, for flour and bread, followed by sugar, milk, coffee and lard in 1916, potatoes and marmalade

---

[39] ÖStA, KA, AOK GZNB 1917 carton 3749, #4588. Censor's report on the mood of the people. March, 1917.

in 1917, and meat in 1918.[40] By contrast, Paris had only two rationed products, sugar beginning in 1917, and bread beginning in 1918, in addition to other less stringent meat and dairy controls. The food situation was even less restrictive in London, where rationing was not introduced until February, 1918. Bonzon and Davis report that Londoners faced inflationary food prices and inequality of access to certain foods, but "[a]part from the disappearance of a few items such as butter, the overall level of food consumption in London was not reduced drastically." In fact, "there were even some gains in nutritional intake" among the working classes.[41] Viennese rations were smaller than those in Berlin, which was undergoing its own wartime food crisis.[42] It may have come as a surprise to Berliners to learn that many Viennese considered the German food distribution system to be a model one. One angry letter-writer wrote to the Viennese War Profiteering Office a typical comparison: "[T]his is a *Schweinerei*... In Germany there is much better order and justice... there they wouldn't have something like this."[43] As table 1.2 makes clear, once ration cards were instituted in Vienna for a certain product, residents could count on steady reductions in rations.

The rationing system itself grew more complicated as new foodstuffs were added and the amounts rationed decreased. Ration cards for Vienna bore the imprint of the Lower Austrian governor's office, but required the stamp of the municipal government. Cards for bread, issued on a weekly basis, entitled their holder either to a loaf of a certain weight or an equivalent amount of flour. They specified the *amount* to which the holder was entitled but not the *price* of the particular good, which was regulated separately. This was an important distinction; inflation at the market stall was the very last hurdle in the distribution chain and prevented some urban consumers from obtaining the foodstuffs they had been rationed on paper. Warnings on the cards that read, "Non-transferable! Keep secure! Copying forbidden!" suggest that a black market had developed for ration cards themselves. In 1917, a new system of color-coded cards was introduced that corresponded to four tiers of family income, and the lowest tier (*Mindestbemittelten*) was allotted extra rations.[44] Such "special treatment"

[40] Hans Hautmann, "Hunger ist ein schlechter Koch: Die Ernährungslage der österreichischen Arbeiter im Ersten Weltkrieg," in Gerhard Botz *et al.* (eds.), *Bewegung und Klasse: Studien zur österreichischen Arbeitergeschichte* (Vienna: Europaverlag, 1978), 661–81, 666–7.
[41] Bonzon and Davis, "Feeding the Cities," 319–20, 315.
[42] Davis notes that during the last phase of the war, a person on the "basic ration" in Berlin was allotted 35.7g of meat, 8.9g of fat and between 375g and 500g of potatoes daily. Davis, "Home Fires Burning," 568. Compare these figures to table 1.2. The ration of flour/bread in Vienna and Berlin was comparable.
[43] AdBDW 1917 V/7 #5385. Anon. letter to Kriegswucheramt Wien, August 1917.
[44] Belinda Davis has written of World War I Berlin that the *Minderbemittelte*, or "women of lesser means," constituted a powerful new consumer-based identity among women of the

Table 1.2 *Declining rations of essential products in wartime Vienna*

	At time of introduction of ration cards		At end of war	
	Daily amount	Calories	Daily amount	Calories
Flour	100g	300	35.7g	107.1
Bread	140g	350	180g	450
Lard	17.1g	153.9	5.7g	51.3
Meat	28.5g	28.5	17.8g	17.8
Milk	1/8 l	82.5	–	–
Potatoes	214g	171.2	71.4g	57.1
Sugar	41.6g	166.4	25g	100
Marmalade	23.8g	47.6	23.8g	47.6
Coffee	8.9g	–	8.9g	–
Total		1300.1		830.9

Source: Hans Loewenfeld-Russ, *Die Regelung der Volksernährung im Kriege*, Carnegie Endowment for International Peace (Vienna: Hölder-Pichler-Tempsky, 1926), 335. These figures are for a "non-self-providing" consumer. The other two rationing categories were "self-providing" agricultural worker and heavy laborer.

for the poorest Viennese was intended to offset price by increasing amount, but had the effect of turning the *Mindestbemittelten* into a "privileged" group in the eyes of other consumers. Middle-income consumers felt they were being squeezed between the very wealthy, who could always make do and the very poor, whom the state was favoring.[45] Inflation, as measured both in prices and amount of currency in circulation, collapsed the distance between lower- and middle-income consumers, leaving the latter disgruntled over their relative loss of status (see table 1.3). As so frequently occurred during the war, this loss was translated into greater perceived "sacrifice."

Key to the food distribution network were the *Zentralen*, established by the government for the management of essential goods. Despite their name, the *Zentralen* were not centralized, but functioned in the following way: private businesses specializing in a certain good would form a government-sponsored cartel that served as the clearing-house for that product. While sanctioned by the government, the *Zentralen* were thus administered by private business interests.[46] Over the course of the

lower classes. See Davis, *Home Fires Burning*. Unlike in Berlin, the term *Minderbemittelte* did not become a significant social category in the vocabulary of the food crisis in Vienna.
[45] See 1918 police report cited in John W. Boyer, *Culture and Political Crisis in Vienna: Christian Socialism in Power, 1897–1918* (Chicago: University of Chicago Press, 1995), 425.
[46] For organization of *Zentralen*, see Loewenfeld-Russ, *Die Regelung*, 71–84; Josef Redlich, *Austrian War Government* (New Haven: Yale University Press, 1929).

Table 1.3 *Wartime inflation (indexed)*

	Prices	Currency in circulation
July 1914	100	100
June 1915	213	208
June 1916	319.4	281
June 1917	394.8	382
June 1918	562.7	741
October 1918	573.3	977

Source: Gustav Gratz and Richard Schüller, *Der wirtschaftliche Zusammenbruch Österreich-Ungarns: Die Tragödie der Erschöpfung.* Carnegie Endowment for International Peace (Vienna: 1930), 184.

war, *Zentralen* were established for at least twenty-seven goods, ranging from leather to cotton to sugar. The "Miles" (Ministerium des Inneren legitimierte Einkaufsstelle) and its successor "Oezeg" (Österreichische Zentral-Einkaufsgesellschaft) handled imports of fats, pork products, beef, butter, cheeses, fish, eggs, fruits and vegetables from outside of Austria.[47] The system was improvised; not surprisingly, those running the *Zentralen* were accused of taking sizeable cuts before the goods actually reached consumers at the market. Black marketeering (*Schleichhandel*) was broadly defined as circumventing the *Zentralen* altogether and marketing goods that had not made their way through the government-sanctioned clearing-house.

Imports of nearly all foodstuffs into Vienna declined sharply during the war, while the population of the city was actually growing. The number of refugees entering Vienna was greater than the number of men leaving for military service.[48] Consider the decline of milk imports to Vienna, between 1915 and 1918 in figure 1.1.

[47] Ludwig von Nordeck zur Rabenau, *Die Ernährungswirtschaft in Oesterreich* (Berlin: Verlag der Beiträge der Kriegswirtschaft, 1918), 117–18.
[48] See Wilhlem Winkler, *Die Totenverluste der öst.-ung. Monarchie nach Nationalitäten* (Vienna: Verlag von L. W. Seidl u. Sohn, 1919) for conscription statistics; and Beatrix Hoffmann-Holter, *'Abreisendmachung': Jüdische Kriegsflüchtlinge in Wien 1914–1923* (Vienna: Böhlau, 1995) for refugees. The system of registration (*Anmeldung*) seems to have broken down with the massive movements of refugees and military conscripts. Those calculating food rations did not have an accurate count of the number of people actually living in the city. Population statistics from mid-1914 cite a total population of 2,149,834, of which 2,123,275 were civilian and 26,559 were active military. Despite an influx of at least 70,000 refugees in the fall of 1914 and the departure of thousands of men for the front, city statisticians recorded little change. By October, 1914, they marked an increase of only 17,453 people, and the military figure remained at its

Milk supply to Vienna (liters)

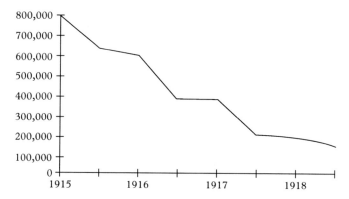

Figure 1.1. Declining milk imports in wartime. Source: Loewenfeld-Russ, *Die Regelung*, 222.

When milk ration cards were first instituted in May, 1916, each resident was allotted (although not *guaranteed*) $\frac{1}{8}$ liter per day, but by the end of the war, no dairy products at all were rationed to the general public. Production of milk-based foods such as cheese and chocolate were restricted. Milk, when it could be secured, was reserved for the "dairy privileged" – nursing mothers, children and the seriously ill. Like the imports of fruits and vegetables, which also declined markedly over the course of four years, the statistics on Viennese imports of beef and pork were bleak (see figures 1.2 and 1.3).

The municipal government instituted official "meatless days" (Fridays) with certain meat products (blood sausage, liverwurst, canned fish) allowed on Mondays and Wednesdays. Restaurants and cafés were restricted to "lardless Saturdays." But these intricate regulations could not hide the fact that for many residents of Vienna, "eating" had become a mathematical exercise in consuming any available calories, no matter how disagreeable their source.

However much Habsburg officials would have liked to blame the food crisis on the "starvation war" pursued by Britain, the shortages in Vienna were, in fact, home grown. When it came to food, Austria-Hungary was at war with itself. Citizens of Vienna who felt they were living in a city besieged by supposed allies pegged the Hungarians and the local farmers of

prewar level. *Mitteilungen der Statistischen Abteilung des Wiener Magistrates*, Monatsberichte, August 1914, 161; and October 1914, 203.

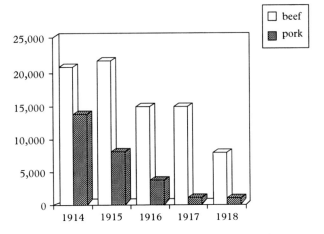

Figure 1.2. Beef and pork imports to Vienna (tons).

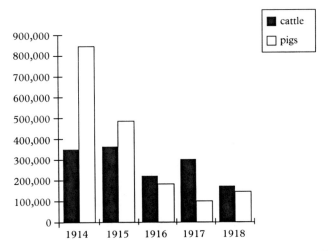

Figure 1.3. Livestock imports to Vienna. Source: Loewenfeld-Russ, *Die Regelung*, 205.

lower Austria as callous victimizers. The Viennese police received unconfirmed reports from the Austrian Food Office that Hungarian children traveling through Austria had been stoned by local residents chanting "Curse Hungary!"[49] "Eine Wienerin" sent an anonymous letter to Viennese Mayor Weiskirchner in April, 1918, expressing typical outrage

---

[49] AdBDW 1918 St./18 #55440.

Table 1.4 *Prewar Austrian food imports from Hungary*

Average Austrian consumption in years 1909–1913 of	% grown/produced in Austria	% deficit to import	% of deficit covered by Hungary
flour	68	32	92
beef	29	71	97
pork	48	52	99
milk	99	1	85
potatoes	97	3	40
corn	39	61	56

Source: Loewenfeld-Russ, *Die Regelung*, 31

at Hungarian greed, which had left the Viennese scrambling for inedible corn bread. Rumors circulated in the city that even the cornmeal was running low, and that Viennese bread would soon be made from hay. She had heard that in Bratislava, only 75 kilometers away and under Hungarian control, every resident could buy poppy seed and nut strudel made with white flour. Reaching her own conclusions, the letter-writer asked rhetorically, "Is the other half of the empire (*die andere Reichshälfte*) in cahoots with the enemies trying to starve us?[50] This question was on the minds of many.

Historian István Deák has cautioned against using the term "Habsburg Empire" after 1867 because the Habsburg head of state was the king, but not the emperor, of Hungary.[51] While he is correct in warning historians against anachronistic use of the word "empire," residents of World War I Vienna – such as "Eine Wienerin" – used the term indiscriminately and clearly included Hungary in its parameters. Living in the largest city in the Habsburg lands, at the symbolic center of political power, the Viennese felt emotionally entitled to the resources of this (misnamed) empire. They were not, however, *legally* entitled to the goods produced there. Economic relations between agricultural Hungary and more industrialized Austria were heavily contested with each ten-year renewal of the 1867 Compromise, the treaty that established dualism. Hungary managed to secure an Austrian market for its agricultural goods, on which the urban population of Vienna was heavily dependent.[52] The great majority of foodstuffs imported to Austria in the prewar period came from Hungary (see table 1.4).

[50] AdBDW 1918 V/1 #55592. Anon. letter to Mayor Weiskirchner.
[51] István Deák, *Beyond Nationalism: A Social and Political History of the Habsburg Officer Corps, 1848–1918* (New York: Oxford University Press, 1990), 11.
[52] On economic relations between Austria and Hungary, see Péter Hanák, "Hungary in the Austro-Hungarian Monarchy: Preponderance or Dependency?" *Austrian History Yearbook* 3, part 1 (1967), 260–302; Géza Jeszenszky, "Hungary through World War I and

However, Loewenfeld-Russ, head of the wartime Food Office, explained the glitch in this arrangement: Hungary had the *right* to sell to Austria, but was under no formal obligation to do so.[53] This arrangement would haunt the Viennese during World War I, and cause them to finger Hungary as the great victimizer of the Austrian people.

Austria-Hungary did not have a unified food policy, and in 1914 the existing improvised arrangement came under enormous stress.[54] First, Austria lost a great deal of the foodstuffs from its most agricultural province, Galicia, due to the war against Russia, which rolled back and forth across the north-eastern territory. Galicia accounted for one-third of all Austrian farmland and had produced a large grain surplus before the war. When we read, for example, that in 1918 "Austria" was harvesting only 41 percent of the grain it had produced in 1914, much of this loss stemmed from the agricultural crisis in Galicia. In addition to the battles being waged on their lands, Galician farmers lost farm labor to conscription and farm animals and machinery to military requisition.[55] When eastern Galicia and Bukowina were recaptured from the Russians after the failed Kerenski offensive in the summer of 1917, farming conditions there were bleak. "The terrain had been devastated [and] a large section of the population had fled and was being housed in refugee camps in the Monarchy's interior."[56] Second, but less central to the food crisis than the government would have it, was the blockade which prohibited Austria-Hungary from importing supplies from abroad. Third, Austria and Hungary combined had to feed the millions of men and thousands of animals of the Habsburg armies.[57] Hungary would claim throughout the

the End of the Dual Monarchy," in Peter Sugar *et al.* (eds.), *A History of Hungary* (Bloomington: Indiana University Press, 1990), 267–94.

[53] Hans Loewenfeld-Russ, *Im Kampf gegen den Hunger: Aus den Erinnerungen des Staatssekretärs für Volksernährung, 1918–1920* (Vienna: Verlag für Geschichte und Politik, 1986), 34. Loewenfeld-Russ was one of the first civil servants assigned to the *Amt für Volksernährung*, founded in November, 1916. This observation makes a comparison of the food supply in Austria-Hungary with that in other countries difficult. Thierry Bonzon and Belinda Davis note that France was relatively self-sufficient in food, Britain was highly dependent on imports, and Germany lay somewhere in between. Bonzon and Davis, "Feeding the Cities," 309. Austria-Hungary as a whole might have resembled France in self-sufficiency, but this did not reflect the food trade patterns *within* the dual state.

[54] In 1917, the Hungarians agreed to join a new food committee for the whole monarchy. While they rejected a formal ministry, Prime Minister Tisza agreed to a cooperative *Dienststelle*, to be called Amt der Ernährungsdienst, also referred to as the Gemeinsamer Ernährungsausschuß. General [Ottokar] Landwehr, *Hunger: Die Erschöpfungsjahre der Mittelmächte 1917–18* (Zurich: Amalthea-Verlag, 1931), 8–13.

[55] Isabella Ackerl, introduction to Loewenfeld-Russ, *Im Kampf*, xiv.

[56] Landwehr, *Hunger*, 99.

[57] The monarchy's armed forces fell into three branches: the unified forces under control of the Heeresverwaltung, the Austrian Landwehr, and the Hungarian Honvéd. According

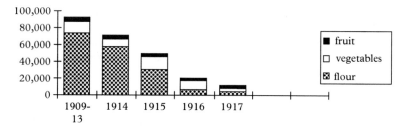

Figure 1.4. Wartime imports from Hungary (1000 Meterznt.). Source: Loewenfeld-Russ, *Die Regelung*, 61.

war that it had taken on the responsibility of feeding the armies,[58] needed to provide for its own hungry population, and could not send as much food to Austria as it had before the war. Indeed, Hungarian exports to Austria fell dramatically between 1914 and 1918 (see figure 1.4).

At the level of high politics, Austrians cited the Hungarian food policy as a key factor in the eventual collapse of the Habsburg state.[59] High-ranking Austrians wondered why the spirit of Austro-Hungarian brotherhood in the field did not carry over to the home front. General Landwehr, head of the Joint Food Commission, recalled, "That Hungary was living better than Austria was on everyone's mind. While the sons of both states fought bravely at the front, this shared *willingness to sacrifice* was missing in the hinterland."[60] At the everyday level, in the angry minds and empty stomachs of shoppers, Hungary played a prominent role in the development of the Viennese victim complex. A thousand listeners gathered at the restaurant "The Green Door" in April, 1915, to hear Hans Rotter, introduced by Vice-Mayor Josef Rain, speak on "Provisioning Vienna in War." "Hungary treats us like a foreign country – like a state of the triple entente," thundered Rotter. Hungary was setting higher prices for grain and squeezing Austria out.[61] A Herr Gabriel who operated a pub on Taborstrasse was arrested and fined for declaring that Hungarian Prime Minister Tisza belonged in the gallows.[62] Many Viennese complained that Austrian leaders had been outsmarted by their cunning Hungarian counterparts. City councilor Goltz described in January, 1915, the growing

to Deák, mobilization brought the number of enlisted men to 3,260,000, and officers to 60,000. *Beyond Nationalism*, 75.
[58] Plaschka *et al.*, *Innere Front*, I, 226–7; and Loewenfeld-Russ, *Im Kampf*, 37.
[59] Loewenfeld-Russ, *Im Kampf*, 33.   [60] Landwehr, *Hunger*, 9 (my emphasis).
[61] NÖLA Präs. "P" 1915, XVb, 1803. Pol. Dir. Wien to Statthalterei Präs., 11 April 1915.
[62] AdBDW 1916 St./9 #28874. Denunciation from Josef Messner to Kriegsministerium, 7 June 1916.

suspicion that Hungary was a state properly *ruled*, while "Austria has absolutely no government."[63]

In letters to various state-level ministries, citizens berated Austrian officials both for cowering before the Hungarians and for profiting personally at the expense of "the people." Viennese citizens declared that the government (*Regierung*), or alternately the rulers (*Herren, Herrschaften*) or statesmen (*Staatsherrn*) had broken an agreement with its citizens. In return for their "hardship and sacrifice" letter-writers demanded sustenance.[64] In fact, they expressed the demand for food in a language of *rights*: an anonymous letter to the Ministry of the Interior signed "One for All" complained in 1917 that the working people "must sacrifice their lives, and for that we are left hungry... Every person, whether rich or poor, has a right to life... Let's turn the spit and let the rulers get a taste of hunger." Authorities filed correspondence of this sort as "threatening letters" (*Drohbriefe*) because they often contained explicit or inferred threats to those who had broken the contract between the state and people. "One for All" concluded menacingly, "We will most certainly recognize the guilty when we come across them."[65] The same year, with unsteady penmanship and many spelling errors, a woman wrote to the same ministry, accusing "the government" – whom she conflated with "the rich" – of betraying the people. "[The poor] have to fight for the rich so that they can fill their sacks while we are ruined... [W]hy does the government let us suffer and starve for so long? [W]hy doesn't the government just have us shot?" She too demanded "equal rights for all" in the distribution of food.[66] In a letter to the Agricultural Ministry in Vienna, anonymous writer/s "Anna and Rasper" asked in desperation whether mothers should offer their own blood and flesh to their hungry children. The government was feeding itself, but had failed to meet the needs of the people. "Do the statesmen only exist," Anna and Rasper wondered, "so that they can eat and drink at will?"[67] It is clear that "the government" had no mechanism for dealing with complaints of this sort. "Equal rights for all's" letter passed to at least three ministries, all of which stamped it "seen," none of

[63] NÖLA Präs. "P" 1915 XVb, 1803. Pol. Dir. Wien to Statthaltereipräs., 11 April 1915. For attitudes in Hungary, see József Galántai, *Hungary in the First World War* translated by Éva Grusz and Judit Pokoly (Budapest: Akadémiai Kiadó, 1989), 192–5. Besides feuding over food supplies, Austrians and Hungarians fought over who would pay for losses and damages caused by war (most destruction of land and property was in Austrian territory).
[64] For similar developments in Berlin, see Davis, *Home Fires Burning*, ch. 9.
[65] AdBDW 1917 St./20 #49367. Anon. letter to MdI, forwarded to police.
[66] ÖStA, AVA, MdI Präs. 22 in gen 1917 carton 2065, #87.
[67] AdBDW 1917 St./20 43367. Anon. letter to Land- und Ackerbau Ministerium, 28 October 1916.

which offered a solution to the woman's troubles. The bureaucrats who
processed citizens' appeals to various layers of government had a bird's
eye view of home-front hardship. In return for hardship suffered – for
the loss of family members, failing health, hungry children and overall
material misery – in short, in return for their *sacrifice* – citizens demanded
food from the state.

With the Hungarians withholding food from the east, and the
Austrian government poised to do little about it, the Viennese victim complex grew to include yet another group: local Austrian farmers who sold
to urban markets at exorbitant prices. Social Democratic city councilor
Skaret noted the "lack of feeling of solidarity" between farmers and the
city population. City residents fantasized about farmers with abundant
stocks; they imagined these farmers were feeding their animals luxury
foods while sending the cattle feed to Vienna for human consumption.
Bitterly eating "war bread" made of a variety of second-rate grains, the
Viennese passed stories about farmers who fed prime barley to their pigs
in the countryside.[68] The lack of solidarity between city and countryside was fueled by city dwellers' sense that *Stand* relations – the class
and status structure of society – had been overturned by the food crisis.
The shortages led to a crisis of value: what had once had value (porcelain
housewares, pianos, fine clothing, and other luxury goods) was traded
ignominiously for eggs, milk and poultry. As residents of one of the most
cultured cities in Europe, the Viennese now had to grovel before local
farmers who held the society's most valued commodities. Anecdotes and
rumors about uncultured farmers stocking their cottages with the finery
of city life circulated in Vienna and became part of the collective memory
after the war. The same few stories were tirelessly retold: the piano teachers who had to move to villages outside Vienna, "following the wealth" to
where the piano owners now lived; the farmer who took delight in watching a "city lady" tramp through his fields in her Parisian shoes looking
for potatoes; farmers with fine carpets, gramophones and opera glasses
whose use they could not fathom.[69] The anecdotes convey the sense of
injustice felt by people far removed from the agricultural sector whose
sense of entitlement as city dwellers was offended by the new economy
of food.

Some farmers delighted in the urban envy of their foodstuffs. In July,
1918, Paula Kaswurm of the village Klausen-Leopoldsdorf wrote to an

[68] WSLA B23/73 Gemeinderat. Protokoll Obmänner-Konferenz, 20 April 1915.
[69] Eduard Ritter von Liszt, *Der Einfluss des Krieges auf die soziale Schichtung der Wiener Bevölkerung* (Vienna and Leipzig: Wilhelm Braumüller, 1919), 53–4; *Wiens Kinder und Amerika: Die amerikanische Kinderhilfsaktion 1919* (Vienna: Gerlach und Wiedling, 1920), 13–14.

Austrian POW in Russia not to believe the stories he had heard about conditions at home. "I'm letting you know that things are still going very well here compared to the cities – they are envious of us all."[70] Another woman farmer who had "amassed wealth in war" expressed to a male relative in captivity that from now on, she no longer wanted to "play farmer." When he returned, she mused, "it won't do you any harm, not to have to play farmer either."[71] That she imagined she was "playing" her role as farmer suggests that notions of *Stand* were indeed in flux.

The actual encounters she may have had with city dwellers took place not on their turf, the city, but on her turf, the farm. In peacetime, with a functioning distribution system, food had flowed into Vienna from the countryside, and farmers and consumers had had minimal contact with each other. The war brought a reversal of this flow; hungry Viennese who felt the farmers were withholding supplies while waiting for better prices set out to secure personally what they could not obtain at the market. Hundreds of thousands of Viennese trekked into surrounding farmlands during the war to buy, steal or extort food from Austrian farmers. The Habsburg state, fighting external battles on three fronts, had to post regiments to guard potatoes from its own citizens.

City dwellers' resentment towards their perceived rural victimizers came to a head in the potato war of 1918. The government and residents of Vienna had long complained that the local farmers were withholding food. In 1915, 1916 and 1917, Viennese Mayor Weiskirchner sent repeated telegrams to all levels of government demanding supplies for his city. The Lower Austrian governor prodded leaders of rural districts to comply: "The city of Vienna has registered complaint that practically no potatoes from the farmers of Lower Austria are reaching the market." Rural district officials replied they had sent all they had.[72] The cycle continued until the summer of 1918, when the rural–urban stand-off began to seriously alarm the Ministry of the Interior, the Lower Austrian government and security forces in the farming villages surrounding the city. A proposed 50 percent reduction in the bread ration caused an explosive increase in the food traffic from Vienna to the countryside. On the night of June 28, "extraordinary throngs" of people headed on foot out of the city towards the villages of Stammersdorf, Königsbrunn, Hagenbrunn, Kleinengersdorf, Flansdorf and Enzersfeld. They were joined in the morning by train after train carrying thousands of passengers, all in search of food. In bands of several hundreds, "the masses of people poured over

[70] ÖStA, KA, AOK GZNB 1917, carton 3752, #4732. Censor's report, July 1917.
[71] ÖStA, KA, AOK GZNB 1917, carton 3751, #4647. Report "Stimmung und wirtschaftliche Lage der österr. Bevölkerung im Hinterland," May 1917.
[72] WSLA B23/74 Gemeinderat. Protokoll Sitzung Obmänner-Konferenz, 3 March 1916.

the lands" of terrified farmers. The behavior and sheer numbers of the strangers led some farmers to stay locked inside their homes. The city dwellers wanted to buy, and where they found a willing farmer, "a lively business...developed." Where they found resistance, violence ensued.

Farmers who refused to sell on grounds that potato trading was restricted or that the crops were not yet ripe for harvest fell victim to the urban scavengers. The Interior Ministry received reports of clashes: "Threats were said to have been made that houses would be burned down or the unwilling would be trampled." On June 29, an estimated 30,000 city dwellers were thought to be in the potato region around Vienna. In many cases "[g]angs swarmed the fields and stole the young potatoes and late potatoes... [W]ide stretches of land were plundered and devastated." The agents in this great potato robbery were women, children, and contingents of military personnel on leave in Vienna. The Military Command in Vienna sent troops to reinforce local gendarmerie and security forces. This would pit some Habsburg troops on security detail against other Habsburg troops looking for potatoes. Onlookers tried to determine the "character of the movement" and some felt it was "Bolshevik" in nature. The report to the Ministry of the Interior rejected this interpretation: despite the fact that the thieves appeared to be working by the thousand in collaborative, Bolshevik-style units, this was mere coincidence.[73] A number of circumstances – the cut in bread rations, the absence of vegetables, fruits, meat and potatoes at Viennese markets and the impossibly high prices of food on the black market – had caused thousands of Viennese "victims" to turn on their perceived victimizers with a vengeance.

The unrest in the farmlands around Vienna continued into July, 1918. Officials took several measures to stop the flow of human traffic between city and countryside. They increased the number of security personnel on foot and on horseback; they curtailed train services to potato-rich villages north of the city; and they resumed debate on the controversial topic of Rucksackverkehr – rucksack travel. Officials of outlying districts had pleaded with the Lower Austrian governor to declare a ban on carrying rucksacks. By denying city dwellers the means of carrying home their loot, the district leaders hoped to discourage the practice of storming the fields. But leaders in Vienna argued that such a ban would punish the most disadvantaged citizens, who would "die a slow, miserable death of starvation" if they were not allowed to use Sunday, their one free day, to travel to the countryside for food. Rucksackverkehr was a difficult, physically

[73] ÖStA, AVA, MdI Präs. 22 (1917–18) carton 2131, #15323 and #16297. Reports from Nö Statthalter to Minister of the Interior, 1 July and 13 July 1918.

taxing lifeline for those who had no other alternatives.[74] City councilor Lowenstein described the brutal tactics of rural security officers: they stopped any civilian carrying a rucksack, basket or bag, demanded to see its contents, and confiscated any foodstuffs that might have come from their district. Throughout the war, members of the Viennese city council and the mayor pressed the Lower Austrian government for an explicit decree legalizing *Rucksackverkehr*. Mayor Weiskirchner protested the planned "illegal measures" to search all hand luggage at Viennese train stations for flour, butter, eggs and legumes. Representatives from other parties on the city council agreed with Weiskirchner that this was a ludicrous plan;[75] while they did not encourage the practice of going to the countryside for food, they recognized it as a city dweller's last resort. By supporting the right to carry a rucksack, Viennese politicians could claim to be representing city interests against those of greedy farmers and brutish rural security forces.

Resentful of the food practices of Hungary and the local Austrian farmers, the Viennese began to see their city as a lonely island surrounded by hostile forces. The terror of being "cut off" would resonate in postwar discussions of the viability (*Lebensfähigkeit*) of Austria, a very small country with an oversized capital. Leopold Blasel, a district representative from Vienna's II district and a vocal critic of wartime food policies, reflected on the danger facing a large urban population disconnected from agricultural supplies. In his 1918 booklet, *Vienna: Sentenced to Death*, he described the tiny new Republic of German-Austria with its massive capital as a dwarf with a hydrocephalic head.[76] During the war, this perceived isolation might have led to an increased feeling of solidarity within Vienna, as residents and the municipal government faced down common foes. One might have expected to see develop among the Viennese and their government a shared identity as fellow victims. But the politics of hunger did not abide by this logic. Struggling throughout the war to establish himself on the side of "the people," Mayor Weiskirchner and his city administrators were unable to duck responsibility for the desperate food conditions. Whether they had any actual control over food imports was irrelevant to wide segments of the Viennese population, who found

---

[74] Heinrich Lowenstein, *Meine Tätigkeit als Gemeinderat 1914–1918* (Vienna: Selbstverlag, 1919), 127–8. From "Interpellation in Angelegenheit der Freigabe des sogenannten Rucksackverkehrs," Gemeinderats-Sitzung, 14 May 1918.

[75] WSLA B23/75 Gemeinderat. Protokoll Obmänner-Konferenz, 24 September 1917.

[76] Leopold Blasel, *Wien. Zum Tode Verurteilt: Eine aktuelle Studie zu den Wahlen in die Konstituante* (Vienna: Heinrich Löwy, 1918), 6.

in their own city government another fine, if vaguely defined, example of
a wartime victimizer.

Members of Weiskirchner's Christian Social party liked to portray their
chief as the only man strong enough to stand up to the Hungarians. With
"weak people at the rudder" of the Austrian government, the mayor had
to do battle with Hungarian Prime Minister Tisza himself. Weiskirchner
defended himself at the 1915 meeting at the "Green Door," saying that,
in his efforts to secure food for his city, he had been groundlessly attacked by Tisza, who claimed Vienna was "spoiled" and needed to learn
to get by on the same kinds of foods eaten in Budapest. The mayor invited Tisza to "try the bread we get in Vienna" and spun a food fantasy
very much like the one "Eine Wienerin" would send to the mayor a few
years later. He had heard that people in Fiume on the Adriatic coast were
eating high-quality *Kaisersemmeln* and sugar croissants.[77] Although po-
sitioning himself against Hungary was a wise public relations move by
the mayor, his own administration would eventually become embroiled
in the growing victim complex as citizens sought to identify the culprits
of their hunger.

The city government began the war on confident footing, boasting that
its "energetic intervention on behalf of consumers" had secured an adequate food supply and kept inflation in check.[78] This optimistic report
from September, 1914, did not take into account that the war would drag
on for fifty months, and the Viennese city government was completely un-
prepared for a war of this duration.[79] Wartime police files show that the
mayor, who cast himself early on as the champion of food provisions, received more abusive, threatening letters than any other public official. He
was denounced in a flood of anonymous correspondence. A "Schmid"
accused Weiskirchner and his pack of "body guard bums" of being in
cahoots with the local farmers. "The *Volk* is patriotic," Schmid wrote to
the Kaiser, "but not towards the scoundrels" of the city government.[80]
Another resident who suspected that city officials had exempted themselves from ration regulations sent Weiskirchner an envelope of worthless
fat ration cards, advising him to "burn the fat coupons and shove them up

[77] NÖLA Präs. "P" 1915 XVb, 1803, Pol. Dir. Wien to Statthaltereipräs., 11 April 1915.
[78] *Die Gemeinde Wien während der ersten Kriegswochen. 1. August bis 22. September 1914.
Nach dem vom Bürgermeister Dr. Richard Weiskirchner dem Wiener Gemeinderate erstatteten
Bericht zusammengestellt vom Sekretariate der Wiener christsozialen Parteileitung* (Vienna:
Verlag des Sekretariates, 1914), 7–9.
[79] On the city government in wartime, see Boyer, *Culture and Political Crisis*, ch. 7.
[80] KA, MKSM 1915 10-1/Nr. 27. Postcard to Kaiser, 22 July 1915.

your ass."[81] In a more desperate tone, an anonymous "Mother Starving
With Her Children" described her plight to the mayor:

From the XIV District! Dear Mr. Mayor! Meat is very expensive and in very
short supply. No vegetables. Potatoes one per day per person. Instead of 1/2 kg.
of flour per week we get more potato flour – to do what? From day to day
hundreds of thousands are waiting for sauerkraut and one sees a tub only once
every 14 days . . . Why so seldom? We can't hold out any longer. We have shown
enough patience and sacrifice, it can't go on. In the whole world, Vienna is the
saddest off. Peace at any price . . . [82]

Another mother wrote to warn Weiskirchner that if the food situation did
not improve she would be forced to abandon her children as wards of the
city.[83] We might ask, if wartime sacrifice was performed as a duty to the
state, why did women who had reached the end of their "willingness to
sacrifice" (*Opferwilligkeit*) target the *city*? This discrepancy tells us something about women's ambivalent notions of the state itself. The war called
women to work for an abstract cause; it required that they expand their
political imaginations beyond the household and the local.[84] But the municipality (*Gemeinde*) had traditionally been the unit of government with
which Habsburg subjects/citizens had the most contact. So to the misery
brought on by state-sponsored war, they attached the human face of the
mayor.

Mayor Weiskirchner defended himself publicly against the countless
rumors circulating about his policies and his person. Although he and
his Christian Social party were no friends to the Jews, he was rumored
to be selling top-quality white flour to Jews for making matzo. He was
so dogged by the persistent rumor that he had offered his daughter as
a down payment for fifteen sacks of flour.[85] For every public statement
in defense of the mayor – for example, a speaker encouraging Christian
Social women to refute energetically the tall tales of "the evil mayor and
the wicked city government" – there were many more letters, rumors and
grumblings that pegged him as a primary culprit of Viennese suffering.[86]
When August Knes, a drunken night tram passenger, announced that
before the war Mayor Weiskirchner had been a known swindler and was

[81] AdBDW 1916 St./16 #34987. Anon. letter to Weiskirchner, Amtsnotiz 8 November
1916, "die Fett Marken selbst einbrennen und am Arsch biken das am Sessel biken."
[82] AdBDW 1917 V/9 #43148. Postcard to Weiskirchner, April 1917.
[83] AdBDW 1917 V/9 #41470. Letter from Mrs. Freudensprung to Weiskirchner, no date.
[84] See chapter 4 on women.
[85] NÖLA Präs. "P" 1915 XVb, 1803, Pol. Dir. Wien to Statthaltereipräs. 11 April 1915.
[86] *Oesterreichische Frauen-Zeitung* 1, no. 9 (1917), 128.

"now an even bigger one," fellow riders were hearing familiar accusations, complaints now common in public discourse.[87]

Bewildered, the mayor and his party found themselves in a perpetually defensive position. Christian Socials protested that they could not very well build potato fields on the Stephansplatz and that decisions about food provisions were made higher up, "completely outside the sphere of influence of municipal government."[88] How, they wondered, had the government of a city with virtually no native food sources become a primary target for the abuse of hungry residents? A cartoon with the heading "Have you any idea of all the things I have to do as Mayor of Vienna?" expressed clearly the mayor's frustration at being blamed for problems he felt were generated at the state level. (See plate 1.1.) It depicted Weiskirchner in various settings, working hard to provision his city: wearing an apron and boots of the common man, he sold flour, drove a coal wagon, hauled potatoes to the market, and unceremoniously herded dairy cows into the city.[89] "And then the people complain," the mayor wondered, "that I don't do anything! I'd rather be a minister!"

The growing divide between municipal and state leaders over food supplies began to cripple Austrian governance from 1915 onwards. In Vienna, regular city council meetings had been suspended at the outset of war, but Weiskirchner continued to meet with advisers and opposition party representatives in the Obmänner-Konferenz until the city council was reconvened in 1916. From the minutes of these meetings it is clear that the business of city government in wartime was almost solely procurement of food. In fact, governance came to resemble the management of a household: politicians discussed shipments of goats, spoilage of produce and even the best recipe for cooking szirok, a mysterious millet from Hungary that had upset the stomachs of diners in Vienna's public soup kitchens.[90] At a party meeting in 1916 the mayor pondered this new, food-focused agenda of local government:

It's strange, I think, in peacetime nobody demanded from me that I should get him potatoes. It didn't occur to anybody that I should provide flour or meat; it was never the legal duty of the municipality to do so . . . It is neither in a statute nor found in law that it is the city's duty to take care of food.[91]

---

[87] AdBDW 1915 St./15 #11529. Police report of verbal denunciation.
[88] *Oesterreichische Frauen-Zeitung* 1, no. 9 (1917), 128.
[89] WSLB Konvolut 73765C, from *Neue Glühlichte*, 18 November 1915.
[90] WSLA B23/75. Protokoll Obmänner-Konferenz, 13 May 1918.
[91] WSLB Kriegssammlung C67052 Konvolut 2. "Zweite Vollversammlung der christsozialen Mandatare Wiens," 9 October 1916.

Plate 1.1. Mayor Weiskirchner as a man of the people. Source: *Neue Glühlichte*, 18 November 1915.

But the angry citizens, hungry mothers and intoxicated grumblers of wartime Vienna were not looking for legal explanations for their hunger. The mayor joined the ranks of the Hungarians, the broadly conceived state "government" and the Austrian farmers as the victimizers of an urban population that felt it had not received food as just return for its wartime sacrifice.

"A sack with a hundred holes"

Was there actually enough food reaching Vienna? Despite the statistics that show sharp declines in all food imports, discussions among the Viennese rarely centered on *supply*. Rather, the wartime discourse on food, conducted in conspiratorial tones, focused intensely on the question of *distribution*. Citizens seemed to believe that in objective terms there might have been enough food reaching the city, but that it regularly fell into the wrong hands. Conspiracy theories spread quickly among residents who had little access to reliable, consistent information, and who contended with multiple "truths" about the food situation each day.[92] In the new vocabulary of the food shortages, victims were pitted against their victimizers in a highly public drama: the hungry cried for fairness and justice in distribution. A police report warned, "The public bitterness is directed...primarily against the 'rich'... The population harbors deep resentment of the supposed unjust distribution of available supplies."[93] Another police report concluded that people were less concerned with the "progression of the war" and more angry about the "inequality in the distribution of war burdens...They stand by the motto 'Equal hunger for all.'"[94] That the Viennese were calling not for equal *food*, but equal *hunger* for all suggests that this was not a straightforward antagonism of the haves against the have-nots. Here, popular conceptions of social and economic justice were refracted through the wartime prism of sacrifice. There was a total sum of sacrifice to be divided equally among civilians. Those thought to be sacrificing too little, profiting too much at the expense of others, were accused of betrayal and, in language reflective of the times, high treason.

As the police noted above, bitterness against the "rich" figured in the struggle between victims and their perceived victimizers. However, in multi-national Vienna, "richness" was more than a purely economic

---

[92] See chapter 3 for discussion of rumors and the crisis of "truth" on the Viennese home front.

[93] ÖStA, AVA, MdI Präs. 22 (1917–1918) carton 2131, #6356. Weekly police report to Ministry of the Interior, 16 March 1918.

[94] Quoted in Unfried, "Arbeiterproteste," 74.

matter; it often included a national or ethnic component as well. For example, when 24-year-old Josephine Wosasek was denounced by a neighbor for exchanging "a box of munitions for groceries," her denouncer pointed out that she was both a "young woman of means" (*ein besseres Fräulein*) and a "radical Czech" (*radikale Tschechin*). Similarly, an "objective and Christian-thinking" denouncer identified Max Resch as both a scoundrel "filling his pockets" in the flour trade and a "typical Jewish parvenu." A denouncer who reported that the lifestyle of Bela Toth, Viennese steamship employee and putative Hungarian, had become noticeably "more luxurious since the beginning of the war" also added that "his wife is said to come from Rumania."[95] Assessing the "richness" of Jewish refugees from Galicia proved especially complicated: some were ostensibly poor but dressed rich – police reported hearing at the market that "many of them receive subsidies" but were "very well dressed, strolling about bedecked with jewelry" – while others were rich but dressed poor – "one also observes in countless cases very poorly dressed refugees with large sums of money."[96] In each of these cases, German-speaking Viennese measured the "richness" of Czechs, Hungarians, Jews, or others suspected of faring well using a combination of economic and national or ethnic criteria.

Individual denunciations show that the victims and victimizers in the food drama did not necessarily fall into recognizable classes such as the *Arbeiterklasse* or *Mittelstand*. Major party-affiliated newspapers of Vienna fingered their usual suspects: the Christian Social *Reichspost* blamed Jews for the food shortages while the socialist *Arbeiterzeitung* blamed big business and farmers.[97] But consumers had much more nuanced and fluctuating views of who was to blame for their hunger. Consumers made class assumptions based on appearances rather than on concrete differences in income level. Those who *looked* rich or appeared to be seeking advantage (buyers or sellers) were enemies of "the community," a fleeting and unstable collective of fellow sufferers. Consumers claimed membership in the "suffering people" (*das leidende Volk*) or simply the "population" (*Bevölkerung*), which was juxtaposed to the profiteer (*Wucherer*). Consumers policed who was included in, or excluded from, this "imagined community" of sufferers far more vigilantly than they policed

---

[95] AdBDW 1918 St./17 #55110. Pol. Dir. Wien report of telephone denunciation from Ferdinand Neunteufel to police in Alsergrund; 1918 V/1 #52176 anon. letter of denunciation, May 1917; 1916 St./9 # 33652, anon. verbal denunciation to Wachzimmer in II district.

[96] AdBDW Stimmungsbericht, 21 January 1915.

[97] See the Kriegssammlung collection at the Wiener Stadt- und Landesbibliothek, "Marktwirtschaft" volumes for party opinions on the food crisis.

membership in specific classes. Anyone seeking advantage, whether a powerful grain magnate or a small-time egg peddler, could be excluded from it. As we will see, it was often the smallest players who were most harshly punished for unfair food practices.

Some officials worried that the reconvening the parliament in 1917 had turned the food question into a "political matter" (*ein Politicum*). The government price regulation agency warned that the food crisis must be handled "objectively" without consideration of the "political questions of the day."[98] But food already *was* the political question of the day. It was politicized beneath the level of party politics, a fact that irritated men used to shaping public discourse. Hans Loewenfeld-Russ, the head of the Food Office, criticized Helene Granitsch and the women of the Imperial Organization of Austrian Housewives for meddling in affairs that ostensibly should not have concerned them: "The fact that every person must eat does not make of every person an expert in matters of food policy. But when it comes to food, everyone believes he is called to voice judgment and criticism."[99] The food crisis introduced to Viennese politics unfamiliar voices and new perspectives. On the matter of who belonged to the ephemeral collective of the "suffering people" most anyone felt entitled to judge and to criticize.

Had the state developed an efficient system for distributing scarce goods, the Viennese might have had a better sense of how much food was actually available. But as it was, state agencies overlapped, countless unenforceable laws were written and government agents themselves came to describe the state food effort as "a sack with a hundred holes."[100] Irate consumers lambasted both the *Zentralen* and the black marketeers (sometimes understood to be one in the same) for cheating "the people" of goods rightfully theirs. Leopold Blasel, a local district councilor, spearheaded a grassroots attack on the *Zentralen*. He spoke to gatherings of several thousand people, using a language of military struggle: the small shop owners who could not get adequate supplies from the *Zentralen* and their customers had to mount an offensive on the *Zentralen* and be prepared for counter-offensive. "Down with the kraut, potato, flour, vegetable and meat doctors!" Blasel thundered at one of his rallies to wild applause, "Businessmen to the front!"[101] Interestingly, he proposed

[98] AdBDW 1918 V/4 #122a. Report of k.k. Zentral-Preisprüfungs-Kommission, March 1918.
[99] Loewenfeld-Russ, *Im Kampf*, 70.
[100] AdBDW 1918 V/4 #122a. Report of k.k. Zentral-Preisprüfungs-Kommission, March 1918.
[101] "Der Kampf gegen die Zentralen," *Neue Freie Presse*, 24 March 1918.

front service as punishment for home front crimes. In 1918, the Ministry of the Interior recommended that Blasel himself be deported from Vienna for his political agitation, but not before he had spoken before thousands in at least five rallies.[102] Blasel and his supporters voiced complaints very familiar to government officials: the *Zentralen* system, even after the establishment in 1916 of an umbrella agency for food, was failing. Government officials had to be careful in breaking up black marketeer rings, because these unsanctioned rings had come to serve a vital role in provisioning Vienna. The Austrian Price Regulation Commission acknowledged in a bleak report in March, 1918, that "the cities, especially in the big industrial regions, are today supported to a considerable degree by black marketeers." The government would have to tolerate the services of black marketeers until it was ready to "guarantee the essential needs of the population" itself.[103]

At all levels of government, officials working the food crisis resorted to a familiar technique: they issued innumerable laws, decrees and local ordinances. This "paper solution" to the food shortages yielded few results. Mayor Weiskirchner complained about laws coming down from Lower Austrian bureaucrats that did not take into consideration the special circumstances of Vienna.[104] In the city, a maze of contradictory regulations governed the selling, buying or using of essential goods: there were twenty-four laws concerning flour, twenty-three on bread, fourteen on milk, thirteen on sugar and eight on alcohol.[105] The Price Regulation Commission conceded that the food laws had become impenetrable and that it was nearly impossible for consumers to know what was allowed and what was forbidden.[106]

Price control generated some of the most complicated regulations on the wartime home front. Starting in November, 1914, the government set maximum prices for many goods and required sellers to post their prices on boards. Agents combing the markets searching for price violators were aided by shoppers eager to report their fellow citizens for price infractions. Thousands of profiteering (*Preistreiberei*) cases filled the dockets at the

[102] ÖStA, AVA, MdI Präs. 22 (1917–1918) carton 2131, #8685. Police report to MdI on Blasel and MdI response, 13 April 1918.
[103] AdBDW 1918 V/4 #122a. Report of k.k. Zentral-Preisprüfungs-Kommission, March 1918.
[104] WSLB Kriegssammlung C67052 Konvolut 2. "Zweite Vollversammlung der christsozialen Mandatare Wiens," 9 October 1916.
[105] *Alphabetisches Verzeichnis der wichtigsten in Wien geltenden gesetzlichen Vorschriften auf dem Gebiete der Kriegswucherbekämpfung und der Versorgung der Bevölkerung mit Bedarfsgegenständen* (Vienna: Kriegswucheramt der Polizei-Direktion Wien, 1919).
[106] AdBDW 1918 V/4 #122a. Report of k.k. Zentral-Preisprüfungs-Kommission, March 1918.

local district courts; in an average week in 1917, 320 people were charged
with violating price ordinances.[107] Typically, the amount of money and
food involved was minuscule. Farmer Petronella Leopold was sentenced
to three-day arrest for selling goose meat at 4 crowns per kilo instead of
3.8 crowns. In February, 1915, grocer Barbara Krzal became embroiled
in a case over a piece of buttered bread she had sold a customer for 14 hellers. A market inspector determined that she had marked her price up
by 318 percent. Krzal protested that the bread had been "thickly covered
with butter," and the case devolved into a debate on whether the poor
quality "war-bread" could even be cut properly into measured slices.[108]
Bread seller Julie Matras was fined 20 crowns and sentenced to a night
in jail for failing to give a customer 1heller change.[109] A related crime
involved falsifying or watering down one's product. In a typical day at the
Margareten district court:

Milk merchant Emme Kosel, who skims off the milk, sells the cream, and waters
down the remaining milk was sentenced to three days' arrest and fined twenty
crowns. Because she mixed twenty-five liters of milk with two and a half liters of
water, milk merchant Anna Vogel was fined forty crowns ... Milk dealer Josefine
Tomas watered down her milk with no less than forty-two percent water. She was
sentenced to only three days arrest and fined thirty crowns.[110]

Incidents of this sort added another layer to the Viennese victim complex.
They were being cheated not only by big-time dealers in the *Zentralen*
but by the local neighborhood merchants. Minor incidents were cast in
press reports not as crimes against the individual consumer, but as crimes
against "the people" or the general public (*Allgemeinheit*).[111]

Crimes large and small fell under the heading profiteering, which included black marketeering, mark-ups by middlemen, hiding supplies and
failing to comply with requisition quotas. Some came to believe that profiteering was a psychological phenomenon, "rooted deep in human ego-
ism," that could lead to "psychosis and a brutal disregard for one's fellow
man."[112] Whether profiteering was a psychological illness or a social malady, the profit-seeker showed no "willingness to sacrifice," which placed
him or her in opposition to the community of sufferers. The profiteers

[107] Amtsblatt der k.k. Reichshaupt- und Residenzstadt Wien 26 (30 March 1917), 19–22.
[108] WSLB ZAS Marktpolizei I, *Neues Wiener Tagblatt*, 4 May 1915.
[109] WSLB ZAS Marktpolizei I, *Fremdenblatt*, 18 July 1915.
[110] WSLB ZAS Marktpolizei 5, *Arbeiterzeitung*, 16 May 1916.
[111] For example, one newspaper claimed that the chemists working to track down food-
falsifiers were fighting "a battle for the well-being and contentment of the widest public,
the *Volk*." WSLB ZAS Marktpolizei 3, *Die Zeit*, 19 December 1915.
[112] AdBDW 1918 V/4 #122a. Report of k.k. Zentral-Preisprüfungs-Kommission, March
1918.

were "greedy hyenas on the battlefields of our times" and constituted for the civilian population "the worst of all our enemies."[113] Profiteering was a public crime, and it demanded public punishment.

In a Foucauldian twist, residents of Vienna began demanding public displays of justice. Newspapers in 1916–17 reported on some of the new ideas in circulation, which included calls for the return of the stocks at Vienna's Hohe Markt and Schottentor,[114] and Hungarian suggestions that profiteers be hanged, flogged or placed in cages for public viewing for a small entrance fee.[115] Journalists recalled methods of punishing profiteers in times past: in the seventeenth century a wooden cross had been erected on Vienna's Graben to which unscrupulous bakers were bound before their customers. Others were dunked in the Danube. As enticing as these methods appeared in the face of public rage against wartime profiteers, there was also considerable objection to reverting to such *vormärzlichen* punishment methods. Pillory did not mesh with the "refined customs and views" of the modern age.[116] One newspaper considered the calls for premodern forms of bodily punishment "grotesque," but concluded that such suggestions were to be expected from a public exasperated with profiteering.[117]

The pillory-decree (*Pranger-Erlaß*), a Lower Austrian ordinance from January, 1917, sought to appease the Viennese appetite for public justice. Rather than erecting stocks, the new law mandated that the names of convicted profiteers be printed, along with their crimes and punishments, in a "pillory list" (*Prangerliste*) in local newspapers and on notice boards in the profiteer's home district.[118] Profiteers would be branded and suffer humiliation through the publication of the lists, and the suffering citizens would have a clear account of the crimes being committed against them. The law was initially hailed as a positive step against these "traitors of the hinterland."[119] But the Viennese very soon grew suspicious that only the names of the small-time profiteers were being published. Where were the big fish? The food tycoons and the heads of the corrupt *Zentralen*? A month after the enactment of the decree, several Viennese newspapers registered protest. The Christian Social *Reichspost* lamented that while small offenders suffered public disgrace, "felons acting against the economic interests of the public good" were spared the glare of publicity.[120]

[113] WSLB ZAS Preistreiberei 1, *Reichspost*, 24 October 1915.
[114] "Mehr Öffentlichkeit!" *Der Morgen*, 22 January 1917.
[115] WSLB ZAS Marktpolizei 7, *Die Zeit*, 17 October 1916.
[116] "Mehr Öffentlichkeit!" *Der Morgen*, 22 Janaury 1917.
[117] WSLB ZAS Marktpolizei 7, *Die Zeit*, 17 October 1916.
[118] Rund-Erlaß Nö Statthalterei, 9 January 1917, #W/II-482.
[119] *Oesterreichische Frauen-Zeitung* 1, no. 1 (1917), 5.
[120] WSLB ZAS Marktpolizei 8, *Reichspost*, 1 February 1917.

Der Abend noted that the punishments listed were between 2 and 50 crowns, relatively minor infractions. While "public opinion" had supported the lists, "one surely imagined a different scenario."[121] In short, the Viennese wanted fewer cases of buttered bread, and more cases of high-level corruption. Occasionally, newspaper readers were treated to larger cases, like the one of Josef Kranz, a banker with "influence" in military circles who was given a government contract to supply "ice-cold beer to the trenches," but ran the scheme at enormous profit to himself.[122] For the most part, though, readers were given only lists of petty crimes. The Lower Austrian government acknowledged public dissatisfaction with the pillory lists, but maintained it did not have jurisdiction to publicize certain court rulings.[123]

The *Reichspost*, the most vocal newspaper on the pillory issue, clearly wanted to see more Jewish names in the lists.[124] Mayor Weiskirchner spoke in typically Christian Social terms about the big fish running Viennese food scams. "I want to tell you about another case," he told followers in 1916. "A Polish Jew in the V district gets butter from the Butterzentrale. Never before had he traded in butter, but the Zentrale gives him butter anyway. What does he do? He sits in a coffeehouse and lets people gather in front of his stand. Only when he's good and ready does he pay for his coffee and finally hand over the butter."[125] Descriptions of profiteers often included code words connoting Jews. One was "refugees"; another was "men in coffeehouses." One administrative report on the proliferation of middlemen stated, "Refugees formed the core of the rings of middlemen. Their turf was at first the street and then the coffeehouses."[126] This stereotype of the profiteer as male and probably Jewish conflicts with the pillory lists, which contained the misdeeds of a great many women. In a typical week in March, 1917, 51 percent of the named violators were women who had committed small crimes like the milk handlers noted above.[127] Readers of the pillory lists seem to have lost interest when the lists failed to expose the shady underworld dealings of "men in coffeehouses" and big-time food swindlers. The public debate

---

[121] WSLB ZAS Marktpolizei 8, *Der Abend*, 6 February 1917.
[122] WSLB ZAS Marktpolizei 8, *Frankfurter Zeitung*, 11 April 1917.
[123] WSLB ZAS Marktpolizei 8, *Reichspost*, 2 February 1917.
[124] The *Reichspost* had been printing names of people fined for municipal violations since 1915. Its lists contained dozens of Jewish names and the designation "Galicia," which linked the food crimes to (mostly Jewish) refugees from the East.
[125] WSLB Kriegssammlung C67052 Konvolut 2. "Zweite Vollversammlung der christsozialen Mandatare Wiens," 9 October 1916.
[126] U. Langer, *Kettenhandel und preistreiberische Machenschaften* (Vienna: Manzsche k.u.k. Hof- und Universitäts-Buchhandlung, 1917), 7.
[127] *Amtsblatt der k.k. Reichshaupt- und Residenzstadt Wien* 26 (30 March 1917), 19–22.

on pillory, and the lists themselves,[128] disappeared after 1917, another failed state attempt to remedy perceived injustice in the distribution of food.

A number of other government schemes, some much more elaborate than the pillory lists, also failed to solve the distribution crisis. These included additional rationing restrictions, police inspections of private kitchens, and the establishment of public war cafeterias. In addition to the rationing program discussed above, certain basic products fell under a stricter form of rationing (*Rayonierung*), whereby customers could only use their coupons at an assigned shop.[129] As the incensed writer who sent worthless ration cards to Mayor Weiskirchner pointed out, rationing only worked if the rationed goods were actually available. As was often the case, either the goods had never been delivered from the *Zentralen* to the shops or, as customers suspected, the shop owners were hoarding, stashing goods for "special customers." A woman signing as "a widow who is not very wealthy but who would at least like a little bread" wrote to the Viennese police about problems at her assigned shop. "Although I am unfortunately assigned" to the bakery of Johann Georg Löws-Erben, she wrote, "I can only rarely get bread there." Instead, the bakery used its flour to make "expensive tarts." She'd heard other "simple people" on the street discussing plans to break the shop windows at Löws-Erben, where "huge profiteering" was taking place.[130] A similar writer who spoke on behalf of "we poor people" warned officials of shady business being conducted by milkman Anton Kirschner. She saw privileged customers carrying "whole cans of milk" out of Kirschner's shop, while regular customers only got the rationed $\frac{1}{4}$ liter. She tracked one of these privileged customers, who went from shop to shop getting large quantities of milk for her children. Rationing failed on account of "these people who know no war and no government," who hoarded milk at the expense of poor children, and who defied the unwritten law of the home front that sacrifice "should be equal for all people."[131] Once again, it was not the supply of

---

[128] Publication of the lists appears to have been voluntary, and most newspapers stopped printing them.

[129] Many Viennese already belonged to consumer cooperatives (*Konsumvereine*) and had thus voluntarily "assigned" themselves to a shopping locale. The city government estimated that in 1915, one-third of Viennese households belonged to such cooperatives. Wartime *Rayonierung* would assign the other two-thirds of households to specific shops for specific goods. WSLA B23/73 Gemeinderat. Protokoll Obmänner-Konferenz, 27 October 1915.

[130] AdBDW 1917 V/9 #41135. Anon. letter to Pol. Dir. Wien, 12 February 1917.

[131] AdBDW 1917 V/9 #5905. Anon. letter to Ernährungsamt no date, likely October/November 1917.

foodstuffs, but perceived unequal distribution, even among those who lived on the same block and frequented the same shops, that defined the parameters of the community of sufferers.

Inequality in food distribution kindled the imaginations of many hungry Viennese and fostered a peculiar wartime phenomenon: food fantasies. Residents who felt slighted by unfair rationing sometimes developed fanciful convictions that fellow citizens were not just getting *more* to eat, they were hoarding unimaginably large stores of food. In letters to police, hungry complainants reported quantities of food held by neighbors or local shopkeepers that bordered on the absurd. Richard Freiherr von Ripp, an imperial bureaucrat, was accused in an anonymous denunciation of stockpiling "enormous quantities" of lard, flour, sugar and coffee. "He stocked the back room of his spacious apartment up to the ceiling with groceries..." the letter-writer maintained. In the face of such outrageous charges, police investigated; they found only two small hams, six salamis, a little flour, some legumes and wine.[132] A bitter, anonymous letter, full of angry, underlined details recorded the "crimes" of shopkeeper Maria Eiler. Her basement and store room were said to be full of the most luxurious products to be found anywhere. She had chocolate pralines for which she charged five times the legal price. The letter writer listed Eiler's other goods, all available for astronomical prices. But this too was a food fantasy; when police investigated the shop, they found no delicacies and everything to be "in order."[133] Of course, not all accusations were fantastic. During a typical week in 1918, police searched sixty-three homes and businesses for illegal goods and found food and other supplies.[134] From time to time they hit the jackpot. An anonymous denunciation led police to grocer Luise Milt, whose "special room" did indeed contain vast supplies.[135] But the food fantasy – rooms full of divine delicacies, rich people repeatedly gorging themselves and then inducing vomiting, "so as not to get fat from this gluttony"[136] – derived from a broken distribution system that created not only hunger, but envy and imaginative tales that explained that hunger.

The quest for food not only pitted customers against shop owners and customers against each other, it also raised tensions within families. City

---

[132] AdBDW 1917 V/9 #41902. Anon. letter to Pol. Dir. Wien, 29 March 1917.
[133] AdBDW 1917 V/7 #5385. Anon. letter to Kriegswucheramt, August 1917.
[134] WSLB ZAS Preistreiberei III, *Fremdenblatt*, 4 September 1918.
[135] WSLB ZAS Marktpolizei 9, *Fremdenblatt*, 31 May 1917. Milt had stored 118 kg white flour, 2 kg barley flour, 2 kg dark flour, 36 kg grits, 55 kg coffee, 170 kg salt, 155 kg powdered sugar, 4 cartons sugar cubes, 75 kg green beans, 25 kg fig coffee, 30 kg rice, 20 kg noodles and 10 kg soap.
[136] AdBDW 1917 V/9 #41902. Anon. letter to Pol. Dir. Wien, 29 March 1917.

officials calculated rations by the number of members in a household: babies, children, normal adults and heavy laborers were deemed to have differing nutritional needs, but a family's ration cards were bundled together in one unit. This assumed that food would be distributed fairly *within* the family – that members of a household shared a common interest – which was not necessarily the case. Historian Reinhard Sieder has shown that food distribution in wartime Vienna broke down within families along age and gender lines, with women sacrificing food first in deference to the male head of the family and then to their children.[137] By instituting rationing by household unit, the state found itself in the uncomfortable position of having to mediate disputes among family members. Officials in the XXI district reported that fourteen women had arrived to complain about husbands who picked up the family's rations at their place of work in other parts of the city and did not save any bread for their wives and children.[138] In "large households" with twelve members or more – concentrated in the wealthy I district and the refugee-heavy II district – it was especially difficult to know if individuals were being well served by the household category.[139] Rationing by household also intensified antagonism between servants and their employers. In a scathing denunciation, "Curious," possibly a servant, described the unequal distribution in a household in the I district, and asked police to intervene. "A shocking detail" of the food situation in the household was "that the three servants have to provide for themselves outside the home and [could] only smell the roasts and chickens consumed by their masters."[140] The World War I view, novel to many, that individuals on the home front had to sacrifice for the state, and that this sacrifice was to be shared evenly among civilians, clashed with the existing structure of the European household, in which inequality in distribution was the norm.

While the state wanted to avoid intervention in the distribution conflicts within households, it did not hesitate in other ways to intervene inside the home. In one of the stranger attempts to manage the food shortage, the Viennese police began inspecting private kitchens. In pairs, police agents searched homes looking for violators of city-wide "meatless days." Begun around 1916, the meat police did not leave extensive records; most of the information on the program comes through a complaint from a woman

---

[137] See Reinhard Sieder, "Behind the Lines: Working-Class Family Life in Wartime Vienna," in Richard Wall and Jay Winter (eds.), *The Upheaval of War: Family, Work and Welfare in Europe, 1914–1918* (Cambridge: Cambridge University Press, 1988).

[138] WSLA B23/73 Gemeinderat. Protokoll Obmänner-Konferenz, 20 April 1915.

[139] WSLA B23/75 Gemeinderat. Protokoll Obmänner-Konferenz, 23 March 1917. The II district had 159 "large families", the I district 116, the III district 89 and the IV district 60. The remaining districts had between 10 and 50.

[140] AdBDW 1917 V/9 #41902. Anon. letter to Pol. Dir. Wien, 29 March 1917.

who felt her home was improperly searched. The police arrived in the afternoon for a "look around" and "according to assignment" inspected not just a few residences but an entire building on the Porzellangasse, one apartment of which belonged to a German officer. Although his wife let the inspectors in, and politely "invited [them] to the kitchen" she later complained that as a legate of the German government, her husband's home should have spared such a search.[141] Because the police department was short-staffed due to military conscription, the inspection program could not have been very extensive. But it was a symbolic effort on the part of the state to calm the hoarding fantasies of hungry residents. Knowing that police were looking behind the closed doors and into the hidden cabinets and "special rooms" of their neighbors reassured the Viennese that sacrifice was being shared evenly, or at least that non-sacrificers would be exposed.

The private kitchen itself seemed a possible war fatality when the Food Office urged regional governments in 1917 to "force the establishment of public dining facilities." This decree, which speculated that if the war dragged on, a total ban on "the preparation of food in small, private households could be necessary," grew from the conviction that the private household was inefficient at preparing and distributing society's scarce resources.[142] Activities in the private kitchen had come under close scrutiny during the war. Early on, women's magazines impressed upon their readers that the kitchen was a small unit in a much larger economic network. "Today every smart woman knows that the small household economy over which she presides is a part of the large global economy. It is the smallest molecule from which the whole is formed."[143] But in a time of severe shortage, the private kitchen was wasteful of heating supplies, left-over foods and women's labor. The 1917 decree, which elicited a "strong response from the population" and generated "an unusual amount of discussion" urged expansion of the existing network of public war cafeterias.[144]

Public kitchens fell into several categories. By mid-1917 the Viennese municipal government was already operating forty-seven "people's kitchens" at which residents could obtain warm, inexpensive meals, and 131 "dining rooms" where the food was free. In addition, cooperatives

---

[141] AdBDW 1917 St./6 #52140. Report from k.k. Polizeikommissariat Alsergrund, 4 January 1918.
[142] January 1917 decree from Amt für Volksernährung, cited in Sigrid Augeneder, *Arbeiterinnen im Ersten Weltkrieg: Lebens- und Arbeitsbedingungen proletärischer Frauen in Österreich* (Vienna: Europaverlag, 1987), 146.
[143] "Die Hauswirtschaft im Krieg," *Arbeiterinnen-Zeitung*, 2 February 1915.
[144] "Die Sozialisierung der Küche," *Der Morgen*, 5 February 1917.

ran sixty-two "social kitchens" and fifteen factories had in-house cafete-rias.[145] But resistance to more public kitchens came from many corners. Social democratic leaders complained early on that the public kitchens were too large – dishing up mass-feedings for 1,500 people at a time – and that their constituents were humiliated by the dining halls, which had the "character of charity."[146] The food was also notoriously bad: a "vegetable soup" of warm water, stalks and stems, or a "tea" of light brown warm water. Wealthier Viennese were equally reluctant to appear at war kitchens. *Der Morgen*, a newspaper affiliated with the Imperial Or-ganization of Austrian Housewives, hypothesized on the panic that the 1917 decree had caused in certain circles. "How will the biggest event of the day – my lunch . . . be affected? Will I no longer be able to visit my cozy, warm pub or enjoy the usual dishes in unlimited quantities at the *Stammtisch* of a luxurious restaurant?"[147] "Big-eaters and epicures" were already eating in public – recall the Stürgkh assassination – but a public very different from the assembly-line mass-feedings of the war kitchens.

In the end, it was not reluctance from the poor or the rich that scuttled the plan to abolish private dining and create mess-halls for civilians. The city of Vienna did not have public spaces large enough to accommodate two million diners per day.[148] More importantly, the arbitrary decisions of outside food suppliers, the improvised network of *Zentralen*, the over-lapping and sometimes contradictory set of wartime food laws and the substantial influence held by non-governmental black marketeers made the creation of more war kitchens an impossibility. *Der Morgen* concluded there could be no realistic talk of the "forcible implementation of war kitchens. The important preconditions for that are missing."[149] It was clear that local, regional and state authorities did not have *control* over the supply and distribution of food in the capital city. The government's failed food management, a self-described "sack with a hundred holes," eroded civilians' commitment to, and practice of, the two key tenets of the home front: "holding out" and the "willingness to sacrifice."

---

[145] *Denkschrift über die von der k.k. Regierung aus Anlaß des Krieges getroffenen Maßnahmen* (Vienna, 1918), 4, 272–3.

[146] WSLA B23/73 Gemeinderat. Protokoll Obmänner-Konferenz, 14 October 1914. Work-ers in prewar Vienna often took meals outside the home at inexpensive Gaststätten. Josef Ehmer, "Die Entstehung der 'modernen Familie' in Wien (1780–1930)," in Laszlo Cseh-Szombathy and Rudolf Richter (eds.), *Familien in Wien und Budapest* (Vienna: Böhlau, 1993), 18–19. Resistance to war kitchens stemmed, then, not from their publicness, but from the atmosphere of "mass feeding" and the poor quality of the food.

[147] "Die Sozialisierung der Küche," *Der Morgen*, 5 February 1917.

[148] WSLA B23/75 Gemeinderat. Protokoll Obmänner-Konferenz, 6 March 1917.

[149] "Die Sozialisierung der Küche," *Der Morgen*, 5 February 1917.

The home front "psychosis"

Two police surveillance photographs from 1916 show the Viennese doing what they did most during World War I: standing in line. (See plate 1.2.) At the Yppenplatz market in the XVI district, shoppers waiting for potatoes could at least see the goods they hoped to buy, should there be any left when they got to the front of the line. The same day, at the Karmeliten market in the II district, the potato lines were so long that most shoppers could not see potatoes. All they could see were hundreds of people in front of them, waiting for the same goods that would surely run out before the product ever came into view.[150] These scenes, repeated thousands of times all over the city, were an essential element of the landscape of wartime Vienna. It was to the food lines that police informers went to gather evidence for their reports on the "mood of the people," and it is to the same food lines that the historian must go to gauge the climate of the home front.

The political agents in lines were primarily women and children. Late in the war police would report that shabbily dressed soldiers of the lower classes on leave incited home front crowds in the food lines with tales of officers' extravagant lifestyles,[151] but for the most part, lining up was the business of women and children. These denizens of the food lines came from various classes. Women working in the war industries were well represented. "Unfortunate disruptions and delays" at Vienna's main artillery factory were attributed to food lines, because women laborers stuck in line "come late or don't appear at work at all."[152] While police reports often mention women of the "lower classes" agitating in lines, they also refute the notion that only the poor engaged in food-line politicking. "Women of the *Bürgerstand* were represented," one police report noted of a food demonstration, "in the same proportion as working-class women."[153] In another investigation of a food-line disturbance, police concluded that "very many upstanding *bürgerliche* people" were among those assembled.[154] Sometimes the German-speaking police personnel attributed food-line agitation to specific groups of women: "It is observed," recounted one agent, "that among the women there are always just a few who stir up the others and seek to agitate. In many cases, these were women of Czech origin, based on the accent."[155] While many

---

[150] AdBDW Nachlaß Pamer, carton 2: Photos. Yppenplatz and Karmelitenmarkt, both 13 September 1916.
[151] ÖStA, AVA, MdI Präs. carton 2131/22, #6356. Stimmungsbericht 16 March 1918.
[152] WSLA B23/74 Gemeinderat. Protokoll Obmänner-Sitzung, 29 September 1916.
[153] Cited in Unfried, "Arbeiterproteste," 27–8.
[154] AdBDW 1917 V/7 #46281. Letter on Anstellen in Brigittenau district, 23 June 1917.
[155] AdBDW. Report of the Zentralinspektorat der k.k. Sicherheitswache, 18 May 1916.

Plate 1.2. Lining up at Vienna's Yppenplatz and Karmeliten markets, 1916. Source: AdBDW Nachlaß Pamer, carton 2, photos.

grumbled that "the rich" never waited in line, the practice of lining up brought women of the lower and middle classes and of different ethnicities together in large numbers. They moved beyond their own neighborhoods and outside of their home districts in search of food. The flawed distribution network that "rationed" to people supplies that were not actually available led women to shop outside their local neighborhoods,[156] bringing them into contact with other women whom they might not have encountered in peacetime.

Children standing outside all night in lines became a symbol of the breakdown of social order in Vienna. The wartime discourse of child delinquency frequently drew on the image of the hungry child waiting in the cold for food.[157] One of the most vocal critics of "lining up" (*Anstellen*) was Social Democratic representative and *Arbeiterzeitung* editor Max Winter, who interviewed children and sent scathing reports of market conditions to high-ranking statesmen. In 1915 he wrote to Prime Minister Stürgkh that over 200 people, many of them children, were observed in a food line at two o'clock in the morning:

Child Murder!
An upsetting thing can presently be observed in Vienna. It concerns us all – fathers, mothers, the authorities and citizens. The public nuisance of "lining up"...has taken on forms that have become unbearable...In the proletarian districts children are lining up...shortly after 10 p.m. in order to get flour when the...shops open at 7 a.m.

In his nightly investigations in several Viennese neighborhoods, Winter found cold, wet children, some of whom spent several nights a week outside, clumped together on sidewalks. He concluded that lining up was a "crime against humanity," and likened the situation to the eastern front. "I actually found this to be the saddest action I have undertaken in a long time – and I've just come from the Russian-Polish war zone where I have seen much misery." He appealed directly to Stürgkh: "As first officer of the Empire, you surely consider yourself to be a patriot... [but] it's a poor patriot who abandons the children whose fathers are fighting and dying on the battlefield, endangering their health and their lives."[158]

---

[156] In 1916, the newspaper *Der Abend* began publishing an evening guide that advised shoppers which markets and cooperatives around Vienna would be selling which products the next morning. Police requested the paper stop publishing the guide so as not to "raise expectations." AdBDW 1917 V/9 #22826. Memo from Marktamtsdirektor to Weiskirchner, 19 November 1916.

[157] See chapter 5 on children.

[158] WSLA B23/73 Gemeinderatsausschüsse 1892–1919. Protokoll über die Sitzung der Obmänner-Konferenz, 27 October 1915.

Thus, the shortages that generated "lining up" threatened to undermine the commitment to sacrifice on home front *and* front. Failing to provide food for civilian family members, the state was dishonoring the sacrifices of soldiers in the field.

The rationale behind "lining up" elicited much speculation. Both the children and the policemen who stood watch over the crowds each night knew why people lined up so early. A watchman explained to Max Winter that those who arrived after 3 a.m. would likely miss out the next morning. Nighttime *Anstellen* was, despite the health risks it posed, a way to better one's chances of getting food. City officials argued that the roots of the lining-up epidemic lay elsewhere, in the depths of the Viennese psyche, where rational measures did not penetrate. "The reason behind *Anstellen* – fear and the desire to acquire – which again is rooted in only fear – cannot be driven away by theoretical measures."[159] The theoretical measures referred to were, of course, the failed government schemes and laws discussed above. Mayor Weiskirchner took the psychological interpretation a step further, stating, "If you want to cure an illness, you must first recognize the cause of the illness. *Anstellen* is an illness; it is a kind of war psychosis which springs from the fear of imminent starvation." He considered lining up to be an irrational act on the part of people who actually had enough to eat. Panic, not demonstrable need, drove women to the lines. Speaking before a Christian Social gathering in 1916, Weiskirchner recounted tales of female irrationality: a salt panic, when Austria was well endowed with salt; several hundred women "guaranteed" a meal at a war kitchen, who nevertheless lined up because they feared their portions would disappear.[160] His comments drew "amusement" from his (presumably male) audience, but they were tinged with frustration that this psychological malady supposedly afflicting Viennese women had the power to invalidate his government's best-laid, bureaucratic solutions to the food crisis.

In the tradition of Central European bureaucrats, officials in Vienna tried to solve the "lining up" problem by *forbidding* it. They received encouragement from the Women's War Aid Committee, an umbrella organization headed by the mayor's wife, Berta Weiskirchner. The women, concerned about the health risks *Anstellen* posed to mothers and youth, "the future of the fatherland," proposed that nighttime lining up

[159] WSLA B23/74 Gemeinderat. Protokoll über die Sitzungder Obmänner-Konferenz, 12 September 1916.
[160] WSLB Kriegsammlung C67052 Konvolut 2. "Zweite Vollversammlung der christsozialen Mandatare Wiens," 9 October 1916.

be "strictly forbidden" and combated with "effective measures."[161] But what could these measures be? How could the state forbid a practice by which citizens procured something as essential as food? Indeed, an early 1918 ban on lining up shows that official decree was powerless to change public behavior. Parliamentary representative Karl Volkert described the scenes following an attempted ban on lines in Vienna's XVII district as "simply hair-raising." Policemen had closed off a street leading to a butcher where women habitually waited overnight. The women congregated instead in the surrounding alleyways, while police "brutally hunted down" and arrested those who got too close to the butcher shop. As 6 a.m. approached and the women were permitted to approach the shop, about 500 of them stampeded through the streets. All of this to get a piece of horse meat, if lucky. In the shouting, shoving and pushing that ensued, policemen grabbed women, inflicting arm sprains and injuries. A follow-up report on the failed ban noted that in addition to the women injured, policemen had been knocked to the ground and their uniforms torn.[162] There were, in fact, no "effective measures" to be taken against lining up. Lawmakers faced a truth daunting for the prospect of stability on the home front: shoppers' determination to find food was stronger than the force of law.

Within the food lines, we see the damaging effect of war on Viennese social relations. The lines offer a glimpse of civilians gripped by incivility, and of the rupture of peacetime behavioral norms that governed community life. Viennese legal theorist Josef Redlich noted that by the second half of the war, inflation and hunger had left Vienna in a state of "social decomposition."[163] Rudeness, envy and violence, manifestations to some degree of hunger itself, marked civilians' interactions with each other. Relations between shopkeepers and their customers had grown so hostile that the Lower Austrian government stepped in with a civility decree, "Against the harsh treatment of customers." It ordered grocery cooperatives to warn their members against abuse of customers, which often led to "disturbances of public peace and order."[164] Taking account of the "nervous atmosphere" in the lines, the Vienna Grocers' Association urged sellers to display "necessary politeness" in their interactions with

[161] AdBDW 1917 V/9 #35583. Letter from Berta Weiskirchner to Police President Edmund Gayer, 17 September 1917.
[162] AdBDW 1918 V/1 #53781. Appeal of Abgeordneter Karl Volkert to Minister of the Interior, 23 February 1918.
[163] Redlich, quoted in Ernst Hanisch, *Der lange Schatten des Staates: Österreichische Gesellschaftsgeschichte im 20. Jahrhundert* (Vienna: Ueberreuter, 1994), 202.
[164] WSLB ZAS Marktpolizei 7, *Österreichische Volkszeitung*, 1 November 1916.

Plate 1.3. Chaos at the market: shoppers and security personnel.
Source: AdBDW Nachlaß Pamer, carton 2, photos.

customers, a message lost on sellers who felt threatened by encirclement
by swarms of hungry, impatient shoppers. (See plate 1.3.)

During a flour altercation, grocer Marie Heiß declared to the crowd,
"All the businesses should close up and let the people starve – that would

be best of all." Grocer Albine Fischer verbally assaulted a customer with the statements, "You are worse than the Jews!" and "Get out of here or I'll chop your paws off!" Such ethnic slurs, often directed at refugees, were not uncommon; Franz Steiniger retorted, "You Jewish pig!" when a customer stuck her head into his shop asking for flour.[165] We know that these incidents, while relatively minor, were representative of shopkeeper/customer relations in wartime Vienna because they filled the dockets of the local courts. While rudeness was not technically a crime, "withholding essential foodstuffs" – often accompanied by insult – was.

Relations among shoppers were equally uncivil. Police investigated a gas attack at the Grossmarkthalle in the III district, where 500 people were in line at a butcher stand. The attack was carried out by an anonymous culprit, either as a joke or "to secure a better place in the line of shoppers."[166] Because one's place in line could mean the difference between eating and going hungry, the Viennese abandoned the prewar courtesy of letting the elderly or infirm step ahead of the line. Shoppers were equally intolerant of pregnant women, who received special passes from the state to avoid waiting. The police had to revise this program – limiting it only to women late in their pregnancies – because the passes provoked "countless complaints at the markets" that pregnant women left nothing for the remaining "unprivileged" shoppers and led to more "disturbances of the public peace and order."[167] An anonymous writer railed against privilege at the market, and in doing so struck at the pro-natalist discourse of the home front: "In the name of 'children and pregnant women' too many sins have been committed. Making babies (*Das Kindermachen*) is now a social crime, because for years, even after the peace, we will suffer from food shortages." Having children "should not be supported, but rather limited as much as possible."[168] The writer differentiated between "pregnant women" and "we poor people in line," momentarily shutting pregnant women – with their market privileges – out of the community of sufferers.

As prewar acts of courtesy disappeared in the competition for food, new codes of behavior, and means of enforcing these codes, evolved in the food lines of Vienna. Shoppers policed the police watching over them. They detected in policemen men of privilege, and, as they had done with

[165] WSLB ZAS Marktpolizei 7, *Die Zeit*, 21 October 1916; *Arbeiterzeitung* 27 April 1917; *Arbeiterzeitung* 7 November 1916.
[166] NÖLA Präs. "P" 1918 XIX, 2976 Pol. Dir. Wien to Statthalterpräs, 4 August 1918.
[167] WSLB Kriegssammlung C67052 Konvolut 5. Kundmachung from Pol. Dir. Wien, 30 April 1918; and AdBDW 1918 V/1 #39/378a. Letter from Kriegswucheramt to Amt für Volksernährung, 12 March 1918. There were about 10,000 passes for pregnant and nursing women in circulation by 1918.
[168] AdBDW 1918 V/1 #39/378a. Anon. letter to the k.k. Amt für Volksernährung in Wien.

pregnant women, rhetorically cast them out of the community of sufferers. The police reported in 1916 that keeping order in the food lines
was "becoming increasingly difficult." Shoppers hurled "derogatory and
insulting remarks" at policemen such as, "Of course, you don't need
[to wait in line], you'll be fed anyway...Get to the front..."[169] Shoppers also policed each other, watching for violations of the unwritten
rules of *Anstellen*. The morning arrivals differentiated themselves from
the evening arrivals in verbal exchanges that degenerated into skirmishes.
While these categories were, of course, ephemeral, individuals who did
not fit into them were subjected to citizen-administered charivari justice.
Such was the case of Barbara Stuchlik, who, in May, 1917, arrived at a
butcher stand on the Eugenplatz at five o'clock in the evening, placing
herself in prime position for the next morning's shopping. But arriving
fifteen hours before sales were to begin was *too* early according to the
judgment of her fellow citizens. Stuchlik's strategy aroused the indignation of neighbors, who rebuked her, and then set upon her in a pack. She
fled by tram with several hundred schoolboys following close behind. An
hour later, 400 heckling, stone-throwing schoolchildren had assembled
in front of her house and had to be dispersed by security personnel.[170]
In the politics of lining up, individual interest might momentarily mesh
with – or clash with – an unstable, fleeting collective interest.

If lining up created any sense of lasting solidarity, it was among shop
owners and neighbors who lived around sites of heavy congregation. Shop
owners repeatedly appealed to authorities for more police presence to
manage large, unruly crowds in the streets. The owner of a carpet shop
in the I district, whose store was near a shop selling sugar, wrote of typical
disturbances: "For many weeks more and more scandalous occurrences
have been taking place in front of our shops." From early morning till
late in the evening his entryway was "blocked by masses – in many cases
youths – who behave shamelessly...roughhousing is not uncommon."
He felt "endangered" by the food crowds, and feared that his carpet
customers, "mostly of the higher social classes," shared this fright.[171]
A paper shop owner, a drapery cleaner and a tailor in the XV district
registered similar complaints, noting that the police were "practically
powerless" to control the food crowds.[172] Residents complained that they
could not sleep because of the noise, and that their pleas to those in line

---

[169] AdBDW Stimmungsbericht, 26 October 1916.
[170] AdBDW 1917 V/9 #32385. Memo from Pol. Dir. Wien to Statthalter, MdI and others,
15 May 1917.
[171] AdBDW 1917 St./1 #47363. Letter from Wacker & Schuschitz Tapeten-Haus to Polizei
Präsidium, 25 June 1917.
[172] AdBDW 1918 V/20 Kriegswucheramt #8/757a.

were met with insults and obscenities. But police concluded in at least one case that "the residents from surrounding houses are themselves to blame when it comes to brawling, because they often dump water and ashes . . . onto the people below which leads to heated arguments . . ."[173] That the Viennese were brawling in the streets – driven to dump waste onto their fellow citizens – demonstrates the extent to which prewar norms of social behavior were abrogated by the food shortage. The food lines undermined any pretense of a unified home front; this was a home front divided, not only along traditional class and national lines, but perhaps more importantly in the millions of daily fissures that divided the Viennese from one another.

Contemporaries used various terms to describe the violent actions of women and children originating in the food lines; riots, demonstrations, disturbances and excesses were the most common. Riots perhaps best encapsulates the spirit of violence that prevailed when a food line broke its boundaries. Historian Tyler Stovall's definition of riots as "conflicts involving sustained fighting over at least several hours by large numbers of participants on both sides of the battle" would fit nicely, except that there were not discernible "sides" in World War I Vienna.[174] The opponent of a group of rioters could be one or more fellow citizens, policemen or "the state" as embodied in government buildings in Vienna's I district. Several elements contributed to the atmosphere in the food lines, which police described in gendered terms as "nervous" or "excitable." Hunger, fatigue, hostility from sellers or aggression from fellow "waiters" or nearby residents raised the metaphoric temperature in the crowd. This depiction of the crowds, which, like Elias Canetti's crowds, seem to become political entities in themselves, is colored by the language of these police reports.[175] Individual names, even of those arrested, are *never* mentioned. State authorities could admit that "the population" was a player in wartime politics, but not individual women or children.

The spark most likely to ignite a riot was the news that the desired product was sold out. This news left a certain number of "unsatisfied

---

[173] AdBDW 1917 V/7 #46281. Report to Polizei Präsidium, 23 June 1917.

[174] Tyler Stovall, "The Color Line Behind the Lines: Racial Violence in France during the Great War," *AHR* 103, no. 3 (June 1998), 737–69, 738. John Bohstedt offers a more general definition of riot, "an incident in which a crowd of fifty or more people damaged or seized property, assaulted someone, or forced a victim to perfrom some action." "The Myth of the Feminine Food Riot: Women as Proto-Citizens in English Community Politics, 1790–1810," in Harriet B. Applewhite and Darlene G. Levy (eds.), *Women and Politics in the Age of Democratic Revolution* (Ann Arbor: University of Michigan Press, 1993), 28.

[175] Elias Canetti, *Crowds and Power* (London: Gollancz, 1962).

persons" – a number police accorded great importance. As early as 1915, security reports noted how many "unsatisfieds" were left on the streets. For example, police calculated for each district the number of loaves of bread received, and subtracted this from the number of people in lines, to measure the potential for unrest on a given day, which could be quite large.[176] On a typical day in 1917, shoppers had formed 783 lines outside of shops or market stalls around Vienna. Of the approximately 250,000 people (about 12 percent of the city's population) waiting in line, police estimated 36,000 "unsatisfieds." A few months later, the numbers were slightly higher. Of about 350,000 people waiting in 1,100 lines, 47,000 were sent away empty-handed.[177] A small group of "unsatisfieds" might hi-jack a food wagon; hi-jackings were so common during the war that one of the city's main bread suppliers instructed drivers to surrender bread "in cases of attack" in order to avoid damage to the wagons. Hi-jackers employed military language – "Charge!" or "Fire away!" – when storming transports.[178] Larger groups of "unsatisfieds," which police described as swelling bodies, provided the material for a riot. Dissecting such a body allows us to see that women and children of the food lines were dictating politics in Vienna.

The following series of riots is both specific and representative. The events described here occurred May 11–16, 1916, but almost identical events are frequently recounted in police reports from the second half of the war.[179] The agitators moved in and among working-class neighborhoods (Favoriten-X, Rudolfsheim-XIV, Ottakring-XVI, Brigittenau-XX and Floridsdorf-XXI) with forays into the city center and seat of state power (Innere Stadt-I). The action began when an "excited mood" among the population at the Eugenplatz in the X district led to late-morning "hunger riots." A band of women who set out to voice their grievances at the city hall was dispersed by police in the IV district, but a smaller group of poorly dressed women with their children made it to the Ringstrasse and sent a representative to see the mayor. Back in the X district, stone-throwing youths broke shop windows and stole 350 pairs of shoes. Actions continued into the night with countless arrests. That evening and in the following days, the unrest spread to Rudolfsheim

[176] AdBDW, Stimmungsbericht, 16 April 1915.
[177] AdBDW, Stimmungsbericht, 1 March 1917; 24 May 1917.
[178] AdBDW Stimmungsbericht, 8 February 1917; 1917 V/9 #46735, report from k.u.k. Bahnhof-Kommando to Platzkommando Wien, 25 June 1917.
[179] Random police reports from 1917–18 mention the following number of food demonstrations and riots by district: II District – 1; III District – 3; IV District – 2; X District – 6; XI District – 1; XII District – 2; XIV District – 4; XV District – 1; XVI District – 11; XVII District – 3; XX District – 6; XXI District – 3. ÖStA, AVA MdI Präs. carton 22/2131.

and Schmelz. Roaming demonstrators destroyed signs and broke windows and street lanterns. Police imposed an 8 p.m. curfew, which caused "countless disputes," and restored order only through "energetic intervention." Simultaneously, the districts of Ottakring, Brigittenau and Floridsdorf were host to "gatherings of embittered masses" which were quelled by "quick and energetic intervention by large contingents of security personnel." On the same day, a tram accident in the XX district led to food demonstrations. A crowd gathered at the accident site was incited by calls against inflation and food shortages. Security personnel dispersed the gathering, mostly children, who fled down side streets. "A veritable hunt ensued." Shop windows and trams were damaged by stones. In total, besides material damage and stolen goods, eleven security personnel and two civil servants were lightly injured. In the "unaffected" districts, a different kind of security threat developed: rumors of violence. Residents spread exaggerated rumors that in the "affected" districts, weapons had been used against the crowds, women had been injured and large military contingents had been deployed.

The participants, causes and demands of these 1916 riots did not vary considerably from those that came later. At all sites "primarily women, but also a very large number of youths and schoolchildren of both sexes" engaged in stone throwing, which caused "considerable damage." Demonstrators came from the "poorer population" and were "sanctioned by a majority of the middle class." Persons from "higher social classes" did not begrudge demonstrators, but rather "[had] lost all faith in the government" for letting things get to this point. Soldiers were also seen in the crowds. They were "for the most part passive" but indirectly supported the demonstrators. Individual women agitators voiced critical remarks about the quality and price of food and tried to "attract followers." Hatred of shop owners "undoubtedly contributed to the movement," as did rumors about food demonstrations in Berlin in which police "took the side of the demonstrators." Another underlying cause was the general anger of "the poor population" at the luxurious living of "rich people" who did not feel the pain of shortage at all. As we have seen, "rich" was not a purely economic category, but often included a national or ethnic component. In this instance, police noted that bitterness against Jews, accused of not buying war bonds, but buying their way out of military service, was also a factor.

Rioters demanded improvement in food provisions and an increase in state subsidies for young children. Cries from the crowd included "We are hungry!," "We and our children are starving!," "Give us something to eat!," "We want peace!" Emergency shipment of fats and eggs to demonstration sites increased suspicion among the crowd that profiteers were keeping an otherwise sufficient food supply from the market. They expressed the general view: "The more we demonstrate, the better it will be." In two locations, leaflets with "incendiary contents" were found.[180] Particularly noteworthy in this series of riots, as in many others, was the participants' attempt to reach the center of the city. Women and children looking for "the state" in wartime Vienna thought they had found it in the fortress-like buildings, of the Ringstrasse. Like demonstrators from previous eras, they considered the I district, which housed the city hall, the Food Office, the War Ministry and most other government buildings, the ideal place to voice demands.[181]

If we compare these incidents to the "workers" strikes of 1918, which historians have pinpointed as a crucial turning point in wartime domestic politics, we see that Viennese food rioters had in fact set the stage and shaped the discourse of Viennese politics. Two waves of strikes in January and June threatened to paralyze Austrian industry. But it was food, and not industrial working conditions, that initially sparked the actions. An Interior Ministry memo to the Kaiser outlined the course of events in the first wave of strikes: "It began with complaints about insufficient food supplies, but spread just as quickly into the political realm and evolved finally into a peace demonstration in which 550,000 workers [from around Austria] took part."[182] The crowds, numbering around 113,000 in Vienna, were described by Socialist party leaders, worried that they had lost control of the situation, as elements "unknown to the party," and comprised agitated, "sensation-hungry womenfolk."[183] A police report entitled "Mood of the Workers – Strike Movement," detailing the next round of strikes, which could just as easily have been called "Food Riot," tells a familiar story. In mid-June 1918, numerous bread trucks were ambushed by large crowds of "mostly women and children." Policemen were pelted with stones, stores were looted, and there were injuries and arrests (again, no names) of *Frauenspersonen* and youths. The one novel feature of the rioting was a crowd of 150 which agitated for a work stoppage by "hooting and hollering" in front of a factory. At the time of the disturbances there were already 45,689 (male and female) workers

[180] Riot report from AdBDW Stimmungsbericht, 18 May 1916.
[181] For women in earlier street actions, see Gabriella Hauch, *Frau Biedermeier auf den Barrikaden: Frauenleben in der Wiener Revolution 1848* (Vienna: Verlag für Gesellschaftskritik, 1990).
[182] Interior Minister to Kaiser, 10 February 1918, cited in Rudolf Neck (ed.), *Österreich im Jahre 1918: Berichte und Dokumente* (Munich: R. Oldenbourg Verlag, 1968), 34–5.
[183] Police report on Social Democratic party meeting, 1–3 February 1918, cited in *ibid.*, 26, 27.

on strike.[184] Agitating for a work stoppage did *not* signal a change in the rioters agenda; rather, just as they sometimes headed to the city center to confront the "state," rioters now had an alternate, equally charged destination, the factory. Nor was this a new development. As early as 1916, individuals had been arrested for trying to commandeer riotous food crowds to factories.[185]

The personal and collective experiences of the World War I food line were taken seriously as matters of state, and caused imperial, regional and local officials to reconsider the relationship of front and home front. Half of the "total war" equation – a stable, productive, passive home front – was negated by a civilian population in revolt. Habsburg authorities had once been careful to shield civilians from the disturbing, bloody reality of battlefield violence; field reports were sanitized, death was euphemized and civilians received from the press an "ideal type" picture of life at the front. Now the same concern operated in reverse. Censors worried that news of the home-front reality would "infect" soldiers with poor morale. Letters from the home front that mentioned food shortage and hunger were confiscated, so as to not to "endanger the discipline of front troops and negatively affect their spirits."[186] Authorities also feared that too much home front "exposure" was dangerous for soldiers on leave. This was a dramatic change from the early days of World War I, when the stable, passive, "not war" realm of civilians was regarded as the place to which soldiers would return once the "war" was over.

A 1914 women's magazine warned its readers not to bother their men in the field with frivolous questions and concerns. "No complaints in the letters and reports to the men in the field: in order to carry out their difficult duties, they must have strength, readiness and quiet. They have

[184] AdBDW Stimmungsberichte, February–December 1918, here 19 June 1918. Unfried has elucidated some of the links between food riots and strikers. Food, not industrial concerns, lay behind the strikers' demand for the freedom to carry a rucksack. And the strike movement of June, 1918 "clearly broke out on account of the reduction in bread rations." "Arbeiterproteste," 24, 171.
[185] AdBDW 1916 St./14 #31593. Report k.k. Bezirks-Kommissariat-Floridsdorf, 15 August 1916. Karl Zouhar of Vienna was being trailed by a police informer, who reported that he planned to steer a gathering of women and children, "which at the beginning had the character of a food demonstration" into a "revolution." Women would shield themselves with their children in the event of police attack. KA MK-KM 1918 #18391, memo from Pol. Dir. Wien, 10 April 1918, Johann Straub of Vienna was arrested for trying to route a food demonstration to the factories with the aim of launching a work stoppage.
[186] AdBDW Stimmungsberichte, January–April 1917 (misfiled). Letter from Marie Krbuschek in Vienna to brother Anton Wolf; and censor's memo, 27 March 1918.

to know, and be convinced, that their women at home are faring as well as they can by themselves."[187] Here, women's wartime burdens were regarded as so minor that they could not be spoken of. As this chapter has shown, home front sacrifice underwent a significant transformation. From the early view of home front sacrifice as secondary (or even inconsequential) in comparison to soldierly sacrifice, there emerged a volatile civilian population which demanded something the state could not provide. As a consequence, they embarked on what can be considered a civilian mutiny – a failure to carry out the passive duty of "holding out," a reluctance to display a "willingness to sacrifice," and a refusal to obey superiors.

As the incivility in the food lines and the subsequent descent into violence demonstrate, the Viennese did not take their victimhood sitting down. But victimhood rooted in hunger made for a strange collective. Solidarity was fleeting in a climate in which "the maintenance of one's own life" was the overriding concern of many citizens.[188] Communities of shared interest broke down and re-formed daily. While we have seen that hungry women and children formed a new political arena in Vienna, theirs was not a politics of "new opportunities" or "emancipation" but rather of basic survival.[189] Unlike postwar veterans, pensioners, widows and orphans who organized across Europe in the 1920s, demanding compensation for wartime losses, the community of sufferers in Vienna was a fragile, unstable entity without an organizational base.[190] The working-class neighborhoods where food riots occurred most frequently were also Vienna's most nationally and ethnically diverse neighborhoods. The strength and direction of consumer-based protest against the state were muted by in-fighting among consumers who felt little lasting solidarity among themselves.

---

[187] *Wiener Hauswirtschaftliche Rundschau* 10 (15 October 1914), 89.
[188] NÖLA Präs. "P" 1917 VI, #3807. Letter from Nö Statthalterei-Präs. to Minister of the Interior, 3 August 1917.
[189] On the pitfalls of viewing women's participation in World War I as "emancipatory" or classifying their protests as "resistance," see Ute Daniel, *The War From Within: German Working-Class Women in the First World War*, translated by Margaret Ries (Oxford, New York: Berg, 1997), ch. 6.
[190] The food demonstrators did not have an official organ, such as a newspaper, to voice their demands. The *Arbeiterinnen-Zeitung*, the party-affiliated paper for women workers, steadfastly ignored women's politics in the streets during the war. Coverage of food issues was limited to prices, monopolies, the structure of distribution and the consumer cooperatives.

2 Entertainment, propaganda and the Vienna War Exhibition of 1916–17

Government officials responded in two ways to the breakdown of law, order and social norms resulting from food scarcity. As we saw in the previous chapter, some officials confronted the problem directly, struggling against competing bureaucrats within the Habsburg civilian and military hierarchies to secure more food for the capital. But if they could not effectively control the supply and distribution of food, some officials reasoned that they could at least try to control how people *perceived* the crisis and what they said about it. This second approach, which involved the production and management of information, aimed to remind civilians of their "place" in war and to eradicate civilians' growing belief in their own victimization. The state waged an information war to combat residents' waning interest in events beyond their city, as typified by the comments of Viennese diarist Demophil Frank. Writing at the end of 1915, Frank explained, "In world affairs nothing much new is happening, the local story is more interesting. And here I must start with our stomachs."[1] Through propaganda, much of it presented in the form of entertainment, state officials attempted to reverse this development; they sought to draw civilians' attentions away from their own stomachs and focus them on the larger, transcendent events of a world war.

On the morning of July 1, 1916, prominent members of Viennese high society gathered in a large imperial park not far from the center of Vienna. This park, the Prater, had been the sight of many fairs, exhibits and festivals in the nineteenth and early twentieth centuries. It accommodated the World's Fair in 1873 and since then had housed circuses, variety shows, children's exhibits and the Luna Park amusement complex.[2] The

---

[1] Demophil Frank (pseud.), *Wien ... Taumel–Qual–Erlösung, 1914–1918* (Vienna: Anzengruber Verlag, 1928), 82.

[2] Like other European powers in the late nineteenth century, Austria had staged imperial exhibitions. Paul Greenhalgh concludes that Austria and Russia could not compete with Britain and France, the leading sponsors of such exhibitions, because "the nature of their respective empires rendered them generally unsuitable for most exhibitions." In other words, they could not produce the "exotic," non-European material that drew crowds.

Prater was a favorite destination of Viennese of all classes in search of recreation and entertainment. On this particular morning, those in attendance were more notable than usual; they included Archduke Franz Salvator, War Minister Alexander Krobatin, Education Minister Max von Hussarek, the Austrian Defense Minister, ambassadors of several allied countries, and local and regional government officials. They were on hand to celebrate the grand opening of what sponsors promised would be an exhibition unlike any Vienna had ever seen. At 11 a.m. the prestigious entourage entered the first hall of the grandest entertainment spectacle of the wartime home front: the Vienna War Exhibition.

Within two months, 500,000 Viennese had passed through the turnstiles, and within a year the number of visitors had reached one million. In a city with a prewar population of about two million, the War Exhibition can be counted as a small but integral part of the war experience for a good many residents. Covering an area of 50,000 m^2, the massive complex boasted forty display halls and theme rooms, several outdoor plazas, a theater, a cinema, two restaurants, two coffeehouses, several souvenir stands, a naval pavilion, a panorama of a mountain battle site and an overhead observation skydeck. Visitors could admire heavy artillery pieces captured from the enemy or view crafts and trinkets made by prisoners of war. Outside the complex, they could tour an "authentic" recreation of a network of battle trenches. The War Exhibition truly promised something for everyone – the visitor could learn about previous Habsburg wars, digest information about the present war, play war with his or her schoolmates or simply relax at a concert given by "war-damaged" musicians with new prosthetic limbs (see plate 2.1). The Exhibition, a Disneyland-like theme park, served war as entertainment to the Viennese.

A remarkable display of state-sponsored propaganda transmitted through channels of popular entertainment, the War Exhibition reveals the complex, mutually dependent relationship of propaganda and entertainment during World War I. Historians have examined the intense interest of state authorities in propaganda and "psychological warfare" during World War I, as well as the influence of war on popular culture in different European countries. Gary Stark notes of Germany, "Popular entertainments and amusements became an important battlefield on which . . . psychological battle was waged."[3] The Viennese

See *Ephemeral Vistas: The Expositions Universelles, Great Exhibitions and World's Fairs, 1851–1939* (Manchester: Manchester University Press, 1988), 73–4.

[3] Gary D. Stark, "All Quiet on the Home Front: Popular Entertainments, Censorship, and Civilian Morale in Germany, 1914–1918," in Frans Coetzee and Marilyn Shevin-Coetzee (eds.), *Authority, Identity and the Social History of the Great War* (Providence: Berghahn, 1995), 57–80, 76.

Plate 2.1. Horn player with prosthetic arm. Source: *Das interessante Blatt*
3 (1916), 12.

Exhibition – the largest war-related entertainment spectacle in Europe –
was a showcase for this marriage of propaganda and entertainment.[4]

[4] For review of propaganda efforts on the Austrian home front, see Mark Cornwall, *The Undermining of Austria-Hungary: The Battle for Hearts and Minds* (New York: St. Martin's Press, 2000), ch. 2; for Germany, see Jeffrey Verhey, "Some Lessons of the War: The Discourse on Propaganda and Public Opinion in Germany in the 1920's," in Bernd Hüppauf (ed.), *War, Violence and the Modern Condition* (Berlin/New York: Walter de Gruyter, 1997), 99–118. On entertainment and popular culture in World War I, see Aviel Roshwald and Richard Stites (eds.), *European Culture in the Great War: The Arts, Entertainment, and*

To understand the context of the War Exhibition, we must trace the
debates on wartime entertainment and charity as they evolved prior to its
opening.[5] That exhibition sponsors were able to open a war theme park
in wartime and that visitors flocked to it in such numbers underscores
the extent to which war had come to dominate the entertainment and
leisure activities of the Viennese by 1916. The Viennese understood entertainment to include all "those undertakings which promote enjoyment
(*Vergnügen*) and amusement (*Unterhaltung*)."[6] We shall consider as sites
of public entertainment (*öffentliche Lustbarkeiten*) a wide range of venues
such as coffeehouses, pubs, wine cellars, theaters, cabarets and circuses.
While elements of all these places of entertainment were eventually incorporated into the War Exhibition, particular attention is devoted to cinema
as one of the most popular forms of home-front amusement.

We begin with Viennese efforts in 1914 to establish a "serious mood"
(*ernste Stimmung*) in the city as a way of respecting and honoring the
sacrifices soldiers were making in battle. Entertainment venues such as
theaters, cabarets, dance halls, cinemas, bars and restaurants were closed
down or operated on reduced hours. City authorities and ordinary citizens agreed that fun and good times were not appropriate in wartime.
This was true for both men and women. Women were expected to demonstrate a willingness to sacrifice commensurate with their gender. Giving
up amusement was clearly not equivalent to the sacrifices being made by
men in uniform, but it was expected of women, by women. Men amusing themselves on the home front also came under close scrutiny. They
were denounced by fellow citizens for a double failure to sacrifice; first,
for not serving in the field, and second, for not honoring the sacrifices
of others through modest behavior. This rhetoric of sacrifice proved to
be quite damaging for those owners and operators who made their business selling amusement. In response, cinema owners repackaged their
entertainment offerings as war education, and entertainment gradually
reappeared under the guise of charity fundraising.

Having set the stage, so to speak, for entertainment's normalized place
in wartime, we will be able to explore more fully the content of the War
Exhibition, noting what visitors saw and, equally importantly, what they
did *not* see as they made their way through its halls, restaurants, shops

Propaganda, 1914–1918 (Cambridge: Cambridge University Press, 1999); Hubertus F.
Jahn, *Patriotic Culture in Russia During World War I* (Ithaca: Cornell University Press,
1995); and George L. Mosse, *Fallen Soldiers: Reshaping the Memory of the World Wars*
(New York: Oxford University Press, 1990), ch. 7.
[5] On the difficulty of settling on suitably patriotic "Austrian" (as opposed to "German")
programs, see Steven Beller, "The Tragic Carnival: Austrian Culture in the First World
War," in Roshwald and Stites, *European Culture in the Great War*, 127–61.
[6] *Kinematographische Rundschau*, 2 August 1914.

and special attractions. If entertainment was the medium, the message was a propagandistic celebration of the unity of front and home front. The sponsors of the War Exhibition had lofty intentions: they promised it would enable visitors to understand the meaning of the war in its totality. This peculiar Viennese undertaking – staging World War I as it was happening – allows us to query how the concept "total war" was understood by contemporaries and how it should understood by historians. For sponsors, who promised exhibits depicting the "perfect union of front and hinterland," total war was one in which a mobilized home front always worked in the service of the front. Home front and front shared a common goal (defeat of the enemy) and home front played a necessary "back-up" position. Historians investigating total war have similarly focused on civilian mobilization in the service of a greater cause.[7] But the War Exhibition itself demonstrates the inadequacy of studying the home front solely through the prism of *mobilization*. When the Viennese looked at displays of the hinterland, which celebrated the accomplishments of "mobilized civilians," they were not seeing reflections of their own war experiences. This leads us to two conclusions: First, sacrifice is a key theme in understanding civilian participation in "total war." Second, the most convincing argument for the totality of this war was not the union of front and home front depicted in the exhibits, but the fact that the Viennese looking for entertainment during the second half of a long war sought their amusement at a war theme park.

Historian Jay Winter, writing on collective remembrance, notes, "The search for the meaning of the Great War began as soon as the war itself."[8] Vienna's War Exhibition can be seen as an orchestrated attempt to construct the meaning of the war through the vehicle of entertainment spectacle. It attempted to synthesize the many facets of war into a unified event, held in a single complex, comprehensible to the individual viewer. Stressing the interrelation between front and home front, the show reminded viewers that, despite the many confusing elements of the war, it was indeed *one* war, comprised of two halves (front and home front) that worked in union. As an attempt to construct meaning, it was preliminary and imperfect, constricted by the dictates of the war in progress. It wanted to offer an Archimedean point outside of war, an opportunity to gain distance, and hence perspective, on the events as they happened. One way of creating this illusion of distance was to bill the war as history. Reviewing the Exhibition, one journalist wrote, "[B]efore the eyes of

---

[7] See the essays in John Horne (ed.), *State, Society and Mobilization in Europe During the First World War* (Cambridge: Cambridge University Press, 1997).

[8] Jay Winter, *Sites of Memory, Sites of Mourning: The Great War in European Cultural History* (Cambridge: Cambridge University Press, 1995), 78.

the visitor, the immediate present is already transfigured into history."[9] Encouraging civilians to forget their "immediate present," marked by hunger, social instability and rebellious actions against authorities, and to imagine themselves as participants in a transcendent, world-historical event was a key aim of the state's information war.

Amusement and the spirit of sacrifice

Vienna in 1914 was an entertaining city. In addition to its famous opera, theaters and coffeehouses, it boasted a wide range of entertainment venues such as variety shows, cabarets, singing halls, dancing halls and pubs, and an impressive number of cinemas, circuses and museums. An English travel guide written in 1914 praised the friendly and festive atmosphere of the city:"[T]here is something strikingly pleasurable and Austrian about merry-making here."[10] The successive declarations of war on Serbia, Russia, France and Britain in late July and August were an immediate blow to Vienna's entertainment culture. Newspapers noted that many venues had closed "on account of the war." The reported "serious mood" of the population was hailed as a sign that the citizens understood the grave circumstances of war and were prepared to sacrifice their amusement to its cause. But this unofficial consensus on maintaining a serious and somber atmosphere on the home front was very short-lived. By the fall, citizens were already complaining to the police that other citizens, in pursuit of amusement, were "making a terrible mockery of the sorrow and mourning with which we honor the fallen heroes."[11]

Leading the "serious mood" campaign were bourgeois women's groups – the League of Austrian Women's Associations, represented by Marianne Hainisch, and the Imperial Organization of Austrian Housewives, represented by Fanny Freund-Markus and Helene Granitsch. These women wrote to the police that the re-emergent nightlife in Vienna, "under the influence of certain unscrupulous and greedy elements," was an assault on the serious mood maintained by the "truly patriotic population."[12] They cited coffeehouses that had been transformed "by the dozen" into cabarets and all-night amusement houses. Using Berlin as an example, they demanded that the Viennese police set strict, early closing hours for these offensive locales. Military authorities had already sounded the alarm about the inappropriate atmosphere of frivolity in Vienna; they

[9] WSLB ZAS, Ausstellung I, *Österreichische Volkszeitung*, 25 June 1916.
[10] G. E. Mitton, *Austria-Hungary* (London, 1914), 100.
[11] NÖLA Präs. 1914 2730 XII 162–85. Letter from women's groups to k.k. Polizeipräs., 26 November 1914.
[12] *Ibid.*

had noticed women joy-riding through the streets in military vehicles and ordered that the practice be stopped.[13] Some Viennese cited a lusty appetite for amusement among refugees from Galicia, who reportedly had a "predilection for nightlife."[14] The police responded to these concerns by requiring 2 a.m. closings for most Viennese bars and entertainment locales and by banning all forms of dancing, whether in staged dance productions or in halls. This move did not satisfy the women's groups (who were pushing for 11 p.m.) but seemed to mollify some critics. One newspaper wrote approvingly that when the shutters closed at 2 a.m., "every citizen would have a duty to fulfill: the duty of sleep . . ."[15]

While consumers of entertainment debated its merits, producers of entertainment suffered the same labor disruptions as other sectors of the economy. Conscription took musicians, actors and cinema owners away from their positions.[16] Museums had to close because there were too few employees to guard their works. Further staff reductions occurred when the police made efforts to rid the entertainment industry of enemy elements. Artists in this multi-national city found themselves under scrutiny; citizens of enemy states were banned from performing and either "interned" or "confined." The hardship this caused entertainment workers is evident in the case of Maria Swiatopulk-Mirska, a performer at the Cabaret Simplicissimus. An Austrian singer and pianist, she had once been married to a Russian, and, even though divorced, she was still considered a Russian citizen. Forbidden as an "enemy" from performing on the Vienna stage, she wrote to the police, "I have made the greatest material sacrifice to acquire training as a cabaret artist, with the conviction that it would enable me to secure a livelihood for myself and my child."[17] She cited the medals her male relatives had won in combat for the Habsburg army, and was eventually granted the right to return to her piano. In other similar cases, police sometimes went to absurd lengths to ensure that any entertainment venues still operating were clean of enemies. The owner of Zirkus Busch had to appeal for special permission to

[13] NÖLA Präs. "P" 1914 389P. Order from Militär- und Landwehrstationskommando concerning "Misuse of autos in military service," 10 September 1914.

[14] NÖLA Präs. 1914 2730 XII/162–85. Letter from k.k. Statthalterei to k.k. Pol. Dir. Wien, 9 August 1915. By September, 1914, there were between 60,000 and 70,000 refugees from Galicia already in Vienna, with more expected with the evacuation of Cracow. WSLA B23/73 Gemeinderat. Protokoll Obmänner-Konferenz, 29 September 1914.

[15] WSLB ZAS Rechtsleben und polizeiliche Maßnahmen I, *Neues Wiener Tagblatt*, 13 December 1914. See also NÖLA Präs. 1914 2730 XII/162–85.

[16] *Der Kinobesitzer*, a trade journal for cinema owners, claimed that by 1917, 50 percent of cinema owners had been conscripted into the military or were performing other war service (*Kriegsdienstleistung*).

[17] NÖLA Präs. "P" XVIII, 396. Letter to Statthalterei, via the Pol. Dir. Wien, early September 1915.

keep one of his performers, a dwarf who was a citizen of an enemy state, on the payroll. He wrote to the Viennese police that the dwarf, François Leporati, was "the only citizen of an enemy state in the whole operation, and we only want to employ him because it's the only way the poor cripple can earn a living."[18] Many entertainment venues closed down altogether, and those that remained open through the first year of the war had undergone a rigorous "Austrianization."

This did not quell the protests of citizens who objected to the very notion of cabarets and circuses in wartime. Critics of wartime entertainment differentiated little between what they considered to be socially or politically unconscionable (enjoying oneself while the troops suffered and died at the front) and the moral threat that entertainment posed for the community. Those advocating a "serious mood" in Vienna focused their attention primarily on evening entertainment. The women's groups mentioned above linked a lust for amusement with lust in general, and thus their campaign against entertainment moved seamlessly into an attack on prostitution and sexual lasciviousness on the home front. Prostitution was on the rise, according to police, because the economic upheaval of war had drawn more women (refugees, wives of reservists and the unemployed) into the business. The client base for prostitution had also grown considerably. Hundreds of thousands of troops were passing through the capital, either in transit or for convalescent medical care. For many of them Vienna represented the "big city," and, as the provincial governor's office explained to the Viennese police, these men sought out entertainment and wanted to enjoy "the pleasures and hustle and bustle of the metropolis."[19] The military commander for Vienna agreed, linking leisure time, entertainment venues and the presence of so many men to the growing problem of immorality (*Unsittlichkeit*):

Often even officers cannot resist the temptations of the many night-spots. These officers, who have come here from the theater of operations, whose wounds have not healed and who have not yet been restored to health, would do better to save their strength and to get a good night's rest in order to return quickly to fitness. A radical remedy of this unfortunate situation, the redress of which is of great military importance, could be achieved by closing such locales at an earlier hour ... Surely such places of amusement provide profit for their owners and tenants; for the general public they spell only harm.[20]

---

[18] AdBDW 1915 V/12 #37/15336. Letter to Pol. Dir. Wien, 20 September 1915.
[19] NÖLA Präs. 1914 2730 XII/162–85. Letter from k.k. Statthalterei to Pol. Dir. Wien, 9 August 1915.
[20] NÖLA Präs. 1914 2730 XII 162–85. Letter from k.k. Stadtkommandant in Wien to Pol. Dir. Wien, 22 November 1914.

Soldiers were warned of the deleterious health effects of too much amusement, but the "unfortunate situation" was blamed primarily on women
who had not adopted the proper spirit of sacrifice. Police and morally
high-minded citizens sought a reduction in the number of women present
in the entertainment venues. This focus on women highlights the gendered notions of sacrifice in total war: women could not serve the state in
the same way as men (by fighting), but could perform a kind of second-
order sacrifice by foregoing amusement and other inessential pursuits in
the city.

A police decree on December 1, 1914 announced that prostitutes
registered with the morality police (women under "*sittenpolizeilicher
Kontrolle*")[21] were forbidden to frequent restaurants, coffeehouses, buf-
fets or "entertainment locales of any kind" in which singing or musi-
cal productions were held.[22] This decree left a fundamental question
unanswered: how were the police, owners and other customers at these
venues supposed to recognize a prostitute? Not only were many prostitutes working outside of the state regulation scheme, but single women
and women whose spouses were serving in the military often went out
unaccompanied. According to one newspaper, it had become a "practical
necessity" for women and girls to visit coffeehouses and restaurants alone
"to grab a meal or an hour of relaxation."[23] In trying to eliminate the sexual stigma of entertainment venues, police cast a shadow of immorality
over women and girls out alone at night.

Two cases demonstrate the consequences for women of entertainment
venues being linked in the public imagination with sexual promiscuity. In a letter to the police, a woman calling herself "Banker's Wife
Zschörner" described with outrage the treatment she had received at the
Café Carlton. Her husband away at the front, Frau Zschörner sometimes
headed to cafés to drink a coffee or a whiskey for "a little amusement in
the evening." A waiter at the Carlton informed her that he was forbidden
to serve women alone, but when she returned to the same café another
evening with friends, she noticed several unaccompanied "coquettes" being served. Indignant, she wrote, "There must be the same rights for all.
Either no lady without accompaniment can be served, or all ladies of all
rank!" She went on to differentiate herself (respectable) from coquettes
(flirtatious behavior, conspicuous clothing and hair) and to justify her
right to amusement. "It can't be demanded of a young, vivacious woman

[21] On state-regulated prostitution in Austria, see Karin Jusek, *Auf der Suche nach der
Verlorenen: Die Prostitutionsdebatten im Wien der Jahrhundertwende* (Vienna: Löcker, 1994).
[22] NÖLA Präs. 1914 2730 XII/162–85. Kundmachung from the Pol. Dir. Wien.
[23] *Neue Freie Presse*, 12 October 1916, 11.

that she'll stay cooped up at home for two years, since the beginning of the war – she'll just become melancholic."[24]

Frau Zschörner's case was not an isolated one. Coffeehouse customer Anna S. brought a lawsuit against an establishment on the Mariahilfer-strasse for failing to serve her.[25] In the course of the proceedings, Karl Attila, the waiter who had asked Anna S. to leave the coffeehouse, explained the policy on serving women. Employees, instructed to ensure that "certain ladies" did not stay too long at the coffeehouse, used the following strategy: they let an unaccompanied woman sit for a long time before taking her order; if she did not leave, they would serve her, then quickly and abruptly present her with a bill, a rude practice at odds with coffeehouse culture. The owner of the establishment defended his right to protect the upstanding image of his coffeehouse, but the judge responded, "Even for a waiter, it is terribly difficult to decide on first glance if a lady belongs to so-called 'easy world.'" The very women who had advocated closing down (or at least cleaning up) the entertainment venues in order to maintain an appropriately "serious mood" in the city had now become victims of policies targeting any woman who appeared to be relaxing or enjoying herself. When claiming in 1914 that "the dreadful gravity of the battlefield should and must find recognition in the mood of the population behind the lines," women's groups were not anticipating a war that would last four and a half years. Could women really honor the soldiers twenty-four hours a day? Could they maintain a stance of full-time, patient suffering? A woman like Frau Zschörner was depressed by this prospect, and Anna S. conceded she needed a little amusement once in a while.

For men on the home front, the pursuit of amusement clashed even more directly with the duty to sacrifice. Throughout the war, authorities fielded citizen complaints about drunken soldiers and officers on leave behaving recklessly or frivolously. In 1916, police had to intervene when loud, intoxicated, singing officers returned from the wine cellars of Grinzing, irritating other tram passengers and nearby residents.[26] The following case of a dancing policeman shows that men who were not in military service (those found "unfit" or exempted on grounds of occupational indispensability) provoked particular ire when amusing themselves. The Viennese police chief received an anonymous letter detailing

---

[24] AdBDW 1916 St./13 #34578. Letter to Polizeikommissariat I district, 11 October 1916.
[25] "Aus dem Gerichtssaale," *Neue Freie Presse*, 12 October 1916, 11. Anna S. and her lawyer made the interesting decision to base the suit not on an "insult to honor" (*Ehrenbeleidigung*), but on "denial of access to necessary foodstuffs" (§482, Strafgesetz).
[26] AdBDW St./16 (no doc. #). Police report, 21 September 1916.

the exploits of policeman Johann Blank. It read:

At midnight... I was on my way home with my wife... As we passed the Gastwirt Kuttelwascher on the Erdbergstrasse I heard dance music and saw through the window several people dancing. Out of curiosity I (went in) and bought myself a 1/4 (liter) of wine. To my astonishment I saw security patrolman Blank, familiar to me from the neighborhood... and several other gentlemen of his age fully immersed in dancing with several girls... I've had enough – so many thousands of our brothers are bleeding on the battlefield and here the patrolmen are staging dances. I can't sit by and watch that. I am convinced that Mr. President knows nothing of these sorts of amusements.[27]

The letter writer juxtaposes home-front amusement to frontline sacrifice. If these could not be reconciled, entertainment in wartime would remain a taboo. But a reconciliation did take place. Whereas many Viennese felt initially that war *precluded* entertainment, they gradually accepted the notion that war could *provide* entertainment. They justified the pursuit of amusement in wartime as long as the theme of the amusement was war itself.

War entertainment

This shift in attitude is particularly evident in the development of wartime cinema. Bernhard Denscher notes that entertainment venues such as circuses, variety shows, operettas and theaters began to market the "martial mood" of the times, and "made their business with the *Heldentod*."[28] The cinema industry merits particular attention because cinema owners spearheaded the move towards war-oriented entertainment. Even before the actual declaration of war, cinema operators occasionally suspended programs out of respect for the "seriousness of the times." For example, they did not show films on the burial day of Archduke Franz Ferdinand and his wife Sophie, assassinated in Sarajevo. But they were the first in the entertainment industry to defend amusement as a necessary component of life on the home front, and the first to realize that their survival would depend on integrating the war into their product. The film production companies were very quick to adapt to the new conditions; already in August, 1914, they advertised *Kriegsfilme* (war-related films) to their customers, the cinema operators. Boldly challenging the assumptions of the "serious mood" advocates, cinema operators argued that they, and their colleagues in theater and music, had a "moral duty" to provide

[27] AdBDW 1915 V/23 #7516. Police report on anonymous letter, 15 March 1915.
[28] Bernhard Denscher, *Gold gab ich für Eisen: Österreichische Kriegsplakate, 1914–1918* (Vienna: Jugend & Volk, 1987), 13.

amusement to the public. Opportunity for "diversion" (*Ablenkung*) was especially important for people coping with the difficult times.[29] They insisted that a woman like Frau Zschörner should not have to sit at home in a state of melancholy; she deserved the opportunity to unwind. Cinema operators explained early in the war, "In times of peace we discovered that the great mass of the public sought and found its amusement in the cinema. The cinema has become spiritual nourishment – the great public longs for it and considers it indispensable."[30] They repackaged their films as war education so that such indispensable pleasure could be combined with valuable instruction. The cinema owners' stance exemplifies one of the key ambiguities of wartime entertainment. Could one program provide diversion – a momentary opportunity to forget the war – while simultaneously providing instruction about the war?

Vienna had a surprising number of cinemas; by 1918 it boasted 160.[31] Not all of these were as grand as the Zentralkino or the new Kino at the Vienna War Exhibition. In fact, some of them were merely rooms, cellars or tents where viewers gathered in somewhat unpleasant conditions. One newspaper described the lesser known Phönix-Kino on Lerchenfelderstrasse as a threat to public health. An overcrowded cellar, accessible by a series of narrow passageways, it "resembled a catacomb," where in the case of fire "the visitors, mostly women and children" would be trapped and would stampede to the cramped stairwell.[32] Richard Guttmann, a Viennese social philosopher, described, somewhat critically, a typical cinema experience in wartime Vienna:

Kino is understood to mean a space that is easily accessible from the street, either at street level or in a cellar, sometimes also a wooden hut or a festive tent... Windows and door are closed. The air is polluted with a disinfectant spray and young and old people alike sit in cramped rows. Expectation waves its gentle wand over spirits suddenly removed from the world. It becomes dark, the music sounds, and a cinematic projector casts his whirring pictures onto a white screen.[33]

This scene was repeated hundreds of thousands of times. An average cinema showed about sixty programs per year, and the Viennese public

[29] *Kinematographische Rundschau*, 23 August 1914, 1.
[30] *Kinematographische Rundschau*, 6 September 1914, 1.
[31] *Der Kinobesitzer*, 15 April 1918, 5. In comparison, Gary Stark estimates that Germany had 2,400 cinemas during World War I, 200–350 of them in Berlin. "All Quiet on the Home Front," 58. Arthur Marwick puts the number of cinemas in Britain in 1914 at 3,000. *The Deluge: British Society and the First World War* (London: Bodley Head, 1965), 140.
[32] *Reichspost*, 23 February 1918, 3.
[33] Richard Guttmann, *Die Kinomenschheit: Versuch einer prinzipiellen Analyse* (Vienna, 1916), 5–6.

displayed an unexpected hunger for films. A commission that studied the wartime cinema boom noted, "Cinematic theaters have unexpectedly recorded mass attendance as never before." The Educational Council, a body of 434 delegates from educational, religious and social service associations in Vienna, focused on "educational matters of a general nature" and took specific interest in cinema and children's welfare. In 1915, E. Hany, a female teacher, presented to the council a lecture on "Cinema and War," in which she speculated that "in many ways the cinema today represents an even greater necessity (*Lebensbedürfnis*) than food."[34] Clearly, the strategies of cinema owners and film producers and the attitude of viewers and state authorities towards film would shape considerably the larger debate on wartime entertainment. Whether viewers, those amusement-seeking "spirits suddenly removed from the world," could also cognitively absorb war education was not addressed.

Just as the cinemas varied in size, so did the films. Some were marketed as blockbusters ("the film event of 1915") while others seem to have come and gone with little fanfare. All passed before the eyes of the Viennese police, who continued to censor films as they had before the war.[35] Surprisingly, films from enemy countries were not automatically banned. Rather, if their content was deemed acceptable, all signs of their "enemy origin" – titles, subtitles, credits – had to be removed. Thus, the film industry did not undergo the same the "Austrianization" as live entertainment, although it may have appeared so to the viewers. A typical weekly censor's report notes that eight films of enemy origin were approved, but viewers enjoying *Auto Racing, Berta's Birthday* and *Dirty Business* had no idea they were watching French productions.[36] The films shown in Vienna fell into three broad categories: the *Spielfilme* (feature films), the "assembly line" films, which showed how army uniforms were assembled and how bullets were manufactured, and the *Kriegswochenschau* (weekly war-film programs). These were not strict genres; segments of the assembly line films and weekly war footage were sometimes woven into feature films that did not have an otherwise explicit war orientation. Thus, it was likely that every trip to the cinema meant viewing a film with at least some war content.

---

[34] ÖStA, AdR, k.k. Min. f. soz. Verwaltung 1918, carton 1590, #1702–18. *Große Kommission des Kaiser-Jubiläumsfondes für Kinderschutz und Jugendfürsorge. Tätigkeitsbericht des Erziehungsrates, 1915,* "Kino und Krieg," 3.

[35] Ministerialverordnung, 18 September 1912, RGBl. 191, §17. The Viennese police published a weekly report of their findings, broken into three categories: films totally banned; films that would be approved with changes (offensive scenes removed); and films that were appropriate for children.

[36] "Zensurergebnisse," 21 August 1917. In *Der Kinobesitzer,* 8 September 1917, 25.

Audiences continued to enjoy detective films and family dramas, but film producers began to make films in which war figured prominently in the plot.[37] *War in the Nursery* (*Der Krieg in der Kinderstube*, 1915) showed the creative ways children had found to play war in their homes. "Out of every possible household appliance they construct a submarine, and they use a great bunch of balloons to create a Zeppelin." In order to construct their theater of operation, the two boys rearrange their entire apartment, which meets "with little understanding from their parents." Although they are sent to their rooms for punishment, the film celebrates the ingenuity and "lively war enthusiasm" of children.[38] Sometimes war was woven more abruptly into feature films. Crudely inserted into *Soldier's Children* (*Soldatenkinder*, 1915), ostensibly a story of two children who want to send cigarettes to their fathers in the field, were scenes from weekly war footage. "In the film we see transport convoys, wonderful airplane ascents and our soldiers at rest." The finale of the film abandons the child-centered plot altogether and shows "really first-class shots" of a dogfight and the downing of an enemy airplane.[39] As will be noted shortly, feature films without a war-oriented plot or at least a little war footage provoked the ire of child welfare advocates.

The assembly line films offered viewers a chance to see the processes of war at work. In these films the war was all about production (*Leistung*). How was the cloth one donated really going to help the troops? How did the nine million men in Habsburg uniform actually receive the cigarettes civilians were rolling for them? Films such as *War Metal Collection* (*Kriegs-Metallsammlung*, 1917) answered these questions.[40] In this film, viewers saw the complicated process by which household materials could be turned into bullet casings. The film begins with people lining up to donate their metal goods; some offer pots and pans, another gives a bird cage, and a little boy offers his trumpet. The items are weighed and the donors receive receipts for their goods. Copper wiring from underground cables on the home front also gets added to the stock. The items are transported, melted down and turned into bullet casings and mortar shells, which, in the last scene, are in a freight transport headed for the front. To preserve the upbeat message that war is productive, the film neglects the second half of the metal-collection story – that pieces

[37] Most films shown in Vienna were produced in Austria, Germany, Hungary and Scandinavia. See Walter Fritz, *Kino in Österreich, 1896–1930: Der Stummfilm* (Vienna: Österreichischer Bundesverlag, 1981) for developments in Austrian film production.

[38] *Österreichischer Komet. Fachblatt für Kinematographie* 8, no. 255, 3 April 1915.

[39] *Österreichischer Komet. Fachblatt für Kinematographie* 8, no. 245, 23 January 1915.

[40] Österreichisches Filmarchiv, *Alltag in der öst.-ung. Monarchie* series, roll 6, *Kriegs-Metallsammlung*, 1917.

of the little boy's trumpet will end up lodged in the skull of an enemy soldier.

The *Kriegswochenschau*, a weekly program of war footage, was the mainstay of wartime cinema. Several film companies were involved throughout the war in putting these series together, and photographers needed the permission of the Army High Command to film scenes involving the armed forces.[41] The 1915 Commission studying "Cinema and War" had only the highest praise for their product. Film advocates noted again and again the incredible, unmediated "reality" which the war footage opened up for the viewer, using the term *naturwahr* (true to nature) to describe the quality of the shots. By 1915, five million meters of war footage had been shown in Vienna theaters.[42] A typical program, advertised outside the cinema on a poster, included the following clips:

1. Infantry under good cover stands before a city left in flames by the Russians; 2. Extinguishing a house fire; 3. Shooting a breach into a house; 4. Farmyard in flames; 5. Issuing an important command; 6. In the early morning hours under the protection of fog an infantry unit and a machine gun division undertake a "leap forward" against the enemy; 7. Building the feared 30.5 cm mortar shells; 8. Our troops firing 15 cm howitzers from good position onto the later captured Magyar foothills; 9. Field howitzer on fire in open terrain; 10. A pilot receives an order for a reconnaissance flight over enemy territory; 11. Departure; 12. High in the stormy clouds; 13. Happily returning with important news and a couple of hits on the wings of the airplane.[43]

A Frau Mohr, visiting the Zentralkino in 1914, did not need to be convinced of the reality of what she saw in the weekly program. In a scene of the storming of Lüttich she recognized her husband in a long row of marching soldiers. She did not believe it at first, but the gait and movements were undeniably his. Herr Mohr appeared later in the same film carrying a flag.[44] Frau Mohr was delighted at seeing her man in action, and afterwards requested still shots from the film. This was a moment where film seemed incredibly "real" – the soldiers were not actors, and a viewer like Frau Mohr could believe she caught a glimpse of her husband's authentic battle experience.

---

[41] The series changed names several times. An early series was the *Kriegs-Journal*. The *Kriegswochenschau* became the *Kinematographische Kriegsberichterstattung* in 1915, then changed to *Sascha-Kriegswochenbericht*, and finally the *Sascha-Meßter Woche* in 1918. Fritz, *Kino in Österreich*, 69.

[42] *Große Kommission*, "Kino und Krieg," 4–5.

[43] *Kinematographische Rundschau* no. 348, 8 November 1914, 24. Cited in Walter Fritz, *Dokumentarfilme aus Österreich, 1909–1914*, Schriftenreihe des österreichischen Filmarchivs, 5 (Vienna: Gesellschaft, 1980).

[44] "Wie seltsam...," *Kinematographische Rundschau*, 11 November 1914, 6.

The weekly film programs, as well as the other venues that offered war as entertainment and promised to bridge front and home front, left out what was certainly the hallmark of the World War I battle experience: killing. It is very, very difficult to find, in any archival or published materials from the Viennese home front, any mention of killing. Certainly, censors made sure there was no trace of killing, even of enemy soldiers, in the films shown in Vienna cinemas. A censor approved one of the weekly war footage programs from the Italian front with the following qualification: "With exclusion of the scene from the first sequence (close-up), in which the distorted faces of dead Italian soldiers are seen ... With exclusion of the scene (close-up) in which the Italian lying on the ground is bandaged by his comrades."[45] The Education Council's 1915 study of cinema and war noted that two kinds of films were being shot: some violent film footage was headed for the war archive, where it would be stored as a "special kind of war documentation." In the second kind, destined for public consumption, it was "obvious" that no scenes of brutality and bloody atrocity could be depicted. The schoolteacher E. Hany argued before the Council that heroic soldiers were not sacrificing themselves only to have their last moments on earth displayed for the "sensation-seeking curiosity of idle viewers." In addition, she hoped that filmgoers would be happier to see soldiers performing the "peaceful labor of war" such as rebuilding bridges, stationing their heavy machinery and digging trenches.[46] The Viennese *were* hungry for carnage, however; police warned newspapers to stop announcing when wounded troops would be arriving at train stations because huge crowds of "the curious" were gathering to get a glimpse of these men.[47]

Although they could not satisfy this particular desire of "the curious" because carnage was censored out of films, cinema operators were pleased to expound on the educational benefits of motion pictures. They disseminated education in various forms, including plots with plausible war scenarios, characters with "war enthusiasm" and news shows to keep viewers up to date on current events. Cinema owners argued for the benefits of "seeing" over other modes of learning. "The children should see the soldiers in action," they wrote. "We read that our soldiers are triumphant – our children should see this and learn from film how gallant men behave, and how cowards ... are punished."[48] As an educational medium, film was ideal because of its mass audience. The Viennese police decided to air public service announcements in the cinemas (pictures

---

[45] Cited in Fritz, *Kino in Österreich*, 70.   [46] *Große Kommission*, "Kino und Krieg," 4.
[47] NÖLA Präs. "P" 1914, 841. Letter from Pol. Dir. Wien to Nö. Statthalterpräs., 16 September 1914.
[48] *Kinematographische Rundschau*, 23 August 1914, 4.

of missing persons, escaped criminals and stolen goods) because these messages would reach "the masses" who rarely or never read a newspaper, but certainly went to the cinema.[49] Sometimes audiences reacted just as authorities hoped they would. A cinema owner reported how deeply affected he was by the reaction of boys and girls in his cinema. Watching a drama about an Austrian woman who was charged with spying by the Russians, the children "followed the events with bated breath." When the woman was narrowly saved by her husband, who managed to take the whole Russian unit prisoner, the children "jumped from their seats and clapped and cheered with excitement."[50] The educational project of an action film could be as simple as getting children to identify correctly the heroes and villains.

One problem with promoting film as war education was that those producing and showing the films could not control audience reaction to them. What if the intended messages of the films were misinterpreted? What if audience members spoke these misinterpretations aloud, spoiling the educational moment for those sitting around them? Audience reaction is difficult to reconstruct, but two incidents suggest that viewers did have verbal reactions to the images they saw, and that these reactions sometimes countered the educational intent of the weekly war programs. In the first case, Stanislaus Grendecki, a nine-year-old Polish-speaking refugee from Czernowitz, attended a show at the Margareten Bürger Kino in 1915. During one of the clips, when Emperor Franz Joseph appeared on the screen, Grendecki blurted out, "Here's where they report on the Emperor – the Emperor should be shot down. He should have been shot down a few years ago." Ten-year-old Mathilde Cul, a fellow Polish-speaker, warned him that he could be punished for making such statements. Grendecki continued, "He should be shot down. My father is sick and he's lying in a hospital." An acquaintance of Cul's mother denounced Grendecki (the youngest victim of wartime denunciation I have discovered), and he was called, along with his mother, to the police station where he admitted making the statements at the cinema.[51] Whether he held the Emperor responsible for his father's wounds could not be determined because the police did not have a Polish interpreter. What is clear is that filmmakers (in this case, probably an imperial photographer) could not control audience reception at the movie house. Between the filmmakers and the audience they hoped to "educate" about war might come live, unpredictable reactions of fellow viewers.

[49] *Der Kinobesitzer* 1, no. 5, 29 September 1917, 5.
[50] *Der Kinobesitzer* 2, no. 33, 15 April 1918, 5–6.
[51] AdBDW 1915 St./15 #4361. Report from Johann Pewner (also Pöwner) to k.k. Bezirkspolizei-Kommissariat Margareten, January 1915.

A similar incident took place a few years later at the Votivkino. Lieutenant-Colonel Franz Nückerl reported to police the comments of Katarina Hahn, who was sitting near him at the cinema.[52] During a film clip in which Emperor Karl was greeting visiting dignitaries, Hahn exclaimed, "Look how many medals he has!" Later she added, "Look how friendly he is!" Nückerl wrote to police (after his own investigation to figure out the identity of his neighbor) that "these perhaps harmless-sounding comments" had been made in a sarcastic tone. In other words, Hahn had been mocking the film. She admitted having made the comments, but claimed she meant them earnestly. This may have been a misunderstanding, a case of an overzealous patriot overreacting at the cinema, but the incident reminds us again that while films could reach a mass audience, the audience itself had the power to disrupt the intended educational message of the films.

Cinema owners were fairly successful at promoting the educational benefits of film, showing the public "the wonder of technology, which war has spurred to great capacities."[53] But two factors provoked continued skepticism about film's positive educational virtues and left cinema operators on the defensive. First, children were spending a great deal of time at the cinema and, like Stanislaus Grendecki and Mathilde Cul, they were often unaccompanied by adults. Although the censors designated only certain films appropriate for children, cinema operators, who relied on ticket sales to children, were letting them in to view adult films.[54] Second, not all of the feature films were about war. The children in the cinemas were also viewing criminal and detective movies that cinema opponents blamed for the staggering increase in youth crime during the war. Youth delinquency (Verwahrlosung) was one of the most widely debated social problems in World War I Vienna. A main theme of the delinquency discussion was – along with lack of supervision for children, the transformation of schools into military hospitals, the increase in youth smoking and the reading of "smut-literature" – the pernicious effects of too much cinema. Juvenile court proceedings often recorded the tag Kinobesucher

[52] AdBDW 1918 St./17 #58677. Letter from Franz Nückerl to Pol. Dir. Wien, 25 July 1918.

[53] WSLB ZAS, Ausstellung II, Neues Wiener Tagblatt, 1 September 1916.

[54] Police tried to catch violators, but they did not have the manpower to monitor cinema entrances. In "Kino Besuch der Kinder" the trade journal Kinematographische Rundschau reported on October 11, 1914, that a veteran cinema operator had been fined 200 crowns when a policeman caught him admitting two children, ages six and seven, to a show after 8 p.m. Protesting moves to further restrict youth access to the cinema, owners wrote, "Unsere Besucher sind heute nur die Frauen, die Kinder und die Jugend. Wenn wir nicht zusammenbrechen sollen, dann muß die Jugend unbehindert ins Kino gehen können." Kinematographische Rundschau, 20 September 1914.

(cinema-goer) as one of the traits of the young law breaker.[55] A Vienna schoolteacher who set out to demonstrate the dangers of cinema published statistics based on the viewing habits of his students: he estimated that "over a short period of time" they had viewed more than 1,600 programs, which included 600 acts of theft, 500 murders and violent acts and 400 other crimes.[56] Cinema owners denounced these statistics as wildly fanciful, but they could not permanently dispel the public association of film with youth delinquency.

The schoolteacher and other cinema critics weighed the business interests of the film industry against the greater moral interests of the community, and called for stricter regulation (or outright closing) of cinemas. Just as they had taken the lead in justifying the need for amusing "diversion" in wartime, and in promoting entertainment as war-education, cinema owners were quick to see the charitable potential of the entertainment business. If not all entertainment could directly incorporate war as a theme, revenues from entertainment could be channeled into the war effort, and this would blunt the taint of profit at the expense of the community. The business of entertainment, repackaged as charity, became an indispensable source of funds for the state and private charity organizations serving war victims.

Charity was big business in wartime Vienna. The state-run War Relief Office was a complex organization with sixteen divisions which raised money and collected donated goods for a wide variety of war causes.[57] But it faced competition from other municipal and private charities. The Red Cross and the Women's Aid Association were competing for donations from the same citizen pool as the War Relief Office, whose prospective donors were also being encouraged by the state to invest any excess money in war bonds. That these organizations all managed throughout the war to continue their operations is partly due to the revenues brought in by entertainment venues, which began to hold benefits in the name of charitable causes. The Viennese expressed widespread suspicion and criticism of anyone thought to be profiting at the expense of the community. Indeed, in wartime discourse, personal profit was almost universally condemned as incompatible with the interests of the general public. Sponsorship of war-related charities enabled entertainment operators to combine profit and public service.

By 1916, it was very difficult to find a concert, theater production or puppet show that was not performed in sponsorship of one of the

[55] "Der Kampf gegen das Kino," *Kinematographische Rundschau*, 18 June 1918, 1.
[56] "Dummheit oder Bosheit?" *Der Kinobesitzer*, 15 April 1918, 5–6.
[57] *Bericht über die Tätigkeit des Kriegsfürsorgeamtes während der Zeit von seiner Errichtung bis zum 31. März 1917* (Vienna, 1917).

war causes. Cinema owners designated special "*Kinotage*" (cinema-days) on which proceeds were donated to a given charity, and they published weekly in newspapers the sums they had donated to the war effort. Theater owners followed suit. When the theater Hölle was closed down by the authorities (the coal shortage of 1917–18 made it illegal to heat certain "inessential" spaces), the owners wrote in protest: "We would also like to note that we consider it our honorable duty in these momentous times to devote our art and our talents even more to publicly beneficial and charitable purposes. Our theater shall not only be available for charity activities, but we will also stage charitable productions as we have already seized the initiative to do."[58] They added that Frau Mela Mars, one of their artists, had been decorated for her Red Cross Service. This was quite a different strategy than that taken earlier by pianist Maria Swiatopulk-Mirska, who based her appeal to return to the Vienna stage on her male family members' military service. Here, the owners of the Hölle argued that their club, as well as their employees, were performing art and providing entertainment in the spirit of war charity. Coffeehouse owners could make similar arguments. By offering the "black and gold" receipt (the Habsburg colors) to customers who paid an extra "war fee" of 2 hellers, they could portray an evening at the coffeehouse as a patriotic occasion.

One further option remained for owners of entertainment venues eager to prove their public-mindedness: They could hire the very people the war charities sought to help. Once again, cinema owners took the lead, this time hiring crippled soldiers to work as ushers and ticket takers. In 1915, the General Assembly of Cinema Owners voted to offer positions to the "war-damaged," and the program proved successful, with more than 2,000 invalids obtaining cinema work in Vienna.[59] Herr Krall, a cinema owner pleased with the "good experiences" he had had with his new employees, wrote to encourage his colleagues to try the new hires.[60] Other popular ways of integrating the "war-damaged" into entertainment were to hire musicians with prosthetic limbs, or to use orphans as assistants, as happened at a venue offering evenings of charity bingo where orphan boys drew the bingo numbers.[61]

For customers, the linking of entertainment to charity took the guilt out of activities that might have otherwise seemed self-indulgent in wartime.

---

[58] AdBDW 1918 V/1 #33/278. Letter from owners of Hölle to k.k. Ministerium für öffentliche Arbeiten.

[59] *Große Kommission*, "Kino und Krieg," 7.

[60] "Kriegsinvalide als Kino-Angestellte," *Kinematographische Rundschau*, 2 January 1916, 14.

[61] WSLB Kriegssammlung 67052C, Konvolut 7.

By 1916, the Viennese had reached a sort of public consensus on the question of entertainment; the "serious mood" debate had faded. Good times were permitted, as long as the entertainment served the war effort in some way. The entertainment could offer war-education, it could be staged as a war fund-raiser, or it could employ "war-damaged" people. Thus, when the great War Exhibition opened in 1916, it was an amalgamation of all the wartime entertainment possibilities the Viennese had experienced to date. It could not have been staged as it was if the Viennese had not already worked out some of their anxieties and ambivalence about entertainment during the preceding two years. It offered coffeehouses, a cinema, music concerts and outdoor shows, as well as marvels they had never seen before. The War Exhibition took entertainment to a new height: it promised to give visitors an understanding of the very meaning of the war.

Exhibiting a war in progress

A closer examination of the Vienna War Exhibition should dispel any notion that state-sponsored propaganda in World War I was a dry, didactic or colorless undertaking. Rather, the message Habsburg authorities wanted to propagate (and it was a very specific message) was transmitted through the medium of an amusement park. Propaganda is a term whose meaning has changed over time according to historical circumstance and the value judgments of its user. It is used here to mean the presentation of a one-sided story, a "dissemination of information – facts, arguments, rumors, half-truths, or lies – to influence public opinion."[62] The one-sidedness of the Exhibition, its half-truth or lie, lay in its relentlessly optimistic, positive depiction of a losing war. The project was sponsored by the military administration, but we have little documentation of its planning or the rationale of its developers. The head of the organizing committee, Freiherr von Bukovic, explained the grand mission of the show:

The effective and harmonious collaboration between army and people, the intimate interrelation of front and hinterland, the mobilization of all economic and

---

[62] *New Encyclopedia Britannica. Micropedia* (Chicago: Britannica, 1987) 9: 728–9. In *The Birth of the Propaganda State: Soviet Methods of Mass Mobilization, 1917–1929* (Cambridge: Cambridge University Press, 1985), Peter Kenez cautions that we have no definition of propaganda "that would be value free and valid regardless of time or political culture," but offers the general definition, "(P)ropaganda often means telling less than the truth, misleading people, and lying." For full treatment of the historical development of the term propaganda in Germany, see Wolfgang Schieder and Christof Dipper, "Propaganda" in Otto Brunner, Werner Conze and Reinhart Koselleck (eds.), *Geschichtliche Grundbegriffe* (Stuttgart: E. Klett, 1984), V, 69–112; see also Jeffrey Verhey, "Some Lessons of the War."

spiritual resources for a resolute and noble goal, the harnessing of all strength rooted in the people to a powerful Whole have produced splendid successes at the front that were hardly imaginable. They elicited heroic deeds and have aroused a steady, determined will among the people to hold out for a victorious end.[63]

But even before it opened, the unity of the show was jeopardized when the Hungarians decided not to participate. They cited the exclusively Austrian direction of the project, the fact that proceeds would benefit only Austrian charities and the inadvisability of publicly displaying new war technology.[64] The Exhibition, minus the Hungarians, was based on the premise that citizens understood some aspects of war, but not others. By providing a total overview – by fitting together the many pieces of the war from the front and home front – the War Exhibition would reassure visitors that the war, in its totality, made sense.

When the prestigious entourage assembled for the opening tour of the War Exhibition in July, 1916, the mood was at once festive and somber. Festive, because the Prater was Vienna's best-loved fairground; it connoted amusement and conviviality in the public imagination. A tourist guide from 1914 describes how the Viennese of various classes spent their leisure time at this park:

Even those who have never been to Vienna have heard of the Prater... Here the fashionable Viennese ride and drive. The entrance to the Prater is usually rather surprising, as the first part is a veritable fair dedicated to shops and book-stalls. At festival times with the flaring illuminations, the noise and fun and jollity, it resembles nothing else, but has an atmosphere peculiarly its own. The open-air cafés and seats and bands are much patronized by the lower middle classes in the evening...[65]

Even as von Bukovic, chairman of the organizing committee, tried to stress in his opening remarks that the purpose of the War Exhibition was *not* amusement,[66] the decision to stage it at the Prater made it *de facto* an entertainment event. But as they stood before the main entrance, visitors could not help but notice the stark, somber lines of the exhibition architecture. Designed by architect Carl Witzmann, the exhibition broke with tradition. Journalists recording their first impressions of the sight were uniform in their appreciation for the novelty of the concept: "Nothing this strange has ever been seen before in any of the countless earlier exhibitions at the Prater, or in any other place on earth."[67] Spectators were

[63] *Offizieller Katalog der Kriegsausstellung* (Vienna, 1916), 3–4. This is one of the few statements I have been able to locate on the visions of Exhibition organizers.
[64] Cited in Denscher, *Gold gab ich für Eisen*, 75.   [65] Mitton, *Austria-Hungary*, 99–100.
[66] V. Bukovic quoted in the *Illustrierte Kronenzeitung*, 2 July 1916, 3.
[67] WSLB ZAS, Ausstellung I, *Österreichische Volkszeitung*, 9 June 1916.

awed by the monumentality and austere simplicity of the buildings, which seemed to offer a "unified whole."[68] These reactions delighted exhibition sponsors, who intended to convey that front and home front were unified – that this was *one* war – and to help individual visitors understand their relation to the whole.

The social democratic newspaper, *Arbeiterzeitung*, was one of the few organs critical of the project and its lofty goals. "A war exhibition in the middle of wartime," the editors maintained, "even when it aims to serve charitable purposes, is in itself a problematic thing."[69] They warned that the war "as it really is," carnage uncensored, could not be represented to those on the home front, and that to attempt such a representation was an insult to that reality. Despite such misgivings, 22,000 visitors lined up to enter on opening day, and the Exhibition continued to attract hordes of visitors for weeks.[70] On occasion the crowds at the entrance grew so thick that the ticket windows had to be temporarily closed. While we do not have demographic information about the visitors, it is likely that in addition to permanent Viennese residents, the show attracted out-of-town guests, including war refugees from other parts of the Empire and soldiers and officers on leave. Refugees from Galicia, for example, might have been interested to see the life and customs of their region on display in the Galician exhibit. Soldiers, likewise, might have been drawn to the "re-creations" of their front quarters.

Not only did the Exhibition advertise the seamless union of "the front and Hinterland finally come together," but it also depicted the civilians on the home front as a unified body, working in harmony for a single cause. In addition, the show was meant to combat a problem increasingly distressing to Habsburg authorities: civilians' waning interest in "the war." Austrian censors, who read mail sent between front and home front, concluded from home-front letters, "In low spirits [sic] any and all interest in the big events has disappeared. Enthusiasm for the grand affair has disappeared along with a belief in holding out."[71] A tour of the Exhibition reveals the contradictions inherent in an attempt to represent a devastating war, as it was happening, in a positive light. Like the assembly line films, the Exhibition depicted war as a productive, rather than a destructive, enterprise.

---

[68] This design recalls the severity and austerity of commemorative war memorials from the immediate postwar period. See Winter, *Sites of Memory*, ch. 4.

[69] *Arbeiterzeitung*, 29 June 1916, 7.

[70] *Neues Wiener Tagblatt*, 2 July 1918. Estimates of the number of visitors on opening day varied wildly. The *Österreichische Volkszeitung* put the number at 61,000.

[71] ÖStA, KA, GZNB 1917 carton 3749, #4588. Censor's report on the mood of the people, March 1917.

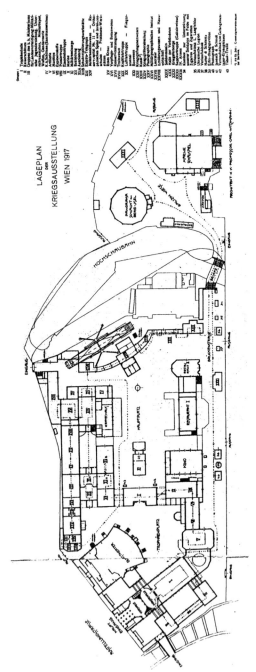

Plate 2.2. Layout of the War Exhibition. Source: *Kriegsausstellung Wien 1917*, exhibition catalog.

With five entrances and five exits, it was possible for visitors to the Vienna War Exhibition to chart any number of courses through the massive complex (see plate 2.2).

The course charted here, which requires a bit of reader imagination, leaves out dozens of attractions, but is intended to reveal some of the inherent contradictions and "half-truths" of marketing World War I as an amusing, relentlessly positive undertaking. In the absence of any concrete reception evidence, the contents of the displays are juxtaposed with information gathered on everyday life external to the show. In light of the resulting "clash of truths," we can conclude that the Exhibition may have been more entertaining than successful at propagating state positions.

Those who entered the War Exhibition had likely been to similar, smaller events; there were at least fifty-four other exhibitions held in the city between 1914 and 1918. These minor shows were held in galleries or public spaces, and ranged in theme from "Turkey in the World War" to war art of the military press corps, dog shows featuring Dobermann pinschers trained for military service, children's wartime artwork or the cumbersomely named "Exhibition of Works by Soldiers with Head Wounds Suffering Speech and Hearing Disabilities."[72] Visitors might also have witnessed other "reality programming," including an April, 1916 theater performance in which "a group of soldiers on leave, survivors of the battle of Uszieczko, were prevailed upon to appear on the stage of a Viennese theater and re-enact the events of the battle."[73] Nor was the War Exhibition the first war entertainment staged at the Prater. In 1915, an elaborate network of war trenches had opened for public view (and play) not far from the War Exhibition site. Authorities from the Ministry of the Interior, who had not been informed of the plan to open trenches, wrote to the Viennese police asking whether the undertaking was not somehow "dubious." They raised a familiar worry about wartime entertainment, cautioning that "it could provoke scandal if these trenches were to be made accessible for public amusement (*Belustigung*) in the evening hours."[74] But the impressive compound was allowed to stay; its educational value outweighed protests about its suitability as entertainment. People winding through the trench network, which had a backdrop painted to look like the landscape of the northern front with houses in

---

[72] WSLB ZAS, Ausstellung I and II.

[73] This incident drew the ire of Viennese satirist Karl Kraus, who considered the packaging of suffering as entertainment a betrayal of human dignity. See Edward Timms, *Karl Kraus, Apocalyptic Satirist: Culture and Catastrophe in Habsburg Vienna* (New Haven: Yale University Press, 1986), 327.

[74] AdBDW 1915 V/25 #11445. Letter from the Kriegshilfsbüro of the MdI to Pol. Dir. Wien, 21 May 1915.

ruin and smoking tree stumps, were promised a valuable, unmediated war experience.[75]

The trophy hall

The first stop inside the main entrance of the War Exhibition was the trophy hall and plaza. Exhibition sponsors knew the Viennese public had a fondness for war booty; in 1914, when thirty-six captured Russian canons were transported to the city for storage, they "naturally attracted a great deal of attention." The three canons put on display had been "visited by thousands . . . (and) were naturally most admired by the boys."[76] The captured treasures on display at the War Exhibition included pieces of enemy heavy artillery and a shot-down airplane. The trophy room, one newspaper wrote, was a place not to "satisfy one's curiosity" but rather to pay homage to the "heroes who gave their lives to win these pieces."[77] In other words, viewers were supposed to see embedded in the machines remnants of human sacrifice and glory. An illustration with the caption "Direct Hit" shows a woman in a Sunday bonnet examining a Belgian target that had been hit by an Austrian 30.5 mortar (see plate 2.3).

Was she thinking about the heroes who had fired the shell that scored the direct hit? The men who perished inside the machine? Was she simply awed by seeing close-up, for the first time in her life, such large, odd, metal contraptions? The critical *Arbeiterzeitung* was unconvinced that displaying enemy war booty honored one's own soldiers; its editors noted that no damaged pieces of Austrian machinery were on display and that in the "now lifeless pieces" of enemy booty, there was no sign of the men who had died defending them.[78]

The POW hall

The identity of this enemy became clearer in some of the other halls. One could take home a painting (lay-away financing available) of "Effects of 30.5 Mortar on Belgrade" or "Imprisoned Russian." Visitors to the War Exhibition might have lacked empathy for the men who died inside or alongside the trophies, because these men were portrayed as utterly different, only marginally human. Passing through a number of other halls, the visitor arrived in room 22, the enemy POW hall, where on display

---

[75] WSLB ZAS, Hilfsaktionen II, *Fremdenblatt*, 16 May 1916.
[76] *Arbeiterzeitung*, 12 September 1914, 7.
[77] WSLB ZAS, Ausstellung I, *Fremdenblatt*, 21 November 1915. Preview of the planned exhibition.
[78] *Arbeiterzeitung*, 29 June 1916, 7.

Plate 2.3. Civilians admire war booty at the Vienna War Exhibition.
Source: *Illustrierte Kronenzeitung*, 2 July 1916, 1.

were the "anthropological findings" of university professor Rudolf Pöch, who had conducted extensive "measurements in the study of the different Russian races." He had photographs of Russian heads and bodies and, to ensure that visitors noticed the special features of these men, he presented plaster replicas of their heads. Those unable to make it to the POW hall might have viewed Dr. Pöch's research in the 1916 film, *Kriegsgefangenenlager* (*Prisoner of War Camp*) at the Exhibition cinema not far from the trophy hall.[79] In the film, two scientists in lab coats take a live "specimen" POW, encase his head in plaster as a fellow prisoner stands by holding the clay, and then crack the mold. The bewildered prisoner is led away as the scientists begin to chisel their work. In a savage ending,

[79] Österreichisches Filmarchiv, *Alltag in der öst.-ung. Monarchie* series, roll 5, *Kriegsgefangenenlager*, 1916.

they triumphantly hold up the "head" of the still living prisoner. The POW hall, which also housed a model showing living conditions of enemy prisoners at an Austrian camp, sought to assure visitors that Austria treated its enemy decently. The overall aim of displaying enemy prisoners of war is apparent in other scenes from the film *Kriegsgefangenenlager*. The POWs are filmed at rest, at work and at play, but in the background, from the waist down, we see an armed Austrian patrol striding confidently back and forth in front of the fence that encloses the prisoners. Visitors were to take away the impression that the enemy, no longer a threat, was securely contained by competent Austrian authorities.

The sanitation hall

One central aim of the War Exhibition was to assure civilians that their family members were receiving excellent care in the hands of military authorities. The sanitation hall, directly behind the coffeehouse, gave an overview of the first-rate medical care available to injured and sick men. By emphasizing exclusively the regenerative powers of Austrian medicine, the display risked espousing the untenable position that war was an exercise in healing, rather than wounding. The *Arbeiterzeitung* complained, "Health services and war surgery take up a large space at the exhibition – a larger space than they can be afforded in the horrifying reality."[80] The sanitation hall housed a model of a reserve hospital, x-rays of body parts, and "an especially noteworthy display of a collection of various foreign articles (nails, screws, glass shards) from the stomach of a mentally ill soldier. Removal by operation allowed for the man's complete recovery."[81] Here, the one-sidedness of state propaganda stretched the limits of credibility, as injured bodies were considered only in relation to their healing; sickness was presented only to showcase the miracle of recovery. For the visitor, the confidence that pieces of metal could be removed from the body of a family member was meant to pre-empt the fear that the metal could end up there in the first place.

The prosthetic pavilion

The repair of damaged bodies was similarly the highlight of the prosthetic pavilion, attached to the sanitation hall. In the display of the latest prosthetic devices and orthopedic apparatuses for men missing limbs, the

---

[80] *Arbeiterzeitung*, 29 June 1916, 7.
[81] *Kriegsausstellung Wien 1917*, exhibition catalog, 30–31.

tone was relentlessly optimistic.[82] Like the assembly line films and the
exhibits of the wonders of the Austrian war industry and technology, the
prosthetic pavilion stressed *Leistung*, the productive nature of war. One
journalist promised that anyone who entered this hall would leave it full
of admiration for the accomplishments both of the men who designed the
devices and the men who would wear them.[83] All kinds of replacement
parts were on display; with them, and with the help of careful training
and re-education schemes, also sketched in the prosthetic pavilion, the
damaged men would once again be *leistungsfähig*. Visitors learned that
nearly half of the crippled soldiers were farmers who could be fitted with
the new "farmer's arm" and returned to their fields.[84] The display worked
hard to spin the tragedy of war-induced physical deformities (with which
visitors were quite familiar by 1916) into a story of rejuvenation with a
happy ending. While it is impossible to reconstruct the actual reception
of this story, it surely clashed with visitors' common sense and first-hand
knowledge of men with war injuries. In this situation, the propagandistic
half-truths of the exhibit competed with other truths beyond the control
of its sponsors.

The war graves hall

If the medical procedures on display in the sanitation room failed, or
if more was missing than just a limb – should a loved one actually die
in the field – the visitor might find comfort in the war graves hall, located down the corridor. The display, set up by the war graves division of
the War Ministry, emphasized the state's efforts to give soldiers a proper
and dignified burial, wherever they might fall. They intended the display to give relatives the "comfort that not even a very devoted family
would be in a position to provide a more worthy resting place for the
dead hero."[85] Such reassurance was needed to combat rumors that were
circulating in Vienna. Soldiers on leave had started rumors that "health
conditions among the troops on the south-western front are very bad.
Since February corpses of the fallen have been lying unburied before the
trenches. Due to the prevailing heat the air has become so fouled that
people are fainting."[86] At the War Exhibition the picture looked quite

---

[82] For a similarly optimistic approach to treating newly crippled men in Britain, see Seth
   Koven, "Remembering and Dismemberment: Crippled Children, Wounded Soldiers,
   and the Great War in Great Britain," *AHR* 99, no. 4 (October, 1994), 1,167–1,202.
[83] WSLB ZAS, Ausstellung II, *Neues Wiener Tagblatt*, 23 August 1916.
[84] *Kriegsausstellung Wien 1917*, exhibition catalog, 72.
[85] WSLB ZAS, Ausstellung I, *Neues Wiener Tagblatt*, 17 May 1916.
[86] AdBDW, Stimmungsbericht, 19 July 1917.

different. Viewers learned that the Education Ministry had sponsored a competition to design war memorials and war graves. Exhibiting these plans was meant to soothe Viennese residents who would never receive the corpses of their loved ones for family burial. The individual viewer would have to weigh the image of bodies rotting in the open air against the image of a state so attentive to its war dead that it provided for them more extravagantly than any single family ever could.

The hall of the War Relief Office

Heading out of the war graves hall, it might have been time for a break. Visitors might have had a snack, entered a raffle, listened to a military band, relaxed on a bench, or taken a walk to see the view from the overhead skyway. Then it was time for visitors to look for themselves on display, in the halls celebrating the accomplishments of the home front. These exhibits posed the greatest challenge to the Exhibition organizers. How to present the "home-front experience" in a refreshing, optimistic light to people who were living it? The solution was to presume that civilians did not "understand" the war based on personal experiences. One journalist impressed by the show declared, "This exhibition will make the person in the hinterland more aware than ever how deeply and widely the war has encroached on all of aspects of life."[87] Would not civilians in 1916 and 1917 already have been aware of this encroachment? The displays sought to obscure the personal in favor of the collective by shaping a narrative of unified, harmonious mobilization.

The hall of the War Relief Office, on the perimeter of the complex, displayed the civilian contributions to the war effort. Like historians who have sought to demonstrate the importance of civilian mobilization in aggregate numbers, this exhibit measured their financial and material contributions in sums and tonnage. The display celebrated civilians' generosity: by 1917, the War Relief Office had received 26,590,972 crowns in cash donations. Civilians had given 1,280,086 pairs of socks and 277,246 pairs of underwear to the *Liebesgaben* project, which, along with their other donations including 34,176 harmonicas, 16,667 liters of wine and 277,514 handkerchiefs, were transported in 125,721 cartons on 978 wagons to soldiers in the field.[88] Aggregate numbers do indeed convey "mobilization," and the statistics in the War Relief Office display surely impressed some visitors. These numbers suggest a harmonious, unified home front giving generously to a deserving front. But while the

---

[87] WSLB ZAS, Ausstellung I, *Die Zeit*, 2 July 1916.
[88] *Bericht über die Tätigkeit.* These figures include donations to the *Weihnachten im Felde 1914–1916* program.

sum of cash donations looks impressive, the Exhibition did not reveal the reality of collection drives. It did not mention, for example, that the War Relief Office collection tins had to be tethered down with chains because people were stealing them.[89] It did not portray the darker side of mobilization – the fact that the Viennese had grown weary of giving, and that collection drives caused tensions within the community and among neighbors. Even at their most vulnerable moments, the Viennese were asked to give. The War Relief Office included a plea for cash donations in death notices sent to families. Its letter began, "Regarding the distressing fatality, of which you are notified in the enclosed," and went on to request that, should families decide to forgo the expense of a burial wreath, they could send this money to the War Relief Office by way of the attached deposit slip.[90] With the Viennese being asked to sacrifice at every turn, who was giving what, and how much, to which causes became divisive questions.

Several examples from the metal collection drives not on display at the Exhibition shed light on the degree to which the Viennese monitored the "generosity" of fellow citizens. A common theme in many of the letters of denunciation sent to the Viennese police was a reported "failure to donate" on the part of a fellow citizen, in this case, usually someone with a Slavic or Jewish last name. The collection drives exacerbated existing ethnic and nationalist tensions in this multi-national city. The War Exhibition did not include the scandals, large and small, that grew out of solicitation and collection of donations. "Gold gab ich für Eisen," a program by which residents gave their gold valuables, including wedding bands, to the state in return for a "commemorative" iron ring caused – along with the pride that came with sacrifice – a great deal of resentment. By September 1914, 90,000 people had already given their wedding rings or other precious metals to the cause.[91] While the iron ring initially carried great symbolic value for its wearer, imitation rings began to proliferate on the home front. The sponsors of "Gold gab ich für Eisen" complained about another charity that planned to introduce "Lucky War Rings" which could be bought for a pittance. Those who had given their wedding bands, and had even had the iron replacements consecrated by priests, could not be distinguished from those who wore the imitations.[92] By 1916 and 1917, when visitors passed through the

[89] AdBDW 1914 St./14 Rotes Kreuz. Letter from KM to Pol. Dir. Wien, 21 October 1914. The War Relief Office sent notice to businesses which displayed the tins, requesting that they secure them "not with string or ribbon, but wire or chain."

[90] WSLB Kriegssammlung 67052C, Konvolut 5.

[91] ÖStA, AVA, MdI Varia carton 71, 1914–1918 Kriegshilfsbüro, no. 783. Letter from the Society of the Austrian Silver Cross to the Kriegshilfsbüro, 19 September 1914.

[92] For discussion of the symbolism of women donating wedding rings to the state, see Victoria de Grazia, *How Fascism Ruled Women: Italy 1922–1945* (Berkeley and Los Angeles: University of California Press, 1992), ch. 4.

War Relief hall, which depicted an orgy of civilian giving, they had very little left to give.

The cigarette room

The situation was the same three doors down at the cigarette room. The "Committee to Supply Our Troops With Cigars and Cigarettes" could boast that, by 1917, Habsburg troops had received through civilian donation 198,400,240 cigarettes, 17,209,432 cigars and 4,917,246 packets of tobacco.[93] There was a European-wide consensus that an army that smoked well fought well, and civilians in Vienna took pride in supplying their men with tobacco products. Soldiers sitting around a campfire relaxing with a smoke was a popular image on wartime postcards. But to amass such a supply of tobacco for the troops, civilians had had to curtail their own tobacco consumption. The aggregate numbers in the cigarette room could not capture the strains that the tobacco shortage had caused on the home front. In April, 1917, in front of a tobacco shop on the Wachaustrasse in Vienna's second district, very close to the War Exhibition itself, 300 women were waiting in line to buy cigarettes. Denied, they began shouting that they wanted the cigarettes for their men and threatened to demolish the shop. When a passer-by made the remark that the women did not really want the cigarettes for their men, but intended to resell them on the black market at higher prices, he was "attacked by the women and mishandled." Security policemen arrived quickly, "freed the captive," and arrested two women. In the ensuing scuffle, a policeman "had to draw his sword to defend himself" and was later pelted with stones.[94] Clearly, the cigarette room did not display the Viennese anger and sense of injustice caused by the tobacco shortage, nor did it aim to. But visitors' knowledge of conditions outside would surely have weakened their receptivity to the state's message. Like the War Relief Office hall, the cigarette room portrayed a "spirit of donation" on the home front that no longer existed outside the walls of the War Exhibition complex.

The souvenir stand

Before leaving the complex, visitors could stop at a souvenir stand to buy a wide range of "official" war trinkets sold by the War Aid Bureau

---

[93] These figures combine *Liebesgaben* donations and donations to the *Weihnachten im Felde 1914–1916* program. *Bericht über die Tätigkeit*, 58, 61.
[94] NÖLA Präs. "P" 1917, XIX, 2554.

(Kriegshilfsbüro). Despite its name, this association, a branch of the Ministry of the Interior, was nothing more than a glorified purveyor of trinkets. Throughout the war it contracted with private firms to produce hundreds of official war items: paperweights, jewelry, commemorative coins, framed drawings, lamps, playing cards, even perfume packaged in wooden bullets.[95] Like a modern-day Olympic Committee, the War Aid Bureau spent a great deal of energy protecting its rights as the "official sponsor" of war trinkets. It faced competition from hucksters peddling imitations, and ran a campaign to encourage consumers to "buy official." Its strongest competition came from a different source, however, one that privileged the "real" over the "official."

Residents in Vienna had begun collecting illicit war paraphernalia early on. By January 1915, the Viennese police had received from neighborhood patrolmen over a hundred reports of sightings of illegal "war booty." A typical report read: "In the late morning on 22 December 1914 I noticed on my rounds a Russian gun displayed in the window of the department store of Josef Linzbauer, II district, Taborstrasse Nr 46."[96] Other items sighted included buttons, medals, bullets, bayonets, uniforms and caps, mostly of Serbian or Russian origin. The Ministry of the Interior tracked the case of Ignaz Kerndler, who was sending to his wife, Rosa, in Vienna, "suspicious packages" thought to contain war booty. Inside they found a jacket, buttons and dishes, and ordered the items sent to the military depot in Vienna.[97] The Military Command in Vienna ordered the police to get the problem under control. The "problem" was not necessarily one of public safety, for many of the items were not weapons. Why would authorities have been so concerned about civilian possession of enemy buttons or dishes? It seems that civilians wanted to possess a "real" piece of the war, but a decree from the Viennese police headquarters to its local branches spelled out the logic behind the prohibition: "The military authorities have made it known that there is no such thing as war booty belonging to the individual (*Kriegsbeute eines Einzelnen*), so that no one may be in legal possession of these spoils."[98] In other words, war booty belonged solely to the state. This raised an interesting dilemma for customers at the souvenir stand. They wanted something authentic, but had to settle for the official. In practice this meant that they might leave the War Exhibition not with a Russian bullet, but with a replica of an Austrian bullet with a pop-up pencil inside. The War Aid Bureau promised that

[95] KA, MKSM 1915 69-8/10; and AVA MdI Varia carton 71, 1914–1918 KHB, no. 1659.
[96] AdBDW 1914 St./6, Kriegsbeutestücke.
[97] AdBDW 1914 St./6, Kriegsbeutestücke. Letter from MdI to Pol. Dir. Wien, 7 May 1915.
[98] AdBDW 1914 St./6, Kriegsbeutestücke. Runderlaß, 27 November 1914.

with the purchase of any of its items, customers were buying a small but "authentic" piece of the history of "these momentous times."

The Exhibition ran through November 1916, closed for the winter, and then re-opened for spring and summer 1917. While there were certainly updates that could be made during the winter of 1917–18, the War Exhibition ran concurrent with the war itself, and to promise that it would open again the following spring was tantamount to saying that the war would still be going on, a prospect few welcomed no matter how splendid these improvements and new displays might be. As it turned out, the War Exhibition did not reopen in 1918. The course of wartime entertainment, and its interrelation with the discourse of sacrifice, gives us some clues as to why the great project to represent the war as it was happening could not survive the war itself. Early on, entertainment and amusement had seemed an affront to the notion of sacrifice. Residents of Vienna held the belief, albeit only briefly, that life on the home front should mirror in tone the conditions on the front. This belief implied a *choice* – one could voluntarily adopt a stance of sacrifice by giving up certain activities, products and possessions. Entertainment operators eventually found a way, by weaving war into their product, to relieve people of the onerous burden of this choice. One could be amused and educated while contributing to worthy causes. The possibilities of wartime entertainment narrowed and eventually dried up, however, when sacrifice was no longer a choice but a fact of life. Already in 1916 and 1917, the War Exhibition, with its triumphant language of harmonious "mobilization," was not able to capture in its home-front displays the painful sacrifices people had made. Home-front sacrifice was initially supposed to be a gesture to the front. When material conditions got so bad that civilians began complaining that they would "rather be at the front," the vision of home front playing supportive back-up to front was no longer tenable. The "intimate interrelation between front and hinterland" praised by the Exhibition-organizing committee on opening day could not be plausibly represented, because it did not exist in reality.

Had there been a War Exhibition of 1918, it would have been a grim affair. It is not clear that sponsors would have been able to procure coal to heat the cinema, theaters, panoramic halls and restaurants. Inside the restaurants, people would have been bickering with staff and each other about who was eating what and who was taking the extravagant step of adding scarce milk to his coffee.[99] The children might not

[99] In 1917 and 1918, Viennese police received a flood of food denunciations reporting petty violations of ration laws.

have had the energy to play in the trenches because many were suffering from malnutrition; the average eleven-year-old weighed 15 kilograms less and was 10 centimeters shorter than in 1914. The earlier comments by Viennese writers that entertainment (and film in particular) was a life necessity "more important than food" were forgotten by the summer of 1918. The closest thing to a War Exhibition in 1918 was the Exhibition of Substitute Goods (Ersatzmittelausstellung), which was held at the very same spot in the Prater. Gone were the raffle tickets, music and souvenirs – this was an educational show of a purely practical sort, meant to demonstrate the latest discoveries from the world of substitution. Visitors could see displays of cardboard shoes, and learn how to make baked goods without flour, fat, eggs and sugar. The ever-critical *Arbeiterzeitung* canned the show, suggesting it should be replaced by an ersatz exhibit.[100]

The Vienna War Exhibition and the debates about entertainment that preceded it belong to the cultural history of World War I. Across Europe, governments worked to present deliberate versions of the war to their home-front populations. By dressing official truths as colorfully and amusingly as possible, the Exhibition was an ambitious attempt to mute competing truths visitors had acquired elsewhere. If propaganda was a "psychological weapon" developed for a mass audience in Europe's first total war, then forms of popular entertainment provided an effective delivery system. This development depended, however, on a reconciliation between amusement and home-front sacrifice. A journalist writing in November, 1918, when the war had just ended, but the material conditions in Vienna were continuing to worsen, challenged the project of packaging war as entertainment. He suggested that a trip to the Exhibition had been a chance for people to enjoy the show and forget about the war, even though they were looking at it. Visitors had been like the viewers in a cinema, "spirits suddenly removed from the world." War entertainment succeeded at diverting attention from – at helping people forget – the very war it purported to represent. He then likened all of Vienna to an exhibition; the foreign relief workers arriving in the city in 1918–19, dumbstruck by the miserable health conditions of its population, were seeing an exhibition, not of how war was waged, but of what it led to.

[100] WSLB ZAS, Ausstellungen II, *Arbeiterzeitung*, 23 June 1918.

3   Censorship, rumors and denunciation: the crisis of truth on the home front

The state's sanitized portrayal of home-front life at the Vienna War Exhibition was an attempt to steer viewers back to a version of the war that it desperately needed them to adopt. By celebrating civilians' "holding out" and their "willingness to sacrifice" in 1916, when commitment to these duties had clearly begun to wane, and again in 1917, when police reports describe a socially atomized population consumed with the self-interested business of survival, state officials were inadvertently furthering social instability. They were producing "truths" that clashed with people's first-hand experiences, second-hand knowledge and third-hand suspicions. The dizzying amount of information circulating in wartime Vienna, and the multiple and contradictory truths contained therein, contributed to social atomization by denying Viennese residents a psychological common ground. During the second half of the war it became increasingly difficult for people to coordinate their realities with those of neighbors, co-workers, acquaintances or strangers because there was no reliable standard against which to measure perceptions. Communities that formed around rumors were powerful but short-lived.

Information came from all directions. On August 9, 1918, a squadron of Italian planes, one of them carrying famed nationalist poet and pilot Gabriele D'Annunzio, flew over Vienna and dumped their "weapons," which consisted of bright leaflets in the colors of the Italian flag. Written in German and Italian, the leaflets appealed to the city's residents:

Viennese!
... If we wanted to, we could drop tons of bombs on your city, but we are sending only a greeting of the tricolor, the tricolor of freedom. We Italians are not waging war against citizens, children, old men and women. We are waging war against your government, the enemy of national freedom ... [1]

---

[1] ÖStA, KA, MKSM 1918 11-2/10. Police and War Ministry reports. D'Annunzio, who had penned some of the leaflets himself, was unable to fly (he had lost an eye in combat), but arranged to ride as a passenger in a two-seater plane during the raid on Vienna, which he had been planning since 1917.

D'Annunzio's stunt over the home front was part of a much wider Italian campaign to undermine Austrian morale on the battle front. The message to the Viennese was similar to messages that the Italians and British had been dropping on Austrian troops in the field.[2] When air raid sirens warned of a similar "attack" several weeks later, many Viennese failed to follow official air raid procedures. Some took cover as directed, but others, more curious than afraid, "ran to open places or to windows and onto balconies, just like on August 9, to see the planes." In harsh language, one leading newspaper criticized the "careless fools" who disregarded safety and "ran into the streets to enjoy a rare theater," perhaps hoping to catch the leaflets raining on their city.[3] These Italian propaganda spectacles demonstrate some of the difficulties Viennese authorities had controlling the content, transmission and citizen reception and reproduction of information in the capital during World War I. Even if they could confiscate some of the contraband leaflets (which they did), authorities could not control the effects of D'Annunzio's message or the stories residents would tell about the incidents afterwards.

Throughout the war, Habsburg officials operated a system of information management whose twin pillars were propaganda and censorship. Propaganda entailed the production and presentation of war-related materials in a way that cast the war effort in a positive light. The state-sponsored War Exhibition was a prime example of this positive or "offensive" information management. Censorship, which we might think of as a negative or "defensive" technique, entailed the identification and suppression of materials critical of the state or its war aims. These negative techniques were unevenly applied throughout the war; measures were strict during the initial period from 1914 to 1916, but relaxed once Emperor Karl came to power and restored elements of constitutional rule. They were also unevenly applied throughout the realm, with the Slavic-language post and press coming under greater surveillance than the German.

Despite the existence in Austria of an elaborate state censorship apparatus, certain kinds of unofficial information, not sanctioned by censors and transmitted orally in the form of rumor, or in writing in the form of

[2] See Mark Cornwall, *The Undermining of Austria-Hungary: The Battle for Hearts and Minds* (New York: St. Martin's Press, 2000), chs. 5–8 on Italy's information war and the Austrian response. Cornwall identifies the Italian front as the site of "the most sophisticated wartime campaign of front propaganda" in World War I, 175. The D'Annunzio leaflet was unusual in that it targeted a German-Austrian audience; the majority of Italian leaflets sought to exploit national sentiment among Habsburg Slavs.

[3] WSLB ZAS, *Neue Freie Presse*, 23 and 24 August 1918. The second attack was a false alarm. Viennese residents had seen their first "fliegende Menschen" in air shows, staged as entertainment, in the years preceding World War I.

anonymous leaflets, letters and graffiti, were difficult to trace back to a point of origin and even more difficult to eliminate once in circulation among the population. Unlike the D'Annunzio leaflets and other forms of anti-Austrian propaganda smuggled in from abroad (by French nuns, Russian officers dressed as sheep herders and spies posing as Galician refugees, according to security reports), much of the unsanctioned information of concern to authorities was generated within Austria by citizens themselves.

Although Austrian censorship regulations looked quite formidable on paper, Vienna was alive with information, official and unofficial, true and untrue, expressed publicly (though often anonymously) and circulating with great speed. Next to food, information was the most politicized commodity on the home front. It was produced, traded and regulated like a commodity, and aimed, delivered and feared like a weapon. Despite the state's repressive efforts, information did not flow only from the top down, with the government feeding news and opinions to the governed and the latter "resisting" by spreading contradictory information of their own. Rather, information flowed in three general directions: it was channeled from the state and organs supportive of the state (notably the Catholic Church and much of Vienna's German-language press) to the population as propaganda; it circulated among the population in the form of rumors; and it flowed from the population back to the state through the widespread practice of denunciation.

Examining these channels in turn, we will see that the instability and unreliability of circulating information led to a crisis of truth in Vienna that contributed to the dissolution of social relations at the local level. Without a stable consensus on which stories were true or untrue, residents succumbed to fantasies and conspiracy theories that were as harmful to neighbors and acquaintances as they were to authorities. The state agency most responsible for the control of information was the War Surveillance Office (Kriegsüberwachungsamt). Similar to censorship offices in other belligerent countries in Europe, Austrian censors had as one of their many tasks the monitoring of the millions of letters and postcards sent between front and home front during World War I.[4] Over the course of the war, censors discovered that this correspondence could be of great

---

[4] The massive correspondence between front and home front has proven to be a useful source for writing the history of everyday life in wartime. See Bernd Ulrich, *Die Augenzeugen: Deutsche Feldpostbriefe in Kriegs- und Nachkriegszeit, 1914–1933* (Essen: Klartext, 1997); Christa Hämmerle, "'...wirf ihnen alles hin und schau, daß du fort kommst': Die Feldpost eines Paares in der Geschlechter(un)ordnung des Ersten Weltkrieges," *Historische Anthropologie* 6, no. 3 (1998), 431–58. See also Marie-Monique Huss, "Pronatalism and the Popular Ideology of the Child in Wartime France: The Evidence of the Picture Postcard," in Richard Wall and Jay Winter, eds. *The Upheaval of*

use to a government intent on ascertaining the "mood" of the people. Accordingly, they shifted focus from what historian Peter Holquist calls censorship (merely controlling the content of letters) to perlustration (intercepting and reading mail "for the express purpose of discovering what people were writing and thinking"), and compiled voluminous reports of their findings.[5] But despite their devoted reading of tens of millions of pieces of citizen mail, as well as their monitoring of press and film, Austrian censors did not create what historian Gustav Spann has called "an almost complete net of censorship over the whole Monarchy which, when compared to other belligerent states, can be described as nearly perfect."[6] Historians of censorship sometimes overestimate the efficacy of censors because they examine only what the censors were supposed to do in theory, based on a reading of the procedures and laws governing censorship institutions, while not probing what actually happened in practice.[7]

By examining the spread of rumors on the home front, we see that in practice the censors' net had many holes. It was not well designed for catching orally transmitted information, which could reappear in written form and vice versa. Letter-writers, for example, often prefaced their news with "We've heard that..." or used the oblique German construction "*Man sagt...*" Had censors been able to locate this elusive, anonymous *man*, one of the great sources of news in wartime and a key player in the transmission of rumors, their work would have been a good deal easier. Instead, rumors proliferated. In her study of the German home front in World War I, Ute Daniel draws a link between overt censorship and

---

War: Family, Work and Welfare in Europe, 1914–1918 (Cambridge: Cambridge University Press, 1988), 329–67.

[5] Peter Holquist, "'Information is the Alpha and Omega of Our Work': Bolshevik Surveillance in Its Pan-European Context," *JMH* 69 (September 1997), 415–50, 421. Holquist argues in his very useful comparative essay that while the content of "mood" reports might interest the historian, "surveillance as a project (rather than simply as a source) requires analysis." He contends "that the desire to generate such material is in fact of far greater significance than the material itself," 416–17.

[6] Gustav Spann, "Vom Leben im Krieg: Die Erkundung der Lebensverhältnisse der Bevölkerung Österreich-Ungarns im Ersten Weltkrieg durch die Briefzensur," in Rudolf Ardelt et al. (eds.), *Unterdrückung und Emanzipation: Festschrift für Erika Weinzierl zum 60. Geburtstag* (Vienna/Salzburg: Geyer, 1985), 149–65, 149.

[7] An example of the top-down approach to the study of censorship is Wilhelm Deist, "Censorship and Propaganda in Germany during the First World War," in Jean-Jacques Becker and Stéphane Audoin-Rouzeau (eds.), *Les Sociétés européennes et la guerre de 1914–1918. Actes du colloque organisé à Nanterre et à Amiens du 8 au 11 décembre 1988* (Publications de l'Université de Nanterre, 1990), 199–210. More accurate is John Halliday's depiction of the personal and somewhat arbitrary work of Viennese press censors in "Satirist and Censor: Karl Kraus and the Censorship Authorities during the First World War," in Sigurd Paul Scheichl and Edward Timms (eds.), *Karl Kraus in neuer Sicht* (Munich: edition text+kritik, 1988), 174–208.

the increasing appearance of rumors. Knowing the censors were at work, ordinary people lost faith in the credibility of information from official channels and experienced a heightened "need for information," which was satisfied in part by rumors. A counter-public (*Gegenöffentlichkeit*) consisting of rumors, jokes, anecdotes, grumbling and criticism generated, supplemented, or in some cases supplanted, official news sources.[8]

From the war's beginning to end, Vienna swirled with rumors, not all of them oppositional to the state, but worrisome to authorities precisely because of their potential for introducing competing realities. The history of rumors during the war resembles the history of food: just as procurement and preparation of food had once been considered a (female) household matter, hardly worthy of the attention of important politicians and statesmen, but soon became *the* defining issue of wartime politics, so rumors took on increased political significance. The informal passing of information at markets or in the streets, traditionally disregarded as *Weiberklatsch*, the idle chat of womenfolk, commanded attention in the top echelons of government once it became clear that men – including military personnel – were involved in transmission.

The image of a government presenting carefully filtered news to a population that, in turn, spread unofficial information orally and in writing to the chagrin of censors is, however, a somewhat misleading picture of home-front information channels. Unofficial information did not always flow *among* the population *against* state authorities; information passing was not necessarily an act of resistance to the censorship apparatus. This becomes clear when we examine a third major channel of information, denunciation, which flowed from the population back to state authorities. Avidly writing letters denouncing neighbors, co-workers and acquaintances, some residents of Vienna used information to bind themselves to the state at the expense of fellow citizens. Through study of this practice we can see that the wartime relationship of the government and the governed, at times hostile and at times conciliatory, was mediated through information.

Propaganda and censorship

Habsburg authorities did not have a well-coordinated program for promoting supra-national Austrian patriotism during the war. Energetic

---

[8] Ute Daniel, "Informelle Kommunikationen und Propaganda in der deutschen Kriegsgesellschaft," in Siegfried Quandt (ed.), *Medien, Kommunikation, Geschichte* (Gießen: Offset Köhler, 1993), 76–89.

programs directed at schoolchildren (see chapter 5) and soldiers either came too late in the war or were met with resistance from nationalist programs competing for the same hearts and minds. This is not to say that there was no state-sponsored propaganda – witness the War Exhibition and the government publication of thousands of poems, stories, calendars, chronicles, commemorative maps and souvenir cards – but it was not well-coordinated for the Herculean task of keeping a multi-national population focused on a supra-national war cause.

At the grassroots level, the state's patriotic message was delivered by official "information workers" who, in uplifting shows to soldiers and civilians, presented sanitized versions of life on one side of the war to the other. Dr. Rudolf Peerz, one of many thousands of these wartime information workers, logged 25,000 kilometers of travel around the Habsburg lands presenting lectures, readings and slide shows to front and home front. (He is singled out here only because he left meticulous records of his work, in part due to a pay dispute with employers.) Peerz, who presented lectures on "The Thankful Hinterland" to troops, assessed the needs of his audience: "The man in the field," he explained, "is primarily worried about his family's suffering, and his own, should he return home as a cripple." He used his multi-media shows to "cheer up the troops by showing the hinterland in awe of [their] bravery." The civilian population, he maintained, would "hold out, buy war bonds, subordinate itself to everything the war demands if [the war] is properly explained."[9]

Much of the "explaining" on the Viennese home front came not from the state itself, but from two reliable sources of support: the Catholic Church and the German-language Viennese press. The Church had long been an essential pillar of support for the Habsburg dynasty, and its representatives in Vienna turned out to be excellent transmitters of propaganda during the war.[10] Just under 87 percent of Vienna's prewar population was Roman Catholic.[11] Early in the war, church attendance spiked. Overflow

[9] In 1917, Peerz reported having presented his multi-media show 175 times in 111 locations in 9 Austrian crownlands. AdR 1918, k.k. Min. f. soz. Verwaltung – Jugendfürsorge, carton 2472, #6912, "Bericht über die Propagandareisen des Prof. Dr. Rudolf Peerz . . . 1917."

[10] For the equally reliable pro-Habsburg stance of the Viennese Jewish organizations, see David Rechter, *The Jews of Vienna and the First World War* (London: Littmann Library, 2001). Staunch dynastic patriotism was one point on which Viennese Jews across the political spectrum could agree, 23.

[11] "Ergebnisse der Volkszählung vom 31. Dezember 1910," in *Statistisches Jahrbuch der Stadt Wien* (Vienna: Verlag des Wiener Magistrates, 1912), 908–9. Nearly 9 percent were Jewish, and the remaining 4 percent belonged to Evangelical or Greek churches or were recorded as "confessionless."

crowds came to hear masses that mixed faith and patriotism.[12] While
it is difficult to reconstruct the religiosity of individual parishioners, we
can assess the kinds of messages they were hearing from the pulpit. At
the outset of war, Viennese Cardinal Friedrich Gustav Piffl gave a number of instructions to Church leaders: the *ex missa tempore belli* was to
be inserted into masses at appropriate moments; in every church a daily
prayer was to be spoken aloud with the congregation, "Let us pray to God
our Father for our Emperor, our sons and brothers in the field, and our
fatherland . . . "; and during sermons, priests were generally to inspire the
flock to offer prayers, good works and sacrifice to the fatherland.[13] A few
months later, the cardinal delivered a war sermon at the St. Stephen's
Cathedral that equaled in patriotic verve anything that official state propagandists had produced. He spoke of the state in organic terms: its ruler
and peoples were bound together through "inborn dynastic sentiment" as
an "organism of inexhaustible life-force."[14] More practically, he extolled
the patriotic duty to buy war bonds. With Italy's entry into the war in
1915, the cardinal redoubled the Church's patriotic position: "With the
new, difficult challenges that have befallen our fatherland it is our solemn
duty to strengthen the followers' faith in God, to fulfill patriotic duties
and to exhort them to renewed sacrifice and works of love."[15] Catholic
bishops even weighed in on the food shortages, reminding their followers that hunger did not justify unlawful behavior. "Honest, reasonable
criticism" of the food situation was allowed, but "grumbling, threats, rebellions and strikes will bring not a single grain of wheat nor a potato
to the country."[16] While not officially coordinated by the state, Church
efforts to discourage lawlessness and preserve social order on the home
front served state interests well.

Once the "long war" had set in, the Church's message oscillated between patriotism – "As terrible as the war might be, it has also demonstrated one thing for sure, that Austria-Hungary is undefeatable," Piffl
preached in June, 1915 – and pronouncement of collective guilt for
the sins that preceded the war. By casting war as result of accumu-
lated sin and the decline of morals, rather than the decisions of Austria's government, the Church may have helped deflect criticism away

[12] Martin Krexner, *Hirte an der Zeitenwende: Kardinal Friedrich Gustav Piffl und seine Zeit*
(Vienna: Dom-Verlag, 1988), 104, 117. On the Church in wartime Vienna generally,
see Krexner, 101–209.
[13] *Wiener Diözesanblatt* 15, 14 August 1914, 129–30.
[14] *Wiener Diözesanblatt* 20, 28 October 1914, 1.
[15] August M. Knoll (ed.), *Kardinal Fr. G. Piffl und der österreichische Episkopat zu sozialen
und kulturellen Fragen, 1913–1932* (Vienna: Reinhold Verlag, 1932), 12–13.
[16] *Wiener Diözesanblatt* 15/16, 24 August 1918, 103.

from state authorities. In January, 1915, Cardinal Piffl asked followers at St. Stephen's Cathedral,

Is there even one among us who could maintain with good conscience that...these miseries of war strike us undeservedly? Has not heaven heard deafening cries of crass unbelief [and] defiant rebellion against God and his eternal moral law? Wasn't cynical blasphemy the order of the day? Hadn't countless suicides, the frightful decline of the birth rate, and fickleness in marriages and separations poisoned and contaminated moral life in the deepest way?[17]

While such sentiments did not constitute positive propaganda for the state, they benefited the state indirectly by refocusing the attention of war-weary Viennese Catholics onto their own moral failings.

Intuitively, one would expect believers to turn to the Church for spiritual comfort in times of loss and hardship. Church leaders, however, saw their mission as larger than that of offering succor to grieving followers. Throughout the war, they continued to sing the praises of the Habsburg state and remind the flock of its obligations to God and Emperor. Clergy made frequent reference to Romans, 8:31, asking, "If God is for us, who can be against us?" Franz Joseph was the *Friedenskaiser*, the Emperor of Peace, and the only wish of his successor, the "beloved Emperor Karl," was "to consecrate his stricken peoples with the palm of an honorable peace."[18] Even as late as August 1918, the Church proclaimed Austria had a "providential mission to fulfill as the pre-eminent Catholic power in the heart of Europe." Austria's strength, according to a pastoral letter, "lies in the unity of its peoples and this [in turn] rests on Catholic faith."[19] In these patriotic wartime teachings, however, we see little mention of how non-Catholic elements fit into the heralded organic union of ruler and peoples. Occasional anti-Semitic rants that appear in Viennese pastoral letters[20] and that may have been voiced from the pulpit remind us that as a transmitter of war propaganda, the Catholic Church supported the state, but had interests that were not always at one with the state's.

A second reliable source of support for the state and the justness of its war cause was the Viennese press itself. If we imagine war propaganda as an apparatus, we need not assume that state authorities were necessarily the ones "feeding" it. Even newspapers such as the socialist *Arbeiterzeitung* spent the first years of the war essentially supporting the cause. "Under the patriotic leadership of Victor Adler," writes historian

---

[17] Krexner, *Hirte an der Zeitenwende*, 129, 125.   [18] Knoll, *Kardinal Piffl*, 15.
[19] "Hirtenbrief," *Wiener Diözesanblatt* 15/16, 24 August 1918, 105.
[20] "Christian believers! The war profiteers are worse than the hyenas of the battlefield; usurers are venal *Judasseelen*, ready despicably to betray their own people, fatherland, and all of humanity." "Hirtenbrief," *Wiener Diözesanblatt* 24, 27 December 1916, 216.

Edward Timms, "the Social Democratic organizations had thrown their weight behind the Austrian war effort. As official party newspaper the *Arbeiterzeitung* had also initially supported the war."[21] Even more consistently loyal to the Habsburg state over the course of the war were the Christian Social *Reichspost* and the liberal *Neue Freie Presse*, a paper so wholeheartedly engaged in war that Viennese satirist Karl Kraus initially held its editors and journalists (rather than statesmen and military officials) *responsible* for the war. According to Timms, we find in Kraus's critique of the Viennese press a number of groups not employed by the state but responsible for the "input of information into the apparatus." These included owners and editors with commercial or political motives; journalists "remarkable for combining fluent professional skills with a lack of responsibility;" and "writers and intellectuals who so readily bent their pens to propagandistic purposes."[22] As with the Church, the state had in the press a body of willing propagandists with the technical means to reach a very large audience. On this point, Vienna was not at all representative of the other cities of the Habsburg Empire; state authorities did not expect the propagandistic zeal of Vienna's major German-language newspapers to be replicated elsewhere, and censored more strictly the Slavic and Latin presses.[23]

The Habsburg state did not have a very effective or well-developed domestic propaganda operation of its own, and so relied on the Church and the press to create and convey much of the "positive" coverage of the war in Vienna. The same cannot be said for censorship. In the "negative" management of information, the state took a much more proactive role. The War Surveillance Office, a "completely unlawful creation," according to contemporary constitutional historian Josef Redlich, was a murky governmental organization born of secret 1912 war contingency plans.[24] Comprised of representatives from the War Ministry, the General Staff and civilians working under the auspices of the War Ministry, the office employed thousands of people in its five divisions: censorship, politics, imports and exports, technology and miscellaneous matters. While it had

---

[21] Edward Timms, *Karl Kraus, Apocalyptic Satirist: Culture and Catastrophe in Habsburg Vienna* (New Haven: Yale University Press, 1986), 361.

[22] Timms, *Karl Kraus*, 284. See ch. 16 for the propagandistic contributions made by Austria's literary elites.

[23] See Mark Cornwall, "News, Rumour and the Control of Information in Austria-Hungary, 1914–1918," *History* 77, no. 249 (1992), 50–64, on the more vigilent censorship of Slavic and Latin publications.

[24] Josef Redlich, *Österreichische Regierung und Verwaltung im Weltkriege* (Vienna: Hölder-Pichler-Tempsky, 1925), 94. Once the parliament was reconvened in 1917, the extra-legal Kriegsüberwachungsamt was renamed the Ministerialkommission im Kriegsministerium (MK/KM) and continued its surveillance operations under a different command structure.

a vague mandate to use all available means to prevent "espionage, disturbances and unauthorized disclosures" in wartime, this mission statement
was written before its authors could have foreseen the course the war
would take and the role the blossoming field of surveillance would play
in it. With hindsight, we see that one of the overarching aims of the state
surveillance effort in "total war" was to demarcate the two theaters of
war – front and home front – and to control the flow of information
between them.

In a total war, in which all members of society were engaged in war-
making in some capacity, regardless of age or gender, no individual could
experience first-hand all facets of the war. People gathered some information from personal experience, while other information necessarily came
from second-hand sources. The Austrian surveillance project aimed to
sanitize versions of all those aspects of war of which people had no direct
knowledge or experience. In practice this meant "protecting" civilians
from disturbing information from the front (military defeats, high casualties, poor living conditions and disaffection among troops), and "protecting" soldiers from home-front conditions (scarcity, hunger, civilian
unrest and violence). If shielded from information that could damage
morale, soldiers would continue to fight and civilians would continue to
perform their primary duty to "hold out." Of course, the imaginary line
between front and home front war was permeable, and a great deal of human traffic flowed between the two realms. In fact, enemy propagandists
counted on this traffic. Italian and British propagandists calculated that
their subversive messages to Austrian troops on the Italian front would
loop back to Austria's unstable hinterland, fermenting in a "common
yeast" to undermine morale in both realms.[25]

The greatest challenges to state censors trying to maintain an information barrier between front and home front were the unofficial stories in
circulation. Residents of Vienna heard and retold stories daily that clashed
with official news. When Marie Krbuschek, a soldier's wife from Vienna's
XVI district, wrote in 1918 to her brother in the field, "[W]e are healthy,
but for how long I don't know, because we are really hungry... Hunger
and misery is widespread... Nothing good awaits us," she was arrested,
not because her information was *false*, but because it stood "to threaten
the discipline of front troops and to negatively influence their morale."[26]
Josef Stary from the V district, angry about bread and cigarette shortages in the capital, wrote ominously to his brother in the field, "Economically and industrially, the whole state will come curiously crashing

[25] Cornwall, *The Undermining of Austria-Hungary*, 437.
[26] AdBDW Stimmungsberichte 1917 (misfiled), #54676.

down."[27] Equally devastating information was sent in the opposite direction. Soldier Otto Wessely wrote home:

Going to the field for the fourth time. I feel like a felon being dragged to the scaffold... Everything for the Fatherland! What a strange word! Is there such thing as a Fatherland? A Fatherland doesn't let people be frivolously slaughtered and starve for no reason.[28]

Censors may have intercepted Wessely's letter, but many similar stories about soldiers without shoes, trainloads of perishable food going to waste, and corpses rotting in the open air circulated in Vienna in a kind of "black market of information" which challenged the state's version of events.[29]

Censors were divided into three units – press, letters and telegrams – to combat this black market of information. Viennese residents knew very well that censors were at work during the war, monitoring the information they received and, in turn, the information they sent. Empty white spaces (weiße Flecken) appeared in newspapers, and mail arrived (or was returned to sender) bearing the censor's stamp. Residents did not necessarily know who was doing the censoring, or under whose authority censors operated. In an effort to humanize the institution that had become an obvious, but still mysterious presence in people's lives, the Neues Wiener Tagblatt was permitted in 1916 to run a human interest article entitled "The Blue Pencil," documenting the work of censors and named for their most famous tool. Although Redlich describes the War Surveillance Office as a sinister institution, veiled in secrecy, and striving for "frightful, absolute power," we will see that citizens came to talk back, with increasing audacity, to the unknown figures of the censorship division.[30]

The blue pencil had a stifling and homogenizing effect on the Viennese press. Many newspapers, especially those with a nationalist bent or known for class agitation, disappeared from circulation at the outset of war. Vienna's sizable Czech community, as well as other Slavic groups and pockets of radical socialists and anarchists, were hardest hit by these measures.[31] Although Viennese newspapers of the prewar period often

[27] AdBDW Stimmungsberichte 1917 (misfiled), #54583.
[28] KA, AOK, GZNB 1918, carton 3759, #5174. July 1918, report from k.u.k. Zensurstelle Wien.
[29] The phrase "black market of information" is Jean Nöel Kapferer's. Cited in Andreas Würgler, "Fama und Rumor. Gerücht, Aufruhr und Presse im Ancien Régime," in Werkstatt Geschichte 15 (1996), 20–32, 21.
[30] WSLB ZAS Kriegsgefangene Bd. I, Neues Wiener Tagblatt, 2 January 1916; Redlich, Österreichische Regierung, 126.
[31] The Czech bourgeois daily Videňský Denník and the Czech social democratic Dělnické Listy were permitted to continue publishing, but other Czech publications were "eingestellt" on grounds of political unreliability.

reprinted borrowed stories, the wartime press was especially repetitive. Reports from the fronts, published daily under the banner "Authentic War News from the Press Bureau of the War Ministry," appeared in identical format in newspapers of all political persuasions. Censors banned market updates, after thousands of shoppers began arriving at markets to buy advertised products which were in fact not available, and casualty lists, which quickly became too long (and demoralizing) to print in newspapers.[32] They even scrutinized the classified advertisements, investigating suspicious ads reading: "Looking for 2,000 cartons of sardines in tomato sauce," or "Selling 5,000 kg white cream soap," suspecting that they were coded messages for spies.[33] Writer Alfred Polgar noted, however, that censors were inconsistent: articles forbidden in one journal were sometimes accepted for publication with only minor changes in another.[34] Finally, "white spaces" appeared when censors rejected articles that had already been formatted onto a page. Save for the masthead, the whole front page of a newspaper might appear blank (see plate 3.1).

Some Viennese journalists appear to have avoided white spaces by practicing what John Halliday calls "pre-confiscation." They submitted copies of their works to the censor, who performed a preliminary reading before the final article was typeset.[35] When they did appear, white spaces were detrimental to the state's propaganda efforts. They alerted newspaper readers to the fact that the "authentic" news was not always the whole news, and left readers to fill the spaces with their imaginations. The *Arbeiterinnen-Zeitung*, the newspaper of German-speaking Social Democratic women, was permitted to publish during the war but was littered with white spaces. Its editors took to filling these spaces with commentaries on the practice of censorship, which, strangely, were not censored. Under the heading "Confiscation," they wrote: "Many of our comrades have asked us in letters, what dangerous thing had been there? We are pleased about this. We have always been of the opinion that confiscations have a more provocative effect than the content [of the article] itself." A year later they used a white space to publish an editorial on censorship:

The lead article of this edition has been completely confiscated...In order not to delay the appearance of the paper, we will have to forego offering an alternate lead article – perhaps also bound for the censor. Comrades! Be convinced that

---

[32] Residents could view casualty lists at their local municipal offices between 8 a.m. and 2 p.m. *Kriegszustand. Instruktionen für Polizeiorgane* (Vienna, 1914), 26–7.
[33] AdBDW 1916 St./5 Pressewesen, #27640. Pol. Dir. Wien to Pol. Dir. Prag.
[34] Alfred Polgar, *Hinterland* (Berlin: Rowohlt, 1929), introduction.
[35] See John Halliday, "Satirist and Censor," 201–4. The author presents evidence that Karl Kraus, a well-known critic of the war, had a rather cozy relationship with the censors in Vienna.

Arbeiterinnen-Zeitung

Sozialdemokratisches Organ für Frauen und Mädchen

Die „Arbeiterinnen-Zeitung" erscheint alle 14 Tage am Dienstag. — Abonnementspreis für Oesterreich-Ungarn: Ganzjährig Kr. 3·40; halbjährig Kr. 1·70. — Für Deutschland: Mk. 3·20. — Für alle anderen dem Weltpostverein angehörenden Länder Frcs. 3·80.

Mit den Beilagen „Für die Jugend" und „Freie Stunden"

Redaktion, Administration, Expedition und Inseratenaufnahme VI/1, Rechte Wienzeile 97. Sendungen sind nur an die Administration zu richten. — Reklamationen sind portofrei. Postsparkassen-Scheck-Konto Nr. 15.905. — Telephon Nr. 900.

Nr. 15.   **Wien, Dienstag den 27. Juli 1915**   **24. Jahrgang.**

Ein Jahr.

Genau vor einem Jahr ist die Note Oesterreichs an Serbien überreicht worden. Dann folgte Schlag auf Schlag; wilde Gerüchte wogten herum und am 31. Juli wurde Jean Jaurès, der unermüdliche Kämpfer für die Verbrüderung Frankreichs mit Deutschland, ermordet. Die Phantasie schwebte zügellos, alle möglichen Leute sollten ermordet sein, man nannte Poincaré und den serbischen Peter. Mit Bomben ließ man — in der Phantasie — Nürnberg von den Franzosen bewerfen und Japan wurde schon beinahe als Bundesgenosse der Zentralmächte gefeiert. Nur die Mobilisierung blieb kein Märchen; sie erfolgte und zerriß die Bande der Familie und des gewohnten Trottes im bürgerlichen Leben. Millionen Menschen folgten dem Ruf zu den Fahnen und im deutschen Reichstag bewilligten die Sozialdemokraten der Regierung die erforderlichen Milliarden für die Kriegführung. Der belgische Neutralitätsbruch war, jedoch erfolgt, deutsche Soldaten standen schon auf belgischem Boden und der Reichskanzler rechtfertigte diese Tat gegen das Völkerrecht mit Berufung auf den Zwang der Not. Die Sozialdemokraten fügten ihrem Votum für die Kriegskredite die Verwahrung bei, daß sie jede Eroberung verwerfen und nur dem Verteidigungskrieg die Mittel gewähren. „In der Stunde der Gefahr lassen wir das Vaterland nicht im Stich" ließen sie durch ihren Vorsitzenden, Genossen Haase, erklären. England aber trat auf die Seite Rußlands und Frankreichs, Japan gesellte sich ihnen zu. Gegen vier Großmächte, Rußland, Frankreich, England und Japan, gegen Belgien, Serbien und Montenegro hatten sich Deutschland und Oesterreich-Ungarn zu wehren. Italien, das immer als der dritte Bundesgenosse der Zentralmächte galt, hielt sich neutral, was man heute so nennt. Hin und her wogten die Armeen, Belgien, Nordfrankreich, Galizien, Russisch-polen und Ostpreußen wurden in Blut getränkt, Witwen und Waisen ringen verzweifelt die Hände um den verlorenen Gatten und Vater. Invalide, auf Krücken gestützt, werden im Straßenbild immer sichtbarer und Zug um Zug rollt mit Verwundeten. Massengrab reiht sich an Massengrab. Und das Kriegsglück kam und ging. Sieger wurden zu Besiegten und umgekehrt. Auch Italien trat aus der Neutralität heraus und wendete sich gegen die Bundesgenossen von gestern, es gesellte sich zu den Feinden Deutschlands und Oesterreichs. „Viel Feind, viel Ehr'", sagt ein Sprichwort; die Ehre ist aber in diesem Fall eine furchtbar kostbare Sache. Mit warmem Menschenblut muß sie aufgewogen werden, und immer mehr und immer mehr Soldaten. Bald werden alle bis zu 42 Jahren unter Waffen stehen, die Achtzehnjährigen folgen ihnen und die Dreiundvierzig- bis Fünfzigjährigen beschließen den Reigen.

Hier wurde eine halbe Seite konfisziert

Plate 3.1. "White space" in a censored Viennese newspaper. Source: *Arbeiterinnen-Zeitung*, 27 July 1915, 1.

our newspaper will not fail to express that which all women wish for, but there are powers against which ours do not suffice ... [36]

By allowing this sort of retort, the censors appear to have been willing to absorb public criticism, and to serve from time to time as a vent for readers' frustrations. But the white spaces also had the unintended effect of politicizing readers. Katarzyna Titz wrote from Vienna's IV district to a family member in captivity in Russia of the effects that press censorship had on her understanding of politics. A budding Polish patriot, she explained her

realization that the Polish nation cannot be deterred by any power in the world, not least by the censor, who does not understand that the heart cannot be silenced by the censor's pencil. I'm telling you, I have the censor to thank – the white spaces and so forth – for the fact that I've acquired full national consciousness.[37]

In Titz's case, white spaces sparked a process of questioning; they exposed the state's dubious claim to be a purveyor of truthful news. By suppressing some information, censors in a sense invited readers to seek it from unofficial channels.

Titz's feelings about press censorship are available to us only because a letter censor saw fit to record them. The censors' reading of millions of pieces of private correspondence in wartime was another ambitious component of information management. While press censors monitored big stories that might reach thousands of readers, the letter censors focused on the small but still dangerous fragments of information that might reach only a single reader. The volume of materials they handled was mind-boggling: the unit overseeing foreign correspondence (primarily letters from the home front to Austrian POWs, and enemy POWs in Austrian captivity to their home countries) employed around 3,000 people in its three offices, which each processed between one and three million pieces of mail per month.[38] They also reviewed the photos and drawings on thousands of wartime postcards, weeding out those images deemed detrimental to the Austrian war effort. One postcard, for example, was banned on grounds that it was "intended to undermine the peace of mind and moral strength of our soldiers." The postcard showed a Russian POW "wrapping his arms around the wife of an Austrian soldier, surprising the husband as he came home on leave."[39] In addition to the international

[36] *Arbeiterinnen-Zeitung*, 27 July 1915; 22 August 1916.
[37] KA, GZNB 1917 carton 3749, #4578. Censor's report, March 1917, on the "Polish Question."
[38] Spann, "Vom Leben im Kriege," 149–50. The offices of the gemeinsame Zentralnachweisbüro were in Vienna, Budapest and Feldkirchen.
[39] NÖLA Präs. "P" 1917 XIIIa, 2301. MdI to Statthalterei, 16 May 1916.

mail, the Viennese police ran its own censorship operation for domestic mail, reading about 2,000 pieces a day, sent to or from residents on a continually updated list of suspected agitators.[40] The mission of letter censors expanded over time: initially, they were charged with removing all false, anti-state or simply "damaging" information from circulation. After 1916, they used citizen letters to compile reports on the mood of the population.

As a source, the reports are valuable but limited: they focus unusual attention on matters of everyday life, giving us the voices and activities of "the people," but always as filtered through the eyes and ears of state agents. Taken as a whole, the reports suggest that the state failed to control the flow of information between front and home front, but it failed with a twist. Whereas its original aim was to prevent civilians from receiving unofficial information about the front, the state was helpless to combat a new kind of information obstacle: apathy. According to the reports, civilians had ceased by 1916 to *care* much about what happened at the front. "While in the first year of war concern about family members in the field [ensured] that events at the fronts held the spotlight, already by the second year circumstances had fundamentally changed," wrote the governor's office.[41] Despite their sporadic propaganda efforts, state authorities were unable to curb the encroaching apathy; like a bad play that goes on too long, the state at war was losing its audience.

Suffering from war-weariness (*Kriegsmüdigkeit*), the population had lost interest in both the "war" and "politics," as traditionally defined. Censors noted in 1917 that

complaints about economic difficulties have become increasingly coarse, while discussion of great political and military events become ever more rare. The failed enemy offensives in the east and west [and] the continuing liberation of East Galicia and Bukowina hardly receive any notice. [C]onvening and activities of the parliament are seldom mentioned.[42]

Censors explained the disappearance of battles and high politics from citizens' letters: "This silence is rooted in the fact that all letter-writers are ruled by only one concern, the concern over daily bread.... everything else falls by the wayside... Any interest in the big events has disappeared."[43] And a month later, they concluded, "[F]rom now on, worry over the maintenance of one's own life is the defining factor for the general

---

[40] AdBDW 1915 V/23 #7535; St./15 #3326.
[41] NÖLA Präs "P" 1917 VI, #3807. Statthaltereipräs. to MdI, 3 August 1917.
[42] KA, GZNB 1917 carton 3752, #4766. "Stimmung und wirtschaftliche Lage der österr. Bevölkerung im Hinterlande," July 1917.
[43] KA, GZNB 1917 carton 3749, #4588. Censor's report, March 1917.

mood."[44] When we read, therefore, that in a sample of 1,000 censored postcards, 941 contained no "mention of war and peace"[45] we can conclude that state authorities and the population had come to define war differently. The former failed to count hunger news as war news, while for the latter, war and hunger had become synonymous. This inability to set and maintain the terms of war on the home front marked one defeat for the state's program of information management.

One feature that distinguished Austrian censorship in World War I from the more rigorous surveillance regimes that followed in later periods in Europe was the apparent lack of fear the surveillance apparatus inspired in the population. Despite its dictatorial ambitions, the Austrian war government was not a terror state.[46] Letter-writers seem to have been rather more annoyed by than afraid of the censors, and often directed remarks specifically to them. A letter sent to Viennese student Franz Hradetschny in 1915 contained typical jabs at the censor. The writer accused censors of having opened his mail and drawn obscene cartoons on his correspondence. "I didn't know that the gentlemen censors have so much time," he wrote sarcastically, "that they include a dedication on the letters. In any case, they must be fine people."[47] Such provocation became steadily more abusive as the war progressed. Censors reported being the targets of increasingly hostile remarks by 1917, noting, "More than a few writers are especially annoyed by the actions of the censorship offices, which create bad blood with their prohibitions."[48] By 1918, letter-writers seem to have declared open season on the censors. "The tone of the letters becomes ever more irritable and rebellious, not only in civilian but also in military circles. Fear of the censor, which until now inspired a certain reserve when discussing public matters among the majority of the population, no longer has any effect."[49]

Some residents turned against the censors upon discovering that not all mail was censored uniformly. Viennese resident Adolf Brecher claimed he was initially willing to tolerate the four- to five-day postal delay caused by censors because he thought it was for the common good. "In light

---

[44] NÖLA Präs "P" 1917 VI, #3807. Statthaltereipräs. to MdI, 3 August 1917.

[45] KA, GZNB 1917 carton 3752, #4766. "Stimmung und wirtschaftliche Lage der österr. Bevölkerung im Hinterlande," July 1917.

[46] Sheila Fitzpatrick defines terror as "extralegal state violence against groups and randomly chosen citizens." *Everyday Stalinism: Ordinary Life in Extraordinary Times. Soviet Russia in the 1930's* (New York: Oxford University Press, 1999), 7.

[47] AdBDW 1915 St./9 #15972. Militärkommando Krakau to Pol. Dir. Wien, 19 Feb 1915.

[48] KA, KüA 1917 #108758. May 1917, report "Stimmung und wirtschaftliche Lage der österreichischen Bevölkerung im Hinterlande."

[49] KA, AOK GZNB 1918 carton 3759, #5174. July 1918, report from k.u.k. Zensurstelle Wien.

of the serious circumstances in which we currently live, I tolerated this process in silence." He soon learned that his neighbors were not being monitored in the same way. "As I realized, however, that letters in general are not processed as they are in my case, I became particularly attentive to the matter." He concluded that either he had been the target of a denunciation, or that police had confused him with someone of the same name. "Because I have absolutely no doubt that I've never done anything in my life that would violate the duties of an enthusiastic patriot, the measures taken against me have deeply offended me ... "[50] Censorship in principle had not made Brecher indignant, but rather the discovery that censors practiced their trade in an uneven fashion, targeting some citizens but not others.

Brecher's case offers the first crack in the thesis that Austrian censors created a kind of totalitarian surveillance that left no room for open expression of opinion. Censors did not manage to read all private correspondence in wartime, especially mail sent from one home-front location to another. One of the great obstacles to total surveillance – more challenging in Austria than in any other belligerent country – was the number of languages used by the population. There were eleven recognized nationalities in the Habsburg realm, each with a corresponding language: German, Hungarian, Czech, Slovak, Polish, Ruthenian, Italian, Romanian, Slovenian, Croatian and Serbian.[51] Within Vienna, where German and Czech were dominant, but certainly not the only languages in wide use, the prospect of censorship was daunting from a linguistic standpoint. In the fall of 1914, the city had absorbed between 50,000 and 70,000 mostly Polish- and Yiddish-speaking refugees from the east.[52] Censorship required adequately trained personnel who knew the languages well enough to detect even cleverly disguised messages and jokes, and the Viennese police had trouble finding what they considered to be "politically reliable" employees, especially for the Slavic languages. The

---

[50] AdBDW 1915 St./9 #13061. Adolf Brecher to Staatspolizei, 21 June 1915.

[51] On language and politics, see Emil Brix, *Die Umgangssprachen in Altösterreich zwischen Agitation und Assimilation* (Vienna: Veröffentlichungen der Kommission für Neuere Geschichte Österreichs, 1982). For the GZNB, the offices that handled all mail coming into or going out of Austria (including POW correspondence), the list of languages was even longer. Mail was sorted into the following twenty-five categories: German, Russian, Italian, Czech, Polish, Slovak, Ukrainian, Serbian, Croatian, Romanian and Bessarabian (Romanian in Cyrillic), Hungarian, French, English, Swedish, Hebrew, Sephardic, Spanish, Latvian and Estonian, Bulgarian, Greek, Albanian, Arabic, Turkish, Persian and Tatar. *Jahresbericht der Auskunftstelle für Kriegsgefangene des gemeinsamen Zentralnachweisbureaus sowie des österreichischen Fürsorgekommittees für Kriegsgefangene für das Jahr 1916*, 6.

[52] On war refugees, see Beatrix Hoffmann-Holter, '*Abreisendmachung': Jüdische Kriegsflüchtlinge in Wien, 1914–1923* (Vienna: Böhlau, 1995).

case of Viktoria Wasservogel demonstrates how the dream of total surveillance clashed with practical security constraints. Claiming she knew four languages, Wasservogel, a Serbian citizen by birth and an Austrian citizen by marriage, applied in 1915 to work as a police translator in Vienna. Although a background check found her "unobjectionable" and her husband was serving in the Austrian army, her "fitness for public service as a translator [was] in question" because she had been born a Serb, and she was ultimately denied the position at a time when police needed Serbian translators.[53] Authorities were in a catch-22: who but a native Serb knew the language well enough to read between the lines of censored mail, but who could be trusted less to work for the Austrian state in wartime than a native Serb?

Language was not the only stumbling block in staffing the censorship offices. The work was considered highly sensitive and suitable only for those with impeccable *Gesinnung*, or attitude towards the state.[54] In an ideal world, all potential censors would be subjected to rigorous background checks, including the "inconspicuous observation of [their] private lives" and investigation of their "character, prewar life and political attitudes." They would be responsible, "free of nervous disorders" and physically fit enough to carry out strenuous night shifts. In reality, the censorship offices reported employees with "low intelligence," some of whom stole from the packages they were supposed to be censoring. Two-thirds of censors working in Vienna were not originally from the city and had difficulty coping with the food scarcity and high inflation in their temporary home; there was talk of a censors' strike. Finally, censors registered such frequent absenteeism that soldiers recovering in the city's hospitals were sometimes called to perform censorship duties.[55] This rather chaotic staffing situation reminds us that censorship as an abstract system is always subject to human constraints. In the case of Vienna, censors faced the same precarious food, health and employment conditions as the population they censored.

Overestimating the scope and success of the Austrian censorship apparatus, the American ambassador in Vienna was reported to have noted in 1916 that any public expression of opinion or political discussion were "absolutely impossible" in the capital city.[56] He failed to appreciate not only the human constraints that made "total" censorship unrealizable, but also that not all expression was subject to the censorial scrutiny. Much

---

[53] AdBDW 1915 V/12 #15972. File on Viktoria Wasservogel.
[54] For detailed discussion of *Gesinnung* and citizenship, see chapter 4.
[55] KÜA guidelines and memos, cited in Gustav Spann, "Zensur in Österreich" (Ph.D. diss., University of Vienna, 1972), 102, 150–53.
[56] *Ibid.*, 386.

unofficial information, in the form of rumors and anonymous writings, circulated under the noses – but beyond the reach – of censors. An Army High Command memo from 1918 acknowledged an inverse relationship of censorship and rumors: the stricter the censorship, the more expansive the black market for unofficial information. "However difficult rumors are to combat," the memo stated, "their suppression is essential at a time when unavoidably stricter operations of the censor have caused people to lend [rumors] even greater credibility."[57] Despite the efforts of thousands of employees who reviewed millions of newspapers and private letters during the war, sensational stories about people collapsing in the street from hunger, women baking cakes with clay instead of flour, and starving Viennese residents gnawing the bark off of trees slipped through the censors' nets, passed between front and home front, and thwarted the state's ambitious project of information management.

The censors' original mission was made significantly more difficult by political developments during the second half of the war, most notably Emperor Karl's agreement to reconvene the Austrian parliament (*Reichsrat*) in May, 1917. One of a series of liberalizing moves taken by the new regime, the decision to reconvene added a new chorus of voices to Austrian public life: the nationally polarized parliamentarians. They sprang to life, making uncensored speeches from the floor, the substance of which was then reported in the press. Not surprisingly, the legally dubious War Surveillance Office was the target of immediate parliamentary criticism; its name was changed to the Military Chancellery of the War Ministry in September, and the Army High Command's role in information management was curtailed.[58] Representatives of Austria's non-German nationalities used the parliament as a forum to air grievances against the multi-national state. Historian Manfried Rauchensteiner, pointing to the larger political implications of this new realm of uncensored speech, writes, "The nationalities first began to turn away from the Habsburg Monarchy not in 1918, but already at the end of May 1917."[59] The effects of this nationalist parliamentary agitation on the mood of home-front residents was likely more dramatic in Prague, Krakow, Ljubljana or other non-German cities in Austria than it was in Vienna. In other home-front cities, taking a stand against "Vienna" – not a particularly resonant position in Vienna itself – was a shorthand way of taking a stand against the imperial state or its German backers. For German-speaking Viennese readers, the published claims of Czech,

[57] KA, MK-KM 1918 #28306. AOK memo, July 1918.
[58] Cornwall, "News, Rumour…," 59.
[59] Manfried Rauchensteiner, *Der Tod des Doppeladlers: Österreich-Ungarn und der Erste Weltkrieg* (Graz: Verlag Styria, 1993), 450.

Polish or South-Slav national representatives had a different effect, serving to strengthen the suspicion that one's own Slavic neighbors and co-workers constituted a treacherous internal enemy.

Rumors

On November 2, 1918, shortly before the signing of the armistice that ended the war, many residents of Vienna believed their city was being taken over by militant Italian prisoners of war who had escaped from camps outside Vienna. At 10 o'clock in the evening, news of the breakout was spreading among people on the streets and in coffeehouses and pubs. In a state of "great excitability," residents heard and passed on the information that the POWs were plundering and burning their way towards the capital. By the quarter hour, the information became simultaneously more detailed and less consistent. The Italians numbered 10,000, then 13,000, and then were said to be working in conjunction with escaped Russians. Between 10 and 11 o'clock "messengers" appeared in coffeehouses on the Ringstrasse and ordered the officers and soldiers there to report to police headquarters immediately for "instructions." Many complied. Two officers in a speeding car warned guests leaving the opera of the impending attack, and civilians were told to go home and lock their doors. Around 11 o'clock, police chief Schober consulted state authorities about "the defense of Vienna against eventual threat from escaped prisoners of war." By midnight, the Minster of the Interior announced that the reports were "strongly exaggerated ... and thankfully do not reflect the truth." The next day, the Viennese press reported on "the most unbelievable rumor" that had spread through the city the night before.[60]

This series of events contains several features common to rumors on the World War I home front. First, a piece of rapidly spreading information was labeled as rumor in hindsight, once it appeared not to "reflect the truth," as determined by state authorities. As we will see, however, information that was not wholly true was often not wholly false either. Second, the prisoner of war rumor, coming as it did shortly before the collapse of the Habsburg state, developed in an atmosphere of *insecurity* – state authorities and residents were faced with myriad unconfirmed stories about the course of events within and beyond the city – and the rumor reflected a sense of *threat*. Both insecurity and threat were typical features of rumors. Third, typical of late-war rumors, civilians and military personnel participated in the same information networks, which made the

[60] WSLB ZAS Kriegsgefangene Bd. III, *Neue Freie Presse*, 3 November 1918; *Arbeiterzeitung*, 3 and 4 November 1918.

information all the more alarming to high level officials. And finally, in this case and in many others, the press was used to "combat" the rumor, exposing it as such once officials declared it false.

Government reports of rumors in Vienna (which are the only source we have on the subject) described them in colorful, qualifying terms. A rumor was never just a rumor. The prisoners of war stories above were "unconfirmed" and "unbelievable." Rumors about military disaffection were "wild" and their spreaders were "defeatists" (*Flaumacher*). Tax and rent rumors were "uncontrollable." Some disease rumors were "improbable," others "fantastic." Stories of defeats at the front were "ridiculous," "absurd" and "lacking any foundation." Officials called rumors of military incompetence "groundless" and called on the press to squelch the "scare-mongering" (*Tartarnachrichten*). Rumors were even qualified in the Austrian legal code, which prohibited the spreading of "false, disturbing" rumors. This raises the question of whether, in official terms, there could be such a thing as a "true" rumor, or whether falsity was constitutive of rumor.

Contemporaries and historians have offered various definitions of rumors. In 1915, one Viennese women's magazine adopted the common-sense stance that you know a rumor when you hear one: "You know what a rumor is. A bit of news surfaces – we don't know where from – and passes with lightning speed from one person to the next; usually it's bad news that depresses the spirit and dampens courage." Its editors traced the genealogy of rumors, beginning with fear: Out of fear, one woman might wonder aloud what would happen *if* the Russians came. Another would change tense, predicting *when* the Russians come, and a third would speculate on *how close* the Russians were to Vienna. "[A]nd so it spreads until the whole place is wringing its hands, filled with foolish rumors."[61] Scholars have similarly viewed rumors as networks of informal communication that represent people's attempts to retrieve some sort of *reality* when their sense of reality has been destroyed by "official" information that does not correspond to their knowledge of events. Ulrich Raulff has explored the psychological dimensions of rumors, focusing on situations of insecurity (such as wartime) in which they tend to develop. He proposes a recipe: take a community in danger, or one that imagines itself to be in danger, one in which members are experiencing isolation, loss of normal social contacts, exhaustion and fear, and add to it a sense that information is either being withheld or falsified. Rumors grow as people whose critical faculties are weakened try to establish reliable truths. Raulff is interested less in the content of rumors than in what

[61] *Arbeiterinnenblatt* 2, no. 2 (1 June 1915), 18–19.

they reflect about the psychological condition of the community.[62] Historian Jacob Vogel points to the difficulty of defining what constitutes a rumor, because we often classify only untrue pieces of information as such, while we consider true information to be "news."[63] Jean-Nöel Kapferer offers the useful distinction: "Rumors are not necessarily 'false': they are, however, necessarily unofficial ... [T]hey challenge official reality by proposing other realities."[64] In all of these examples, rumor-spreading is directly related to a population's lack of faith in the veracity of officially circulated information.

By examining a few specific cases from Vienna, we see that Kapferer's definition of a rumor comes close to the working definition used by Austrian legal authorities during the war. The full text of the law prohibiting "false, disturbing" rumors read:

Whoever, by way of public announcement (posters, public speeches or lectures and the like) spreads a false rumor [or] a rumor that disturbs public security, without sufficient grounds to believe it true, or whoever disseminates unfounded predictions or spreads them further is guilty of a misdemeanor punishable by eight days' to three months' close arrest.[65]

When Friedrich Kast, a resident of Vienna's VIII district, announced in a hotel lobby in September, 1914 that Russia was "gobbling up" Austria, that the country would be divided into four zones, and that Germany was poised to benefit from Austria's losses, he was arrested under this law. His actions met the two criteria of a rumor: the information he passed was "false" in that it clashed with official press versions of the progress of the war in the east, and it was "public" in that he spread it to "the guests present in the hotel," who experienced "uneasiness" at hearing the news.[66]

While Kast's violation was fairly clear cut, most rumor cases were not. In the case of Alfred Frankl, accused in August 1914 of spreading "false

---

[62] Ulrich Raulff, "Clio in den Dünsten: Über Geschichte und Gerüchte," in Bedrich Loewenstein (ed.), *Geschichte und Psychologie: Annährungsversuche* (Pfaffenweiler: Centaurus, 1992): 99–114, 99, 104. See also Franz Dröge, *Der zerredete Widerstand: Soziologie und Publizistik der Gerüchte im 2. Weltkrieg* (Düsseldorf: Bertelsmann Universitätsverlag, 1970).

[63] Jacob Vogel, "Die Politik des Gerüchts. Soziale Kommunikationen und Herrschaftspraxis in Frühneuzeit und Moderne," *Werkstatt Geschichte* 15 (1996), 3–10.

[64] Jean-Nöel Kapferer, *Rumors: Uses, Interpretations and Images*, transl. Bruce Fink (New Brunswick, NJ: Transaction Publishers, 1990), 263.

[65] §308 St.G. Verbreitung falscher beunruhigender Gerüchte. Ludwig Altmann and Karl Warhanek (eds.), *Das Strafgesetz und die Strafprozeßordnung* (Vienna: Verlag der patriotischen Volksbuchhandlung, 1911), 183.

[66] AdBDW 1914 St./8 #1103. k.k. Landesgendarmeriekommando to Pol. Dir. Wien, 25 September 1914.

rumors" on a tram about the treason of a high-ranking officer, authorities ruled that his comments lacked the requisite "public" quality. "The incriminating conversation took place between only two people," a judge ruled, "and was hardly carried out in loud tones."[67] For the great majority of rumors, authorities could not identify a single perpetrator or the origin of the information. And sometimes, stories that did not "reflect the truth" were not necessarily totally false. In the earlier-noted rumor about escaped Italian POWs, officials confirmed that, indeed, there *had* been some sort of action at a POW camp outside Vienna on the night in question, but even the official versions contained inconsistencies. In one report, Italian prisoners had "disarmed" the camp guards and hoisted Italian flags, while in another report the Slavic guards and their Czech camp director had simply abandoned their positions "in order to return to their homes."[68] Finally, not all rumors that disturbed "public security," according to the law, could be considered *disturbing to the public*; to the contrary, some rumors sparked joyful celebrations. In October, 1916, rumor of an impending peace spread through the crowds at a local racetrack. The information, said to originate at the War Ministry, caused "joyful proclamations" among the fans in the three-crown seats, and "appeared to have spread widely around Vienna," as many district police offices received inquiries about its veracity.[69] While the disappointment following this rumor might have been disturbing, the information itself was not.

Though we normally think of rumors as being transmitted orally, Austrian law counted other forms of "public announcement" as rumor. In wartime Vienna, citizens transmitted unofficial information and opinions via anonymous posters, leaflets and graffiti, which often urged readers to direct action. In October, 1915, flyers reading "People – Kill your generals, privy councilors and the Jews," and "To the People – Break with the government, the murderers and scoundrels," were posted on house doors in five districts. The same year, hand-written signs in the XII district encouraged women to confront their government: "Attention! We want bread and freedom. Women and mothers of Meidling. Sunday, April 18, meeting at 2 o'clock at the city hall."[70] All of these messages were quickly confiscated by police, who sometimes had to search the unlikeliest

---

[67] AdBDW 1914 St./9 #1424. Police file on *Neues Wiener Journal*, 11 October 1914.

[68] WSLB ZAS Kriegsgefangene Bd. III, *Neue Freie Presse*, 3 November 1918; *Arbeiterzeitung*, 3 and 4 November 1918.

[69] AdBDW 1916 St./15 #34496. Police memo to Statthaltereipräs., MdI, KüA, etc., 28 October 1916.

[70] AVA, MdI Präs. carton 2130/22, #22822. Pol. Dir. Wien to MdI, 25 October 1915; NÖLA Präs "P" 1915 XIIIe, 2046. Pol. Dir. Wien to Statthalterei, 22 April 1915.

places for contraband materials. An official investigation of a men's bath-room near the Schönbrunn palace turned up a wall of anti-state graffiti. Police determined, based on spelling errors, that the many contributors likely stemmed from the lower classes, but never identified any culprits.[71] Anonymous postings, like information passed by word of mouth, were beyond the censor's net, and provided erratic but visible challenges to official information sources.

An increase in rumors might be expected during times of war. Many Viennese spent the war in insecure circumstances, worrying about food, housing, health, heat, clothing and the fates of their family members in the field or in captivity. From personal experience, they had reason to doubt official proclamations on any or all of these matters. "The concentrated appearance of rumors," historian Andreas Ernst explains, "is evidence of a lack of confidence in the usual channels of information."[72] What seems to have surprised Viennese officials more than the increased number of rumors in wartime was their content. In Europe's first total, modern war, residents of Vienna reached back to themes of threat and danger that had surfaced since the middle ages. On August 5, 1914, the Austrian Interior Ministry issued a note to regional officials about the first widespread rumor of the Great War: citizens feared that the enemy had poisoned the drinking water. "In Vienna, erroneous rumors have been spreading for days about an apparent attempt to poison the drinking water with cyanide."[73] Officials from the sanitation department denied any such poisoning had taken place and wondered at the medieval quality of the stories. "We have at hand only rumors, old fairy tales that the people have taken from the imagination of the middle ages and seized upon anew with wars and epidemics."[74] Despite the particular details of the Viennese rumors in World War I, they indicated widespread insecurity and followed time-honored themes of threat and danger.

Ernst has identified several rumor archetypes that have appeared at different times and in various historical contexts: suspicion of minorities (the "fifth column," often ethnically defined); threats to health (myste-rious diseases, poisonings); and deviance and conspiracy theories (often involving politicians or leaders.)[75] Among Christian, German-speaking Viennese, Jews and Czechs were the choice targets of those looking for

[71] AdBDW 1916 St./16 #35,807. Police memo, 29 November 1916.
[72] Andreas Ernst, "Mutmassungen über Gerüchte. Zu Jean-Noël Kapferer's Untersuch-ungen über das Gerücht," *Werkstatt Geschichte* 15 (1996), 105–8.
[73] AVA, MdI Präs. 1914, carton 22 in gen 2047, #9627. Memo from MdI to regional leaders, August 1914.
[74] AVA, MdI Präs. 1914, carton 22 in gen 2047, #9627. Sanitation Department, 8 August 1914.
[75] Ernst, "Mutmassungen über Gerüchte," 105–8.

an internal enemy. By October, 1914, rumors of treasonous Jews betraying the war effort in Galicia were in full circulation in the capital. A police informer noted that the stories were spreading "unbelievably quickly," taking root especially among the "under classes."[76] The rumor that Czech soldiers had declared they would not shoot at Russians and Serbs because they were "Slavic brothers" was one of the most oft-repeated among German-speaking Viennese. Rumors about the internal enemy make difficult the argument that rumor-spreading is an act of "resistance" on the part of the people against the state's repressive information management, because many of the stories were directed by one segment of the population against another. The severe food shortages in Vienna sparked countless rumors of conspiracy and hunger-related illnesses. In 1917, officials tried to combat a particularly stubborn rumor, circulating even among "serious, thinking persons," of an epidemic of "hunger typhus," a disease which, according to leading doctors, "[did] not exist."[77] A year later, officials suspected that rumors of large shipments of Serbian pork, which drew thousands of shoppers to the markets in anticipation, were planted by "certain elements" in order to "incite agitation among the masses."[78] All of these rumors reflect the insecurities, personal and political, that hung over Vienna throughout the war.

From the first rumors in 1914 about poisoned water to the last rumors in 1918 about an attack on the city by enemy POWs, officials worried about how these pieces of unofficial information would affect public morale and encroach upon their positions as purveyors of the truth. However, if we compare early responses to rumors to those from 1917 and 1918, we see that this form of communication attracted steadily more attention in official circles over time. As rumors began to "jump" the civilian/military barrier, circulating among civilians and military personnel simultaneously and feeding on the knowledge of each, they became correspondingly more dangerous. Perceived originally as irrational and linked to women's predilection for idle chatter, rumors came to threaten the foundations of the state itself.[79]

[76] NÖLA Präs. "P" 1914 #994, Pol. Dir. Wien to Statthaltereipräs., 1 October 1914.
[77] AVA MdI Präs. carton 2131/22, #4499; NÖLA Präs "P" 1917 XIIIc, #1844. Correspondence of MdI, Statthalter, Stadtphysikus, March 1917.
[78] AdBDW 1918 V/20 #8/260a. Memo from Kriegswucheramt, 30 January 1918.
[79] KA, MK-KM 1918 #27870. MdI memo, 4 July 1918. Anti-dynastic rumors were intended "eine der stärksten Grundfesten unseres Staatswesens, nämlich das unbegrenzte Vertrauen der Bevölkerung zur Allerhöchsten Dynastie, wankend zu machen und die Verehrung, die dem Allerhöchsten Kaiserhauses bisher allenthalben entgegengebracht wurde, abzuschwächen."

Women have often been considered the key agents in rumor and gossip networks.[80] But historically, in Austria as elsewhere, men's words have carried more public weight that women's. This explains why rumors became correspondingly more "dangerous" in official estimation, once men joined women in the practice of rumor-spreading. In peacetime Vienna, women passing information at markets and in semi-public places were thought to be perpetuating the traditions of old wives tales; women, inclined by their female temperament to idle chatter, passed trivial information of no consequence for politics or the state. In 1915, when Viennese resident Franz Malik tried to dismiss shirking charges against him as "stories from womenfolk at the markets" he was drawing on this prewar paradigm.[81] State authorities, too, drew on this association of women with unfounded or unsubstantiated information to combat, on gendered grounds, a rash of late-war rumors. "We are no longer talking about the transmission of thoughtless gossip," the General Staff wrote in 1918, in reference to reports of rumor-mongering within the military. "Whoever collaborates in the creation and spreading of disturbing rumors works directly into the hands of the enemy and commits a crime against the Fatherland." Loose-lipped conversations of military personnel in coffeehouses, pubs and trams threatened the honor of the officer class and had sparked "the most absurd and damaging rumors" in civilian circles. Officials repeatedly appealed to the *manliness* of officers and soldiers, urging them to take responsibility for the accuracy of information they transmitted. "It is unmanly to place the responsibility for news and rumors on the shoulders of others by hiding behind the phrases 'it's said . . . ' [and] 'I've heard . . . '"[82] While the content of rumors did not change drastically over the course of the war, official estimation of them did, once the habits of womenfolk became matters of military discipline.

To combat rumors, public notices around the city warned people of the dangers of intemperate speech. In a Czech pub, guests were sternly advised to "refrain from all political discussion," while soldiers were reminded, "Use caution when speaking! Danger of spies."[83] Lacking any

[80] See Arlette Farge and Jacques Revel, *The Vanishing Children: Rumor and Politics Before the French Revolution*, transl. Claudia Miéville (Cambridge, MA: Harvard University Press, 1991), ch. 4; Melanie Tebbutt, *Women's Talk? A Social History of "Gossip" in Working-class Neighbourhoods, 1880–1960* (Brookfield, VT: Scholar Press, 1995); Temma Kaplan, "Female Consciousness and Collective Action: The Case of Barcelona, 1910–1918," *Signs* 7, no. 3 (1982), 545–66.
[81] AdBDW 1915 St./13 #15692. Malik file.
[82] KA, MKSM 1918 10-2/1-3. Chef des Generalstabes to MKSM, 20 July 1918; 10-2/1-9, KM memo, 11 September 1918.
[83] AVA, MdI Präs. carton 2130/22, #18079. Report on Narodní Dum; KA MS/1. Weltkrieg Flugschriftensammlung, carton 19, Wien: Stellungskundmachungen.

more effective means of stopping orally transmitted information, authorities relied most heavily on the press. As in the case of the escaped Italian POW rumor, newspapers often carried official negations of the unofficial stories in circulation. Several newspapers carried a government press release on the duty of the whole population to "suppress radically" the rumors in its midst and to cooperate with officials, who promised to supply the "most authentic news on war-related events." They stated disingenuously that information in the press was presented "without cover-up and distortion" and admonished the public to "limit itself . . . , with fullest trust, to information from the official news sources."[84] Such promises and admonitions glossed over the key difference between "authentic news" and truth.

A top-secret memo from Vienna's police chief in the summer of 1918 shows authorities issuing helpless paper threats against the mouth-to-mouth weapon of the rumor. Police Chief Schober demanded unrealistically that "founders and malicious spreaders" of rumors be arrested and punished, not acknowledging the independent power of rumors, whose elusive founders and malicious spreaders might simply be "*man*."[85] At war's end, Catholic clergy warned their followers of the seductive power of "the many wild rumors that are now swirling around, and that are, despite their frightfulness, often accepted as true by the overheated fantasies of the excited masses."[86] Rumors fed on and fostered insecurity in a dual sense. On one hand, panicked authorities devoted increasing attention to rumors, and spoke of them in more urgent terms, the closer the state came to defeat. On the other hand, rumors could damage social cohesion among the population. Lacking a mechanism for determining which stories were "true," the Viennese had difficulty establishing a common ground with neighbors, acquaintances, co-workers or strangers. Rumors thus undermined civic cohesion. In this atmosphere of uncertainty, some Viennese displayed a remarkable penchant for "overhearing," believing and spreading information about their fellow citizens.

Denunciation

As officially sanctioned information flowed from the state and press to the population during wartime, and unsanctioned information flowed freely among the population partly in response to the conditions of censorship, a third channel, denunciation, linked the population back to the

[84] "Eine Kundgebung gegen die Verbreitung falscher Gerüchte," *Neue Freie Presse*, 5 August 1914.
[85] AdBDW Nachlaß Pamer. Karton 3: Akten, Runderlaß, 27 July 1918.
[86] *Wiener Diözesanblatt* 21/22, 18 November 1918, 123.

state in the project of surveillance. Scholars have noted that denunciation has flourished in other European contexts when opportunities for participation in formal politics and legal avenues for redress of grievances have been limited.[87] Both of these conditions existed in wartime Vienna. Besides the menacing but imperfect operations of the War Surveillance Office and local censors, the parliament was suspended, civilians were placed under the jurisdiction of military courts for state-related crimes, and many associations were banned. Those that were allowed to meet were monitored more closely by police than they had been before the war. As the traditional political sphere dried up and avenues of expression were circumscribed, Vienna witnessed the emergence of a culture of denunciation.

In 1914, an anonymous tip promised to lead Viennese authorities to one of the many "founders and malicious spreaders" of rumors who haunted the city during World War I. "A Good Patriot" suggested to the War Ministry that fellow resident Johann Geisler warranted scrutiny for spreading rumors. "Such people who spread these disturbing rumors belong at the front," the patriot opined, adding that it was much easier to spread rumors than to win a war.[88] The following year, Viennese police received a similar report about a certain Frau Knie from the IX district who was spreading rumors from her butcher shop. A letter writer, also choosing the pseudonym "A Good Patriot," described Knie as an agitator who "yesterday held a whole lecture in her shop that the women shouldn't be so dumb and let it pass that the government simply calls up all men to get shot up and then sends them back home as cripples..." The writer wanted police to "stuff the mouth of this Czech woman (*Böhmin*)" so she would not incite women any further.[89] And a year later, in 1916, "A Patriot" wrote anonymously to warn Viennese police about mysterious sounds coming from a neighbor's apartment. The writer explained that during the night strange noises came from the apartment, which was occupied by "a Czech family," and that according to "hearsay" (*Hörensagen*) in the building, the sounds resembled those of a printing press in operation. "Without accusing the family of treasonous things, a prompt search of the house would perhaps be in order," the patriot suggested. Police investigated, found the apartment to be infested with insects, and

---

[87] See the essays in *Journal of Modern History* 68, no. 4 (December 1996), a volume devoted to "Practices of Denunciation in Modern European History, 1789–1989." Sheila Fitzpatrick notes in "Signals from Below: Soviet Letters of Denunciation of the 1930s," 831–66, "[F]or the great majority who were not powerful or well connected, denunciation was one of the few available forms of agency, a way that the little man (as well as the malicious one) could hope to impose himself on his environment," 866.
[88] AdBDW 1915 St./15 #4267.   [89] AdBDW 1915 St./13 #9498.

determined that the mysterious sounds came from the family's electric fly swatter.[90]

Each of these cases is about information in a dual sense. First, each shows citizens monitoring the information production of fellow citizens (two cases of rumors and one of a suspected printing press); second, the letters of denunciation are themselves examples of information transmission from citizens to the state. Sheila Fitzpatrick and Robert Gellately offer a definition of denunciation which applies to the practice in wartime Vienna:

> ... denunciations may be defined as spontaneous communications from individual citizens to the state ... containing accusations of wrongdoing by other citizens or officials and implicitly or explicitly calling for punishment. ... They are likely to invoke state ... values and to disclaim any personal interest on the part of the writer, citing duty to the state (or the public good) as the reason for offering information to the authorities.[91]

Based on a sample of 200 written denunciations from the police and Lower Austrian regional archives, we see that wartime surveillance involved a fair amount of cooperation and collaboration between state authorities and the population. Of the sample letters here, 62 percent were sent directly to the Viennese police headquarters or to one of the local neighborhood police branches. The other 38 percent were originally sent to other government bodies (often the War Ministry or the mayor of Vienna) and were forwarded to the police for investigation. Nearly 70 percent were anonymous or signed with a pseudonym, and judging from the spelling and written style of the letters, they came from people of all classes.[92] While we have seen that the censorship apparatus was imperfect, especially for catching and stopping rumors, denunciations show that many sets of eyes and ears were at work, feeding information back to authorities.

Denunciations of fellow citizens tell us not only about citizens' assumptions about state authority, but also about how fellow citizens related to each other. In other words, they allow us to probe the depth of loyalty to fellow citizens and ask to which entity, the citizenry or the state, letter writers felt they most belonged. This is an important distinction during wartime, when rhetoric about the "common good" (*Gemeinwohl*) and the "community" (*Gemeinschaft*) was at a high. Historian Colin Lucas has suggested that "denunciation lies along the fault line dividing those who

---

[90] AdBDW 1916 St./9 #26904.

[91] Sheila Fitzpatrick and Robert Gellately, "Introduction to the Practices of Denunciation in Modern European History," *JMH* 68, no. 4 (December 1996): 747–67, 747.

[92] Not included here is the practice of verbal denunciation, in which a citizen would make an *Anzeige* against another citizen in person, often at the neighborhood police branch or to a passing police officer.

find themselves in tension with the state and those who see some of their own identity in the state; it marks the division between a state that is 'externalized' and on that is 'internalized' by the citizens."[93] Although the state in question here, the Habsburg Monarchy, was soon to collapse, the letters from Vienna show clearly that citizens wanted and expected top-down interventions by state authorities when dealing with each other.

Denunciations fell into several categories, the most common being attacks on fellow residents' *Gesinnung*, or attitude towards to the state. Other popular denunciation themes were food hoarding, shirking and bad-mouthing the royal family.[94] *Gesinnung* denunciations, often targeting Czechs, highlighted the patriotic intentions of the denouncer and the nationalist or anti-state predilections of the denouncee. The Czech writer J. S. Machar, a Viennese resident of thirty years before his imprisonment in 1916 for writing anti-state poetry, described the blanket of suspicion hanging over Vienna's Czech community during the war. "[P]eople of all classes and ranks lived under continual police observations...there was a deluge of anonymous accusations on all sides, and as a result of them, cross-examinations, domiciliary searches, arrests and imprisonments took place."[95] Using denunciations of Vienna's Czech-speaking residents by German-speakers as a case study, we can examine the pernicious effects of denunciation on morale and civic cohesion on the home front.

In the two decades leading up to the First World War, German–Czech relations in the city were marked by continual low-level violence over questions of Czech-language schooling, Czech cultural institution building and access to state services and civil service positions. Bands of Germans and Czechs challenged each other over the controversial Czech private schools in Vienna and gathered for occasional brawls outside of taverns known to be meeting places of the other. German nationalists in Vienna had warned for years of the dire consequences of the "Slavization" of Central Europe. How many Czechs actually lived in Vienna, and how "Czechness" was determined were subjects of fierce debate. There is no objective number to arrive at because the counting of people was a highly politicized undertaking in late imperial Austria. Although Czech-speakers had migrated to Vienna from Bohemia and Moravia in large numbers in the decades before the war, German-speakers had an interest

---

[93] Cited in Fitzpatrick and Gellately, "Introduction to the Practice of Denunciation...," 763.

[94] See chapter 1 for discussion of food fantasies and denunciations born of hunger; chapter 6 for shirking; and chapters 4 and 6 for attitudes towards the royal family.

[95] J. S. Machar, *The Jail Experiences in 1916*, transl. P. Selver (Oxford: Basil Blackwell, 1921 (orig. 1919)), 16.

in keeping the official count low to deny Czech aspirations for language parity in state institutions. Based on residents' "language of common use" (*Umgangssprache*) the 1910 census listed just under 100,000 Czechs in a total population of around two million. Based on place of birth or family history, some Czech advocates put the number at 250,000, and others as high as 500,000, or one-fourth of the Viennese population.[96]

Two external events during the war heightened German-speakers' convictions that Czechs constituted a dangerous internal enemy. In April, 1915, Austrian Infantry Regiment 28 deserted *en masse* to the Russians on the eastern front. Most of the officers and troops of IR 28 were Czechs drawn from the area around Prague. The desertion was well publicized. News of these events "made a deep impression in Vienna. The Viennese began to demonstrate vehemently against the 'Czech traitors.' "[97] Not a month later, news of a second scandal involving Czech sedition raced through the streets of Vienna. Karel Kramář, one of the leaders of pan-Slav and Czech national politics before the war, was accused of treason and brought to Vienna for trial. A military tribunal found him and several colleagues guilty and sentenced them to death. When Kramář was eventually amnestied by Emperor Karl in 1917, news of his release outraged German-speakers in Vienna. Police reports on the mood of the people noted that "the German population is agitated by the complaisance of the government... it is said that the amnesty decree will only sharpen the antagonism between Germans and Czechs." In a clear example of the convergence of high politics – the release of a prominent national leader – and the realm of everyday life – women shopping at the market – a police report one week later noted, "Germans are still talking about the amnesty and maligning Czechs. At the market in the XVI district it has even come to pass that Czech women (*Tschechinnen*) have been openly insulted."[98]

---

[96] Josef Sulík, *Proč máme vychováti sve děti v českých školách?* (Vienna: Vídeňská Matice), 1914, 1. See Wilhelm Winkler, *Die Tschechen in Wien* (Vienna: Alfred Hölder, 1919), 6–7 for figures wildly at odds with Sulík's; see also *Ergebnisse der Volkszählung vom 31. December 1910 in der k.k. Reichs-Residenzstadt Wien* (Vienna: Verlag d. Wiener Magistrates, n.d.). For overview of Czech presence in Vienna, see Monika Glettler, *Die Wiener Tschechen um 1900: Strukturanalyse einer nationalen Minderheit in der Großstadt* (Munich: R. Oldenbourg, 1972); Michael John and Albert Lichtblau, "*Česká Vídeň*: Von der tschechischen Großstadt zum tschechischen Dorf," in *Archiv 1987: Jahrbuch des Vereins für Geschichte der Arbeiterbewegung*; and Karl M. Brousek, *Wien und seine Tschechen* (Vienna: Verlag für Geschichte und Politik, 1980); on national attribution more generally, see Emil Brix, *Die Umgangssprachen in Altösterreich*; and Gerald Stourzh, "Ethnic Attribution in Late Imperial Austria: Good Intentions, Evil Consequences," in Ritchie Robertson and Edward Timms, eds. *The Habsburg Legacy: National Identity in Historical Perspective* (Edinburgh: Edinburgh University Press, 1994), 67–83.

[97] *Das Verhalten der Tschechen im Weltkrieg. Die Anfrage der Abg. Schürff, et al* (Vienna, 1918), 50.

[98] AdBPDW, Stimmungsberichte, "Nationale Verhältnisse," 19 and 26 July 1917.

The Czech-speaking community in Vienna was scattered over several districts and did not have a stable associational base or recognizable leadership. Historian Monika Glettler characterized the migrant Czech community before the war as "a hotel that was at once fully occupied, but always by different people."[99] The daily newspaper *Česká Viděň*, which ran pro-Czech and anti-German articles until July 1914, was suspended by censors for the duration of the war. The less outspoken Czech-language newspaper *Vídeňský Denník* continued to publish, and urged its readers to defend themselves from attacks by sticking together. It encouraged consumers to "buy Czech," and ran articles reminding readers to bring Czech-language books and newspapers to wounded Czech soldiers convalescing in Vienna's many makeshift military hospitals. *Vídeňský Denník* was also fervent in denouncing denunciation, perhaps because so many Czech-speakers had been targeted. It called on people "of character" to reject the path of hatred, malice, spitefulness, vindictiveness, avarice and dishonesty, the hallmarks of denunciation.[100]

When employed by German denouncers, "Czech" was a slippery term used interchangeably with "Slav," "serbophile," "russophile," or as a catchword for anyone suspected of weak or non-existent loyalty to Austria. Recall Frau Knie, the alleged *Böhmin* accused above of defaming the state from her butcher shop. What made Knie a *Böhmin*? Was she speaking in Czech? Did she speak German with an accent? Could anyone critical of the government be lumped into the category "Czech?" Born in Croatia/Slavonia, a Slavic region quite distinct from Bohemia, Knie denied making inflammatory speeches and added plaintively, "I'm not a *Böhmin*, so this part of the accusation is also untrue."[101] Similarly, a woman identifying herself as a "true Austrian" (*echte Österreicherin*) denounced a Herr "Maschik" (later Mařík, according to police) as "thoroughly Russian-oriented," for reading Russian newspapers and having Russian "connections." While she was confident of his reading habits, this "true Austrian's" unfamiliarity with Slavic languages caused her to misname her target. Coach driver Jakob Kucera, denounced for a having "Czech-national" *Gesinnung*, was said to make frequent comments such as "So much for Germany and Austria, in 14 days the Russians will be in Vienna." Karl Klusaczek was denounced by a neighbor for playing the Russian and French anthems on his gramophone. In other instances, a whole building or block might be summarily denounced. "The whole of Lerchengasse appears to be overrun with Czechs. The milk lady Anna

[99] Monika Glettler, *Sokol und Arbeitervereine der Wiener Tschechen bis 1914* (Munich and Vienna: R. Oldenbourg, 1970), 13.
[100] *Vídeňský Denník*, 8 January 1916, 4.
[101] AdBDW 1915 St./13 #9498. Letter to Viennese police, 19 April 1915.

Scholz across from House No. 25 has never made a secret of her love for Russians and Serbs," wrote the anonymous "*Kaisertreu.*"[102] The attraction of a *Gesinnung* denunciation was that one did not have to identify an actual act of wrongdoing; the denouncee was guilty of a certain state of mind. One's own Austrian loyalty – "I couldn't sleep knowing this and not reporting it" or "I am only thinking of my beloved fatherland" – justified whatever harm might come to the denouncee.

As these examples demonstrate, German-speaking denouncers often cast their actions in patriotic terms. Writing denunciations could be an expression of one's love of country, a practice that allowed those far from the front to feel they were contributing to the war effort and the protection of the state. Denunciation was a *participatory act*; for civilians, and women in particular, this might explain its popularity in wartime. In 53 percent of the letters in which the gender of the writer could be guessed (letters, for example, stating, "As a mother and a good Austrian," or signed "*Patriotin*"), women were the denouncers. As women in Vienna were constantly reminded, their duty in war was *durchzuhalten* – to hold out. But holding out connoted a dull, plodding, passive contribution to the war effort. While women participated in other essential ways in the making of war, denunciation offered a particularly active, even exciting means of taking part: speaking out as a citizen for the public good, hunting down the enemies of the state, protecting the interests of the royal family. There was a heady exuberance in the language of denunciation, a conviction that transmitting information to the state, even at the expense of fellow citizens, was warranted by the dangerous conditions of the times. Denunciation was a duty.

When denouncers weighed duty against the distastefulness of denunciation, duty prevailed. In 1917, a woman denounced a Herr Nowakovics from the III district, labeling him a "Serb" and accusing him of hoarding eggs:

Allow me to note that it is not at all customary for me to engage in denunciation. But the fact that I have often personally been witness as masses of people have had to line up, and after a long wait receive only a few eggs from this egg dealer – while an enemy foreigner gets such large amounts – has prompted me to write these lines.

I stress again that I consider it a duty to report such an occurrence to the ... authorities, [and make] the additional request that necessary steps be taken to verify the truth of my claims, and that appropriate punishment be issued for this type of action.

---

[102] AdBDW 1914 V/9 #9868; 1915 St./12 #2897; 1916 St./20 #18476; 1914 St./9 #3565.

I don't consider it necessary to sign my name because it concerns the general interest and is not malice on my part.[103]

It was not the law, but rather the wartime discourse of duty, which likely compelled her to write, for in fact she was not legally obliged to do so. According to Austrian law, certain civil servants had an obligation to notify authorities of wrong-doing (*Anzeigepflicht*), but this obligation did not extend to the general public.[104]

Along with many other writers, Nowakovics' denouncer expressed the powerful conviction that authorities *welcomed* her information and would put it to good use. This was not necessarily the case, however. The Viennese police, already experiencing manpower shortages due to military inscription, spent a great deal of time investigating the individual tips offered by citizens, but many of these investigations were inconclusive. It is not possible to determine the total number of denunciations police received, or what percentage of these cases they decided to pursue. The denunciation paper trail is incomplete, but a number of investigations appear to have ended with the police ruling that the denouncee was "*unbedenklich*," unobjectionable or harmless. The seeming inaccuracy of information offered in denunciation letters suggests that the information flow between citizens and the state was imperfect. Gaps in transmission occurred in countless denunciation cases: the street knowledge of what citizens saw, heard or imagined in their everyday environment was not easily utilized by police, whose investigatory techniques were quite unsophisticated. Such breaks in transmission are evident in the denunciation of Milli Jankovitz, in which a "confidential source" gave detailed information about the "immoral lifestyle" and shenanigans of Jankovitz, reputed to be a Serbian citizen escaped from an internment camp, who took refuge at the Café Hausner in the II district.[105] She was considered a gossip-monger and "an enemy of Austria, as she herself has expressed many times!" The denouncer gave police specific times when they might find Jankovitz at work. The result? Police found that Jankovitz was not employed at the café and that nobody there seemed to know such a person. The basic tools of police work at the time consisted of a handwriting collection, used to track down the writers of anonymous letters (catching the

[103] AdBDW 1917 V/7 #45316.
[104] Elgin Drda cites an 1873 law (StPO §86): "Wer immer von einer strafbaren Handlung, welche von amtswegen zu verfolgen ist, Kenntnis erlangt, ist berechtigt, dieselbe anzuzeigen," and concludes that citizens were *authorized*, but not *required*, to report wrong-doing. *Die Entwicklung der Majestätsbeleidigung in der österreichischen Rechtsgeschichte unter besonderer Berücksichtigung der Ära Kaiser Franz Josephs*, Ph.D. diss., University of Linz, 1992, 160–61.
[105] AdBDW 1917 St./27 #47902.

denouncer) and the *Meldezettel,* by which police could track down anyone
officially registered in the city (locating the denouncee.) Considering the
time it took to write a letter to the authorities, and the passion of the
accusations and self-justifications contained therein, it would be wrong
to conclude that Milli Jankovitz and countless other denouncees whom
police could not find were "imagined" by their denouncers. Rather, the
street knowledge of the citizenry was too rich and too fragmented to be
usefully channeled into the rudimentary police apparatus.

Lacking direct policy statements from state or local authorities, we
do not know whether denunciation was officially encouraged or discour-
aged, but we can gauge public discussion of the phenomenon through
the Viennese press. Some newspapers encouraged vigilance and promoted the idea of citizen–state cooperation, not only for catching spies
but for the more mundane work of catching the ubiquitous figure of the
Kriegswucherer, or war-profiteer. The *Fremdenblatt* wrote,

In the battle against the profiteer, officials require the support of the population –
without its reports or tips (*Anzeigen*) officials are helpless, because in most cases,
pretext for an intervention is lacking. The saying, where there is no plaintiff there
is also no judge, should be kept in mind by all those who attach great importance
to the improvement of conditions.[106]

The tabloid *Illustrierte Kronenzeitung* ran a regular column called "Who
Knows What?" which solicited citizen participation in police investigations. Other newspapers, however, warned of the erosion of community
spirit that resulted from citizens passing information to the state. In addition to protests from Czech newspapers, the German-language *Der
Morgen* ran a piece highly critical of denunciation, calling the practice a
disease which had developed into a "spiritual epidemic" in wartime. It
criticized the cowardly "patriots" who sent their poisoned words from
behind shelter of anonymity, and compared denunciation to a Pandora's
box, which, once opened, had released hatred, greed and envy into home-
front social relations.[107]

Denunciation was a local affair: denouncers knew their denouncees,
if not personally, then from the neighborhood or workplace. Neighbor
denunciations, of which the case of midwife Ludmilla Kubart is typical, show us that an air of suspicion enveloped everyday encounters with
acquaintances and colleagues. Kubart was denounced by a neighbor "because in early 1915 she said to two women in the doorway of her apartment building, 'Germany and Austria will become this small,' whereby

[106] WSLB ZAS Rechtsleben und polizeiliche Maßnahmen Bd. III, *Fremdenblatt,*
31 December 1916.
[107] "Denunzianten im patriotischen Gewande," *Der Morgen,* 3 July 1916, 5–6.

she traced a circle on her palm."[108] The number of letters against neighbors, in addition to those filed by maid servants against employers and vice versa, makes clear that even domestic spaces were not safe from the suspicious, vigilant eye of the denouncer. These letters should dispel nostalgia about life *am Gang*, in the hallways of communal apartment buildings in late imperial Vienna. Michael John writes, "Culture in the tenement house has rightly been characterized, above all, by the key words *help and sociability*."[109] But for those overheard in their stairwells, in courtyards and through open windows, social relations in wartime Vienna might be described otherwise.

In 1918, the newspaper *Der Morgen* published a piece entitled "Why am I afraid of my landlady?" in which the author confessed, "I'm afraid of my landlady. I could just as well have said the cleaning lady, the coffeehouse waiter, the greengrocer, any bureaucrat, tram conductor or barber." From all of the characters of his everyday life the author feels cold, suspicious stares. "I see this cold, compassionless hatred between people all around."[110] The hostility and mutual suspicion the author describes are hallmarks of the atomized communal relations of late-war Vienna. Denunciation stood in paradoxical relation to the notion of community. While writers frequently claimed to be writing in the name of "community well-being" or the "general interest," their letters point to the difficulty of defining the general interest in this multi-national city. Like the writer above who, in the process of defining *her* idea of the general interest, denounced Nowakovics as an "enemy foreigner," letter-writers often imagined a community in which they and state authorities worked in tandem to catch enemies in their midst. Denunciation was a means of delineating community, of establishing which "patriots" were included in and which "traitors" excluded from it.

Late in the war, the information citizens passed to authorities sometimes bordered on the absurd. The letters reveal the degree to which citizens had lost the ability to problem-solve in everyday life situations. One frustrated customer wrote in 1917: "Notice! I am bringing charges against the below-named because I had to pay K1.80 for a glass of Malaga wine at the Café Museum, I Operngasse. Allow me to note that the average price asked in highest quality locales is K1 to K1.20. Seeking intervention..."[111] Another had been overcharged at the Café Gröpl,

---

[108] KA, MKSM 1917 85-1/89.
[109] Michael John, "'Kultur der Armut' in Wien 1890–1923. Zur Bedeutung von Solidarstrukturen, Nachbarschaft und Protest," *Zeitgeschichte* 20, no. 5/6 (1993), 158–86, 164, citing Reinhard Sieder.
[110] *Der Morgen*, 27 May 1918, 5.   [111] AdBDW 1917 V/7 #43970.

sending a denunciation and the drink bill to the police for resolution.[112] These cases are significant because they are so insignificant. The wartime conditions, the atmosphere of suspicion and aggression born of severe material shortage, had stretched the social fabric to the point where people were resorting to police intervention over disputes of 60 hellers. Quick resort to police intervention into seemingly trivial matters points to a lack of communal consciousness in Vienna's neighborhoods. Although residents were suffering under the same difficult living conditions, many of their letters express a vertical affinity with state authority rather than a horizontal comradeship with each other.

The military planners who conceived of Austria's War Surveillance Office in 1912 had foreseen that information management would be an important factor in an upcoming war. As they designed an agency responsible for preventing "espionage, disturbances and unauthorized disclosures" in wartime, they could not have imagined the forms espionage would take, the magnitude of home-front disturbances, or the multiple means by which citizens would make unauthorized disclosures. In the tightly controlled information system they envisioned, information would flow only from above. But as Gabriele D'Annunzio's 1918 propaganda stunt over Vienna demonstrates, even "from above" was no longer a secure position for the state. The enemy leaflets falling on Vienna serve as metaphor for the obstacles the state faced: its information-management scheme was challenged from all sides, in unexpected ways. What was to be a top-down system looked more like a cycle, with channels of information flowing between the state and citizenry, but controlled by neither.

Study of these channels offers one link between "high" and "low" politics on the home front. That is, the management of information brought state authorities into the management of everyday life. Story-telling, letter-writing, gossiping, grumbling and rumor-spreading were interpreted as matters of state in ways unforeseen in peacetime. Information – even of a personal or ostensibly apolitical nature – had more value in wartime. As with any other commodity, shortage of a desired good (accurate news) produced increased demand that was met through a black market (rumors and anonymous writings). State officials themselves were willing to admit that their censorship measures were responsible, in part, for the higher premium placed on information. This rich trade of unofficial information in Vienna mandates consideration of practice as well as theory: even during the first half of the war, when the state censorship

---

[112] AdBDW 1917 V/7 #45180.

apparatus had its widest powers on paper, information management in practice was a mutual affair between the government and the governed.

As we have seen, passing unofficial information might subvert government regulations, but it was by no means a gesture of solidarity among the governed. Information did not need to drop from an enemy airplane to constitute a "weapon." Residents of Vienna used the heightened premium on information to attack foes in their midst. Rumors sometimes centered on a "fifth column," and denunciation became a means for delineating "patriots" from "enemies" within the city, the neighborhood, or the apartment building. In the end, passing information of this sort was even more damaging to the local community than to the state.

State and family

4   Sisterhood and citizenship: "Austria's Women" in wartime Vienna

In late July, 1914, upon partial mobilization of the Austro-Hungarian army, an urgent appeal to "Austria's women" circulated widely in the Viennese press. It urged women to "perform service in the time of war" and reminded them that in this moment of state peril, women had to suppress their "differences" and display the "strongest solidarity" among themselves. "Women's unity, women's energy and women's work" would be crucial for the survival of Austria.[1] The notice was published by one of the women's groups in what would become the Frauenhilfsaktion Wien, an umbrella organization founded in early August, comprising all the major women's groups in the city. Together with similar, subsequent appeals to *duty, service, sacrifice* and an *inner bond* uniting all women, the notice marked the beginning of World War I as a potential turning point in women's relationships to each other and to the state. Across the political spectrum, noble, bourgeois and working-class women, Christian and Jewish, German-speaking and others, were asked to put aside their differences and perform war service as "Austria's women."

The term "Austria's women" offers an opening for the study of women's place in wartime politics. It contains a number of assumptions, contradictions and possibilities about women's potential solidarity (sisterhood) and their relation to Austria (citizenship). Dissecting the term "Austria's women" allows us to see that contemporary beliefs about women's nature licensed but limited their place in the polity. Although Austrian women became politically enfranchised in November, 1918, they did not become citizens overnight. Their citizenship was a *process of becoming*, which began in the prewar period and intensified during the war as women forged new links with the state. In her study of American women, historian Nancy Cott has proposed that citizenship is not an absolute status, it is "not a definitive either/or proposition – you are or you

---

[1] Reprinted in Helene Granitsch, *Kriegsdienstleistung der Frauen* (Vienna: Hugo Heller, 1915), 8.

are not – but a compromisable one."[2] Her suggestion that citizenship is a spectrum that ranges from the nominal (residence) to the participatory (political rights) is useful in the Austrian context. Although voting rights marked an important change in women's position within the state, suffrage is just one of several ways of approaching women's citizenship. Equally important are the familial, social and administrative components of "Austrianness" that came into play.

What did it mean to be Austrian in 1914? For most inhabitants of the Habsburg lands in the prewar period, one's relation to the state (citizenship) was a far less important category than one's relation to the province and town (domicile) within the Empire, where one had the right to live, work and draw on social services.[3] Although some rights and services extended to all Austrians (allowing people mobility within the state), one's domicile was a more commonly cited attribute of legal identity; in administrative files from the period, for example, a "person" was summarized in shorthand by name, date of birth, religion, marital status and *Zuständigkeit*, one's proper local jurisdiction. Yet in wartime, state citizenship became an increasingly important category. This was due to the growing centrality of the state in public discourse; everyday matters such as work, food, gossip, leisure and mourning became matters *of state*. In January, 1919, a socialist magazine wrote, "In its reality, the war made clear what the state means nowadays for the life of every single person and every family."[4] The fact that there is virtually no historical scholarship on women's citizenship in the Habsburg lands suggests that figuring out how women fit into our understanding of late imperial Austria is no easy task.[5] There is no obvious or definitive set of texts to consult.

---

[2] Nancy F. Cott, "Marriage and Women's Citizenship in the United States, 1830–1934," *AHR* 103, no. 5 (December 1998), 1,440–74, 1,442.

[3] According to the 1910 census – the last before the war – Vienna had a population of 2,004,939. Of these, 1,816,102 (91 percent) had domicile (*Heimatberechtigung*) in Vienna itself or in another part of Austria. Legally, we can consider this group "citizens" of Austria, because in order to possess rights of domicile, one needed to be a citizen (*Staatsbürger*). See law of 3 December 1863, §2 "Nur Staatsbürger können das Heimatrecht in einer Gemeinde erwerben." Leo Geller, *Allgemeines bürgerliches Gesetzbuch sammt einschlägigen Novellen* (Vienna: Verlag Moritz Perles, 1892), 150. Of the remaining population, 148,552 (7 percent) had domicile in Hungary or Bosnia-Herzegovina and 40,315 (2 percent) were citizens of foreign countries. *Statistisches Jahrbuch der Stadt Wien* (Vienna: Verlag des Wiener Magistrates, 1912), 900.

[4] *Der Sozialdemocrat. Monatsschrift der Organisation Wien*, 1 January 1919, 3. Cited in Reinhard Sieder, "Behind the Lines: Working-Class Family Life in Wartime Vienna," in Richard Wall and Jay Winter (eds.), *The Upheaval of War: Family, Work and Welfare in Europe, 1914–1918* (Cambridge: Cambridge University Press, 1988), 132.

[5] In her useful essay tracing the evolution of Austrian citizenship since the late eighteenth century, Hannelore Burger broaches, but does not systematically address, gendered aspects of this citizenship. Hannelore Burger, "Zum Begriff der österreichischen

Nonetheless, the upheavals of war provide a few openings that shed light on women's evolving relation to the state. Women entered the war as incipient citizens, dependents of male family members who represented them politically. Five years later, they emerged from war as more formal citizens whose relationship to the state was licensed but limited by their familial capacities as mothers, wives, daughters or sisters.

Austria was a state, not a nation, and this made the project of mobilizing Austria's women for war different from mobilizing French, British or German women. State and nation allow (or demand) different levels of commitment from individuals; one may be loyal to a state, but one does not "belong to" a state in the same way that one belongs to a nation. In France, Britain and Germany, women were mobilized on behalf of the *nation*, and nation has therefore been the key organizing principle guiding most historical studies of women's mobilization in modern European wars.[6] Within Austria, there were many nationalities, but it was on behalf of the multi-national state that the front and home-front populations were expected to labor and sacrifice in war. An exhaustive literature exists on the conflicts between nationalities and state in Austria, but we know very little about women's roles in these conflicts.[7] This chapter focuses not on Viennese women's national affiliations (if they existed) but on their evolving relation to the state, because during war, the state was the idiom of mobilization. We know that Austrians had struggled since the nineteenth century to articulate a modern *Staatsidee* – an idea of state – that would emotionally bind citizens/subjects to a multinational state in an age of mass politics.[8] Wartime mobilization offers an ideal moment

Staatsbürgerschaft: Vom Josephinischen Gesetzbuch zum Staatsgrundgesetz über die allgemeinen Rechte der Staatsbürger," in Thomas Angerer *et al.* (eds.), *Geschichte und Recht: Festschrift für Gerald Stourzh zum 70. Geburtstag* (Vienna: Böhlau, 1999), 207–23.

[6] See, for example, the recent work of Susan R. Grayzel, *Women's Identities at War: Gender, Motherhood, and Politics in Britain and France during the First World War* (Chapel Hill: University of North Carolina Press, 1999).

[7] Historians have begun to explore links between national identity and women in the Habsburg lands. See Pieter M. Judson, "The Gendered Politics of German Nationalism in Austria, 1880–1900," in David F. Good, Margarete Grandner and Mary Jo Maynes (eds.), *Austrian Women in the Nineteenth and Twentieth Centuries* (Providence: Berghahn, 1996), 1–17; Claire Nolte, "'Every Czech a Sokol!' Feminism and Nationalism in the Czech Sokol Movement," *Austrian History Yearbook* 24 (1993), 79–100; Katherine David, "Czech Feminists and Nationalism in the Late Habsburg Monarchy: 'The First in Austria,'" *Journal of Women's History* 3, no. 2 (Fall, 1991), 26–45.

[8] Hubertus F. Jahn suggests that Russia, too, was struggling to find a workable *Staatsidee* during World War I. He writes, "There was no commonly accepted national symbolic figure such as Uncle Sam or John Bull or the Deutsche Michel . . . The tsar, the monarchy, historical military heroes, and mythological knights were not commonly accepted points of identification, either." Hubertus F. Jahn, *Patriotic Culture in Russia during World War I* (Ithaca: Cornell University Press, 1995), 173.

for investigating how women figure into the discursive possibilities and limitations of "Austria."

Questions of women's collectivity can be examined by juxtaposing the aspirations of organized women's groups with the actions of "women-folk" (*Weiber*) and "female-persons" (*Frauenspersonen*). As we have seen in the previous chapters, anonymous "womenfolk" and "female-persons" (as they were designated by police agents) came to play a central role in public life in wartime Vienna. Without names and without the kind of structures or organization that would make them immediately rec-ognizable as a political group, they forcefully and physically demanded that the state had an obligation to provide food in return for civilian sacrifice. Women's groups, however, overlooked this female protest in the streets and offered a program of wartime action based instead on supposedly universal feminine traits of maternalism, love and selfless-ness. The war exposed strains and cracks in their theories of female collectivity.

The newly founded Frauenhilfsaktion Wien promoted the notion of women's unity (*Fraueneinigkeit*) rooted in the maternal, care-taking in-stincts shared by all women, and predicted that this unity would blossom in wartime. War would give women the power to transcend personal, class and national differences. The natural traits that made women good mothers to their own children would make them good caretakers of sick soldiers, despairing women, and orphaned children. The skills the house-wife employed in running an efficient household were just the skills she would now export to the "public household" of society at war. In this respect, organized women's groups in Vienna, regardless of political af-filiation, adhered to the maternalist principles advocated by women in Europe and the United States in the same period.[9] Yet, if we look beyond their published writings to alternative sources such as police records, court files and correspondence of (anonymous) women with government officials, subjects appear who *are* women but who act with little apparent relation to a (lasting) female collective.

Judging from this second body of texts, this woman-centered Austrian *Burgfrieden* was something of a fiction. Everyday life in a city of acute shortage pulled at the "inner bond" supposedly shared by women; the home front as a domain of sisterly collectivity (*Mitschwestern*) was more evident in pamphlets than in the streets.[10] A competing picture of Vienna,

---

[9] See Seth Koven and Sonya Michel (eds.), *Mothers of a New World: Maternalist Politics and the Origins of Welfare States* (New York: Routledge, 1993); Anne Taylor Allen, *Feminism and Motherhood in Germany, 1800–1914* (New Brunswick, NJ: Rutgers University Press, 1991).

[10] *Frauenkriegskalender 1915. Herausgegeben vom Bund österreichischer Frauenvereine* (Vienna: R. Lechner/Wilh. Müller, 1915), 63.

characterized by acts of betrayal of women by women, personal and political sabotage, and woman-on-woman violence, existed alongside the Frauenhilfsaktion from war's beginning to end. During the war, then, we have parallel developments in women's politics: a vocal minority (the women's groups) with press and publishing access, speaking on behalf of "women," and a large mass of women (the "womenfolk" and "female-persons") speaking and acting in uncoordinated ways on behalf of themselves.

Viennese women's failure to unite in practice did not spell the end for their theories of feminine "nature." As will be shown, these theories formed the bedrock of women's evolving citizenship. Most women under consideration here were (or at least considered themselves to be) Austrian. No woman, regardless of class or of how she perceived herself in relation to other women, could escape the gendered contours and constrictions of membership in "Austria's women." But what made a woman Austrian? At the moment when women were called for the first time in large numbers to serve the Habsburg state, in what capacity did they serve? Few of the hundreds of thousands of women who performed war service in the capital city ever had occasion to question the precise, legal definition of their Austrianness. But family, social and administrative situations particular to wartime allow us to investigate what it meant to be Austrian and a woman.

In four instances during the war we can see women's citizenship unfolding. We begin at the beginning, with legal definitions of citizenship carried over from the prewar period. In cases of marriage to foreigners, we see that women's citizenship was determined by the status of their male family members. With no direct relation to the state as individuals, women were citizens one step removed. In the second instance, state payments to families of soldiers, women's dependent status within the family "went public" when the state stepped in as a surrogate husband in wartime. Third, we see throughout the war that assumptions about women's particular nature remained central to contemporaries' assessment of women's legal and political accountability, even in cases where their speech or actions were deemed harmful to the state. Finally, near the end of the war, we see in the experiences of Women's Auxiliary Labor Force volunteers the limits of maternal ideology for women's public engagement. In all of these cases, a woman's familial capacity largely shaped perception of her citizenship and determined where she fell on Cott's "spectrum" of Austrianness. Thus, as female contact with the state intensified during war, women's groups were partly vindicated: feminine "nature" might not lead to solidarity *among* women, but in the eyes of the state, a woman was all, and nothing but, a woman. Her gender was the primary determinant shaping her Austrianness.

Many of the questions raised here are not unique to Vienna or to Austria. Because women across Europe performed labor in wartime that had previously been categorized as "male," and because they were granted full or partial suffrage in many European countries at war's end, historians have rightly pinpointed World War I as a period of dramatic rupture in women's everyday lives and in European gender relations more generally.[11] Historiographical debate has centered on the lasting consequences of this rupture. One line of inquiry that has generated a rich comparative literature in the past decade asks how this gender rupture of World War I figured in the rise of modern European welfare states.[12] What many historians writing on "women and the state" implicitly mean, however, is women and the nation-state. In Austria, women's legal citizenship hinged on their relationship to the state rather than their membership in a nation. We learn from the study of Austria's women that determining a person's citizenship was a highly subjective enterprise; in addition to legal considerations, there were equally important emotional and psychological components of state loyalty. Citizenship in this part of Central Europe was a matter of feeling rather than solely a matter of law.

The Frauenhilfsaktion Wien

When the Frauenhilfsaktion Wien convened for the first time on August 13, 1914, those in attendance stood poised to overcome some of

[11] A large literature now exists on World War I, women and gender. Margaret Randolph Higonnet et al. (eds.), *Behind the Lines: Gender and the Two World Wars* (New Haven: Yale University Press, 1987); Ute Daniel, *The War from Within: German Working-Class Women in the First World War*, transl. Margaret Ries (Oxford: Berg, 1997); Elisabeth Domansky, "Militarization and Reproduction in World War I Germany," in Geoff Eley (ed.), *Society, Culture and the State in Germany, 1870–1930* (Ann Arbor: University of Michigan Press, 1996); Belinda Davis, *Home Fires Burning: Food, Politics, and Everyday Life in World War I Berlin* (Chapel Hill: University of North Carolina Press, 2000); Mary Louise Roberts, *Civilization Without Sexes: Reconstructing Gender in Postwar France 1917–1927* (Chicago: University of Chicago Press, 1994); Susan Kingsley Kent, *Making Peace: The Reconstruction of Gender in Interwar Britain* (Princeton: Princeton University Press, 1993). For Austria, see Christa Hämmerle, 'Zur Liebesarbeit sind wir hier, Soldatenstrümpfe stricken wir...' Zu Formen weiblicher Kriegsfürsorge im Ersten Weltkrieg, Ph.D. diss., University of Vienna, 1996; Ingrid Bauer, "Frauen im Krieg: Patriotismus, Hunger, Protest – weibliche Lebenszusammenhänge zwischen 1914 und 1918," in Brigitte Mazohl-Wallnig (ed.), *Die andere Geschichte: Eine Salzburger Frauengeschichte von der ersten Mädchenschule (1695) bis zum Frauenwahlrecht (1918)* (Salzburg, 1995), 285–310; and Hanna Hacker, "Ein Soldat ist meistens keine Frau," *Österreichische Zeitschrift für Soziologie* 20, no. 2 (1995 Sonderdruck), 45–63.
[12] See Susan Pedersen, *Family, Dependence and the Origins of the Welfare State in Britain and France, 1914–1945* (Cambridge: Cambridge University Press, 1993); Susanne Rouette, "Mothers and Citizens: Gender and Social Policy in Germany after the First World War," *Central European History* 30, no 1(1997), 48–66; Koven and Michel (eds.), *Mothers of a New World*.

the obstacles that had hindered women's unity in the prewar period. As Harriet Anderson explains, "Ironically it was the war which finally brought together the League [of Austrian Women's Associations], the Social Democrats and the Catholic women's movements, who in the previous twenty years had themselves been fighting a war against each other."[13] Philosophical questions about the role of women in society and the desired shape of society itself, as well as concrete questions of education, employment, suffrage, and marriage reform, had divided Viennese women's groups into camps that resembled the party-political camps of their male counterparts.[14] In Vienna, political discord – whether of the class, national or religious variety – was sometimes referred to as *Parteilichkeit* – a partiality, bias or narrow particularism. *Parteilichkeit* was a pejorative term, which might be applied to the perceived partisanship of one's opponent; its opposite was the non-partisan, transcendent, common good. When war broke out, state officials and representatives of many organized interest groups, including women, issued exhortations to unity. "[A]lmost overnight," according to the Frauenhilfsaktion Wien, war had mandated that women suspend their *Parteilichkeiten* and serve an Austria ringed by enemies. War, they believed, accomplished a miracle in this politically divided capital city; it "united us, men and women, members of all parties, young and old."[15]

Comprising the Frauenhilfsaktion Wien were the Imperial Organization of Austrian Housewives, the Social Democratic Women's Organization, the Catholic Women's Organization of Lower Austria, the Viennese Christian Women's League and the League of Austrian Women's Associations.[16] Ludmila, a small Czech women's charity organization that counted up to 300 members in Vienna in the decades before the war, appears not to have participated in the Frauenhilfsaktion, and may have been disbanded in 1914. Because Austrian law prohibited women

---

[13] Harriet Anderson, *Utopian Feminism: Women's Movements in Fin-de-siècle Vienna* (New Haven: Yale University Press, 1992), 124.

[14] On women in prewar politics, see Anderson, *Utopian Feminism*; Birgitta Zaar, "Dem Mann die Politik, der Frau die Familie – die Gegner des politischen Frauenstimmrechtes in Österreich, 1848–1918," *Österreichische Zeitschrift für Politikwissenschaft* 16 (1987), 351–62.

[15] *Frauenkriegskalender 1915*, 3.

[16] *Die Frauen-Hilfsaktion Wien* (Vienna: Kommissionsverlag Gerlach & Wiedling, n.d.), 15. From my research it appears that the Allgemeiner österreichischer Frauenverein, a very small but intellectually influential group of women (primarily from Vienna), did not officially join the Frauenhilfsaktion Wien, although its members were active in war services. The AöF sent the only Austrian representatives to the 1915 women's international peace conference in the Hague. The group wished to transcend the limits of "Austria's women" and appeal to "women of all classes and all empires." WSLB 145654B, Nr. 38a, *Friedenshefte des Allgemeinen österr. Frauen-Vereins: Frauen auf zum Kampf für den Frieden* (probably 1917).

(as well as children and foreigners) from joining "political associations," all of the member groups operated in the shadow of politics, casting their activities as social or charitable.[17] Police agents observed their meetings and intervened if discussion turned "political." Membership statistics were as follows:

Imperial Organization of Austrian Housewives	30,000 (Vienna plus satellite branches)
Social Democratic Women's Organization	30,000 (Vienna plus crownlands)
Catholic Women's Organization of Lower Austria	12,000
Viennese Christian Women's League	13,000–20,000
League of Austrian Women's Associations	40,000[18]

These numbers are somewhat misleading because the League was an umbrella organization to which eighty smaller groups, including the Housewives, belonged. Seventeen women from the member groups made up the executive committee of the Frauenhilfsaktion Wien, which was housed in the city hall and headed by Berta Weiskirchner, wife of Vienna's Christian Social mayor. The women set up twenty-three branch offices, staffed by 700 volunteers, and offered the following social services: they aided in collection drives, established information bureaus for people seeking employment or advice on matters relating to mobilization or collection of state aid, organized war kitchens in many districts, and provided training and work space for twenty-nine sewing rooms where unemployed "sisters" earned money sewing and knitting war garments.[19] In addition, the group tried to influence morality on the home front, sparking early-war debates on entertainment and leisure by admonishing civilians to maintain a "serious mood."[20]

---

[17] §30 of the Austrian Law of Associations, 15 November 1867.

[18] Because membership in some groups overlapped, "double counting" of members is possible here. Membership figures from the following: Granitsch, *Kriegsdienstleistung*, 10; *Arbeiterinnen-Zeitung* 27, No. 8 (9 April 1918), 1. The number of Social Democratic women may have been higher in 1914 – the women's committee struggled to hold its members during the war; AdR k.k. Min. f. soz. Verwaltung 1918, Jugendfürsorge carton 2472, #289, "Tätigkeitsbericht der katholischen Frauenorganizationen für Niederösterreich 1917"; John W. Boyer, *Culture and Political Crisis in Vienna: Christian Socialism in Power, 1897–1918* (Chicago: University of Chicago Press, 1995), 502 (figures for 1901–1905); Anderson, *Utopian Feminism*, 91.

[19] 7,000 women found employment at these sewing centers, *Almanach des Kriegsjahres 1914–15 der patriotischen Frauen Österreichs*, herausgegeben zu Gunsten des Witwen- und Waisenhilfsfond für die gesamte bewaffnete Macht (Vienna, n.d.), 41.

[20] See chapter 2 for women advocating a "serious mood" on the home front.

While the creation of the Frauenhilfsaktion Wien was a considerable accomplishment and the organization provided vital services during the war, it was not representative. The key problem in using the published writings of women's groups to draw conclusions about women as a whole is that these groups represented only a small fraction of Viennese women. Even if we interpret the membership statistics of the Frauenhilfsaktion very generously, knowing that some women belonged to more than one group, that the membership lists counted women not just from Vienna but from the province of Lower Austria, and that membership may have been exaggerated, the organizations comprising the Frauenhilfsaktion represented no more than 12 percent of Viennese women. It is important to bear this in mind when considering the validity of claims that organized groups made on behalf of all women.

Feminine virtues

Organized women's groups attributed unifying, almost magical powers to war. They described war not as a social process in which they were participants, but as an anthropomorphic teacher of whom they were the students. "For our housewives, the war was a strict master (*Lehrmeister*)," who demanded diligent, efficient performance from his pupils.[21] War revealed to them previously unseen connections between their private lives and the wider world: "With dazzling clarity the war showed us the threads that link our private economic concerns with the whole political economy."[22] What differentiates this war appreciation from the "war enthusiasm" that swept European home fronts in 1914 is the specific emphasis on war's lessons for women. War called women to put aside the "political trivialities of yesteryear," to step out of their roles as private persons disconnected from the "large, serious, earthshaking questions" of the times. Of course, some women had already assumed positions in Austrian public life prior to 1914, notably in campaigns for women's education and employment opportunities, but even these women credited the war with "[teaching] us . . . the triumph of women's work in the service of the whole."[23] In wartime, this service was not a choice, but an

---

[21] *Oesterreichische Frauen-Zeitung* 1, no. 1 (1917), 7.

[22] WSLB B145654, Nr. 87. Helene Rauchenberg, "Erziehung zum Frieden," lecture before the Bund österreichischer Frauenvereine, Vienna 1918.

[23] Katharina Migerka, "Was der große Krieg uns lehrt," *Almanach*, 99. Christian women were careful to note that public-spiritedness did not mandate public action by all women, whose primary place remained the home. In fact, "the vast majority [of women] does not enter the public sphere." The woman who instilled the spirit of *Gemeinsinn* in her own home and in her children, who worked charitably in her own small circle, also "rendered

obligation. Hermine Cloeter, a Viennese war volunteer, explained, "Finally the day came when everything we [did] for ourselves appeared small and worthless: everyone wanted to do something for the whole."[24] While women's groups expressed obligatory regret and sorrow at the coming of war, they also showed great reverence for war and the "lessons" it would impart to them.

To minimize their differences, women's groups cited universal feminine virtues and appealed to each others' shared maternal instincts. One of these virtues was a capacity for love. Historian Christa Hämmerle has noted a love discourse on the World War I Austrian home front in which women's talents for preserving and spreading love were counted as contributions to the war effort. Labor performed and services rendered were cast as "acts of love."[25] As mothers (or potential mothers) all women, regardless of prior affiliation, were experts in nurturing and "drying tears"; they possessed natural defenses against the hate, vulgarity and greed that mushroomed in wartime.[26] Women could soothe the pains of sudden geographic dislocation. A woman-led organization offering services for war refugees explained what would happen when a female refugee arrived at its office:

Here she knocks. She won't be intimidated by the matter-of-fact sobriety of officials; she stands face to face with women, in whose eyes she sees knowing sympathy. She can also reveal her silent suffering to [the women], who take care of everything expeditiously with tact and feminine tenderness.[27]

In this scenario, as in countless depictions from ancient to modern times, women's love is seen as the antithesis of war.[28]

Women's groups so effectively promoted this image of maternal selflessness that constitutional historian Josef Redlich, normally an astute commentator on the time period, reproduced it uncritically. He credited the "selfless devotion of... women of all classes" for their home-front service.[29] Not all male commentators agreed that "love" was thriving on the home front. Viennese diarist Demophil Frank lamented that women and girls had very quickly become militarized in thought and speech. He

---

a great service for the common good." *Oesterreichische Frauen-Zeitung* 1, no. 8 (1917), 97.
[24] *Almanach*, 18.   [25] Hämmerle, "Zur Liebesarbeit," 159.
[26] *Frauen-Hilfsaktion*, 11; *Der Bund. Zentralblatt des Bundes österr. Frauenvereine* XII, no. 9 (Nov. 1917), 12–3.
[27] Anitta Müller, *Ein Jahr Flüchtlingsfürsorge, 1914–15* (Vienna: R. Löwit, 1916), 7.
[28] See Jean Bethke Elshtain, *Women and War* (New York: Basic Books, 1987).
[29] Josef Redlich, *Austrian War Government* (New Haven: Yale University Press, 1929), 104.

wrote on August 14, 1914:

All women and girls have become war and military buffs. There's no more flirting; if a man chats up a young, pretty girl he hears words such as: field company, reserve company, red cross, howitzer, Cossack attack, conscripted army, war service, etc., etc., in short, everything but the word: love.[30]

The difficult material conditions in Vienna also tested the theory that women were "selfless" beings imbued with love. Censors at the War Ministry responsible for monitoring the mood of civilians described the spirit on the home front as anything but loving. The women in their reports are very different creatures from the women in patriotic writings whose "warm blood must now flow with love for all humanity"; who felt "unending sympathy" for "all victims of these times, for all, man and animal, friend and enemy"; who learned in war "the miraculous power of love."[31] Rather, censors who spent their days reading women's letters noted "a marked rise . . . in the anti-social instincts of particular individuals." "Envy and hatred" separated those who had become rich in wartime from those who felt left behind. "Striking are the recurring complaints of egotism, displayed among close relatives, among siblings, between children and parents."[32] The women in the censor's reports are rather more human than feminine; their virtues are balanced by selfishness and pettiness.

Similarly, women who threatened to abandon their maternal duties posed a challenge to the belief that mother love would sustain the home front and provide the grounds for a stable, nurturing postwar society. With too little evidence to call it a trend, but enough cases to make it noteworthy, we find in police and censor's reports strains of maternal defeatism on the home front. That is, women in desperate situations expressed their despair by threatening to kill themselves and their children.[33] Hedwig Dussl, a 37-year old war widow from Vienna's working-class XVI district, notified the Minister-President and the Food Office in March, 1917, that if she did not receive help she would kill herself and her two children within days. Dussl's husband, a baker's assistant, had been

---

[30] Demophil Frank [pseud.], *Wien . . . Taumel–Qual–Erlösung, 1914–1918* (Vienna: Anzengruber Verlag, 1928), 15.

[31] *Almanach*, Käthe Braun, 15; Ella Hofer, 66; Katharina Migerka, 99.

[32] KA, KÜA 1917, #108758. Stimmung und wirtschaftliche Lage der österreichischen Bevölkerung im Hinterland. Mai Bericht.

[33] The statistics on child murder and abortion (which was illegal) in Franz Exner's *Krieg und Kriminalität in Österreich* (New Haven: Yale University Press, 1927) are unreliable. Like many scholars from this time period, Exner draws conclusions about Austria using *German* statistics because the latter are "richer" and better organized according to sex, age and family status. See pp. 146–66 for his discussion of women.

killed early in the war and now her children were sick. Neighborhood
police responded to her threat by delivering coal, lard and vegetables,
and making a note to "keep an eye" on her circumstances.[34] Dussl's call
for help was extreme, but she was not alone. From market and street
demonstrations police reported hearing verbal threats similar to Dussl's:

Many women hold their children above their heads and shout, somebody should
take a look, they're already half-starved[.] [T]hey will hang one in every window,
that's how far the government has driven them.

It would be best to take the children into the Danube or jump from the fourth
floor . . .

The government . . . should give us cyanide instead of potatoes, then we wouldn't
have to wait at 4 in the morning for 2 kg of this frozen rot.[35]

Some women expressed general pessimism: "Someone should just shoot
us or otherwise do us in, but don't just leave us slowly to die,"[36] while others made direct reference to their children. In a coal line in the working-
class X district, a mother threatened, "There's still coal in the cellar but
it belongs to the rich, we can go to hell; I'm going home now to hang my
children."[37] Children had no place in this society, according to one critic
in the XVII district: "Every pregnant woman should abort the child or
strangle it at birth."[38] Such comments draw on, but invert, the maternalist discourse of the organized women's groups. While still identifying
as mothers, women expressing maternal defeatism turned the theory of
mother love on its head, reappropriating it as an instrument of protest.

This same dichotomy – abstract notions of feminine virtue that clashed
with lived experience – is replicated in the realm of women's work. In the
press and in women's published writings, we find praise for women's
innate willingness to "help." Women who stepped into previously male
positions such as tram conductor, coach driver, post and telegraph employee and shop manager were lauded for their "unprecedented, selfless
work" on behalf of the whole. "In offices, shops and workshops, thousands of women have not only carried on the work, they have to a great
extent taken over the daily obligations of those who have been called to
arms."[39] But not all women could see the benefits of the work performed
by their sisters. The uniformed female tram conductor, for example, came
to symbolize the disruptive effect that the war was having on gender roles.

---

[34] AdBDW 1917 St./27 #40663. Police report on Hedwig Dussl.
[35] AdBDW Stimmungsbericht, 8 February 1917.
[36] AdBDW Stimmungsbericht, 1 February 1917.
[37] AdBDW Stimmungsbericht, 8 February 1917.
[38] AdBDW Stimmungsbericht, 23 February 1917.
[39] *Almanach*, Henriette Herzfelder, 57.

She inspired respect in some, but provoked ire in others, and was joined by uniformed female coach drivers, mail carriers and street lamp lighters as a staple of wartime humor. In the 1916 film *War in Vienna*, Ferdl, a happy-go-lucky soldier on leave, finds his city so full of uniformed women that he thinks he is back at the front.[40] In a less humorous vein, police noted that in 1916, "demonstrating women [have adopted] a hostile attitude towards female coach drivers and tram personnel." On other occasions, police reported that tram conductors expressed solidarity with the demonstrators, "encouraging them to hop on, [and] they would bring them over to the city hall." Some women accused the female tram conductors of *prolonging* the war; had the conductors "stayed home and put their stockings in order, then the war would have long been over."[41] Others were apparently envious of the prestige or wages the new jobs brought. In November, 1916, a daycare center in the XVI district which cared for the children of several female tram conductors began receiving defamatory letters. The daycare director suspected that "jealousy" had motivated the anonymous letter writer, who claimed to be a tram conductor herself, and described the secret life of prostitution led by these women in uniform. "Like all tram conductors I walk the streets because this job is perfect for us whores." The writer described late-night sexual encounters "on the outskirts of a park or in a station house," and signed with the names of four conductors, all of whom denied involvement. The four identified Anna Illes, a 26-year-old milliner, as the probable culprit because she was "not well disposed towards [them] and had often insulted the female tram conductors before."[42] By filling gaps in the economy left by men, women were "helping," which women's groups proposed was in their nature, but in so doing they exposed themselves to ridicule, harassment and to the charge (by other women) that they were prolonging the war.

Women's unity

Marianne Hainisch, head of the League of Austrian Women's Associations, claimed before a diverse group in 1915 that all "party squabbles" had ceased among women. "We know no national, no confessional differences. We are women, we want equal rights for all, equal participation for all . . ."[43] Although representatives of the Social Democratic women were present, Hainisch failed to mention class as one of the sets of differences that women had overcome. Was this omission deliberate or an oversight?

[40] Österreichisches Filmarchiv, *Alltag in der öst.-ung. Monarchie*, roll 4, *Wien im Kriege* (1916), Spielfilmfragmente.
[41] AdBDW Stimmungsbericht, 18 May 1916.   [42] AdBDW St./16 1916 #35,864.
[43] *Der Morgen*, 21 June 1915, 11.

It is in class relations where we see the greatest disparity between what women's groups hoped for and what war actually produced. Hainisch and the other women who called for unity in 1914 viewed war as an occasion to bridge class conflict. (Of course, they were in the company of many men across Europe who saw in war the same potential.) Instead, war created countless new opportunities for class antagonism in everyday situations.[44]

One of the first differences to surface was in the way women of various classes conceived of work. In the Viennese press and the writings of middle- and upper-class women, a linguistic turn occurred at the outset of war. The concept of "work" became fused with that of "service," so that many positions, paid or unpaid, were cast as "war service" (*Kriegsdienst*). Women's groups used patriotic slogans to describe this service. "None for herself, all for one, all for the fatherland!"[45] The problem with this wholesale reinterpretation of women's work – everything from knitting to childcare to industrial labor – as patriotic *service* was that a great many women in prewar Austria already performed some sort of wage labor.[46] While some statistics, such as insurance membership rates, suggest that large numbers of women entered paid employment for the first time during the war, it is more likely that women were changing jobs *within* the labor market, moving from domestic work and textiles into industry and municipal services.[47] Working-class women resented the depiction of their labor as "coming from the heart," originating in feminine selflessness.

[44] For class relations in World War I Vienna, see John W. Boyer, *Culture and Political Crisis*, ch. 7.

[45] *Frauenkriegskalender 1915*, 3.

[46] By some estimates, 46.6 percent of Austrian women were employed in 1910. Oskar Lehner, *Familie–Recht–Politik: Die Entwicklung des österreichischen Familienrechte im 19. und 20. Jahrhundert* (Vienna: Springer Verlag, 1987), 63, cites the 1910 census. (This high figure probably includes self-employed women and family helpers). Emmy Freundlich, *Die Industrielle Arbeit der Frau im Kriege* (Vienna, 1918), 4, puts the number considerably lower, at 34 percent. It is unclear whether Freundlich includes domestic and agricultural workers in this figure. For Austrian women's wage labor in World War I, see Sigrid Augeneder, *Arbeiterinnen im Ersten Weltkrieg: Lebens- und Arbeitsbedingungen proletärischer Frauen in Österreich* (Vienna: Europaverlag, 1987); Margarete Grandner, *Kooperative Gewerkschaftspolitik in der Kriegswirtschaft: Die freien Gewerkschaften Österreichs im Ersten Weltkrieg* (Vienna: Böhlau, 1992); Berthold Unfried, "Arbeiterprotest und Arbeiterbewegung in Österreich während des Ersten Weltkrieges," Ph.D. diss., University of Vienna, 1990.

[47] Between 1913 and 1915, women's membership in the Allgemeine Arbeiterkrankenkasse rose by 22 percent. Women made up 36 percent of total insurance membership in 1914 and 47 percent in 1916. (Domestic servants were not insured before the war; neither were most agricultural workers or family helpers.) But Freundlich also notes that scarcity of raw materials for textiles and handwork drove many women to seek employment in munitions factories and in transportation fields. "Fast jede Bezirkshauptmannschaft in den Gegenden Österreichs, wo Textilindustrie vorherrscht, war ein Werbebureau für die Frauen, die der Munitionsindustrie zugeführt wurden," *Industrielle Arbeit*, 24. This

Social Democratic spokeswoman Emmy Freundlich criticized the bourgeois glorification of service: "The woman doesn't go to the factory to satisfy her ambition (*Ehrgeiz*) as it perhaps happens in bourgeois circles." In these circles, she pointed out, "the woman is led out of the house solely by ambition and a longing for a position in public life." The working-class woman was (and had been) compelled by acute material need, not a romantic notion of serving the greater good.[48]

Part of the difficulty in establishing women's cross-class unity lay in the leading roles that middle- and upper-class women assumed they would play in the creation of this unity. At the sewing centers of the Frauenhilfsaktion Wien, where ladies and working-class women came into close contact, the former were in charge while the latter "benefited." "In most districts," one women's group reported contentedly, "ladies, with [their] selfless goodwill took the lead at sewing centers, not only minding the books and cashiering, but also taking energetic, loving care of the women workers."[49] The *Arbeiterzeitung* would challenge the "loving" intentions of the women who ran sewing operations. For example, a certain Frau Rothziegel, who placed a newspaper ad seeking women for "light sewing work," was accused of grossly exploiting the forty-odd women who answered the ad. After agreeing to pay only a "hunger wage," and then reneging even on this, she fired the workers and recruited a new crew of unemployed women.[50] Not all working-class women at the sewing centers found themselves under the tutelage of a "sister" like Frau Rothziegel, but the wartime unity envisioned by ladies was founded on pre-existing class hierarchies. Middle- and upper-class women promoted the societal benefits of new feminine service, but also sought to preserve their prewar positions as benefactors of the poor.

They self-consciously urged each other not to perform labor voluntarily, such as sewing and knitting, for which women of the lower classes could earn a wage.[51] "Don't perform good deeds at the expense of the

---

supports the thesis of Ute Daniel, who has argued that in Germany women didn't move from the home into wage labor during the war, but rather from one kind of wage labor to another. See Daniel, "Women's Work in Industry and Family: Germany 1914–18," in Jay Winter and Richard Wall (eds.), *The Upheaval of War: Family, Work, and Welfare in Europe, 1914–1918* (Cambridge: Cambridge University Press, 1988), 267–96.

[48] Freundlich, *Industrielle Arbeit*, 22.

[49] *Kriegsarbeit des Vereines "Soziale Fürsorge für erwerblose Frauen und Mädchen unter dem hohen Protektorat der Frau Erzherzogin Marie Valerie" 1914–1916* (Vienna, 1916), 5.

[50] AdBDW 1914 St./12 #1494. Follow-up police report on *Arbeiterzeitung* article, 14 October 1914.

[51] Social Democratic city councilor Winarsky complained in mid-August 1914 that "society ladies" had misunderstood the economic consequences of their good deeds, working voluntarily at a time when many women were unemployed. WSLA B23/73 Gemeinderat. Protokoll Obmänner-Konferenz, 12 August 1914.

poor," a women's newspaper warned ladies. "Don't knit and sew for the soldiers and the wounded. By offering such help you are robbing the very poorest – the unemployed – of bread." No matter how enthralling the "newly expanded circle of women's duties" created by war, a selfish or unreflective practice of *Kriegsdienst* could damage the collective. Similarly, in their zeal to sacrifice, ladies needed to be reminded that firing one's domestic help caused more hardship than it prevented. A list of "Ten Commandments for Women Volunteers" noted: "To heal wounds is good; to inflict no wounds is better. She who does not fire her employees or maid servant does more than she who makes ten donations to the unemployed."[52] For women's groups, then, a first step in serving Austria was to consider the consequences of any service on other women.

While ladies of the middle and upper classes weighed their actions accordingly, leaders of the Social Democratic women defended their decision to join these ladies in the Frauenhilfsaktion Wien. Quite simply, the material distress that many working-class families experienced at the beginning of the war due to conscription and the transition to a war economy warranted joining an organization dedicated to providing social services. By participating "from within" the Social Democratic women wanted to ensure that the Frauenhilfsaktion would not become just another charity run by ladies for the benefit of the poor. Their constituents needed convincing. Leaders noted, "To our profound regret, we meet dependents of comrades who would rather starve and carry their hard-earned possessions to a pawnshop than seek out the services" of the neighborhood branches of the Frauenhilfsaktion Wien. Working-class men feared, mistakenly, that accepting help from the Frauenhilfsaktion amounted to taking charity, which would disqualify them as voters under Austrian law. Women leaders tried to assure their followers that the organization was *not* a charitable one, and that visiting a neighborhood branch need not be humiliating:

Often we hear from our female comrades that they don't want to "bow down before the Christians." This attitude has to be combated. First, the money doesn't come from the "Christians" alone, and furthermore, one need not feel humiliated – our female comrades have seen to that.[53]

Nevertheless, they acknowledged that any visit to a committee of the Frauenhilfsaktion – for work, food or advice – would probably entail an encounter with society ladies, since they had the most free time to donate to the cause.

---

[52] *Neues Frauenleben* 16, no. 8–9 (August–September 1914), 236–7.
[53] *Arbeiterinnen-Zeitung* 24, no. 1, 5 January 1915, 3–4.

Though they were ostensibly unified as "sisters" by the war, we see that
the Viennese women's groups themselves maintained the linguistic distinctions "female comrades," "*bürgerliche* women" and "society ladies,"
while religious groups continued to write of "the Christian woman." Organized women were maintaining hyphenated identities, claiming membership in the wartime feminine collective, but simultaneously retaining
affiliation to particular camps. Working together with those from other
camps sometimes brought out class-based tensions that universal feminine virtues could not ease. The Social Democratic women, for example,
were disturbed by the social practices of "society ladies," particularly the
ritual of hand kissing. "These ladies arrive in different districts and the
others slobber all over their hands. *Pfui Teufel*! We don't know for whom
the disgust is greater, for those who do it or for those who allow it to be
done."[54] From the outset, the Social Democratic women seem to have
registered the greatest skepticism about the feasibility of the Frauenhilfsaktion Wien. "Women gathered together, made grand plans, and all the
newspapers were full of praise for the capabilities of women, especially
Viennese women," they wrote. But could the social services the organization offered really do much to combat the upheaval and material distress of war? Despite their somewhat grudging participation, the Social
Democrats doubted early on whether a handful of "well-bred ladies...
countesses and '*Frau vons*'" could speak for a true collective of Viennese
women.[55]

Within the domestic sphere war exacerbated rather than eased class
tensions between maidservants and these well-bred ladies. The maidser-
vant/employer relationship had been a flash point for class and gender
conflicts in many cities in prewar Europe.[56] In 1910, there were 104,364
domestic workers in Vienna, the vast majority of them women who had
immigrated from Bohemia, Moravia and the Lower Austrian countryside.[57] As noted above, many Viennese maidservants lost their positions
in 1914 as a "panic overcame many families, which caused them to fire
their domestic help." This action left "countless women and girls...in
bitter misery."[58] Other maidservants left domestic work voluntarily in
order to seek higher wages in war industries. "Einigkeit," the association

[54] "Händeküssen," *Arbeiterinnen-Zeitung*, 22 September 1914, 6.
[55] *Arbeiterinnen-Zeitung*, 25 August 1914, 4.
[56] See Dorothee Wierling, *Mädchen für alles: Arbeitsalltag und Lebensgeschichte städtischer Dienstmädchen um die Jahrhundertwende* (Berlin: Verlag J. H. W. Dietz Nachf., 1987); and Karin Walser, *Dienstmädchen: Frauenarbeit und Weiblichkeitsbilder um 1900* (Frankfurt/Main: Extrabuch Verlag, 1985).
[57] For history of maidservants in Vienna, see Marina Tichy, *Alltag und Traum: Leben und Lektüre der Wiener Dienstmädchen um die Jahrhundertwende* (Vienna: Böhlau, 1984).
[58] *Kriegsarbeit*, 3.

which represented the interests of Viennese maidservants, dissolved in 1915 because "many of the most loyal and devoted members have left Vienna, many have turned to other occupations."[59] While maidservants were susceptible to the vagaries of the war economy, housewives too were made more vulnerable than they had been prior to the war by the presence of an "outsider" in the home. Snooping, intrigue or indiscretion on the part of a maidservant, which before the war might have caused a housewife social embarrassment, might now, in light of censorship, lead to political trouble for a bourgeois family.

The war allowed maidservants like nineteen-year-old Rosa Krucka to retaliate against her employer, Marie Kolar, after the latter fired her for stealing. Krucka accused her employer of making frequent (and illegal) "Russian-friendly" statements, of scratching out the eyes on a photo of the German and Austrian Emperors, and of saying when an airplane flew overhead, "If only [one] would fly over and drop a bomb on Schönbrunn." Former domestic employees concurred on Frau Kolar's political disposition and she was charged with "insulting His Majesty" and disturbing the peace.[60] Hilda Nowotny faced a similar domestic betrayal from her one-time maidservant, Anna Makowska. Nowotny was arrested for illegal possession of enemy war booty after Makowska reported she was hiding a Russian bayonet and other objects in her apartment.[61] The accusation was supported by Rosa Binder, Nowotny's cook. Similarly, Emma von Schebek, an upstanding woman who had made a name for herself as a matron at one of Vienna's Red Cross hospitals, found herself the subject of police investigation when a maidservant accused her of stealing Red Cross supplies and stockpiling them in her home.[62] As war penetrated the bourgeois home, disputes that might previously have been personal now became matters of state. From their strategic places within middle- and upper-class homes, maidservants discovered in war a means to inflict harm on their otherwise much more powerful employers.

What are called here class tensions bore little relation to the "party squabbles" that the Frauenhilfsaktion aimed to overcome. From an organizational standpoint, women's groups agreed to suspend their differences in the name of home-front unity. Organizational solidarity did not, however, translate into personal solidarity among women. Assessing cross-class cooperation or antagonism is especially difficult for the war years because notions of class were in flux. Middle-class women's prewar conceptions of their status and appropriate place in the social hierarchy were confounded by the new standards of privilege in the war economy. As we have seen in earlier chapters, severe shortage overturned the system by which the Viennese measured outward signs of status. Objects which before the war had a recognizable class coding (a certain style of blouse or make of shoe) were now being worn by the "wrong" women. To the detriment of "sisterhood" women in Vienna daily measured the rise or decline of their own status according to the (perceived) inverse rise or decline of the women around them.

Similarly, Marianne Hainisch's claim that the member groups of the Frauenhilfsaktion had overcome confessional differences also appears dubious. Christian Social women contributed actively to the anti-Semitic discourse of the home front, blaming Jews in the same terms used by their male counterparts. When city councilor Breuer spoke before a neighborhood gathering of the Viennese Christian Women's League in 1917, his anti-Semitic remarks were met with "loud applause," "passionate agreement" and "indignant outcries" from the female crowd. "All over, wherever we look, we see that these foreigners (*Fremdlinge*) are given priority over us, that they fatten and enrich themselves while the sick, hungry, hollow-cheeked Christian *Volk* must wait in long lines for hours for a piece of lard." He appealed to motherly indignation, claiming, "Our sons, the blossom of our *Volk*, bleed on the battlefields, while the offspring of the legendary Maccabees sit in the coffeehouses on the [riverfront] ..." Breuer's cry "Our anti-Semitism is justified!" elicited "stormy applause."[63] In other instances, Christian women had taken matters into their own hands by accosting Jewish refugee women at the markets. "Energetic intervention" by police was sometimes required "to prevent excesses against the Jews." Christian mothers accused Jews of buying up all the food, leaving them and their "three, four and even more children of the most tender ages" to go hungry.[64] Christian women's roles in perpetuating anti-Semitism is an understudied topic in the otherwise rich literature on anti-Semitism in Vienna. In the instances cited here, confessional hatreds trumped common maternal bonds promoted by the Frauenhilfsaktion. We see that Christian motherhood was a forceful position from which to articulate anti-Semitic sentiments.

Reconciling women and "womenfolk"

Some organized women's groups showed surprisingly little interest in the women who would have seemed to be their natural constituents,

---

[63] *Oesterreichische Frauen-Zeitung* 1, no. 9 (1917), 128–9.
[64] AdBPW Stimmungsbericht, 17 February 1916.

and others propagated theories of female collectivity that clashed with women's lived experiences. The Social Democratic women are a case in point. We saw in the earlier chapter on food that tens of thousands of "womenfolk" were waiting in food lines on any given day in wartime Vienna. Many of the discontented shoppers were women of the working classes who, in angry statements to authorities or verbal assaults on shopkeepers, demonstrated a keen "consciousness" of their positions in the war economy. And yet, perusal of the *Arbeiterinnen-Zeitung*, the organ of the Social Democratic women's committee, shows that the committee distanced itself completely from the women in the streets; it held fast to the distinction between women of the underclasses (*Unterschichten*) and women workers (*Arbeiterinnen*). Losing membership during the war, the organization acknowledged that the food crisis was partly to blame. "As every woman has to spend many hours of the day to get a loaf of bread or a half kilo of flour, when is there time left over to think about the organization and newspaper?"[65] Yet there is virtually no mention of (or support for) the forceful, physical presence of women at the markets. Like their male counterparts in the Social Democratic party, the organized women clung to notions of discipline and party structure and distanced themselves from the female rabble in the streets.[66]

The organization which spoke most fervently on behalf of female shoppers was the Imperial Organization of Austrian Housewives. In the interests of consumers, which it equated with women, or more narrowly, "we housewives," it advocated price controls on essential goods and waged a steady press campaign against profiteers: "Since the outbreak of war...we women...have seen it as our task to fight against the internal enemies who, in these important and serious times and in most detestable pursuit of personal gain, have an eye only for their own profits."[67] But the categories "women" and "consumers" were not fully congruent; a considerable number of those arrested for profiteering were themselves women, and marketplace violence often consisted of skirmishes among women shoppers or the demolition of women's stands. In 1917, when a female market seller declared to assembled shoppers, "Somebody should burn this rabble," apparently referring to the shoppers themselves, they destroyed her stall. Only "with effort" could the security personnel who intervened protect the seller from bodily harm. The same day a group

---

[65] "An unsere Leserinnen," *Arbeiterinnen-Zeitung*, 11 January 1916, 1.
[66] Unfried, *Arbeiterprotest*, discusses the key differences in methods and strategy between the *Arbeiter* and organized *Arbeiterbewegung*.
[67] *Der Morgen*, 21 June 1915, 14; 2 August 1915, 12.

of women and children who broke into a shop to steal 300 loaves of bread had the saleswoman "by the throat" when policemen arrived.[68] Here women played protagonist and antagonist simultaneously. As was suggested in earlier discussion of food, solidarity at the market was based on a fleeting "community of sufferers," and this community in no way resembled a "sisterhood" of collective feminine interest.

Nor could women planning a collective action count on female solidarity within the food lines. Josephine Waldhäusl reported to police in Vienna's X district in March, 1917, that she had uncovered a conspiracy at the market:

I overheard a few women, who looked like they belonged to the working class (*Arbeiterstand*), as one said to another, was she also planning to come next Sunday? The one asked where to, and the first answered, "Yeah, on Sunday the fun begins. A demonstration"; another asked what kind of a demonstration, and where? The other: Things are letting loose all over on Sunday on account of food and the like . . . [69]

Waldhäusl could not identify the women because she did not know them and had no association (*Gemeinschaft*) with them. Whether she reported them out of malice, fear or a sense of duty, her situation points to a difficulty in reconciling the Housewives' program of female solidarity based on shared interest as consumers. At the abstract level, the Housewives were right that most consumers were women, who, as a collective, stood to gain by challenging monopolists and power brokers in Vienna's ailing food distribution network. As a lived experience, however, consumer solidarity was not synonymous with women's solidarity. Women themselves played multiple roles in the food crisis: consumer, producer, seller, profiteer and victim.

One way of reconciling the theories about women propagated by organized groups with the (sometimes contradictory) actions of "womenfolk" is to see them both as constitutive aspects of total war. As suggested in the introduction to this book, World War I was "total" in different ways: it was profound, enormous, transcendent of the ordinary on one hand; and it was terribly ordinary on the other, penetrating to the smallest, seemingly insignificant everyday practices. In a 1914 speech, Viennese clergyman Erich Stöckl explained the gravity and scope of women's new public duties, and in so doing presented a version of total war that many women's groups would echo: it was a grand undertaking that would cleanse society

[68] AdBDW 1917 V/9 #32385. Police report, 3 April 1917.
[69] AdBDW 1917 St./20 #32385. Protokoll from Polizei-Bezirks-Kommissariat Favoriten, 30 March 1917.

of particularism, pettiness and everyday conflict. "The war . . . sets aside as worthless all that is weak and cowardly, small and selfish, impure and false, incomplete and lacking in love."[70] Women's groups focused on the war as a big event, and recorded their (literally) big contributions: the Frauenhilfsaktion boasted that it had served up enough portions of vegetables in its war kitchens to fill a pot the size of the Deutsches Volkstheater and that it had distributed enough bread to make a giant loaf the size of Vienna's ferris wheel.[71] But the actions of "womenfolk" also demonstrate the extent to which ordinary, everyday practices became acts of war. Their actions in wartime were precisely "small and selfish . . . incomplete and lacking in love." The women who attacked perceived enemies at the market, the mothers who threatened suicide, the anonymous writers who denounced out of jealousy, the Frau Rothziegels of Vienna who exploited others for profit, the maidservants who saw in war a weapon against their employers – show us that the Great War was waged everywhere, by nameless faces in ordinary places.

In choosing war as a time to celebrate women's unity and enlist their virtues in the service of the whole, women's groups set for themselves a formidable challenge. Their idealistic theories about woman's true "nature" were tested under the most materially difficult circumstances. By the second half of the war acute shortages curtailed the actions of the Frauenhilfsaktion Wien. They lacked food for their war kitchens and cotton and wool for their sewing centers. Marianne Hainisch warned soberly that material shortage posed a danger to women's potential collective spirit. She urged women in economic despair not to forget war's important lesson that the "I" was connected with the rest of society.[72] Viennese women conducted their daily lives in wartime not as a sisterhood, but as a collection of "Is" that sometimes unified along gender lines and often did not.

While organized women's groups failed in concrete ways to integrate women and "womenfolk" into an operative home front collectivity, their theories about woman's nature took firm root at the state level. During war, women came into greater contact with the state authorities and institutions than ever before, and these contacts were bounded on all sides by contemporary assumptions about women's nature. Social Democratic women, who had been the most skeptical members of the

[70] *Der Krieg und die Frau. Vortrag gehalten von Pfarrer Erich Stöckl in der evang. Stadtkirche A. B. zu Wien am 3. Dezember 1914* (Vienna: Selbstverlag, 1914), 19.
[71] *Die Frauen-Hilfsaktion Wien*, 31.
[72] WSLB ZAS Frauenarbeit I, *Arbeiterzeitung*, 9 Feb 1916.

Frauenhilfsaktion Wien, had demanded suffrage before the war "exactly because we are womanly and motherly."[73] These qualities were central to the wartime evolution of female citizenship.

If we look back to the earlier appeal to "Austria's women" we see that, since 1914, Austria had played an important role in Viennese women's conception of the war and their place in it. We might have expected them to mobilize their sisters with an appeal to "Vienna's women." After all, they were organized at the municipal level, and the women of the Frauenhilfsaktion Wien carried out their work at the neighborhood level. For Viennese women, though, one of the truly novel aspects of this war was the way it encouraged, or in some cases forced, them to think beyond their affiliation to community and to consider their relation to the larger polity. War compelled its students to transcend the everyday and the local, to consider matters of Austria and the world. When German nationalist women from the provinces tried at a 1916 meeting in Vienna to have the name "Imperial Organization of Austrian Housewives" changed to "German Housewives," they were met with boos from the crowd and the cry, "The women are all Austrians!" (*Oesterreicherinnen*).[74] The motion to change the name was defeated, suggesting that mid-way through the war, some women were holding on to the possibility of a shared identity as Austrians.

The following four scenarios trace the course of women's Austrianness during the war. In the first instance, where women's legal status was in question, we see that their links to Austria had traditionally been family links. Their relation to the state was mediated through male family members, usually father or husband, and the protective (or restrictive) veil of the male-headed family kept women one step removed from the state.[75] Second, this dependent status within the family was replicated in public on a massive scale with the advent of a wartime program of state payments to families of soldiers. Third, in judicial matters, the state showed leniency towards women precisely because it needed their "womanly" services on the home front more than it feared their anti-state agitation. Finally, we see the limits of maternal ideology late in the war in the example of the Women's Auxiliary Labor Force. As army support volunteers,

[73] Cited in Birgitta Bader-Zaar, "Women in Austrian Politics, 1890–1934: Goals and Visions," in Good, Grandner and Maynes (eds.), *Austrian Women*, 65.

[74] "Eine erfolgreiche bürgerliche Frauenorganisation," *Arbeiterinnen-Zeitung*, 23 May 1916, 1–2.

[75] See Lehner, *Familie–Recht–Politik*; Ursula Floßmann, *Österreichische Privatrechtgeschichte* (Vienna: Springer Verlag, 1983); and Josef Ehmer, "Die Entstehung der 'modernen Familie' in Wien (1780–1930)," in Laszlo Cseh-Szombathy and Rudolf Richter (eds.), *Familien in Budapest und Wien* (Vienna: Böhlau, 1993).

women remained "soaked" in their sex, in the words of Denise Riley.[76] Cumulatively, these experiences demonstrate that the prewar value accorded women's "womanly and motherly" qualities was codified publicly during wartime and formed the basis for women's citizenship in Austria.

Citizenship and *Gesinnung*

Austrian law made passing mention of women "enjoying the rights of citizenship," but these rights were never positively defined. Rather, women's citizenship appears only in a clause on women's *loss* of citizenship through marriage to a foreigner. Conversely, a foreign woman who married an Austrian was assumed to take Austrian citizenship by virtue of the fact that a wife "followed the *Stande* of the man."[77] During World War I, however, law proved an insufficient means of distinguishing between "Austrian" and "foreigner." This distinction, charged in wartime because of the conflation of foreigner with enemy, was as likely to be based on sentiment or insinuation as on the law. Contemporaries accorded great significance to a concept that has since fallen out of use in discussion of citizenship: *Gesinnung*. Difficult to translate, *Gesinnung* referred to one's disposition, attitude or political proclivities. Gerald Stourzh points to the importance of *Gesinnung* in assigning ethnic attribution to individuals in prewar Austria – that is, in deciding to which nationality *within* Austria a person "belonged."[78] Stourzh finds the evaluation of a person's *Gesinnung* to be an insidious, thoroughly subjective process – "one would have to look into their family relations and would have to take into account their behavior, conduct and their views in all national questions" – and calls it "that terrible phenomenon to be found in all illiberal and chauvinistic movements..."[79] In wartime we see that *Gesinnung* was used not only to determine national belonging, but also to test a person's loyalty to the *state*. Widespread in World War I, the discourse of *Gesinnung* permeated popular writings (letters of denunciation, for example) as well as police and court files in which labels such as "Russian-*gesinnt*", "Slavic-*gesinnt*"

---

[76] Denise Riley, *"Am I That Name?" Feminism and the Category of "Women" in History* (Minneapolis: University of Minnesota Press, 1988), 41.

[77] ABGB 34 Patent, 24 March 1832, §19 states, "Die Frauenspersonen, welche das Staatsbürgerrecht geniessen, und welche sich mit einem Ausländer verheiraten, verlieren, indem sie dem Stande des Mannes folgen, hierdurch die Eigenschaft von österreichischen Unterthaninnen." Leo Geller, *Allgemeines bürgerliches Gesetzbuch summt einschlägigen Novellen* (Vienna, 1892), 152.

[78] Gerald Stourzh, "Ethnic Attribution in Late Imperial Austria: Good Intentions, Evil Consequences," in Ritchie Robertson and Edward Timms (eds.), *The Habsburg Legacy: National Identity in Historical Perspective* (Edinburgh: Edinburgh University Press, 1994), 67–83.

[79] Stourzh, "Ethnic Attribution," 71.

or "patriotic-*gesinnt*" were entered alongside objective traits such as date of birth, address, hair color or height. *Gesinnung* was considered an innate trait, and a poor *Gesinnung* could "infect" an entire family.

The centrality of *Gesinnung* to citizenship is evident in the 1917 case of a "foreign-born" woman in Vienna who faced criticism that her commitment to Austria was less than sound. Despite the fact that she had married an Austrian man, and thus by law had become an Austrian citizen, she could not live down persistent rumors that she was "Italian." The rumors continued, despite her husband's proven loyalty to the state and her own impressive involvement in war-related, charitable activities. Like countless women who thought and wrote about their duties toward and feelings for the state during war, the "Italian" struggled to articulate her relationship to Austria. She differed from the many other women grappling with their civic identities at this time only in that she was the Empress of Austria.

The case of Empress Zita highlights some of the key citizenship issues affecting all women, from nobles to those of the lower classes. Married to Franz Joseph's successor, Karl, who became Emperor in late 1916, Zita lent her name to charity organizations and frequently visited soup kitchens and volunteer stations in Vienna in order to boost morale. But she was also the subject of much gossip and could not shake the label "foreigner." A contemporary remembered from an opening of a war kitchen, "[She spoke] with an unmistakably foreign (*fremdländischem*) accent. Perhaps this is one reason why she is considered a foreigner by the population."[80] Zita is remembered in relation to her brother, Prince Sixtus, who negotiated the secret French-Austrian communication (a compromise peace, loosening the German-Austrian alliance) that was later exposed and caused scandal and humiliation for the Austrian imperial family.[81] Her "French" and "Italian" lineage (she was from the house of Bourbon-Parma) did not endear her to Austrian patriots in wartime. A number of sensational stories circulated in the Zita rumor-mill: she was reported to have betrayed Austrian troops engaged in battle against Italians on the Piave river; she allegedly "fired two gunshots" at the German Emperor

---

[80] Hans Loewenfeld-Russ, *Im Kampf gegen den Hunger: Aus den Erinnerungen des Staatssekretärs für Volksernährung, 1918–1920* (Vienna: Verlag für Geschichte und Politik, 1986), 100.

[81] See Erich Feigl, *Kaiserin Zita* (Vienna: Amalthea, 1977); Gordon Brook-Shepherd, *The Last Empress: The Life and Times of Zita of Austria-Hungary, 1892–1989* (London: HarperCollins, 1991); and Emilio Vasari, *Zita: Kaiserin und Königin* (Munich/Vienna: Herold-Druck-und-Verlags-GmbH, 1976). For the growing incompatibility between cosmopolitan, inter-house royal marriages and the nationalist sensibilities of World War I, see Adam Müller-Guttenbrunn, *Völkerkrieg! Österreichische Eindrücke und Stimmungen* (Graz: Verlag von Ulr. Mosers Buchhandlung, 1915), 60–3.

188 Vienna and the Fall of the Habsburg Empire

Wilhelm; and she was rumored to have been locked up in a Hungarian castle to prevent her from doing more damage to the Austrian war effort. In all of these instances, police identified and arrested women of the lower classes for slandering the imperial family.[82] Zita's Christian Social defenders painted her as the mother of Austria. Countering these "most despicable rumors" at a rally, they contended she was the "mother of the poor," who gave Christmas parties for children, founded convalescent homes for soldiers and allowed royal horses to be used to transport coal to poor neighborhoods in Vienna.[83] In Zita's roles as both "first lady" and "state enemy" Austrianness was less a matter of law than of how people in the street evaluated her *Gesinnung*. Zita herself considered her "Italianness" an accident of birth: "[W]e were all 'Austrians' in *Gesinnung*, regardless of where we happened to be born."[84]

Lesser-known women in Vienna faced similar difficulties in establishing their Austrianness. A women's newspaper reported, "The arrangement whereby a woman automatically changes her citizenship to that of the man upon marriage has proven disastrous for women during this war."[85] In the three cases discussed here, those of Maria Mosconi, Frau Chr. P. and Maria Swiatopulk-Mirska, women faced the reverse problem of the Empress: they were "born Viennese" but had married foreigners. Their legal citizenship status (unlike that of the Empress) did not mesh with what they "felt" themselves to be. Mosconi and Swiatopulk-Mirska were both separated, but not legally divorced, from their husbands. Under Austrian law at the time, divorce was illegal for Catholics, and the only possibility for ending a marriage lay in obtaining a legal separation.[86] Bound for life to their foreign husbands, the women in these cases used two strategies for establishing their Austrianness: first, they presented evidence of service to the state by male family members, usually husbands,

[82] NÖLA Präs. "P" 1918 Ib, 2603, police and governor's reports on rumors about the imperial family.
[83] "Eine vaterländische Massenkundgebung in Wien," *Reichspost*, 2 July 1918, cited in Feigl, *Kaiserin Zita*, 336–9.
[84] Feigl, *Kaiserin Zita*, 27.
[85] *Neues Frauenleben. Organ der freiheitlichen Frauen in Österreich* 19, no. 11–12 (November/December 1917), 226.
[86] A legal separation, "Scheidung von Tisch und Bett" (literally, separation of table and bed), allowed partners in a failed marriage to take up separate households. Divorce (Trennung) was permitted only for non-Catholics. ABGB §111, 115. See John W. Boyer, "Freud, Marriage, and Late Viennese Liberalism: A Commentary from 1905," *JMH* 50 (March, 1978), 72–102; and Ulrike Harmat, "Die Auseinandersetzungen um das Ehescheidungsrecht und die sog. 'Sever-Ehen,' 1918–1938" (Ph.D. diss., University of Vienna, 1996). While I show here that the impossibility of divorce made some women's lives more difficult in wartime, Harmat notes a greater public concern for returning "war-damaged" men who were separated and prohibited from remarrying, but who were in need of "häusliche Pflege und Ordnung," 68.

fathers or brothers. Second, in light of the novel labeling of women's work as *Kriegsdienst*, they presented a record of their own service to the state.

In a last-ditch effort to save her reputation and reclaim her job as a bilingual office worker in the Italian war zone, Maria Mosconi penned a dramatic letter to Emperor Karl in 1918. She wrote that she had inherited loyalty to the Habsburg dynasty through her "father's blood," and had ingested it through her "mother's milk." Born in Vienna, Mosconi had married an Italian and was still classified as an Italian citizen, despite having been legally separated for fourteen years. She worked briefly as a "female laborer" (*weibliche Hilfskraft*) in the Italian zone, before military authorities fired her on grounds of "political unreliability." She was allegedly fraternizing with Italian citizens in her free time and was reputed to be a "hysterical" gossip who "prattled on" indiscriminately. While she was technically not considered a spy, her superiors noted that "on account of her verbosity and craftiness she was certainly in a position to do harm here."[87] Back in Vienna, Mosconi mounted a defense which revealed her complicated relationship to Austria, mediated through her male family members. Her Austrian lineage was impressive: she was the daughter of a decorated field marshal and the granddaughter of a general. "[U]pon our heroic march into Italy, I placed myself voluntarily in the service of His Majesty's Army High Command," she wrote, adding that she wanted to "achieve distinction" as an office worker in the same place where her father had done so in battle. But Mosconi was caught between being an Austrian's daughter and an Italian's wife. Despite her claim of willingness "to die for my adored, one and only Austria," she was confined to her Vienna apartment. Unable to support herself financially, she remained under a cloud of suspicion, branded a "traitor" (*Landesverräterin*).[88]

Lamenting the situation of women like Mosconi, Olga Misar, a prominent women's advocate, wrote that the war had forced women to protest "how really shameful it is that a woman does not possess personal citizenship" independent of her husband.[89] Besides affecting a woman's reputation in the community, the citizenship designation could prevent a woman from supporting herself. Frau Chr. P.'s situation highlighted the absurd consequences of the citizenship law in wartime. Described as "ein echtes Wienerkind," she was born in Vienna and had never left the city. A newspaper account of Frau Chr. P.'s case included the obligatory recounting of her male family members' contributions to Austria: her father had served in the Italian campaign of 1859 and had ended his life

[87] KA, MKSM 1918 69-9/47. Report from Walzel, Nachrichtenstelle Udine, 14 April 1918.
[88] KA, MKSM 1918 69-9/47. Letter from Maria Mosconi to Emperor Karl, 24 May 1918.
[89] WSLB ZAS Rechtsleben und polizeiliche Maßnahmen III, *Neues Wiener Tagblatt* (Abend), 26 January 1917.

as a "servant of the state." This was little help to his daughter, however, who had married a Serbian citizen living in Vienna and consequently ran into great trouble at the outbreak of World War I. Her husband was interned in a prison camp in the nearby town of St. Pölten. As a "Serb" Frau Chr. P. was not eligible for community welfare payments, and had to apply for financial support from the Serbian state. She was informed that in order to receive benefits she would have to move to Serbia (not an easy prospect in 1915), where she had never been. She turned instead to a branch of the Frauenhilfsaktion Wien, asking for help in acquiring a sewing machine so she could support herself. The Frauenhilfsaktion was sympathetic, but informed her, "We are unable to grant this favor to the subject of an enemy power."[90] Frau Chr. P. was an enemy in her own hometown.

Women caught in the citizenship trap during the war were left to make the legally irrelevant plea that they "felt" Austrian. Josephine Michelazzi, "Austrian by birth, family and sentiment" but separated from an Italian citizen, had served Austria as a nurse on a hospital ship. When the ship went down, she was "captured" and interned as an Italian, "although she certainly *feels* herself to be Austrian."[91] Many of the arguments made to support this "feeling" are found in the writings of Maria Swiatopulk-Mirska, whose articulate expressions of her relation to the state contain many of the themes relevant to women's citizenship at the time. Branded a "Russian" because of an earlier marriage which ended in legal separation, Swiatopulk-Mirksa employed a wide range of arguments in her campaign to uphold her right to perform on stage in wartime Vienna, though a citizen of an enemy state.[92] First, she stated her pre-marital Austrian credentials: "I have already documented that I am an Austrian citizen by birth." Next, she argued for the irrelevance of her legal status as a Russian, claiming that it had not affected her *Gesinnung*: "As a Pole and an Austrian, I myself am thoroughly patriotic-Austrian *gesinnt*."[93] She

---

[90] "Ein Jahr Frauenhilfskomitee–Die Feindin," *Arbeiterinnen-Zeitung*, 24 August 1915, 3–4.

[91] KA, GZNB, 1917, 4562. Monthly report on "Internierten und Konfinierten in der Monarchie," March 1917. Men also attested to "feeling" Austrian in cases where they were legally foreign. 37-year-old wine cellar operator Josef Podrecca was born in Vienna and had lived there all his life. He was a taxpayer and claimed, "It is only for Austria and Vienna that I live and die." Nonetheless, authorities considered him Italian. In his second appeal for permission to serve in the Austrian army he wrote to the War Ministry in 1915, "I've hated Italy all my life and I've never even been [there]." AdBDW 1915 V/12, #11982.

[92] NÖLA Pras. "P" XVIII, 396. Letter Maria Swiatopulk-Mirska to police.

[93] Swiatopulk-Mirska's claim to be both a "Polin" and an "Österreicherin" was perfectly understandable to contemporaries. Within supra-national Austria, one's loyalty to the state was not incompatible with simultaneous loyalty to one of its nations. Of course, for some nationalities, this system of dual loyalty was severely tested in World War I.

then presented a list of several male family members' military and civil service for Austria. Thus, while she did not want to share the status of her ex-husband, she did want other male family members' accomplishments added to her own citizenship dossier. Finally, she presented herself as a hard-working, single mother whose maternal desire to care for her "Austrian" child was being thwarted by an unjust law. On account of the police ban, she was "completely unemployed and in no position to earn an honest living . . . [for] myself and my child." Her rhetorical strategy was to cast a wide net in hopes that the authorities would find at least one of her arguments compelling. They did. Swiatopulk-Mirska was eventually granted the right to perform; on the surviving copy of her letter, the only bureaucratic markings are blue lines highlighting the service of her uncle and brothers.

We might ask why male service remained so crucial in determining a woman's status at a time when women could claim their own gender-specific *Kriegsdienst* for Austria. The answer to this question goes beyond the patriarchal traditions of Austrian family law, under which women and children were legally dependents (*Angehörige*) of the male head of household. *Gesinnung*, the proclivity for loyalty or disloyalty to the state, was widely thought to be a trait not of individuals, but of whole families. Thus, the logic of *Gesinnung* did not allow for variation *within* families. The problem, of course, for all of the women discussed here was that they belonged to two families – the birth family and the marital family. We see little sign that authorities were eager to factor in a third component – a woman's own proclivities, as demonstrated by volunteer or paid service during the war – in evaluation of *Gesinnung*.

Authorities charted the *Gesinnung* of suspicious families the way turn-of-the-century criminal anthropologists charted generational degeneracy: with the aid of a family tree.[94] Political "unreliables" were interned in prison camps or confined to house arrest in Vienna. With notable exceptions, women were thought to absorb *Gesinnung* from male family

---

[94] For example, in 1917, military authorities made a diagram the size of a field map of the Kreutzenberg-Ecchers, a family accused of Italian irredentism, and provided a key explaining the crimes or suspicious activities of forty-five family members over four generations. The few upstanding members of the family, including a major general in the Austrian army, could not make up for the dozens of bad seeds; the family was incurably "*national gesinnt*." On occasion, it was not the male members whose behavior and attitudes determined the *Gesinnung* of the whole family. In the case of the Kreutzenberg-Ecchers, officials deemed Eugenia von Kreutzenberg, wife and mother, a "fanatical Italian" and "the most politically dubious person, the prime mover in the family, who wielded influence" over her husband and sons. KA, MKSM 69-8/8 1917 Stammbaum der Familie Eccher; k.u.k. 11. Armeekommando to k.u.k. Heeresgruppenkommando FM Freiherr von Conrad, 18 June 1917.

members. In the case of a Russian Orthodox family in Vienna, the father, Paul Barna, had "made himself and his family conspicuous." "This family" the police reported, "is said to be *russenfreundlich gesinnt*."[95] In another case, Sophie Markow, widow of a "Russian agitator," arrived in Vienna as a refugee from Lemberg with her three daughters in 1915. They were placed under police surveillance because "in Lemberg the whole Markow family is known for its avidly russophile *Gesinnung*."[96] An anonymous letter to the police in the Vienna's Favoriten district warned of the arrival of an entire family of suspicious Czechs. The denouncer claimed that "an ultra-Czech, russophile, serbophile family" had recently moved to the neighborhood after things got a little too "hot" for them in Brno.[97] *Gesinnung* was an ambiguously defined, highly charged and officially sanctioned way of reading an individual's loyalty to the state. It passed like a germ, usually from husband or father to the rest of the family, and transformed the family into a unit of guilt by association.

One way that neighbors and police assessed *Gesinnung* was to examine a family's home. Apartment searches, when they yielded contraband materials, were an effective way of ferreting out state enemies. But how could police "read" political proclivities in homes where no such obvious evidence was found? Here, a woman's housekeeping or the arrangement of the furniture might be the deciding factor in whether the family passed the subjective test of *Gesinnung*. The wife of Josef Musil, a man suspected of collecting illegal maps during the war, behaved impeccably during a search of their home just outside Vienna. "The wife herself opened . . . all the drawers and letters," authorities noted. "They live quite unassumingly . . . They have an orderly lifestyle [and] the arrangement of the apartment is simple [and] *bürgerlich*."[98] Similarly, an orderly family life aided Viennese porter Franz Schimak, who had been denounced for his "anti-Austrian *Gesinnung*" by a neighbor. A police agent with no obvious evidence to go on reported that Schimak lived in "orderly circumstances" with his wife and children and found Schimak to be "unobjectionable."[99] Conversely, a questionable living situation might reinforce suspicions that a family had negative proclivities toward the state. An anonymous denunciation from "A Viennese citizen loyal to the Kaiser" warned police that a certain Emil Gerschitz was living with a "foreign

[95] NÖLA Präs. "P" 1915 IV, 297. Report on Barna family.
[96] NÖLA Präs. "P" 1915 VII, 1210. Letter to Statthalterei, 4 March 1915.
[97] AdBDW 1916 St./9 #30703. Anonymous letter from Brünn to Polizei Kommissariat Favoriten.
[98] NÖLA Präs. "P" 1914, 748. Letter from k.k. Bezirkshauptmannschaft Floridsdorf-Umgebung to Statthalterei, 8 September 1914.
[99] AdBDW 1915 St./12 #6675. Report from Pol. Dir. Wien, 2 March 1915.

woman" in Vienna's III district and that the two were "very dangerous for the fatherland." Police inspected the home and found that the pair had lived together before marriage and that "Gerschitz apparently lives beyond his means." They noted in great detail the layout and contents of the luxurious apartment: "living room, parlor, a large atelier set up as a salon with a piano...behind in paying the rent."[100] Although police could find no evidence of anti-state crimes, their critical remarks about the Gerschitz home suggest that domestic "appearances" could factor into evaluations of *Gesinnung*.

These subjective ways of assessing state loyalty in wartime help explain why a woman's legal citizenship was sometimes of secondary importance when compared to other social determinants. On some occasions, as in the case of Empress Zita, rumors of an anti-Austrian *Gesinnung* could seriously undermine a woman's (legally sound) claim to be Austrian. In the other cases, such as Maria Mosconi's, Frau Chr. P.'s and Maria Swiatopulk-Mirska's, women argued that hometown loyalty or patriotic *Gesinnung* trumped their legal status as foreigners. The criteria for identifying a woman's standing *vis-à-vis* Austria included any number of extra-legal determinants: her spoken accent; military or civil service by male family members; her commitment as a mother; the attitudes inherited from generations of descendants; and even her manner of keeping house. Nancy Cott's thesis that citizenship is a spectrum rather than a firm status is useful here for understanding Austrianness. Often it was not a question of *whether* a woman was Austrian (the law was clear enough in most cases) but a determination *how* Austrian she was, based on a host of family-related variables.

The surrogate husband

Going into World War I, then, women's familial roles largely determined their civic identities. With the advent of state aid to families of soldiers, these familial roles became publicly codified in a system of welfare payments. Across Europe, women entered into new financial relationships with states during World War I.[101] In every combatant country, states paid economically dependent family members subsidies to cover some or all of the support they had previously received from their men who were now enlisted. Historian Susan Pedersen describes a situation in

---

[100] AdBDW 1915 V/12 #11949. Letter of denunciation to Polizei-Präsident, 4 May 1915; police report, 5 June 1915.
[101] See Pedersen, *Family, Dependence and the Origins of the Welfare State*; Young-Sun Hong, *Welfare, Modernity, and the Weimar State, 1919–1933* (Princeton: Princeton University Press, 1998); and Elisabeth Domansky, "Militarization and Reproduction".

Britain where the state came to play the role of "surrogate husband," paying wives "because of their husbands' citizenship status and rights, not their own work or needs."[102] In Austria, the logic of the payments, known as the "state support subsidy" (*staatliche Unterhaltsbeitrag*), was similar; women were paid subsidies on behalf of their husbands' service to Austria. The *Arbeiterzeitung* explained, "The state that doesn't protect soldiers' wives against hunger wouldn't be worthy of the spilled blood of its soldiers."[103] The millions of women who went twice a month to pick up their payments, issued by the Austrian War Ministry and distributed by municipalities, were forging a novel but dependent relationship with the Austrian state. According to state censors who tracked public opinions of the payment scheme, the experience led to "disorientation," "bitterness" and profound disappointment for many women.[104]

By June, 1917, the Austrian government had paid out an astounding 3,676,250,342 crowns in support to soldiers' families.[105] By October 1918, Viennese residents, the vast majority of them women, had filed 467,321 applications for the state support subsidy. The payment scheme, first updated for inflation in 1917, was based on a 1912 law which stated:

Family members (wife, children, parents, grandparents, parents-in-law, step-parents, siblings and also illegitimate children) of conscripted Austrian citizens whose livelihood was heretofore dependent primarily on the wage of the conscripted citizen, have a right (*Anspruch*) to a support subsidy, which for each dependent consists of a support payment (88h for Vienna) and a rent subsidy (44h for Vienna.)[106]

With the outbreak of war, the difficulty of implementing the payment scheme for millions of recipients who were now temporary dependents of the state led many women to feel victimized, rather than subsidized, by Austria. Only three weeks into the war, one could hear "bitter complaints"

---

[102] Susan Pedersen, "Gender, Welfare and Citizenship in Britain during the Great War," *AHR* 95, no. 4 (October 1990): 983–1,006, 985.
[103] WSLB ZAS Frauenarbeit III, *Arbeiterzeitung*, 23 June 1918.
[104] KA, GZNB, 1917 carton 3751, #4614, #4675; AOK 1918 GZNB carton 3757, #5033. Censor's reports "Der staatliche Unterhaltsbeitrag," 31 March 1917, 5 June 1917 and 3 March 1918.
[105] *Denkschrift über die von der k.k. Regierung aus Anlaß des Krieges getroffenen Maßnahmen*, 4 vols. (Vienna, 1918), IV, 257.
[106] Law of 26 December 1912 RGBl Nr. 237, cited in *Kriegszustand. Instruktionen für Polizeiorgane* (Vienna, 1914), 19–20. On changes due to inflation, see WSLB 67052C Kriegssammlung Konvolut 2, Law of 27 July 1917, RGBl. Nr. 313, "Neuregelung des staatlichen Unterhaltsbeitrages." Other sources note a raise in April, 1917. WSLB ZAS Staatliche Unterstützung II. A dense 1918 pamphlet "Was bekommen jetzt die Soldatenfamilien," shows that the 1912 law, with its wartime changes and additions, had become indecipherable to the average recipient.

about the mismanagement and injustice of the payment scheme.[107] The
first official review of the program concluded, "It appears to be an undeni-
able fact that, despite its truly humane and social intentions, the program
of state support subsidies has not met with the anticipated popularity."[108]

Problems with the plan fell into three categories: most women felt the
payments were too low, some felt they were wrongly denied payments,
and some challenged the program's public replication of women's familial
dependence. Despite the fact that inflation in wartime Vienna raged as
high as 200 percent, the daily payment rate of 1.32 crowns per dependent
(88 hellers for children under eight) remained set until 1916, when rates
for young children were increased by 25 percent. Only in 1917, with the
reconvening of the parliament, was the rate for women and older children
raised to 2 crowns.[109] Many women complained that when they sought
outside employment to "supplement the supplement" they were denied
state funds altogether. "I'm being punished because of honest work,"
charged one woman.[110] In other instances, a Viennese woman was cut
off for earning small amounts of money as a newspaper carrier; a landlady
was scratched from the rolls because she had a vacant apartment; other
women lost their payments for taking in needlework at home.[111] Mayor
Weiskirchner lobbied the War Ministry on their behalf, noting frequent
cases in which women earning "only modest wages" had been cut off. He
pointed out that the payment was defined as a *Beitrag* – a contribution –
meant only "to prevent a threat to livelihood," not to prohibit women
from earning additional wages.[112]

Other women were frustrated by multiple, unexplained rejections of
their applications for the state support subsidy. Letters from the home
front to men in the field contained "countless cases in which the news read
'[W]e are doing badly, we aren't receiving the support subsidy.'" Authorities summarized complaints in 1918: "Some individuals report... that
they have applied repeatedly, three times, even six times," only to be met
with "rude, arrogant words or to be shown the door" by bureaucrats.[113]

[107] WSLB ZAS Staatliche Unterstützung I, *Arbeiterzeitung*, 22 August 1914.
[108] KA, GZNB, 1917, carton 3751, #4614. Report on state support subsidies, 31 March 1917.
[109] WSLB 67052C Kriegssammlung Konvolut 2, Law of 27 July 1917, RGBl. Nr. 313, "Neuregelung des staatlichen Unterhaltsbeitrages."
[110] KA, GZNB, 1917, carton 3751, #4614. Report on state support subsidies, 31 March 1917.
[111] WSLA B23/73 Gemeinderat. Protokoll der Obmänner-Konferenz, 1 December 1914. Comments of Gemeinderat Reumann and Skaret.
[112] WSLB ZAS Staatliche Unterstützung II, *Neues Wiener Tagblatt*, 5 August 1915.
[113] KA, AOK 1918 GZNB carton 3757, #5033. Third report on state support subsidies, March 1918.

Widespread misunderstanding about who was eligible for the state support subsidies left women frustrated. Some considered the payments
a form of charity, a notion that state officials tried to dispel. Censors
gathered from home-front letters that people were not sufficiently educated about the "character and premise" of the wartime subsidies and
"appear[ed] to see it as a kind of poor relief." This confusion was exacerbated in Vienna by the fact that women picked up their state support subsidies at the same neighborhood offices that dispersed municipal welfare
payments. The city government in turn complained that the inadequate
wartime subsidies were driving people "left completely helpless by the
state" onto traditional city welfare; this was a breach of the state's obligation to soldiers, "whose mighty task should not be made more difficult
by worries about the fate of their dependents."[114]

Although women and children received the state subsidies, the payments were in fact meant as compensation for the missing male wage
earner. If the soldier deserted or otherwise violated military law, payments to his family were suspended. If he died, the payments were reduced by more than half.[115] While scorn for soldiers' wives never reached
the pitch it did in Germany,[116] Viennese women receiving the support
subsidy were criticized for being frivolous with state funds. These "welfare
women" (Unterstützungsweiber) were accused of wasting money intended
for their husbands, money that came into their hands only by chance of
war.[117] Some critics even suggested that women who had married during
wartime had done so to take advantage of the payment scheme. A speaker
of the Association for Reform of Marriage Rights in Vienna complained
about the phenomenon of war marriages, calling them "fleeting, reckless"
unions created only to "activate the support subsidy."[118] This charge is

---

[114] WSLB ZAS Staatliche Unterstützung I, *Fremdenblatt*, 28 January 1915; II, *Amtsblatt
der Stadt Wien*, 14 January 1916.

[115] Widows' pensions varied according to the rank of the deceased soldier. Widows received the following *monthly* amounts: simple infantrist, 9 crowns; lance-corporal or
bombardier, 12 crowns; corporal, 15 crowns; train driver, 18 crowns; higher sergeant
30 crowns. Orphans received an "education supplement" of 4 crowns monthly. Officers' widows and orphans received much higher pensions: lieutenant, 93 crowns; first
lieutenant, 112 crowns. "Was bekommen die Hinterbliebenen der Gefallenen?" *Arbeiterzeitung*, 25 November 1914.

[116] On *Kriegerfrauen* in Germany, see Daniel, *War from Within*, 182–5; and Davis, *Home
Fires Burning*, 33–40. On *soldatki* in Russia, see Emily E. Pyle, "Village Social Relations and the Reception of Soldiers' Family Aid Policies in Russia, 1912–1921,"
Ph.D. diss., University of Chicago, 1997, 198–228; and Barbara Alpern Engel, "Not
by Bread Alone: Subsistence Riots in Russia during World War I," *JMH* 69 (1997),
696–721.

[117] The *Arbeiterzeitung* wrote that the derogatory term "Unterstützungsweiber," was used
by German nationalists. WSLB ZAS Frauenarbeit III, *Arbeiterzeitung*, 23 June 1918.

[118] NÖLA Präs. "P" 1918, XVb, 2176. Police report on meeting of Eherechtsreformverein,
15 May 1918.

hardly credible, considering the agreement across the political spectrum –
from Christian Socials to Social Democrats – that the payments did not
provide subsistence, and the fact that marriage rates did not increase
during the war.[119]

Social Democrat Emmy Freundlich came close to challenging the
whole premise of the state playing "surrogate husband" to women in
war. Austria, she maintained, ought to pay female citizens for their own
hardship, which was equal to, if not greater than, the suffering of Austria's
men:

> [N]obody would be in a position to decide whether it is more painful and more
> torturous to experience the misery of the front, or to sit at home for months
> shaking about the existence and fortune of the family. The daily worries, the
> punishing battle between hope and fear often amounts to more mental suffering
> and spiritual death than does actual death at the front.[120]

Freundlich called for doubling the support subsidy and eliminating the
differentiated pay for younger children: "That is what Austria's mothers
demand from the state, from the government and from society."[121] Her
demand that women be paid for wartime hardship as *citizens in their own
right* fell on deaf ears.

The support subsidies represented a grand-scale intervention of the
Austrian state into Viennese families. It replicated in the public sphere the
dependent status of women within the family, so that women remained,
in the eyes of the state, wives and mothers. The state supported "Austria's
women" only on behalf of "Austria's men."

"Nature" and legal accountability

Because of their special "nature" as dependent creatures embedded in the
family, women in World War I Vienna were held to a different standard of
legal accountability than men for their speech and actions. Naiveté, inability to grasp abstraction, emotional rather than rational thought processes
and capriciousness were attributes that ostensibly justified women's exclusion from official politics in pre-World War I Europe.[122] Women's

---

[119] After a surge in marriages (4,929) in August, 1914, the monthly marriage rate returned
to prewar levels (around 1,000 per month), and did not vary much throughout the
war. Another surge is evident in the second half of 1919. *Mitteilungen der statistischen
Abteilung des Wiener Magistrates*, Monatsberichte, 1914–1919.
[120] WSLB ZAS Staatliche Unterstützungen II, *Arbeiterzeitung*, 24 November 1916.
[121] *Ibid.*
[122] For example, Austrian law held that a woman was less capable than her husband of
administering her own property. And women, along with children, the insane, the blind,
the deaf and the mute (among others) could not legally serve as witnesses. Lehner,

groups declared at the outset of war that women were emotionally and intellectually "ready" for politics, and yet these traditional feminine traits lingered in the minds of state authorities as they weighed the motivations and appropriate punishments for women's wartime deeds.

As we saw with the organized groups of the Frauenhilfsaktion Wien, Austrian women were legally prohibited from participating in political parties or clubs. Women's groups had argued for the abolition of this clause and were close to succeeding on several occasions before the war. Marianne Hainisch, head of the League of Austrian Women's Associations, argued during the war that banning women from official political bodies deprived the state of their services. "With increased zeal, women will give the state that which belongs to the state – their energies, their love, their understanding – when they in turn are given what they are due."[123] She was referring to suffrage and the right of association, political rights of a formal kind. Over the course of the war, however, Austrian authorities were confronted with forms of women's "political" action that fell outside the realm of organized politics: women were speaking publicly about matters of state, criticizing government figures or their policies, and committing deeds (such as harboring deserters) deemed harmful to the state. In assessing how to punish these words and deeds, the state found itself with a conflict of interest. On one hand, to maintain morale on the home front it needed to curb critical (and illegal) statements about the conduct of war, and to punish those who dared to make them. On the other hand, the state needed the services of women as mothers and caretakers on the home front, services it was denied if it imprisoned the thousands of women who spoke and acted critically of the state.

At the center of this conflict of interest were two of the most common "crimes" in World War I Austria: the relatively obscure charge of *Majestätsbeleidigung* – insulting His Majesty – and the charge of disturbing the peace.[124] Some authors have written comic accounts of the absurd application of these laws at the outset of war.[125] The clauses are worth quoting here because they were the means by which many women in

---

Familie–Recht–Politik, 21, 27. For nineteenth-century Austrian discussion of women's inferior brain functioning, see Zaar, "Dem Mann die Politik".

[123] Marianne Hainisch, "Petition an das Abgeordnetenhaus," *Der Bund* 12, no. 9 (November 1917).

[124] These are §63 and §65 respectively of the Austrian penal code. In the years 1909–13 only a handful of people – all of them male – were arrested in Vienna for these crimes. *Statistisches Jahrbuch der Stadt Wien, 1914* (Vienna: 1918), 306.

[125] See Jaroslav Hasek, *The Good Soldier Schweik*, Book I, chs. 1–2; and Karl Kraus, *Die letzten Tage der Menschheit*, Act I, scene 1.

Vienna ran afoul of the law and faced imprisonment. The law on "insult-ing His Majesty" stated,

Whoever damages respect for the Emperor, whether by personal insult, by slander or ridicule in public or in the presence of several people, through printed works, communication or distribution of pictorial depictions or writings, is guilty of the crime of insulting His Majesty and is to be punished by one to five years' imprisonment with hard labor.[126]

In wartime, criticizing the government, the state, the military or even complaining about conditions could be interpreted as an "insult" to the Emperor, in whose name the war was being waged. Comments as vague as "Down with the war!" or as specific as "Emperor Franz Joseph has several illegitimate children," or "Our Emperor ... shouldn't have broken the alliance with Italy – then Italy would have helped us against Russia and I wouldn't have lost my son," landed women in jail.[127] The charge of disturbing the peace was more broadly defined: it included expressing (in print or "in public or in the presence of several people") disdain or hatred of the Emperor, the Emperor's allies, the form of government or the state administrators, disobeying laws, or encouraging others to commit these acts. Viennese women were arrested for comments such as "Germany must be defeated," "The Germans are stupid," "Someone should stick the German Emperor's nose in corn meal!" and "The Sarajevo murders were a good thing ... the poor Serbs [did] too little."[128] Women uttered these and thousands of similar opinions not in print or from podiums, but in food lines, in stairwells and in conversations with "friends" in private apartments.

Assessing the place of women in political history, historian Eve Rosen-haft has asked whether women's *Treppenhausgespräche* (staircase conver-sations) are analogous to men's *Kneipengespräche* (pub conversations) as informal public spheres where women, particularly of the lower classes,

[126] For a full and lively account of this law, see Elgin Drda, "Die Entwicklung der Majestätsbeleidigung in der österreichischen Rechtsgeschichte unter besonderer Berücksichtigung der Ära Kaiser Franz Josephs," Ph.D. diss., University of Linz, 1992. Drda calculates that between 1848 and 1916 around 15,000 people were prosecuted in Austria for this offense and 10,000 were convicted. He does not say how he has reached these figures; he has located only eighty-seven *Majestätsbeleidigung* files in archives. Drda notes that later drafts of this 1852 law allowed for shorter punishments (six months to five years), 147. While his study extends to 1916, he appears not to have considered civilian cases processed by military courts, which for this particular offense would have included most cases after August 1914.
[127] KA, MKSM 1917 85-1/10; 85-1/65. Recommendations for imperial pardon.
[128] KA, MKSM 1916 85-1/36; AdBDW 1916 St./9 # 35306 and # 27535.

exchanged information and exercised social control. The analogy fails in her mind because the pub conversation "is likely to be one about politics" while the staircase conversation is likely to be "about people."[129] But this distinction did not hold true in World War I Vienna, where most any opinion might be construed as "a matter of state." Austrian authorities then faced a difficult question: could and should women making such statements be held accountable for their actions? Critical comments like those above, made in passing, could easily spread as rumors and undermine official proclamations. But the fact that they were made by *women* left authorities in a quandary. First, as noted above, the nineteenth century bequeathed to contemporaries a belief in women's inability to understand the gravity of politics. According to police, women critical of Austria often did not understand the significance of their words or had "lost their heads." Second, jailing female offenders during the war further threatened "the family," a delicate unit already strained by male conscription and youth delinquency.[130] To imprison women who had taken over their husbands' business obligations, who cared for children as the sole remaining parent and who provided for other dependent relatives was, as legal experts acknowledged, not in the best interest of Austria. Ultimately legal authorities would have to decide: should women with critical opinions be held accountable by Austrian law as individuals? Or should they be pardoned because the state valued them more as Austrian wives and mothers?

A set of applications for women's legal pardons and the rulings of imperial advisers on these applications allows us a glimpse of how gender played out in World War I jurisprudence. In the thirty-six cases from 1916 and 1917 under consideration here, women imprisoned for making anti-state comments or insulting His Majesty (23), for harming the state by harboring a deserter (9), for encouraging a man to abandon his military duty (2), for attempting illegally to secure a man's exemption from service (1) and for killing a man in service (1) wrote petitions for leniency (*Gnadengesuch*) to the Emperor requesting a shortening of sentence.[131]

---

[129] Eve Rosenhaft, "Women, Gender and the Limits of Political History in the Age of 'Mass' Politics," in Larry Eugene Jones and James Retallack (eds.), *Elections, Mass Politics and Social Change in Modern Germany* (Washington, DC: German Historical Institute, 1992), 149–73, 156.

[130] See chapter 5 on children.

[131] KA, MKSM 1916, 1917 85-1. The women were tried in army district courts in Vienna, Linz, Brünn, Prague, Theresienstadt, Josefstadt and a few smaller military court branches. The cases *cannot* be considered a representative sample of all women who appealed for leniency because the only cases found in the state archive were those with a *positive* outcome. How many similar requests were rejected cannot be determined. Shortly after these cases were processed, Emperor Karl's general amnesty of

In all of the cases, imperial advisers supported leniency on one of three gendered grounds: as a woman, the accused did not have the mental capacity to understand the gravity of her words or deeds; as a mother, her imprisonment would place her children in peril; or, in the case of harboring a deserter, her loyalty to husband or son "naturally" took precedence over her loyalty to Austria.

In the first instance, women were granted leniency by claiming absent-mindedness, a tendency to become "overly excited" or on grounds of political naiveté. For all of the early-war rhetoric on the ways in which war stirred in women a new political consciousness, these cases show that women were still not considered fully accountable as rational individuals. Therese Bartsch, a 27-year-old grocery clerk in Vienna, found herself in jail for having shouted to four soldiers who marched by her shop with a flag, "Stick the flag in the oven and stay home so the war will finally end!" Her sentence was reduced from six months to six weeks because she had shown remorse and had been in a state of "excitement" at the time of the offense. She was "nervous" because she hadn't heard from her husband in the field in a long while and wasn't sleeping well on account of her worries. Her unpremeditated comments were the product of her "highly agitated mood" and lacked "malicious intent." In this case, Bartsch's feminine attributes – her emotional vulnerability and excitability – reduced the force of her critical comment.[132] The same logic applied to the case of 34-year-old midwife Ludmilla Kubart. As recounted in the previous chapter, Kubart had been denounced by neighbors for criticizing the Central Powers while standing in the doorway of her apartment building. Among the other reasons for her release, advisers noted that she had made "a comment... among women that posed no wider threat." Kubart's eight-month sentence was reduced because she did not show signs of an anti-state *Gesinnung*, and appeared to be an "easily excitable person."[133]

Even in wartime crimes of greater magnitude, women's perceived emotional fragility worked in their favor. In 1915, Marie Wanko stabbed her husband Richard, a military reservist, to death in their Vienna apartment. She received a reduced sentence in part because she had committed the crime in a "highly agitated state," and was judged to have "hysterical tendencies" which were exacerbated by menstruation and alcohol consumption.[134] While mental state was sometimes taken into account when

July 2, 1917, freed many female offenders jailed on charges of "insulting His Majesty" and disturbing the peace.
[132] KA, MKSM 1916 85-1/71.   [133] KA, MKSM 1917 85-1/89.
[134] KA, MKSM 1917 85-1/220.

judging men's offenses, it is particularly evident in women's files. By recommending leniency for a woman on account of her predilection for gossip, her inexperience in "political matters" or because she was judged "incapable of mature reflection"[135] these cases show that state authorities did not share women's groups' newfound regard for women's political consciousness.

The Emperor was equally likely to pardon women on grounds of motherhood. Jailing a woman on the home front might mean removing the only remaining parent in a family already disrupted by conscription. Embarrassing situations arose when women tried to bring their children to jail with them because they had no other childcare options.[136] Authorities needed to protect the state from slanderous remarks, but they also feared an increase in the number of abandoned children that would result from punishing female offenders. They needed women's help in combating the youth delinquency epidemic that had spread through the city in early 1916. Arguing for the early release of a mother of three children, officials noted, "In every single case, where possible, steps should be taken against the ever more alarming [rise of] youth delinquency."[137] The Emperor's advisers recommended early release for Käthe Srsen, the mother of a nine-month-old baby, arguing that the "health and perhaps even the life of the child would be endangered" if she served her full sentence for aiding and abetting a deserter.[138] In the case of Elise Bertagnolli, authorities reduced a two-year sentence, which suggests they considered insulting the Emperor – the offense Bertagnolli had committed – less a threat to Austria than the continued incarceration of a mother of eleven children. Whatever threat to public morale women posed as war critics, the value of their maternal services on the home front weighed heavily in their favor when seeking leniency for these offenses.

Women similarly benefited from the belief that their duty to love and nurture male family members took precedence over other competing duties, such as the duty to protect state interest. Competing loyalties to family and state came to the fore in cases of women charged with aiding and abetting deserters. Desertion became an increasingly serious problem for the Habsburg military as the war progressed. While scholars have focused on desertion of soldiers from non-German-speaking regions, deserters also came from, and sought refuge in, the capital city.[139] Despite the threat that desertion posed to military operations, it appears

[135] KA, MKSM 1917 85-1/28.   [136] AdBDW 1916 St./9 #26483.
[137] KA, MKSM 1917 85-1/220.   [138] KA, MKSM 1917 85-1/29.
[139] On desertion, see Richard Plaschka *et al.* (eds.), *Innere Front: Militärassistenz, Widerstand und Umsturz in der Donaumonarchie 1918*, 2 vols. (Munich: R. Oldenbourg Verlag, 1974). In 1917, the Ministry of the Interior ordered the Statthalterei in Vienna to compile

that Habsburg authorities did not encourage women to report husbands or close family members who had deserted. On the one hand, according to Austrian law one could not offer shelter to or otherwise protect a deserter. According to the penal code, it was illegal

to offer a helping hand of any kind to a serviceman who has fled from the military (fugitive, deserter) by providing directions, by clothing, hiding or offering shelter, and thereby promoting his flight or hampering the investigation and capture of the fugitive.[140]

On the other hand, a 1917 note from the Military Chancellery specified that petitions for leniency in desertion cases involving women were not necessarily to be judged by "the letter of the law" but also by "humane" considerations. "All efforts are being made ... to free the wife and close relatives of the legal obligation to report husbands and relatives."[141] Officials wanted to catch deserters, but not at the cost of breaking family ties. Thus, when Marie Hotton, a 25-year-old feather arranger in Vienna, offered shelter to her fiancé (and later husband), a deserted infantrist, over six months in 1916, offering him "a helping hand" and hindering inquiries into his whereabouts, she was sentenced to four months in jail. Her sentence was reduced on the grounds that she didn't possess "reprehensible *Gesinnung*" but rather had broken the law "only out of love" for her man.[142] In other cases "motherly love" and "sisterly love" were cited as grounds for women's reduced sentences. Maria Slanina, a mother whose nineteen-year-old son, Ludwig, had deserted and hidden his uniform in her Vienna apartment, reported helplessly, "As a mother it would have been very difficult for me to turn him in. I would have probably even let him stay overnight at my place longer." She fed him periodically before he was picked up by the military police.[143] Deserters sought from their female family members food, clothing, nurturance and a "home," just those things that state authorities felt women were "naturally" endowed to provide. These soldiers had broken the law and needed to be apprehended; but for a woman to turn in her husband, son or brother was to break a bond even more sacred, and more important for society in the long run, than military discipline.

In a political atmosphere characterized by anonymous grumbling, intrigue, desertion and myriad other "dangers to the state," authorities

monthly reports about "staatspolizeilich relevante Vorfälle." Aiding a deserter appears frequently in these reports. NÖLA Präs. "P" 1917 VII, 752.

[140] §220 Austrian penal code. Penalty was a fine and six months to a year in prison.
[141] KA, MKSM 1917 85-1/237. Handwritten note relating to case of Sofie Novozamski.
[142] KA, MKSM 1917 85-1/110.
[143] WSLA Landesgericht Strafsachen 1917 Fasz. 514 Zl. 8922, document 21.

204 Vienna and the Fall of the Habsburg Empire

were forced to articulate the standards of legal accountability set for the citizenry. These cases of wartime leniency for women demonstrate that accountability was not gender-neutral; authorities highly valued women precisely for their "womanly and motherly" service to Austria.

The Women's Auxiliary Labor Force

Difficult circumstances late in the war prompted the state to recruit women for positions for which they were not "naturally" suited. In 1917, the Army High Command, looking to replenish the depleted ranks of its soldiers, announced an ambitious program to free up for front service the "greatest possible number of troops" by replacing men in army support positions with women.[144] It established the Women's Auxiliary Labor Force in the Field (weibliche Hilfskräfte im Felde), which came to employ between 36,000 to 50,000 women in 1917 and 1918. As the historiography on World War I has shown, women in many European countries performed tasks in wartime that had formerly been designated "male." The Women's Auxiliary Labor Force merits special attention because it had women serving Austria in ways that so closely resembled military service. Unlike the nurses of the Austrian Red Cross, who had been working under army contract since 1915, and who were publicly celebrated for the specifically feminine virtues of their service, the volunteers of the Women's Auxiliary Labor Force met with official resistance and public derision.[145] As army employees working in regions not actually at the battle front, but behind the lines in support areas,[146] they served as laboratory assistants, clerical workers, technicians and telephone and telegraph operators. They wore uniforms; they referred to themselves as "enlisted"; they were relatively well paid; they traveled far from home and worked alongside men. The public controversy the program generated, and great resistance to it from within the army itself (despite urgent promotion by the High Command) suggest that the definition of "Austria's women" was under great strain by war's end. In the interest of the Austrian war effort, women filled these positions, yet commentators felt the feminine virtues of those who enlisted were jeopardized in the process.

---

[144] KA, GZNB 1917 carton 3750, #4605. KM memo, 3 January 1917.

[145] Next to the public icon of the virtuous "angel-like" nurse, was a counter-image of the nurse as whore. See Ernst Hanisch, "Die Männlichkeit des Kriegers: Das österreichische Militärstrafrecht im Ersten Weltkrieg," in Thomas Angerer et al. (eds.), Geschichte und Recht: Festschrift für Gerald Stourzh zum 70. Geburtstag (Vienna: Böhlau, 1999), 313–38, 329–30.

[146] See introduction for the war geography of the Habsburg lands.

It was paradoxical that volunteers of the Women's Auxiliary Labor Force were perceived by the public as independent adventure-seekers, because they actually gained access to the program through the deeds of male family members. A War Ministry recruiting memo emphasized, "Of the applicants, first priority is given to widows and orphans of active military persons," followed by widows and orphans from previous wars.[147] Although we saw above that citizenship was not a status women possessed independently, the army sought women between the ages of eighteen and forty who were "citizens" of Austria, Hungary or Bosnia-Herzegovina, and who demonstrated strong moral character and "political reliability." The latter were certified by a statement of good character from authorities in the woman's hometown. We do not know precisely how many of the volunteers came from Vienna, but the Army High Command recruited through the press, posters, employment offices and through direct appeal to Viennese women's organizations.[148] Authorities stressed the provisional nature of the assignments, and attempted to quell fears that the service might damage that which was most womanly in a woman – her childbearing potential. "Only older women" were to be stationed in areas with poor hygiene.[149]

The threats that service in the Auxiliary Labor Force posed to a woman's "nature" were numerous. First, did she remain a woman at all? Close reading of army documents on the subject shows that male administrators of the program rarely, if ever, referred to the volunteers as women. Rather, they referred to the volunteers in the plural as female auxiliary laborers (*weibliche Hilfskräfte*), which was shortened to "w. Hk." This abbreviation subtly erased (on paper, at least) the unsettling fact that *women* were being sent into the field. Second, the army was loathe to admit that the volunteers wore uniforms, stating emphatically that the "form of dress is *in no way intended as a uniforming* of the female auxiliary laborers. The aim is rather to simplify the production of garments and to curtail special wishes and demands."[150] Yet sketches and photos of the women's garments show them to be uniforms (see plate 4.1).

Finally, authorities worried that the experience of serving in the Auxiliary Force would spoil women's futures as homemakers. Reports that volunteers had not been keeping their quarters clean prompted fears

[147] KA, GZNB 1917, carton 3750, #4605. KM memo, 3 January 1917.
[148] KA, MS/ I. Weltkrieg Allg. 111, fol. 1–241. "Nachrichtenblatt Nr. 5 betreffend weibl. Hilfskräfte bei der Armee im Felde," 24 August 1918; and AdR k.k. Min. f. soz. Verwaltung Präs. 1917, carton 44, #494, letter to Viennese women's organizations, 17 December 1917.
[149] KA, GZNB 1917, carton 3750, #4605. KM memo, 3 January 1917.
[150] KA, MS/ I. Weltkrieg Allg. 111, fol. 1–241. "Bestimmungen für die Aufnahme weiblicher Hilfskräfte und deren Verwendung im Bereiche der A.i.F."

Plate 4.1. Uniforms for the Women's Auxiliary Corps. Source: Österreichisches Staatsarchiv, Kriegsarchiv.

that women who would return to "normal *bürgerliche* circumstances" at
war's end had lost the feminine touch. Measures were taken to ensure
the women, who lived in sex-segregated military housing, didn't "lose
the look and feel for a cozy home" while they were in the field.[151]

Many contemporaries expressed disdain for the Women's Auxiliary
Labor Force. Some in Vienna resented the relatively high pay for women
in the most technical positions. Laboratory assistants, Hughes telegraph
operators and some office workers earned between 120 and 200 crowns
per month, although most earned far less.[152] The *Illustriertes Wiener Extrablatt* painted a luxurious picture of volunteer life, noting to its readers
that in addition to high pay, the women enjoyed free room and board,
travel to and from their assignments and a yearly clothing allowance.[153]
The same criticism was never leveled at soldiers who received the same
"benefits" for their service. Other complaints came from within the army
itself, from men who understandably felt threatened by the arrival of
the female workers. Stationed comfortably behind the lines in office or

[151] KA, MS/ I. Weltkrieg Allg. 111, fol. 1–241. "Nachrichtenblatt..."
[152] KA, MS/ I. Weltkrieg Allg. 111, fol. 1–241. "Bestimmungen..." Volunteers performing more traditionally "female" work – as mess cooks for officers and soldiers, seam-
stresses, waitresses, launderers and cleaners – earned considerably less, between 40 and
90 crowns monthly.
[153] *Illustriertes Wiener Extrablatt*, 24 April 1918.

support positions with the designation "indispensable," these men were suddenly rendered dispensable by a program whose stated aim was an "increase in troops."[154] They accused the newcomers of being unqualified, frivolous adventure-seekers. The *Reichspost* printed the comments of a man who had allegedly seen one of the women "at work" in a military office. The former waitress

> proudly assured me that after "completion" of a sixteen-hour (!) course [she] now had complete command of typing, stenography, accounting and military business protocol. The Fräulein was in our office one month. During this time she read (in secret, of course) all the novels she could get her hands on, naturally during working hours.

He added that on her first day of service the volunteer requested to leave work early "because she had to go to the cinema."[155]

The high pay and the seemingly glamorous lives of the volunteers fed rumors that the women were prostitutes. An anonymous letter-writer speaking on behalf of "the little people" implored Emperor Karl to intervene in the scandalous arrangement whereby officers mingled with the "30,000 womenfolk who aren't qualified for the work" and who were sent merely to service the whoring men (*Hurenkerle*). "The state pays these women to service the filthy officers."[156] Army authorities worried that contact with the female volunteers had damaged the reputation of the army. "The unhindered trafficking of officers with female auxiliary laborers in the streets and in public places (cinema, front theaters and coffeehouses)" spawned rumors that made their way back to the home front. "This damages most acutely the impeccable reputation of our officer corps and seriously discredits the program of female recruitment, which is necessary...for saving on men."[157] Individual volunteers complained that their honor had been insulted by the sexual innuendo that attached itself to women in service. Olga Fil, a telephone operator with the Foreign Ministry, was apprehended at a train station by a detective who "suspected me to be a lady of quite another profession." A local inspector defended the action, noting that "the monitoring of female persons is quite rigorous, but complies with the wish of the responsible army commanders that women traveling aimlessly in the vicinity of the war zone be kept as far away as possible."[158] The repeated declarations

---

[154] KA, MS/ I. Weltkrieg Allg. 111, fol. 1–241. "Bestimmungen..."
[155] WSLB ZAS Frauenarbeit III, *Reichspost*, 10 October 1918 (*Abend*).
[156] AdBDW 1918 St./16 #55053. Anon. letter to Emperor Karl, May 1918.
[157] KA, MS/ I. Weltkrieg Allg. 111, fol. 1–241. Memo from k.u.k. 11 Armeekommando, 24 August 1918.
[158] AdBDW 1917 St./2 #48164. Letter of Olga Fil and official response, 23 July 1917.

of the High Command that the Women's Auxiliary Labor Force was essential to the Austrian war effort because it freed up troops at a time of manpower shortage could not dispel widely held suspicions that women's "service" in the field was of a frivolous or sexual rather than patriotic or professional nature.

To begin to assess how the women themselves conceived of their service we can look to Maria Mosconi and Countess Marie Anna Rumerskirch, two women who served in the field and left written records of their experiences. In both cases, Austria figures prominently in the women's accounts of their motivations. Mosconi, the aforementioned "Italian" translator who was fired from her job and confined in Vienna as a "political unreliable," expressed desire to serve Austria as her father had in battle. Accused of being a loose-lipped gossip who fraternized with enemy civilians, Mosconi fit the stereotype of a woman who couldn't keep secrets. It was precisely this inability to keep secrets that prompted some army officials to doubt women's capabilities to serve the state in a time of peril. Volunteers in the Women's Auxiliary Labor Force were required to sign an oath to protect state secrets, but male counterparts doubted their trustworthiness. "Especially confidential documents may not be processed by the female auxiliary laborers," a War Ministry memo noted.[159] Mosconi's real or perceived inability to recognize the gravity of state secrets – a "feminine" weakness that echoed nineteenth-century justifications for the exclusion of women from politics – ultimately disqualified her from serving Austria.

Similar feminine political naiveté – this time an inability to distinguish between enemy and ally – was ascribed to Countess Marie Anna Rumerskirch, a hospital volunteer serving near the Russian front. She was fired from her position after rumors, allegedly started by her maidservant, circulated to military authorities. Rumerskirch was accused of making herself unpopular at the hospital by caring exclusively for Russian officers and talking to them on the street. From her temporary residence at Vienna's Grand Hotel she launched an ambitious letter campaign to clear her name. She asked the Emperor to intervene on her behalf, stating that her only aim was "to perform patriotic work in wartime." The malicious rumors could not dampen her "patriotic *Gesinnung*," which compelled her to serve near the front, "where help is most needed."[160] The other letters in Rumerskirch's military file convey her sense of honor at serving her country, and her wounded pride at being banned from sensitive territories near the front. Her articulations of "Austrianness,"

---

[159] KA, GZNB 1917, carton 3750, #4605, KM memo, 3 January 1917.
[160] KA, MKSM 1917, carton 1268, #10–1/23. Rumerskirch letter to Emperor, 19 April 1917.

established in her mind through *Kriegsdienst*, clashed with contemporary
gendered notions of whether (and in what capacity) women were temper-
amentally suited to serve the state. She was never directly charged with
spying, but her reputation was stained by a vaguely defined "suspicion
of espionage" stemming from her flirtations with, and perhaps sexual
interest in, the enemy.

Of "Austria's women," the volunteers came closest to serving the state
in ways that resembled men's service. But clearly, something about the
"w. Hk." was deeply troubling to contemporaries. They were accused
of a laundry list of feminine violations. They didn't display selflessness (adventure-seeking); they were immoral (prostitutes posing as office
workers); they were frivolous (novels and cinema); they didn't dress like
women (uniforms); and they neglected key feminine duties (poor housekeeping). Although we know that family connections were important in
the selection process, the women were not performing their work in a
recognizable family capacity as mothers, sisters or daughters. They not
only worked outside the home, they left the *home front* altogether and
moved into areas where, in the cultural imagination, men waged war.
Vehement opposition to the program suggests that Austrian society in
1917 and 1918 was not ready for women's service that extended beyond
traditional, familial roles.

In November, 1914, 24-year-old store clerk Josephine Cieslak was arrested in Vienna for making anti-state comments. An Austrian citizen
suspected of spying for Russia in a city closer to the front, she had been
relocated to Vienna for "confinement." While in the capital, she struck
up a conversation in a café with soldiers on leave, who later reported to
police that Cieslak despised Austria so much that she "began to shake in
agitation when the word 'Austria' was spoken aloud."[161] This incident,
coming just a few months after the founding of the Frauenhilfsaktion
Wien, suggests that the project of mobilizing "Austria's women" faced
challenges from the very beginning. While some organized women seem
to have found a mission in war, "realizing" a latent Austrianness and
expressing it through public works, no lasting female collectivity took
shape in wartime Vienna. Individual women in the venues of everyday
life practiced a different sort of politics, undermining theories of universal
feminine virtue under the noses of the organized women who advocated
them. War brought out human traits – greed, anger, aggression, jealousy
and selfishness – that did not fit within the theoretical rubric of the feminine. Acts of violence, incivility, betrayal or disloyalty by women should

[161] NÖLA Präs. "P" 1914, 1422. Pol. Dir. Wien to Statthaltereipräs., 27 November 1914.

not surprise us, considering the material scarcities in Vienna and the survival mentality that gripped many residents. The state nonetheless incorporated feminine virtues of maternalism, love and selflessness into its legal and administrative decisions about women's citizenship. From this, we see that the crisis of the Austrian *Staatsidee* was accompanied in its final years by a simultaneous crisis of an Austrian *Frauenidee* – an idea that women could be expected to behave a certain way publicly and politically due to a distinctly feminine nature. This assumption, by no means a new idea in the early twentieth century, was disproved during World War I, and yet it was one of the legacies passed from the old Austria to the new.

5   Mobilizing Austria's children for total war

In 1915, the Austrian War Ministry issued a commemorative certificate in honor of Austria's children. Sketched in a classical style, it showed a child approaching an altar to present an offering to warriors in battle. Encouraged by a woman, the child gazes upward and outward and makes a sacrifice to the men at war. Beneath the sketch, an inscription read:

> To Austria's children
> A lasting memorial
> Of the great war
> As a sign of thanks
> For gifts of love
> And deeds of loyalty.[1]

Like many commemorative prints, cards and trinkets from the War Welfare Office, the certificate was probably mass-produced and sold to raise money for war charities (see plate 5.1). Its text and image provide several clues for understanding one of the key economic and cultural projects in World War I Vienna: the attempted mobilization of children for total war.

The certificate thanks "Austria's children" for contributing to war through acts of sacrifice. As with the term "Austria's women," which, as we saw in the previous chapter, assumed a certain nature for women but elided divisions among them, "Austria's children" appealed to an undefined but ostensibly inclusive collective of young people. Although the sketch tells us nothing about this collective, it does convey the location of children's sacrifice. Typical of official propaganda, the certificate depicts two distinct realms of war – front and home front: the men engaged in battle are elevated above and beyond the placid scene in the foreground, in which women and children participate and contribute, but do not fight. The actions above are heroic and glorious, while those below are mundane, grounded, but also necessary. As will be shown, notions of

---

[1] ÖStA, KA, MS/I. Weltkrieg Flugschriftensammlung. Carton 40, Kriegsanleihe.

Plate 5.1. Certificate commemorating sacrifice by "Austria's children" in wartime. Source: Österreichisches Staatsarchiv, Kriegsarchiv.

children's sacrifice underwent significant change after the printing of this certificate. Urged during the first half of the war to sacrifice, children ended up *being* sacrificed by social and economic decisions of total war that jeopardized their health and education.

Using visual images and a wide range of textual sources, this chapter places children at the center of the social, political and economic maelstrom of the years 1914 to 1918. The primary aim is to underscore the centrality of children – symbolic and real – to adults' assessment of war and their state. As will be made clear, the "Austrian child" at war, a symbolic representative and proto-citizen of the imperial state, grew out of a prewar model of the "imperial child." The same virtues that made children attractive symbols of the prewar state – purity, innocence, promise – made them attractive symbols of war. Adults fantasized about children's natural proclivities for and uncorrupted understanding of war, as evidenced by the unusual fascination that writers on the home front, especially men, had with "playing war." The difference between *playing* war and *making* war was blurred early on, with the appearance of the child hero. Considerable attention is devoted to the story/myth of Rosa Zenoch, the legendary "girl from Rawa Ruska," who was cast by the Viennese press in 1914 as the ideal child of the empire. She inspired numerous copy-cat child heroes, who for reasons of circumstance failed to establish themselves as genuine. While possibilities for individual heroism were limited for children in Vienna because they were far from battlefields and borders, the state developed and promoted the idea of "mass heroism" to tap the economic resources of child laborers and consumers in the capital.

The imperial child discourse assumed that children were a political *tabula rasa*, unaffected by the nationalist, class and religious discord of late imperial Austria. But as a symbol, the apolitical, supra-national Austrian child was weakened by forces that had already claimed children as political weapons in the Empire and within Vienna itself. In other words, "children" as a universal category could not transcend the particularism that characterized the Austrian political landscape.[2] In fact, children themselves participated in nationalist, class and religious agitation at the street level in the capital. From schools and media, their parents and their peers, children in Vienna heard distinctly mixed messages about whose war they were fighting and whose future they represented.

---

[2] Party organizations for children and youth blossomed even more fully in the 1920s. The socialists, for example, offered programs from childhood through young adulthood: the Kinderfreunde (ages six to ten), the Red Falcons (ten to fourteen) and the Socialist Worker Youth (fourteen to twenty-one). Helmut Gruber, *Red Vienna: Experiment in Working-Class Culture, 1919–1934* (New York: Oxford University Press, 1991), 166.

Historians of France, Britain and Germany have noted the political and economic centrality of children to the World War I home front. They have documented children's value as laborers, consumers, and as powerful symbols of the nation and its future. In all three of these cases the nation was the essential link between children and war. Children labored on behalf of the nation, sacrificed in honor of the nation, and provided the fresh, regenerative spirit that would secure the nation's future after the bloody war ended.[3] But the disjuncture in Austria between nation and state raised the question: whose future did Austrian children represent? For those committed to the supra-national state, the model child in war did not *embody* the nation, as in other European cases; he *transcended* it. But as will be seen, the Austrian child at war fell head-first into what Oskar Jászi has called the "chasm between dynastic and national patriotism."[4] The multi-national Habsburg state needed to marshal the economic and symbolic powers of children for the purposes of war. After decades of hollow, uninspiring imperial instruction in the schools, it needed quickly to create imperial patriots out of children who had already been inscribed as political beings.

Schools, the key mediating institution between the warring Habsburg state and its children, were unable to meet this challenge. School authorities attempted to mobilize children and extract labor and money from them under the guise of "war education," but there were two glaring problems with mobilizing children through the schools. First, many young people left school at age fourteen and were thus beyond the reach of school administrators.[5] Across Austria, only 3.3 percent of students went on to a middle school (*Mittelschule*).[6] Second, the school system

---

[3] For France, see Stéphane Audoin-Rouzeau, *La Guerre des enfants, 1914–1918: Essai d'histoire culturelle* (Paris: A. Colin, 1993); and Marie-Monique Huss, "Pronatalism and Popular Ideology of the Child in Wartime France: The Evidence of the Postcard," in Richard Wall and Jay Winter (eds.), *The Upheaval of War: Family, Work and Welfare in Europe, 1914–1918* (Cambridge: Cambridge University Press, 1988), 329–67. For Britain, see Deborah Dwork, *War is Good for Babies and Other Young Children: A History of the Infant and Child Welfare Movement in England, 1898–1918* (London and New York: Tavistock, 1987). For Italy, see Andrea Fava, "War, 'National Education' and the Italian Primary School, 1915–1918," in John Horne (ed.), *State, Society and Mobilization in Europe During the First World War* (Cambridge: Cambridge University Press, 1997), 53–69.

[4] Oskar Jászi, *The Dissolution of the Habsburg Monarchy* (Chicago: University of Chicago Press, 1929), 436.

[5] Legally, Austrian children were required to finish eight years of schooling. Robert Wegs notes of Austria, "Most youth from working-class homes finished their school obligation at age 14 or even 12 under some conditions. A large number of problem youth were expelled from the schools before age 14 as well so that they would not 'contaminate' other students." Robert Wegs, "Youth Delinquency and 'Crime': The Perception and the Reality," *Journal of Social History* 32, no. 3 (Spring 1999), 603–21, 613.

[6] Otto Glöckel, *Selbstbiographie: Aus dem Leben eines großen Schulmannes* (Zurich: Verlag Genossenschaftsdruckerei, 1939), 176, reprint of a parliamentary speech, 12 July 1917.

itself collapsed during World War I under the strain of teacher conscription, militarization of the curriculum and the requisition of school buildings for military uses; this collapse jeopardized the intellectual and moral development of the children who represented Austria's future. Austrian schools lacked any coherent civic education to bind pupils emotionally to the state. Wartime, it seems, would have been an ideal (and necessary) time to implement an imperial civics curriculum to correct the misperception of the average Austrian pupil who "left school with the impression that beyond the Leitha an entirely foreign country began."[7] The war service programs, it will be argued, inverted the traditional order of citizen-building: the state called on civic contributions from pupils before a civic consciousness had been imparted through education.

Adults' early-war enthusiasm for the beneficial educational effects of war on children were replaced mid-way through the war by alarmist concerns over the behaviors of a new breed of *Kriegskinder*. In early 1916, a public scare about delinquency and degeneration erupted and colored nearly all public discussions of children thereafter. We can look beyond the conflict of imperial child vs. particular child to see how the material and emotional deprivation of war reduced the attractiveness of the child-as-regenerative-symbol altogether. The sickly creatures produced by the food shortages in Vienna did not lend themselves to political romanticization. Moreover, the same adults who fantasized about children's purity and innocence, and celebrated their instinctive understanding of war in 1914, wrote volumes on the lawless street bandits of 1916. Once symbolizing all that was right and bright about the future, children came to embody adult disillusion with a war not nearly as regenerative and life-affirming as initially predicted. The mid-war panic, which cast the problem of delinquency as "new" and a byproduct of war, actually signaled a return to earlier debates on youth waywardness that had been in circulation since the late nineteenth century.[8]

In certain respects, the emergence of the child in Austrian political discourse was part of a wider, child-centered discussion in late nineteenth- and early twentieth-century Europe. Under the rubric of "population politics," statisticians had been scrutinizing the birth rate and bodies of children, measuring, weighing and recording the health of the nation;

---

[7] Jászi, *Dissolution*, 438.
[8] In "Youth Delinquency and 'Crime,'" Wegs cites urbanization, poor work ethics, declining quality of training for apprentices, entertainment, degeneration of family, and secularization as important components of prewar debates on youth in Austria. For prewar youth delinquency in a European context, see Derek S. Linton, "*Who Has the Youth, Has the Future*": The Campaign to Save Young Workers in Imperial Germany (Cambridge: Cambridge University Press, 1991); Joan Neuberger, *Hooliganism: Crime, Culture and Power in St. Petersburg, 1900–1914* (Berkeley and Los Angeles: University of California Press, 1993), ch. 4.

robust children would mean strong soldiers and healthy mothers for the next generation.[9] In this competition for a healthy, vital future, Austria was not faring well. Dropping steadily in the prewar period, the birth rate in Austria plummeted from 155,000 in 1913 to 89,000 in 1918.[10] Aping military language, commentators tallied unborn children as *casualties* and alarmists warned that in the first two years of war, Austria had "lost" 1.5 million babies that would have been born in peacetime: "It is quite unnecessary to elaborate further on the consequences of this violent loss of life for the economic and military future of the empire. It far exceeds the bloody losses of the war."[11] Losing its children could be even more detrimental to a state than losing its soldiers. Identical sentiments could be heard on all the European home fronts in World War I. But if we look more closely, those concerned with population, children and the "future generation" in imperial Austria faced complications similar to but ultimately more complicated than their European counterparts.

The imperial child

During his sixty-eight-year reign as Emperor (1848–1916), Franz Joseph and his advisers relied heavily on paternal imagery as an instrument for promoting imperial unity. The father figure Franz Joseph addressed the national and ethnic groups of the monarchy as "my peoples," and continued the Habsburg tradition of linking the interests of state with those of the dynastic family. In time, this Habsburg paternalism was directed more specifically at actual children. After 1900, and in conjunction with the European-wide declaration of the new "Century of the Child,"[12] Franz Joseph was no longer just the figurative father of his peoples; he spoke to the young people of his territories. Although disputes over children's education, particularly language and schooling, had already become focal points in the nationalities conflicts of the empire,[13] and children were

[9] In 1900, Swedish reformer Ellen Key wrote the widely translated and disseminated *A Century of the Child* (New York: GP Putnam, 1909). In it she promoted the idea that the greatest asset of any civilization was its children. The book was part of a much larger literature on the importance of children for the future of the state. Military defeats in 1870 (France) and the Boer War (Britain) heightened the panic about the condition and readiness of the "national physique." See Karen Offen, "Depopulation, Nationalism and Feminism in Fin-de-Siècle France," *AHR* 89, no. 3 (June 1984), 648–76.

[10] Clemens von Pirquet (ed.), *Volksgesundheit im Krieg*, 2 vols., Carnegie Endowment for International Peace series (Vienna: Hölder-Pichler-Tempsky, 1926), I, 17.

[11] ÖStA, AdR k.k. Min. f. soz. Verwaltung, carton 1590, #3826-18, Armeeoberkommando, 14 May 1915.

[12] See Key, *A Century of the Child*; and Eduard von und zu Liechtenstein and Rudolf Peerz, *Die Sorge um das kommende Geschlecht: Entwicklungsgedanken über Jugendschutz und Kriegerwaisenfürsorge in Österreich* (Vienna: Verlag des Kriegshilfsbüros, 1916).

[13] Gerald Stourzh, *Die Gleichberechtigung der Nationalitäten in der Verfassung und Verwaltung Österreichs, 1848–1918* (Vienna: Verlag der österreichischen Akademie der

thus already implicated in particularist politics, a counter-model of the imperial child – defined as a vital, enthusiastic child whose commitment and loyalty to the supra-national state outweighed loyalty to any political grouping within that state – emerged as a unifying possibility in the decade before World War I. At the sixty-year jubilee of his reign in 1908, Franz Joseph "spoke the words that have become famous: 'Everything for the child!'"[14]

The Emperor's "Everything for the child" campaign called for donations from across the Habsburg lands, which were used to establish the Grand Coalition of the Emperor's Jubilee Fund that sponsored orphanages, clinics and children's programs. At the same time, a flurry of other child-centered organizations was born. Joseph Maria Baernreither, a child welfare advocate and member of parliament, organized the first Congress of Child Welfare in Vienna in 1907, and the following year established the Center for Child Protection and Youth Welfare, which served as an umbrella group for regional and local youth welfare branches throughout the Austrian crownlands. In 1908, in conjunction with the imperial jubilee and under the protectorate of the Emperor, the Imperial Union of Patriotic Youth Organizations of Austria was founded with the aim of promoting the "patriotic sentiment, physical development and religious-moral values of Austrian youth."[15] Even military planners saw the benefit of "awakening the interest in youth" in the operations of the Habsburg military. Among other things, the Military-Patriotic Campaign of the prewar period introduced over 140,000 schoolchildren to the "Adria" exhibition on the imperial navy.[16] These youth programs – imperial, associational and military – suggest that children had come to figure prominently in the struggle to articulate a workable Austrian *Staatsidee*.[17] Promoting the symbol of the imperial child and building the support and loyalty of real children was a Habsburg strategy for fighting the forces of national and class fragmentation on the eve of World War I. In a patriotic poem distributed to Austrian children, Franz Joseph proclaimed, "You children are the jewels of all the peoples of mine/ The blessing of their future conferred a thousand times."[18]

Wissenschaften, 1985), discusses school conflicts in relation to §19 of the Austrian *Staatsgrundgesetz*, which outlined equality of the *Volksstämme*.

[14] Liechtenstein and Peerz, *Die Sorge*, 3.

[15] KA, MKSM 1917 29-4/8. In 1917, the organization was renamed the "k.k. österreichischer Jugend-Reichsbund" and Emperor Karl became its new patron. At this time it had 1,825 clubs in the Austrian crownlands, with a total of 142,000 members.

[16] KA, MKSM 1914 33-2/2.

[17] For recent thoughts on the Austrian "idea of state" (*Staatsidee*) see Solomon Wank, "Some Reflections on the Habsburg Empire and Its Legacy in the Nationalities Question," *Austrian History Yearbook* 28 (1997), 131–46.

[18] *Der Brief Sr. Majestät unseres allergnädigsten Kaisers Franz Joseph I. an die Kinder im Weltkriege*, 1914–15.

Beyond devotion to the Emperor or youthful interest in the military, it was difficult to find concrete issues that would connect children, many of whom were raised in a nationalist or class-segregated milieu, to the Empire. F. W. Foerster, a German pedagogue lecturing at the University of Vienna, described in 1914 the pedagogical challenge of educating youngsters to be children of the Empire, a dilemma he called "the Austrian problem." Children needed to be taught that Austria was a state of a "higher order," one that had (or could) overcome the tribal instincts of nationalism and serve as a model for the transnational European future. But as of yet, Foerster lamented, teachers lacked "a concrete definition of the essence of state culture," a definition that could break the particularist grip of *Parteimenschen* and mold children "truly committed to the state ... [to] work for the common good."[19] World War I initially provided a number of potentially powerful links between child and state. First, it spawned in children a novel interest in Habsburg geography. Sarajevo, Przemysl, Piave and countless other distant and perhaps irrelevant places when seen from the prewar Viennese perspective became familiar and closely watched points of interest on the home front. For example, one boy who had been plotting his father's whereabouts wrote:

The first battle that my father was in was near Lublin. My father wrote that he took part in the eighth battle, and during the twelfth he was wounded. The Russian bullet hit my father at the knee – that was in the battle of Pr[z]emysl. He spent the night under the stars and fell asleep ... He stood up and dragged himself to the Red Cross. He was bandaged up there and transported to Birkental in Germany.[20]

Second, war was a cause for which children could work on behalf of the state as apprentice citizens.[21] And finally, the child lent to war the same hopeful, future-oriented, regenerative image it lent to the struggling Empire.

Efforts to establish a model imperial child received a boost from the assassination in Sarajevo of Franz Ferdinand, heir to the Habsburg throne. A month before World War I began, the first "innocent victims" of enemy aggression had already rooted themselves in the Viennese consciousness. In Sofie, Max and Ernst, the orphaned children of the assassinated Archduke and his wife, the first and most widely circulating

---

[19] F. W. Foerster, *Das österreichische Problem: Vom ethischen und staatspädagogischen Standpunkte* (Vienna: Hugo Heller, 1916), 18.

[20] Richard Rothe, *Die Kinder und der Krieg: Beitrag zur grundlegenden Gestaltung der Ausdruckskultur* (Prague, Vienna, Leipzig: Schulwissenschaftlicher Verlag A. Haase, 1915), 140.

[21] This phrase is from Jean Bethke Elshtain, "Commentary: Political Children," *Childhood: A Global Journal of Child Research* 3, no. 1 (February 1996), 11–28, 27.

poster children of the Empire were born. In newspaper headlines, the plight of the orphans rivaled the story of the assassination itself. From the tabloid *Kronenzeitung* to the liberal *Neue Freie Presse*, the Viennese papers offered extensive, sensationalistic and sentimental coverage of the unfolding orphan drama (see plate 5.2).

Readers learned that the children, aged thirteen, eleven and ten, had been playing in the idyllic, fairy-tale rose garden of the family's Konopischt castle at the moment of the bloody deed in Sarajevo. Foreshadowing the wartime trend of portraying dead fathers as model parents, the *Neue Freie Presse* mourned, "Papa will never again look earnestly and lovingly through the [school] exercises done so carefully for him..."[22] Robbed of their innocence, but naive to their plight, the orphans were not immediately told of the tragedy, but were urged to go to church and pray for their parents, who had suddenly "fallen ill." They were placed in the care of their aunt, who, when the children's tutor finally broke the news to them, fainted at the sight of their despair and convulsive fits. When Emperor Franz Joseph spoke with the children and issued a public message of sympathy, journalists marveled at the paternal grace of an elderly man still able to relate fully to the sorrows of youth. In the drama of the royal orphans, the Viennese press found model victims and constructed a narrative of the war orphan that would dominate discourse, if not always dictate child welfare policy, for several years. "These three children," the *Neue Freie Presse* wrote, "whose parents' horrifying destiny it was to bleed to death... on the altar of the fatherland, belong to all Austria. All of us... The love of all Austria will be their guardian."[23] Sofie, Max and Ernst were the first children of the state, and the language of their tragedy became standard rhetoric as hundreds of thousands more children were orphaned during World War I.[24]

---

[22] "Den Waisen von Konopischt," *Neue Freie Presse*, 30 June 1914, 3.

[23] *Ibid.*; There was already an older system of paternal care in place for some "orphans," the unmarried daughters of Habsburg military officers and civil servants. These women received small support payments (*Gnadengaben*) from the court, and were still referred to as "orphans" into old age. Thousands of these orphan women wrote letters of request (*Bittschriften*) directly to the Emperor asking for additional financial support during the war. See chapter 6.

[24] The exact number of orphans and "half-orphans" resulting from World War I is unclear. For the dual Monarchy, the number of men killed was 1,016,200, but it is not clear how many of these were fathers. István Deák, *Beyond Nationalism: A Social and Political History of the Habsburg Officer Corps, 1848–1918* (New York: Oxford University Press, 1990), 192. Based on casualty rates and prewar marriage rates and family sizes, Wilhelm Winkler suggests the war may have left about 400,000 Austrian women widowed and 1,200,000 Austrian children as orphans or "half-orphans." See Winkler, *Die Einkommensverschiebungen in Österreich während des Weltkrieges* (New Haven: Yale University Press, 1930), 23.

Plate 5.2. The drama of the imperial orphans unfolds. Source: *Illustrierte Kronenzeitung* 3 July 1914, 1.

Dead fathers left orphans, and dead men left gaps in the population that optimists hoped children would fill. With these two circumstances in mind, the image of the imperial child, evolving in the decades before the war, became even more potent in wartime. In the first instance, orphans offered a means of paying tribute to fallen heroes. The Widows and Orphans Aid Fund, a fundraising organ of the War Ministry, stressed that orphans were the living legacy of the dead. A 1914 fundraising poster addressed to "fellow citizens" appealed to their reciprocal sense of duty: the soldiers had performed their duty for the state, but they had done so on the assumption that their nearest and dearest would be cared for. "To us, we who are left behind, they have left a precious legacy – their widows and their children! Make good on the trust that these heroes took with them to the grave..."[25] During the fundraising campaign the imperial child and the imperial orphan became one:

It was our illustrious Emperor who at earlier ovations always spoke his wish that any planned dedications be put towards youth welfare, and who coined the glorious phrase: "Everything for the Child."
Demonstrate the never-ending love and loyalty that steadfastly binds the peoples of Austria for all eternity to the royal throne in a new way by caring for *these children*, most dear to the Emperor's heart, as you would care for your own.[26]

Despite its name, the Widows and Orphans Aid Fund rarely made appeals directly on behalf of widows. They were mentioned, for example, in a fundraising poster that pledged to the dead hero: "We want to care for your wives as if they were our wives, and your children are our children." The telling phrase *as if* explains why widows had less public appeal than orphans; the ambiguous notion of a man's wife "belonging" to all limited the marketability of the widow as war victim and communal concern. Like the famous orphans of Konopischt, however, any child whose father had died for the state could be a child of Austria. The Christian Social *Reichspost* urged compensation, stressing that orphans provided the means by which state and society could repay the "deeds of our heroes."[27] In fact, the presence of orphans heightened the tribute to men, making it possible to remember the dead not just as brave soldiers but as loving fathers. Just as Archduke Franz Ferdinand's paternal cachet grew in death, ordinary soldiers were recast as loving fathers. Prince Eduard of Liechtenstein, who headed the youth division of the Interior Ministry, explained, "The great majority of the fallen heroes are men of good standing. They are

[25] KA, MS/1. Weltkrieg Flugschriftensammlung Karton 19. Wien: Stellungskundmachungen.
[26] *Ibid.*   [27] WSLB ZAS Jugendfürsorge II, *Reichspost*, 9 May 1916.

dutiful workers, farmers, small businessmen and members of the higher professions. The child was for them the pivotal point of their lives, their happiness, their hope."[28]

Of course, not all soldiers were fathers. In a more general way, children would replenish what contemporaries called the *Menschenmaterial*, human resources, of the state, filling in the population gaps left by dead men. One of the many clichés circulating in Austria at this time was that war (and death) had taught people the value of life, and the regenerative potential of the child's life was offered as a panacea to population decline in wartime. *Wiener Kinder aufs Land*, a program that sent thousands of urban children to the countryside for rest, nourishment and fresh air during the war, was promoted by the volunteer women who ran it not only as a benefit to individual children's health, but to the health of the whole society. "[E]specially now," wrote one newspaper of the Wiener Kinder organization, "with so many men's lives being extinguished, we must be conscious of the fact that the next generation – the growing child – is called on to fill the deep, painful holes the war has torn in our ranks, to rebuild the future of society, the strength of the *Volk* and the state."[29] With men's lives more or less expendable at the front, children's lives were hailed as a precious state commodity.

One war charity that exemplified the spirit of communal responsibility for "Austria's children" was the Kriegspatenschaft, an organization run by ladies from the "highest social circles." Founded early in the war and inspired by a similar organization in Germany, the Kriegspatenschaft arranged sponsorship for needy newborns and their mothers. For 12–24 crowns a month, a wealthy woman could sponsor a child in need, provided that its mother could prove the father was serving in the military. Although the organization promoted the sponsorships as financial, it also informed sponsors that they could choose a specific child and play a role in the child's life, that they could "watch over their charges," offering personal care and attention to ensure, perhaps, that Austria's newborns were protected from possible ineptness among Austria's lower-class mothers. By 1917, the Kriegspatenschaft had sponsored 9,304 babies in Vienna.[30] Because babies symbolized new life in a time of mass death, they lent themselves well to rhetorical flourish. Playing off the phrase *Gold gab ich für Eisen* ("I gave gold for iron"), a slogan of wartime metal-collection drives, one advocate of the Kriegspatenschaft suggested

---

[28] *Jugend- und Kriegerwaisen-Fürsorge: Drei Vorträge gehalten in der Wiener Urania* (Vienna: Verlag des Kriegshilfsbüros des k.k. Ministeriums des Innern, 1917), 18.

[29] WSLB ZAS Jugendfürsorge II, *Österreichische Volkszeitung*, 18 June 1918.

[30] *Jahresbericht der Kriegspatenschaft 1917* (Vienna, 1918), 7, 10.

Gold gab ich für Lebendiges! ("I gave gold for life!") as a motto for the organization.[31]

If the image of the orphan and the faith in the regenerative spirit of the baby put an innocent face on war, children could also actively use their innocence to further the state cause. Adults repeatedly asked them to pray for victory, since "the prayers of innocent children... move the heart of God, because these prayers are conveyed directly by the guardian angels."[32] An instructional booklet for children whose fathers were away at the front reminded them that even before the duties to work and to obey their mothers, "The first of your duties is: pray!... Perhaps your prayer will provide the shield that diverts a bullet or the bombs dropped by an enemy." In any case, the child's prayer, if it came from a "pure heart," was sure to reach the throne of God.[33] Writing in 1915 to pupils at a primary school in Vienna, Archduke Peter Ferdinand thanked them for sending gifts to his infantry troops, and asked them to pray both for the souls of the heroes who had fallen in the field of honor and for the "complete victory."[34] Even the Emperor called for children's prayers, noting early in the war that "God hears the requests of the innocent" and that in prayer children had a weapon that could protect the Empire.[35] In these instances, we see that the wartime motif of the innocent child was more than an inspirational force for adults; innocence, which put children in God's favor and secured a direct link to him, could be actively utilized in pursuit of victory.

The purity of children's hearts, thought to be so efficacious in prayer, attracted the attention of Viennese commentators in a related field. Some teachers and pedagogues became convinced that children had a different "experience" of war than did adults, one that, if tapped, could teach adults something about the essence of war. Children's understanding of war was thought to be unmediated, uncorrupted by exposure to politics – in short, pure. Viennese art teacher Richard Rothe explained, "Children do not think, nor do they judge, nor do they calculate, but they *know*; they know that we will be victorious. It is from this well of instinctual feeling that all of their actions flow."[36]

[31] "Kriegspatenschaft," *Der Bund: Zentralblatt des Bundes österreichischen Frauenverein X*, no. 2 (February 1915), 3.

[32] *Das gute Kind* (October, 1914), cited in Anton Staudinger, "Die christliche Familie im Krieg," in Klaus Amann and Hubert Lengauer (eds.), *Österreich und der grosse Krieg, 1914–1918* (Vienna: Verlag Christian Brandstätter, 1989), 115.

[33] Johannes Eckardt (ed.), *An das Kind des Kriegers: Kriegsbriefe V* (Salzburg: Verlag von Georg Lorenz, 1914), 3.

[34] *Aus großer Zeit (1914–1916): Ein Kriegs-Lesebüchlein für die Jugend und das Volk* (Vienna: k.k. Schulbuch Verlag, 1918), 34.

[35] *Der Brief Sr. Majestät.*   [36] Rothe, *Die Kinder*, 34.

Plate 5.3. Exhibition of children's artwork: "experiences" of war.
Source: Richard Rothe, *Die Kinder und der Krieg: Beitrag zur grundlegenden Gestaltung der Ausdruckskultur* (Prague, 1915).

This instinct found expression in painting and drawing, and at the
end of 1914, an exhibit of children's war art opened at the Heller salon
in Vienna. Like other wartime exhibits, this one promised viewers on
the home front clues to the meaning of war, clues children were best
suited to offer because they "perceive the war very differently than we
adults do . . . they see it as it really is."[37] Exhibit organizers stressed that
the artworks, produced by ten- to thirteen-year-olds from several local
schools, were free of adult influence. Viewers were assured that teachers
had not interfered in the creative process, and that the works were the
manifestation of "slumbering ur-instincts" awakened by war. If we look
at the pictures from the exhibit, however, the claims about the purity
of children's expression appear dubious; while the exhibit was billed as
a chance to witness children's unmediated "experience" (presumably of
the war on the home front), nearly all of the drawings depict bloody battle
scenes at the front (see plate 5.3).

If, as exhibit organizers claimed, "With children everything is real,
rooted in the genuineness and honesty of perception,"[38] which child had

[37] *Ibid.*, 72.   [38] *Ibid.*, 70.

really been on hand to "perceive" the scenes in the pictures exhibited? Wilhelm Börner, a socialist and opponent of this romanticization of children's war experiences, criticized the art exhibit and the cultural deluge of child-war artifacts that followed:

[I]t is completely incomprehensible how some pedagogues can maintain that these children's drawings are *unbeeinflusst* and *urwüchsig*. It is clear from the start that the sources of these works are the pictures seen in newspapers, postcards and films. It could not be otherwise, because we are talking about the representation of things and events that lie totally outside the realm of children's experience.[39]

But the exhibit marked only the beginning of adults' attempt to see and comprehend the war through innocent eyes.

Children's "experiences" became a boom industry in various media as publishers and newspaper editors clamored for children's essays, letters to men in the field, songs, poems and games. Jingles circulating in Vienna made defeating the Russians and Serbs seem like a playground endeavor:

> Peter, du blöder, mit deinen zwei Buben
> Wir machen von euch saure Ruben!
>
> Heil Wien! Heil Berlin!
> In 14 Tagen
> In Petersburg drinn!
>
> Vater, Mutter, Weib und Kind
> Ihre Lieben, die zu Hause sind,
> Habt keine Angst, wir kehren wieder
> Vorerst hauen wir die Russen nieder.[40]

In nursery rhymes and children's anecdotes, adults found a war that was harmless, poignant, utterly unthreatening. Newspapers printed children's letters, such as the one nine-year-old Josefine Lederer wrote to Emperor Franz Joseph:

Dear Emperor! Please don't be mad that I'm writing to you. Because you are busy with the war, I wanted to make you happy and I wrote a poem. You might want to laugh, but I'm only in fourth grade. With a hand kiss, J. L.[41]

Publishers relished the enthusiasm of child essayists, in whose work "a deep patriotic sensibility [was] unmistakable," such as the boy who

---

[39] "Die Kinder und der Krieg," *Arbeiterzeitung*, 12 Nov 1916, 7.
[40] Bernhard Denscher and Franz Patzer, *Das Schwarz-Gelbe Kreuz*. Catalog of "Wiener Alltagsleben im Ersten Weltkrieg," Wiener Stadt- und Landesbibliothek, 7–9. Flyers with these rhymes sold for 20 hellers to raise money for the Red Cross.
[41] Rothe, *Die Kinder*, 142.

described an Austrian encounter with the Russians and their "vodka Kaiser":

The Austrians stab the vodka Kaiser and his soldiers, and sometimes they also strike the vodka bottle. That's when the Russians are saddest. The Kossacks jump up and say, "Our poor vodka! No worse tragedy could befall us!" Then they die. Amen.[42]

War as interpreted by children had a sweetness seductive to adults. Childhood was founded on naive misunderstandings that should not be corrected, according to Rothe, teacher and organizer of the art exhibit, who explained that these misunderstandings allowed for fantasy scenarios in which "reality is unreal."

Nowhere was adult fascination with children's perceptions of war more focused than in the realm of play. Male writers on the home front produced voluminous, sentimental writings on *Kriegsspiel*, "playing war." The innocent child, simultaneously at play and at war, spawned men's fantasies of boyhood adventure and generated a debate on how play could best be utilized by the state. Before the war, the Lower Austrian school council circulated to teachers a questionnaire to determine which games children played; they wanted to popularize games that maintained and promoted native folklife and folk sentiment.[43] Adults celebrated play as a pure realm of childhood experience, but could not resist the urge to intervene in this realm. This urge was even more pronounced during wartime. Teachers were advised to "use" the illusion at the heart of make-believe games for productive ends. "In the romance of play" a boy would "unconsciously absorb much real soldiering."[44] In *The Last Days of Mankind*, Viennese critic Karl Kraus satirized the romanticization of play:

Frau Wahnschaffe, (a housewife): Oh, here they come now, the cute little kiddies! What's the matter now? Aren't you playing World War?
Little Willy (crying): Mommy, Marie won't stay dead!
Little Marie: We played encirclement, then World War, and now –
Little Willy (crying): But I only wanted a place in the sun, then –
Little Marie: He's lying!
Little Willy: I successfully bombarded her position, and now she won't stay dead!

---

[42] *Ibid.*, 72, 138.
[43] ÖStA, AVA, MdI "S", carton 44, 1911–1918, #2824. The questionnaire asked seventeen questions, among them: What are the names children give to their games? Where are they played? In what season? What are the rules? How many participants? Are toys needed? What is the history and symbolism of the game?
[44] *Verordnungsblatt für den Dienstbereich des k.k. nö. niederösterreichischen Landesschulrates* 1914 Sonderbeilage I, Stück XX, 3.

Little Marie (crying): No, it's not so! It's an enemy lie, just like a Reuter's dispatch. First he took my forward position, and now he attacks from the flank! I effortlessly repelled the attack and now he says –
Little Willy: Marie is lying![45]

At a time when the Ministry of the Interior was publishing children's books such as *Let's Play World War!* Kraus captured the profound ambiguities in the notion of innocence during World War I, but his was a rare voice in an otherwise sentimental discourse.[46]

In the work of Eduard Golias, whose *Die Kinder und der Krieg* is the most extensive treatise on war play from this period, we see how the pervasive rhetoric of frontline heroism and battle-ready masculinity affected men like Golias who spent the war on the home front.[47] Remembering child's play allowed them to remember a time when they, too, had been heroes. Prompted by the children he sees playing around him, Golias reminisces, "We've all lived through days when the world appeared too small, too confined, and our yearnings drew us to distant lands full of lurking dangers."[48] He slips into the persona of a boy as he recounts pirate escapades, Indian raids and the battles he has waged against savage enemies in his exclusively male world of fantasy and adventure. But this world shatters; during a stealthy approach on an unsuspecting enemy, the voice of a woman, the boy's nagging mother, "rips him from his dreams." His male adventure world is blotted out by the most mundane, female of activities: he has been asked do the shopping at the corner store. Returning to his fantasy during his errand, he manages to fend off the knife attack of a "redskin," but absentmindedly buys sugar instead of coffee and is scolded by his mother. The fantasies lived, and humiliation suffered, by the boy mirror those of men like Golias, who claimed to be writing about "the little ones," but who, in this era of the soldierly ideal, could express their own home-front "yearnings" through the prism of the child.[49]

Adults delighted in children's war games for several additional reasons. They detected in *Kriegsspiel* a beneficial leveling of class hierarchy, a solidification of gender roles, and an opportunity to train children for "real

---

[45] Karl Kraus, *The Last Days of Mankind*, transl. F. Ungar (New York: Ungar Publishing Co., 1974), Act III, scene 40.
[46] *Wir spielen Weltkrieg!* (Vienna: Kriegshilfsbüro des k.k. Ministeriums des Innern, 1915), a picture book advertised as "a timely gift for our little ones."
[47] Eduard Golias, *Die Kinder und der Krieg: Ernstes und Heiteres aus der Welt der Kleinen* (Vienna: Verlag F. Tempsky, 1915).
[48] Golias, *Die Kinder und der Krieg*, 7.
[49] See chapter 6 for men's experiences on the home front.

war." Just as military conscription brought together men from different walks of life, war games would bring middle-class children into contact with the poor, "the so-called better children" with the "*Gassenbuben,* also known as *Lausbuben.*"

Those who earlier would never have gotten to know each other because Mama or the nanny forbid it, were now playing war together. Strangely, one has now come to see that children have a right to play with each other and that sometimes the great enthusiasm [of the better children] cannot be satisfied with well-behaved walks in the park.[50]

Here, pampered "mama's boys" would be hardened by contact with their rough-and-tumble lower-class counterparts, learning more naturalness, while the *Gassenbuben* would learn more order. War games fostered comradeship and solidarity among boy soldiers, whose biggest problem was assigning the unfortunate role of the enemy to their fellow playmates.

Further, these war games were thought to awaken the primal gendered instincts of children, making the boys "more active" and the girls, taking part in war games for the first time as Red Cross nurses, "milder and softer." Although Karl Kraus's "Little Marie," above, engages in battle play, most adults posited a stereotypical, nurturing role for girls. According to Golias, war had offered clearly defined gender roles even before the war games boom of World War I. Girls had traditionally been on hand to sew costumes, flags and other military accoutrements and now had a more prominent role as nurses, able "to wrap the many real and imagined wounds of the eager warriors."[51] Boys and girls in Vienna not only dressed up as soldiers and nurses in play, but were also frequently photographed in costume. A typical wartime postcard sent as a greeting "to our fathers in the field" records the unambiguous gender roles for children playing war at home.[52] A few adults protested the dressing of children in miniature soldier's uniforms, saying that it was both a waste of cloth and "from the standpoint of honor, regrettable to turn [the uniform] into a toy,"[53] but the military aesthetic remained a steady influence in children's fashions throughout the war.

Adults also saw in children's war games and toys great educational potential. Imperial military authorities predicted that children would learn through play "how brave the armed forces are, and what great gratitude they are owed," encouraged the production of war-oriented picture books

[50] Rothe, *Die Kinder,* 17.   [51] Golias, *Die Kinder und der Krieg,* 13.

[52] See *Soldatengrüße aus dem Felde: Feldpostkarten und Briefe unserer Vaterlandsverteidiger an die Illustrierte Kronen-Zeitung* 1 (January 1915), 18.

[53] NÖLA Präs. "P" 1915 XVb, 8345. Pol. Dir. Wien to Statthalterei Präs., 18 December 1915. Remarks of schoolteacher Angelo Carraro at meeting of Arbeiterverein "Kinderfreunde."

and puzzles, and praised the battles of the Carpathian Mountains, the Isonzo and Tirol as rich in "historical-geographic content."[54] The imperial child could learn the contours of the empire through board games. A 1917 exhibit of 180,000 toy soldiers on display on Vienna, ostensibly set up for children, was "an even bigger pleasure for adults," who could inspect the historical accuracy of the uniforms and the geographic placement of the tiny imperial figurines. Reporting on the show, one journalist was transported back to his boyhood and wrote with childlike enthusiasm, "[W]aging battles with our armies of lead soldiers was always the greatest fun for us boys! The love of our miniature army went hand in hand with our love for the real, big army."[55] Expressed in 1917, his fondness for war play was apparently undiminished by the war of the "real, big army" which had been underway for thirty-four months.

In these accounts, children are simultaneously the antithesis of war and its most promising recruits. Adults held them outside of war, but attributed to them a sort of sixth sense for its true essence. Playing war was good for the future of Austria: it united children from diverse backgrounds, and trained boys to be men and girls to be women. Adult men on the home front who hailed the cathartic effects of war play found in it a chance to return to their boyhood adventures and heroism. Whether as orphan, artist or playmate, the innocent child was a seductive cultural symbol in World War I because it rendered war harmless and promised Austria a future.

In September, 1914, children in Vienna who enjoyed dressing up in costume and playing war began hearing tales of one of their own – a child – who had crossed the line from the make-believe into the real. She was a twelve-year-old Polish-speaking girl named Rosa Zenoch, "the girl hero from Rawa-Ruska," who became a bona fide hero and model child of the Empire. In order to understand how a child could become a hero – normally the domain of soldiers – we need only look to the German language, which, with its compound nouns, made particularly fertile ground for multiple claims to heroism. The root *Helden-* could be attached to any number of words to create heroic subcategories. There was the *Heldentat* (heroic deed), *Heldenkampf* (heroic battle), *Heldentod* (heroic death), not to mention the *Heldensinn* (heroic spirit) and the *Lehrerhelden* (heroic teachers). What was to stop the invention of the *Heldenmädchen*, the heroic girl? Some of the factual details of Zenoch's story remain vague: newspapers alternately spelled her name Zenoch, Zennoch and Hennoch;

---

[54] KA, MKSM 1917 29-4/4 kuk Armeeoberkommando, Kriegspressequartier to MKSM, 14 May 1917.
[55] WSLB ZAS Ausstellungen II, *Fremdenblatt*, 18 May 1917.

she was sometimes twelve, sometimes thirteen years old; some accounts had her arriving in Vienna directly from the eastern front, while others had her traveling by way of Budapest. But most accounts of Zenoch's story follow the same basic trajectory: Rawa Ruska was a village near Lemberg,[56] where, in the fall of 1914, the Austrians and Russians fought several bitter battles. Attempting to carry fresh drinking water to Austrian troops, Zenoch was caught in the line of fire and wounded in the foot by a piece of Russian shrapnel. En route to Vienna as part of a transport of wounded soldiers, her leg was amputated. She ended up in a city hospital, where Emperor Franz Joseph visited her, bestowed a locket upon her, gave her a large cash prize, and agreed to provide her with a new prosthetic leg.

Despite missing or conflicting details in the story of the real Rosa Zenoch, the myth of the girl hero from Rawa Ruska quickly evolved as numerous wartime writers took liberties to fill in the imaginary details of her heroic actions. Although photos show her to be blonde, the *Neue Freie Presse* wrote that her black braids fluttered in the wind during her "barefoot, breathless" dash into the enemy line of fire.[57] Another writer described Rosa as "calm and unwavering" as she made her way to the troops.[58] Her picture appeared in newspapers and on postcards, and her story became a staple of wartime children's literature (see plate 5.4).

Children's books intimated that she had made her heroic dash many times, running to the troops "every time" the canons thundered.[59] The soldiers who carried her from the place where she fell thought of her simultaneously as an angel and a sister.[60]

Several features of the Zenoch legend lent weight to Rosa as model child of the empire. First, she was not from the center, but rather the periphery of the Habsburg lands. She spoke a strange dialect that even Polish-speaking doctors in Vienna could not initially decipher.[61] This "border child" was the ideal representative in a war ostensibly fought in defense of Austria's borders. One children's story recounted how "the young hero sank to the ground with a cry. Her young blood reddened

[56] Today in Ukraine, Rava-Rus'ka and L'viv.
[57] "Das Heldenmädchen von Rawa Ruska,"*Neue Freie Presse*, 20 September 1914, 8.
[58] Josef Göri and Leo Tumlirz (eds.), *Österreich-ungarisches Kriegslesebuch 1914/17: Als Vorlesebuch für den Schulgebrauch* (Leipzig: Friedrich Brandstetter, 1917), 43–4.
[59] Hans Fraungruber, *Aus dem Weltkriege: Ernste und heitere Berichte* (Vienna, Prague: k.k. Schulbücher Verlag, 1916), 45.
[60] Göri and Tumlirz, *Österreich-ungarisches Kriegslesebuch*, 43–4; and the poem "Rosa Zenoch" in Oskar Staudigl (ed.) *Aus grosser Zeit (1914–1916): Ein Kriegs-Lesebüchlein für die Jugend und das Volk.* Deutsch-Österreichische Jugendhefte, no. 1 (Vienna: k.k. Schulbuchverlag, 1918), 38.
[61] "Das Heldenmädchen von Rawa Ruska," *Neue Freie Presse*, 20 September 1914, 8.

Plate 5.4. Child hero Rosa Zenoch aiding soldiers in battle. Source: *Illustriertes Wiener Extrablatt*, 22 September 1914, 1.

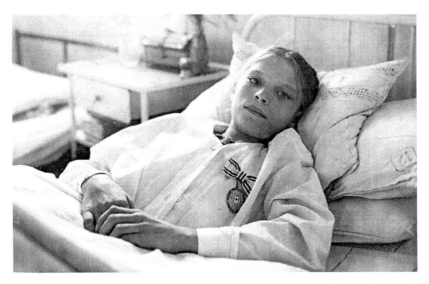

Plate 5.5. Picture postcard of child hero Rosa Zenoch. Source: Postcard in possession of author.

the soil!"[62] Rosa's blood was Habsburg blood, spilled at the far edges of the Habsburg domain. Moreover, the legendary Rosa did not seem to have parents. Although initial newspaper photos showed Rosa arriving in Vienna with her mother, the mother was written out of later versions of the story. With the receipt of a locket with the initials "FJ" she became a symbolic ward of the Emperor himself. Other members of the royal family gave her gifts and cash and her hospital room was overflowing with gifts from "the population." In legend, Rosa belonged to the Emperor and the people.

While it provided adults with a poster-child for the Empire, the legend of the girl from Rawa Ruska posed difficulties for children in Vienna. How could children inspired by Rosa emulate her heroism in the streets of Vienna? How could a Viennese girl like Greti Simon, who, in December, 1914, received a postcard of Rosa (see plate 5.5) from her father with the words "In memory of the World War 1914. I am sending you the girl-hero Rosa Zenoch, who carried water to soldiers in the line of fire" live up to the example of a legend?

Other young heroes appeared in children's literature, but like Rosa they lived on the Empire's periphery, close to battle sites. "Maruska," a fictional girl from Bukowina who saved her father and her village from barbarous Russians before being "impaled on the lance of a Kossak," lived in circumstances unlike those in Vienna.[63] Two cases of failed copy-cat child heroes demonstrate the limits of individual child heroism in the capital city, and suggest that many children in World War I (like their male family members at the front) would have to settle for participation in anonymous acts of "heroism."

Eleven-year-old Heddy Stritzko of Vienna never made it into children's books and she was never memorialized in war poetry. But her wartime exploits earned her a thick police file, and brought her to the attention of Church authorities and high-ranking state officials including the Minister of the Interior and the Lower Austrian governor. Her failed bid for heroism had consequences for the many foreign-born teachers and pupils in Austrian schools. In the fall of 1914, the following anonymous letter was sent to Viennese Mayor Richard Weiskirchner:

Dear Friend!
Regarding our conversation, I am letting you know that a pupil by the name of Heddy Stritzko at the French boarding school "Notre Dame de Sion," Vienna VII, Burggasse, has repeatedly reported that those at [the school] pray for the victory of the Russians.
The following incident is telling:
"The nun said: Now we will all pray for Russian victory, but whoever does not wish to, needn't take part. All the pupils stood up to pray, except the above-mentioned Stritzko. When asked if she wanted to join in the prayer, this pupil hesitated, whereupon the nun proposed a bad grade for conduct!"
I surely don't need to tell you more – this is enough!
Fondly,
Your comrade[64]

The letter might have been filed away and forgotten like hundreds of other anonymous writings received by authorities during the war. But it touched on a topic of public concern in wartime Vienna: foreign influence in the schools. In October 1914, the Education Ministry cautioned that citizens of enemy states, teaching in public and private schools, might negatively influence the "impressionable souls" of Austrian youth. It ordered an institutional cleansing: only subjects (*Angehörige*) of Austria-Hungary, or foreigners who could prove beyond a doubt their "full trustworthiness," would be allowed to remain in the classroom. Further, foreign pupils whose parents were citizens of enemy states were to be identified and

---

[63] "Auch eine Heldin" in Staudigl, *Aus grosser Zeit*, 25–30.
[64] AdBDW 1915 St./12 #3662.

"kept away."[65] The timing of this announcement – and its specific mention of the Notre Dame de Sion girls school as one of the potentially infected institutes – placed fourth-grader Heddy Stritzko at the center of the debate on patriotism and schooling.

When Austrian school inspectors investigated teachers at the Notre Dame de Sion school, the nuns and their Church patrons adamantly denied charges that they had prayed for Russia. Born in Westphalia, Stritzko's teacher Sister Johanna Berchman (suspected of being "French") maintained that her brother and five cousins were decorated soldiers in the German army. The school headmistress testified that Berchman's anti-Russian and anti-French sentiments were so strong that they sometimes had to be "moderated" in the presence of children. The head of Berchman's convent concluded that the anonymous letter to Mayor Weiskirchner, and the rumors it generated, were nothing but "mean-spirited defamation." Austrian school inspectors, working with the Viennese police, concluded that the author of the letter recounting Stritzko's defiance of treasonous teachers and pupils was Stritzko herself.

The letter, coinciding with the "suspicious attitude ... [of] the population about foreign influence on education," created hardship for foreign teachers and students.[66] Stritzko's stories about treasonous teachers and schools "filled with Serbian girls" gained a wider audience among government officials because her father, a Ministry of the Interior employee, passed her accounts to colleagues. In reality, there were only two Serbian girls at her school and these were "carefully observed and held in detention" according to school officials. Questioned by police, Heddy Stritzko admitted her stories were fabricated. When asked why she had made up the stories, she replied, "I don't know. I didn't want to lie."[67] But if we return to her original letter, we see that fabrication and wishful thinking were difficult to differentiate for a girl swept up in the discourse of heroism. Stritzko casts herself as the sole patriot in a sea of traitors. She was paying the price (a bad grade) for her resolute refusal to betray Austria and join the enemy. Identifying a credible enemy was the bane of would-be child heroes in Vienna, who, unlike Rosa Zenoch and other children

---

[65] ÖStA, AVA MdI Präs. 1909–1914, 38, carton 2293, #14,057. Ministerium für Kultus u. Unterricht, 19 October 1914.

[66] NÖLA Präs. "P" 1915 VII, 535. k.k. nö. Statthalterei-Präsidium to Pol. Dir. Wien, 26 December 1914; see WSLB ZAS Schulwesen Bd I, *Neues Wiener Tagblatt*, 1 May 1915 for Education Ministry decree on foreign teachers. Social Democrat Otto Glöckel noted that between January and September 1915, education authorities penned at least four "top secret memos" about the dangers of "enemy" students in Viennese schools. *Selbstbiographie*, 189.

[67] AdBDW 1915 St./12 #3662. Police protocol, 9 January 1915.

from the Habsburg periphery, did not live in close proximity to Russians and wild Kossacks. Perhaps seduced by the discourse of child heroism promoted in official literature, they invented enemies as threatening to themselves and to Austria as those on the battlefield.[68]

When sixteen-year-old Fritz Stanka appeared in the pages of Viennese newspapers in September, 1914, he seemed destined for a public reception more like that of Rosa Zenoch than Heddy Stritzko. The *Neue Freie Presse* carried the headline "A Sixteen-Year-Old War Hero in Vienna." But just a few days later the *Illustriertes Wiener Extrablatt* printed Stanka's photo with the headline "A War Swindler. The Fantasies of a Sixteen-Year-Old." What happened in between was an aggressive police investigation of Stanka's claims and the unraveling of another child "hero." Stanka had arrived in the city dressed in eclectic garb. He donned a German soldier's cap, carried a French bayonet and an Austrian officer's sword, wore a Red Cross band on his left arm and displayed two prominent bandages, one on his knee and the other around his neck. The bandages covered the shrapnel wounds he had suffered in the battle of Lüttich. He told reporters he hoped to have an audience with the Emperor to receive a decoration for his bravery.[69]

The initial public enthusiasm for Stanka's tale evaporated when doctors removed the bandages to reveal "not a scratch on his body."[70] Stanka, police concluded, was not a hero, but a lost soul, a boy from Bohemia whose father had emigrated to America years earlier and whose mother lived in Berlin. He had spent time with a traveling circus and had been a waiter's apprentice. The very week that Rosa Zenoch lay in the hospital receiving gifts and a new leg from the Emperor, the short-lived legend of Fritz Stanka expired in the Viennese press. As journalists and children's authors penned new and sometimes fanciful details about the girl hero from Rawa Ruska, newspaper readers read the final verdict on Stanka: "The young man, who makes an unusually smart impression, but who appears to be a pathological liar, is being held in police custody."[71] The fates of Stanka and Heddy Stritzko held a warning for children in Vienna: *participation* in the war effort was a more realizable goal than acts of individual heroism. Rosa Zenoch filled the role of child of the Empire, and as such was meant to be admired, but not emulated. The state needed her, but it also needed hundreds of thousands of young laborers and consumers to work anonymously for the cause.

---

[68] For a similar case of a student imagining a fellow student to be a dangerous spy, see the denunciation of Georg Widter, AdBDW 1914 St./9 #2538.
[69] NÖLA Präs. "P" 1914, 928. Report of Pol. Dir. Wien, 25 September 1914.
[70] *Illustriertes Wiener Extrablatt*, 24 September 1914, 6.   [71] *Ibid.*

The particular child

Studies of prewar Austrian politics show that the imperial child was not the only child being politically cultivated. National, class and religious interests had similarly recognized in children attractive symbols of the future, and children themselves had imbibed attitudes from across the political spectrum. As historian Gerald Stourzh has demonstrated for the late nineteenth century, tensions in nationally mixed areas of Austria often found outlet over questions of children and language of school instruction.[72] We know that supporters and opponents of Czech-language schools in Vienna had clashed in the streets in the prewar period. Working-class children in the city belonged to gangs (*Kinderbanden*) and defended their streets and neighborhood territories against enemy gangs. They also waged mini-war (*Kleinkrieg*) against unpopular landlords.[73] In addition, socialists and Catholics organized groups such as the socialist *Kinderfreunde* and the Catholic *Reichbund der katholischen deutschen Jugend Österreichs* that, while not anti-state, aimed to inculcate a particular *kind* of child.[74]

In 1915, a member of the German Reichstag spoke before an audience at Vienna's Urania hall about the importance of promoting "state feeling" (*Staatsgefühl*) over "national feeling" (*Nationalgefühl*). The speaker elicited "tremendous applause" when he claimed that historically, states with prominent "state feeling" thrived, while those with stronger "national feeling" declined.[75] His speech, on the education of citizens, addressed a problem peculiar to Austria, one that nation-states like Germany, Britain and France did not face: when speaking of children as *Zunkunftsmenschen* – future people – precisely *whose* future did the children represent? Those promoting the imperial child as a unifying element in war and as an antidote to Austria's nationalities conflicts glossed over the reality that children (and their schooling in particular) had been at the core of nationalist conflict in the Habsburg lands since the late

---

[72] Stourzh, *Die Gleichberechtigung*, 173.
[73] Hans Safrian and Reinhard Sieder, "Gassenkinder–Straßenkämpfer: Zur politischen Sozialisation einer Arbeitergeneration in Wien, 1900–1938," in Lutz Niethammer and Alexander von Plato (eds.), *"Wir kriegen jetzt andere Zeiten": Auf der Suche nach der Erfahrung des Volkes in nachfaschistischen Ländern* (Berlin: J. H. W. Dietz Nachf., 1985), 117–51, 121.
[74] On socialist youth, see Robert Wegs, *Growing Up Working Class: Continuity and Change Among Viennese Youth, 1890–1938* (University Park, PA: Penn State University Press, 1989); on Catholic youth, see Franz Maria Kapfhammer, "Die katholische Jugendbewegung," in Erika Weinzierl *et al.*, (eds.), *Kirche in Österreich, 1918–1965*, 2 vols. (Vienna: Verlag Herold, 1967), II, 23–53. Kapfhammer notes that the first German nationalist *Wandervogel* groups in Austria began in 1911, 28.
[75] WSLB ZAS Schulwesen II, *Neues Wiener Tagblatt*, (*Abend*) 30 November 1915.

nineteenth century.[76] In wartime Vienna, nationalism challenged the dream of using schools to promote "Austria's future."

As we have seen in discussions of food, children were very active in wartime street actions, often leading protests and engaging in violent skirmishes.[77] To the dismay of adults promoting "state feeling" among youth, Viennese children also acted as political agitators. In March, 1915, Vienna's Polish-language newspaper reported a disturbing incident: a fourteen-year-old Polish-speaker, Fräulein M., was attacked by two boys while window shopping. One of them shouted "Polish pig!" as he hit her in the face. The journalist lamented that such behavior from Viennese children was not uncommon: "[C]hildren are usually just a mirror of the attitudes of older people. I must add that I have already witnessed such behavior from Viennese children several times before. As the 'little patriots' heard that I speak Polish they ridiculed me."[78] He was correct that Viennese children were emulating the behavior of adults, who had few qualms themselves about targeting children as enemies. In the presence of Amalie Przybyla, a Polish refugee girl, women in a Viennese shop held Poles "responsible" for the fall of the fortress Przemysl in the east. "All the Poles should be burned. They didn't even help us," the women opined in the spring of 1915.[79] In a more direct encounter, a Polish-speaking high-school student reported that he had been heckled and beaten, denounced as a "Polish cow" and "Polish pig" in a bread line "not only by women, but also small children" who were angry that a Pole had gotten a loaf of bread.[80] The Polish youngsters being beaten by Viennese children were just as "Habsburg" as the legendary Rosa Zenoch, but this counted for little in the politics of the street. Some children similarly took the offensive against Jews in numerous skirmishes. For example, in March 1915, twelve "half-grown boys" gathered before the shop of Jewish retailer Wilhelm Offmann, spat on his display window, and shouted, "Look here – the Jews bake with white flour while we've got nothing to eat!" According to a security policeman on the scene, their actions met with "cheers from the Christian population."[81] By the fall of 1914 there were already between

[76] Stourzh argues that questions of where to send children to school and what sorts of schools to establish had become "ein Politikum erster Ordnung." *Die Gleichberechtigung*, 173.

[77] See chapter 1 on food demonstrations.

[78] ÖStA, AVA MdI Präs. carton 2130/22, #13241, *Wiedenski Kuryer Polski*, 4 March 1915.

[79] ÖStA, AVA MdI Präs 2130/22, #22597. Beschwerde wegen feindseligen Verhaltens sub-alterner behördlicher Organe gegenüber galizischen Flüchtlingen. Protokoll of Jedrzej Przybyla, 27 March 1915.

[80] *Ibid. Wied. Kuryer Polski*, 20 May 1915.

[81] 1914/5 k.k. Sicherheitswache Ottakring #8239, cited in Günther Bögl and Harald Seyrl, *Die Wiener Polizei im Spiegel der Zeiten* (Vienna: Edition S, 1993), 120.

60,000 and 70,000 refugees from eastern Habsburg provinces living in
Vienna, and these incidents suggest that children figured prominently in
making the newcomers feel unwelcome.[82]

Clashes between children of different nationalities were likely to occur in the streets rather than in schools because refugee children had
lowest priority in school placement.[83] But street fights were not a new
phenomenon in Vienna. In oral histories, working-class Viennese born
around the turn of the century have remembered with fondness the
sense of belonging to certain streets and neighborhoods, defending them
against outsiders.[84] Street fighting was an adventurous means of delineating one's community, but the demographic upheaval of war brought
many newcomers and transients to the city, upsetting children's align-
ments and calculations of who was "in" and "out" in the neighborhood.
While the state promoted the idea that the Viennese felt *Mitgefühl* for their
Mitbürger, and that shared suffering in wartime would actually strengthen
ties between peoples with different languages, customs and worldviews,[85]
some children simply added wartime refugees from other parts of Austria
to their lists of neighborhood "outsiders."

Showdowns between German- and Czech-speaking children in Vienna
reflect a larger breakdown of German-Czech relations during the war, and
highlight the increasing difficulty of raising a generation of "Austrian"
children. In July, 1914, as angry German-speakers smashed windows of
Czech schools in Vienna in "retaliation" for the murder of the Archduke
in Sarajevo at the hands of a Slav, imperial officials tried unsuccessfully to quell long-standing German–Czech tensions in the city.[86] In
August, the Ministry of the Interior issued the following order discour-
aging *nationale Hetze*, or national agitation: "In order to maintain the
patriotic unity of the population under the present war conditions, it is
ordered that national agitation be most energetically repressed through

[82] For war refugees, see Beatrix Hoffmann-Holter, *'Abreisendmachung': Jüdische Kriegsflüchtlinge in Wien 1914–1923* (Vienna: Böhlau, 1995); Klaus Hödl, *Als Bett-ler in die Leopoldstadt: Galizische Juden auf dem Weg nach Wien* (Vienna: Böhlau, 1994); David Rechter, "Galicia in Vienna: Jewish Refugees in the First World War," *Austrian History Yearbook* 28 (1997), 113–30; Walter Mentzel, "Weltkriegsflüchtlinge in Cisleithanien 1914–1918," in Gernot Heiss and Oliver Rathkolb (eds.), *Asylland Wider Willen: Flüchtlinge in Österreich im europäischen Kontext seit 1914* (Vienna: 1995), 17–44.
[83] WSLB ZAS Kriegsgefangene II (article misfiled) "Der Andrang zu den Mittelschulen." Some refugee children had private afternoon classes in their native languages; for place-ment in Viennese schools, they had lowest priority behind Viennese and Lower Austrian children, and military officers' children.
[84] Safrian and Sieder, "Gassenkinder–Straßenkämpfer," 120–25.
[85] *Staatliche Flüchtlingsfürsorge im Kriege 1914/15* (Vienna: k.k. Ministerium des Innern, Hof- und Staatsdruckerei, 1915), 4.
[86] See chapter 3 on the size and make-up of the Czech community.

all available means, regardless of which of the nations of Austria it might be directed against."[87] Vienna's Czech community ran several schools through its education association, "Komensky." Czech educators felt that Czech children in Vienna could not receive a proper education at German schools, because they did not foster "Czech sentiment," they neglected the mother tongue, they disregarded or falsified Czech contributions to Viennese history, and they instilled shame in Czech students. Educator Josef Sulík presented conversations between Czech parents and children, in which the latter rejected "being Czech" because of the negative stereotypes they learned in German school. "I'm Viennese. You are the Czechs!" he reported a girl saying to her parents.[88] Shortly before the war, the Komensky school in the working-class XX district was plundered by German-speaking schoolboys who broke windows and shouted, "Down with the Komensky school! We don't need a Bohemian school!" Czech parliamentarians blamed the hateful act on the influence of German schools: Responsibility for the crime lay not with the schoolboys themselves, but with the anti-Czech tirades they had heard in school.[89] The case of sixteen-year-old Bohuslav Simon suggests that the worldviews of some children were so nationally determined that "Austria" was not a consideration. Simon left Vienna without the permission of his parents and tried to join the French army. Rejected for military service because his torso measurement was too small, Simon later explained that he had run away "because I want to fight as a Czech and not as a German."[90]

Austrian school authorities worried that the ideal of the "Austrian child" was slipping away as schoolchildren became more embroiled in political discord on the home front. A group of left-leaning pedagogues issued a decree warning of the consequences of schooling a generation of children in the ethos of hate: "Hate, thirst for revenge, contempt and *Schadenfreude* for enemy nations and chauvinism for one's own nation have expanded to such a horrible degree that it is time to break the silence on this matter and gravely face those who bear the heavy responsibility for education."[91]

Although they may have involved only a small number of Viennese children, the incidents of street violence show that children were employing some of the political terminology of the times, expressing not only

[87] NÖLA Pras. "P" 1914, 611. Letter from MdI to Nö Statthalterei, 28 August 1914.
[88] Josef Sulík, *Proč máme vychováti sve děti v českých školách?* (Vienna: Vídeňská Matice, 1914), 4, 8, 13.
[89] ÖStA, AVA, MdI Präs., carton 2130/22 1911–1916. Interpellation filed by Karl Exner.
[90] ÖStA, AVA, MdI Präs, carton 2130/22, #6176.
[91] WSLB 145654B Pamphlet no. 3, "Aufruf an Eltern, Lehrer und Erzieher."

hatred of "enemy nations" (France, Britain, etc.) but intolerance of nations within the Habsburg state.

Rather than punishing young nationalist agitators in the streets, school officials sought instead to root out non-German nationalism in schools. World War I Vienna saw a rash of closings of Czech language schools on the premise that they fostered anti-state attitudes. With the Komenksy schools in Vienna closed, Czech teachers began offering private schooling in their homes. In October, 1915, police raided the apartment of Professor Franz Doubrava, who was running an afternoon middle school for up to 300 children. The German-speaking police depicted the Czech children as wild and disobedient nationalist creatures. The twenty children they found hiding in a classroom "began to scream and cry and hindered the further activities" of the investigators, and they were practiced in the art of "passive resistance."[92] Authorities also dissolved the Czech teachers' union of Lower Austria, whose headquarters was in Vienna. The teachers were accused of "agitation" and "anti-state behavior" for publishing postcards protesting the closing of Czech schools. One postcard showed a photo of a Komensky school with the caption "Sealed-off Czech school in Vienna"; another caption for the empty school building was "Monument to Austrian Justice."[93] German nationalists in Vienna claimed to have found Czech-language schoolbooks with treasonous content, and military authorities worried that the word "Austria" did not appear in Czech schoolbooks, but only the ambiguous *Vlast* (one's own country, fatherland).[94]

It was partly this ambiguous patriotic terminology, further muddled by problems of translation, that allowed children to be claimed as representatives of competing political projects. Those committed to the supranational state might use the term *Vaterland* to promote children as the future of Austria, but the term took on different meaning in nationalist circles. Each of the Habsburg languages had its own terms for state, nation, people, home and fatherland, for which children constituted ideal symbols. Throughout the war, countless groups made political appeals in the name of children. German nationalists wanted to instill in their children love of the fatherland and counted on children to regenerate the *Volkskraft*;[95] the Czech association *Domov* (home) urged, "The Czech children in Vienna should be organized towards the ideal of becoming

[92] ÖStA, AVA, MdI Präs. carton 2130/22, #23677. Report to the MdI, 30 October 1915.
[93] WSLB ZAS Rechtsleben u. polizeiliche Maßnahmen II, *Fremdenblatt*, 3 March 1916.
[94] ÖStA, AVA, MdI Präs. 1915/16, 15/3, 1645, #11474. Report from Bezirks-Polizei-Kommissariat Margareten, 21 May 1916; KA, MKSM 1916 28-3/1-3. K.u.k. MilKommando Leitmeritz to KM, 30 May 1916.
[95] WSLB ZAS Jugendfürsorge II, *Österreichische Volkszeitung*, 18 June 1916.

mature Czech persons";[96] socialists appropriated the child not for a particular nation, but for the ends of class struggle. "[T]he child," according to socialist Otto Glöckel, "should be the fulfillment of our hopes and dreams, the continuation and completion of our struggle."[97] In a feeble countermeasure to these appropriations of child-oriented terminology, the Ministry of Education endorsed a new children's magazine, *Young Austria*, published late in the war in the different languages of the Empire and ostensibly free of "party politics."[98] But the dream of the "Austrian child" – Franz Joseph's junior army of proto-citizens and loyal state subjects – faced serious competition from groups who recognized and capitalized on the symbolic potency of the child for particular political ends.

The school front

If we return to the War Ministry certificate commemorating children's sacrifice mentioned at the beginning of the chapter, we recall that this sacrifice took place symbolically at an altar. In reality, school was the state's chosen institution for mobilizing children for war. Schoolchildren's organized participation in the war effort can be broken into two broad categories: the labor they performed as "volunteers" and the influence they wielded as economic agents. Historian Christa Hämmerle has suggested that within the Austrian home front, a "school front" operated which led to the increasing encroachment of the state (*Verstaatlichung*) on childhood. She has argued that the Austrian state "instrumentalized" childhood, pulling children into the war economy through school projects and countless service actions.[99]

Organizing Austria's young "human capital" for war was a top priority for school officials, who noted the urgency of "utilizing for the state the slumbering energies of schoolchildren."[100] On August 7, 1914, they announced the creation of the Pupils Volunteer Corps, a program that put thousands of children to work in the service of the public good. The

---

[96] NÖLA Präs. "P" 1918 XVc, 2922. MdI report to Statthalterei, 29 July 1918.

[97] Glöckel, *Selbstbiographie*, 66.

[98] ÖStA, KA, MKSM 1917 29-4/3. The magazine was published in many different languages, but it had a circulation just over 12,000.

[99] Christa Hämmerle, "'Zur Liebesarbeit sind wir hier, Soldatenstrümpfe stricken wir...' Zu Formen weiblicher Kriegsfürsorge im Ersten Weltkrieg," (Ph.D. diss., University of Vienna, 1996), 314–16; also Christa Hämmerle, "Wir strickten und nähten Wäsche für Soldaten..." Von der Militarisierung des Handarbeitens im Ersten Weltkrieg," *L'Homme: Zeitschrift für Geschichte* 3, no. 1(1992), 88–128; and Christa Hämmerle (ed.), *Kindheit im Ersten Weltkrieg* (Vienna: Böhlau, 1993), 267.

[100] MfKuU 1914, cited in Hämmerle, "Wir strickten und nähten...", 98.

work was performed without pay, as a way of serving the state in its time of need. The language of the original call for child volunteers sounded similar to a call for military conscripts; volunteering was both a *duty* and an *honor*. Organized by their schools into brigades, pupils over fourteen were put to work in a number of capacities: as office aides in government and military agencies, as assistants at train stations, post and telegraph offices, as Red Cross workers and as agricultural hands in and around the city.[101] Especially lucky children served in the bicycle brigade, and all Pupils Volunteer Corps participants wore gold and black armbands identifying them in their public capacities. As the war dragged on and adult labor became scarcer, more and more jobs were deemed suitable for schoolchildren. For example, in 1917 children were assigned to Vienna's West, East and South train stations where their "service consisted of carrying or leading wounded or sick soldiers out of the train cars" and delivering them to hospitals and convalescent centers around the city.[102] Earlier fears that the children would be infected by disease-carrying soldiers were shelved in light of the labor shortage. The amount of time schoolchildren should be allowed to spend away from the classroom was contested: some educators argued for one "service day" per week, while others envisioned the work brigades all but replacing school, except for the "smaller sickly and weak pupils," who would be left behind in the classroom.[103]

But what of the children who had already left the classroom? At age fourteen, most Austrian youths left school for work, and were thus beyond the reach of school programs. For this set, military officials conceived of a training scheme that would improve physical fitness and instill imperial-patriotic values. The Austrian Defense Ministry issued a decree in the summer of 1915 that boys who had left school were "voluntarily" to join a military youth preparation course organized through existing youth groups. Historian H. Jürgen Ostler has outlined the program's many failings: working boys had little time or energy to spare for the training; parents were skeptical of militarization, some fearing it would lead to early conscription; and employers were loathe to release their

---

[101] ÖStA, AVA, MdI Präs. carton 1739, 19/1 #9854 "Aufruf betreffend die Gründung eines Schüler-Hilfskorps in Wien"; and *Verordnungsblatt für den Dienstbereich des k.k. niederösterreichischen Landesschulrates* 16, 15 August 1914.

[102] *Verordnungsblatt für den Dienstbereich des k.k. niederösterreichischen Landesschulrates* 1917, 5. Erlaß 32, 22 March 1917. See also Barbara Holzer, "Die Politische Erziehung und der vaterländische Unterricht in Österreich zur Zeit des Ersten Weltkrieges," (Diplomarbeit, University of Vienna, 1987), 150–53.

[103] "Die Hilfstätigkeit unserer Schuljugend für die Landwirte," *Verordnungsblatt für den Dienstbereich des k.k. niederösterreichischen Landesschulrates* 1915, Sonderbeilage V, 7.

young male workers for exercises.[104] In addition, the national and class affiliations of the youth groups through which the program operated rendered many of them unsuitable for the propagation of imperial-patriotic instruction.[105] The program stalled in 1916 and was canceled before the war's end. Officials at the Defense Ministry also worried about the "quantity and quality" of young female *Menschenmaterial*. For girls who had already left school, they envisioned a program of physical fitness training, "naturally taking into account the peculiarity of feminine nature, as well as the innate job of the woman as housewife and mother."[106] The program never got beyond the planning stage.

Too young for the Pupils Volunteer Corps, the 237,744 boys and girls in Viennese Volks- and Bürgerschulen were nonetheless organized by their schools for war service.[107] In the classroom, they assembled *Liebesgaben* ("gifts of love") for the soldiers in the field, with girls knitting socks, scarves and mittens and making bandages from recycled linens, and boys rolling cigarettes.[108] Children's labor was also key to the success of the various collection actions (metal, paper and cloth) on the home front and the initial flourishing of vegetable plots in Vienna's open spaces. Collecting would be "the equivalent of military service for youth," a way for children to express appreciation for soldiers in the field. Enthusiasts for the children's collection programs gushed that the innocence of the rosy-cheeked little collectors would make it hard for any adult to resist giving,[109] while detractors called this marshaling of innocence "exploitation" that led children to "extort" money from their parents in order to meet classroom quotas.[110]

Two aspects of children's war service are noteworthy here. First, children's contributions were not tangential to the waging of war. Military authorities calculated the number of garments schoolgirls could knit and figured this into their provisions. The banal reality that soldiers could not

---

[104] See the thorough study on military preparation for youth, H. Jürgen Ostler 'Soldatenspielerei'? Vormilitärische Ausbildung bei Jugendlichen in der österreichischen Reichs-hälfte der Donaumonarchie, 1914–1918 (MA thesis, Universität Hamburg, 1990).

[105] KA, MKSM 1915 29-4/6 Ministerium für Landesverteidigung to MKSM 5 October 1915. Sokol clubs (the Czech national-cultural association) were not to be given any role in the military youth preparation "because almost without exception these clubs have proven themselves to be politically unreliable."

[106] ÖStA, AdR, k.k. Min. f. soz. Verwaltung Präs. 1917 carton 44, #491, Ministerium für Landesverteidigung to MfKuU, 8 December 1917.

[107] Statistische Monatsbericht der Stadt Wien (October, 1914), 218.

[108] See Hämmerle, "Zur Liebesarbeit," on the reorientation for the purposes of war of "weibliche Handarbeiten," a traditional school subject for girls.

[109] WSLB ZAS Sammlungen II, Neues Wiener Tagblatt, 20 April 1915.

[110] Otto Glöckel described the collections as "extortion" and criticized the state for pressuring children to buy "completely useless things." Selbstbiographie, 182.

fight on the Russian front or in the Tyrolean mountains without socks and
scarves underlines the essential link between children's labor (performed
at school) and military success. Second, the "gifts of love" were not
sent by individual children from their homes, but always *via the school*.
Viennese school chronicles relay the importance of postal correspondence
between soldiers and school classes. For example, a boys' school chron-
icle reported that in 1914–15, pupils had received 120 cards from soldiers, thanking them for their "service." A soldier who came from the
pupils' very own neighborhood wrote to a school in Vienna's X district:

My dears!
Many thanks for the *Liebesgaben*. We distributed them with great pleasure. We're
in heavy combat with the Russians. Only 300–400 steps away.
A thousand greetings and thanks. Happy New Year!
Sender: Fr. Stepan, IR 75, from Vienna X, Favoritenstrasse 139.[111]

In such letters we see that one kind of unit – the school class – was
organized in the service of another – the infantry regiment.

The school was similarly the key institution for tapping the (albeit
limited) financial resources of children. Just as teachers encouraged children to solicit parental donations of cash and valuables to the state, local
school councils were instructed by the Ministry of the Interior to "rec-
ommend strongly" to their pupils the purchase of official war notebooks,
maps and pencils.[112] By 1915, the sale of war bonds to children at school
had generated a discourse about children as proto-citizens. War bond
sponsors had initially been unable to attract children because the min-
imum bond subscription – 100 crowns – was out of their reach. With
the third round of war bonds in 1915, authorities found a way to elicit
money from children while simultaneously binding them to the future of
the state: children would donate a small amount of pocket money and
take out a bank loan to cover the rest of the 100 crowns. The arrangement
met with glowing praise. During the fifteen to thirty years the bond holder
spent repaying the loan, this "young patriot" would revel in the memory
of having come to the aid of "the fatherland in its time of acute need."[113]
By facilitating the sale of war bonds to pupils, the Austrian schools
were "educating citizens of the state": giving money to the state was a

[111] *Dreizehnter Jahresbericht über die k.k. Staatsrealschule im X. Bezirk in Wien* (Vienna, 1915), 21. In the case of girls' schools, there was an effort to promote individual corre-spondence between a girl and "her" soldier. See Hämmerle on the World War I "love discourse" between front and home front, "Zur Liebesarbeit," 111–90.
[112] ÖStA, AVA MdI Varia, carton 71 1914–1918, KHB #2685, Kriegshilfsbüro to local school councils, 10 April 1915.
[113] *Die Schulen Niederösterreichs und die dritte österreichische Kriegsanleihe: Bericht der Anglo-Österreichischen Bank* (Vienna: Selbstverlag, n.d.), 6.

dry run (for boys, at least) for later giving their lives for the fatherland.[114] The Lower Austrian School Council sent a memo to school directors, explaining the educational benefits of war bonds. "The modern state citizen doesn't squirrel his money away in hard times of war, but rather lends it trustingly to the state" to be used "in defense of the Empire."[115] In the first two rounds of war bonds (before the "child bond" was invented) children bought bonds worth 2,589,000 crowns; in the third round this increased dramatically to 13,579,000 crowns. For many of the 82,740 Lower Austrian children who took part, buying a war bond was the first financial transaction of their lives, and it was one that bound their futures to that of the Habsburg state. The motto – *Konnt ich auch nicht Waffen tragen/ Half ich doch die Feinde schlagen*[116] – reveals how bonds offered Viennese pupils a way to participate in war, even if they could not emulate Rosa Zenoch's first-hand battle experiences.

If we look more closely at the role of schools in wartime, however, we see a discrepancy in what they could theoretically do to foster solid future citizens, and the resources they were actually allotted to carry out this task. The project of producing "children of the Empire" through the school system failed in Vienna because the schools were overburdened with a host of war-related assignments. School buildings and the prewar curriculum were sacrificed. In addition to organizing everything from bandage production to war bonds, the schools were expected to perform the following tasks: erect shrines in corridors and courtyards to honor the teachers or former pupils who "fell in the field of honor";[117] stage public ceremonies honoring soldiers;[118] clear space (usually in the gymnasium) for the city's bread commission to distribute ration cards; promote physical fitness so that the boys and girls of the younger generation could refortify the threatened *Volkskraft*;[119] adopt the tenets of "war pedagogy," which revamped the peacetime curriculum to take into account the "lessons of war," integrating war into math, physics, religion, history, geography and literature classes;[120] and more generally, gather

---

[114] *Ibid.*, 7.
[115] K.k. Nö Landesschulrat to school directors, 23 October 1915, cited in *Die Schulen Niederösterreichs*, 10.
[116] *Ibid.*, 3.
[117] *Verordnungsblatt für den Dienstbereich des k.k. nö. Landesschulrates* 1916, Stück XVI, 111.
[118] WSLB 67052 C Kriegssammlung Konvolut 2. K.k. Bezirksschulrat Wien to school directors, 30 June 1916.
[119] ÖStA, AdR k.k. Min. f. soz. Verwaltung Präs 1917, carton 44, #491. K.k. Ministerium für Landesverteidigung to k.k. MfKuU, 8 December 1917.
[120] ÖStA, KA, MKSM 1915 33-1/3. MKSM response to KM memo, 6 June 1915; WSLB ZAS Jugendfürsorge I, decree of Education Minister Hussarek, in *Reichspost*, 3 July 1915. Sample lesson plans adopting *Kriegspädagogik* in *Verordnungsblatt für den Dienstbereich des k.k. nö. Landesschulrates* 1915, Sonderbeilage VIII, 10, and VI, 6.

together unsupervised children dislocated by war and provide appropriate activities and supervision.[121] To perform these varied tasks, schools were allotted far fewer resources than in peacetime.

The Army High Command proposed placing elementary schools, which had been administered on the local level, under state control in order to facilitate proto-military instruction and to weed "politically unreliable elements" out of the teaching staff.[122] Social Democrats were most vocal in protesting this militarization of school life. They questioned the appointment of an active military officer to the Lower Austrian school council, criticized school field trips to the mock trenches in the Prater, and proposed recalling all conscripted teachers back to their teaching posts. Contemporaries estimated that 30–40 percent of the male middle-school teachers in Austria had been conscripted into the armed forces.[123] The same pedagogical journal promoting school shrines, increased physical fitness and a bolstered war curriculum reported that in the years 1914–17, 286 male teachers in Lower Austria had died for the fatherland.[124] The shortage of actual teachers coincided with some pedagogues' increasing conviction that war itself was a teacher, the great *Lehrmeister* of the times. The Ministry of Defense issued the perplexing order that, "Lack of building space, training grounds and equipment should be no excuse for neglecting physical education."[125] Facing these conflicting demands placed on schools, the Central Association of Viennese Teachers began to complain about being expected to accomplish more with less.

Besides the militarization of the curriculum and depletion of the teacher pool, the school buildings themselves had been taken over for military administration and hospitals. By March 1915, 260,000 wounded soldiers had been taken to Vienna's 306 "hospitals," only 40 of which were actual hospitals; the remaining 266 were classified as "other hospital accommodations," more often than not vacated school buildings.[126] Even the flagship orphanage of the 1908 "Everything for the Child" campaign was transformed into an officers' hospital. To make up for lost space, many Viennese schools were running double shifts, which meant that the

[121] WSLB ZAS Jugendfürsorge I, *Reichspost*, 4 March 1916.
[122] Christoph Führ, *Das k.u.k. Armeeoberkommando und die Innenpolitik in Österreich, 1914–1917* (Graz, Vienna, Cologne: Böhlau, 1968), 132.
[123] WSLB ZAS Schulwesen I, *Neue Freie Presse*, n.d.
[124] *Verordnungsblatt für den Dienstbereich des k.k. nö Landesschulrates* 1917, 11–12.
[125] ÖStA, AdR k.k. Min. f. soz. Verwaltung Präs. 1917, carton 44. #491. K.k. Ministerium für Landesverteidigung to k.k. MfKuU, 8 December 1917.
[126] AdBDW 1915 V/23 #7535. Report from Polizei-Präs. to MdI, 5 March 1915, "Die Wirkungen des Krieges in Wien." Vienna had 12 state hospitals, 2 military garrison hospitals, 14 military reserve hospitals and 12 Red Cross reserve hospitals. The remaining 266 were "*sonstigen Spitalsunterkünften.*"

school day and class schedule were shortened for individual students by as much as a third or a half. In 1916, the teachers' association demanded – apparently without effect – that as many school buildings as possible be returned to their original functions.[127] They pointed out that the Habsburg state could not succeed in using the school system to produce loyal citizen-subjects if the children were not physically in school.

In his influential account of the fall of the Habsburg Empire, Oskar Jászi cites the absence of supranational, state-affirming civic education in local schools as one of the keys to its demise.[128] His argument is borne out by the experience of Viennese schools during the war. From a pedagogical standpoint, it was not the long-overdue imperial civics instruction, but war itself that came to dominate the curriculum. The many war-oriented projects and actions that were meant to utilize children's labor and economic resources, and simultaneously link them emotionally to the state, had depended on a well-functioning school system. War may have been a great *Lehrmeister* in theory, but in practice the schools were critically deprived of personnel and materials. By 1917, the old rhetoric of a state deeply committed to its children, and hence its future, could still be heard in some quarters. Emperor Karl and Empress Zita, the new imperial pair who succeeded Franz Joseph in late 1916, harked back to the old Emperor's "Everything for the Child" campaign. They appealed to children to help build for the future a "new, solid, unshakable Austria."[129] But the wished-for children of the empire – hundreds of thousands of anonymous Viennese Rosa Zenochs working on behalf of a supra-national state – were developing instead into menacing "war-children" with political allegiances and social behaviors threatening to that state.

The delinquent child

One drawback during the war of using the child as a symbol or mascot for state, nation or class was that children were, quite literally, becoming less attractive. The unblemished innocence of childhood was acquiring physical blemishes. A typical early World War I postcard of a rosy, cherub-faced baby that read "I'm a war boy!" (see plate 5.6) bore little resemblance to real war babies, who neither looked so healthy nor held such promise for the future.

---

[127] WSLB ZAS Jugendfürsorge II, *Die Zeit*, 15 June 1916.
[128] See Jászi, *Dissolution*, 433–50.
[129] ÖStA, AdR 1918 k.k. Min. f. soz. Verwaltung – Jugendfürsorge carton 2472, #6912. Pamphlet "Schule und Vaterland. Zeitschrift für bodenständige Jugenderziehung und Volksbildung in Österreich" (January, 1917).

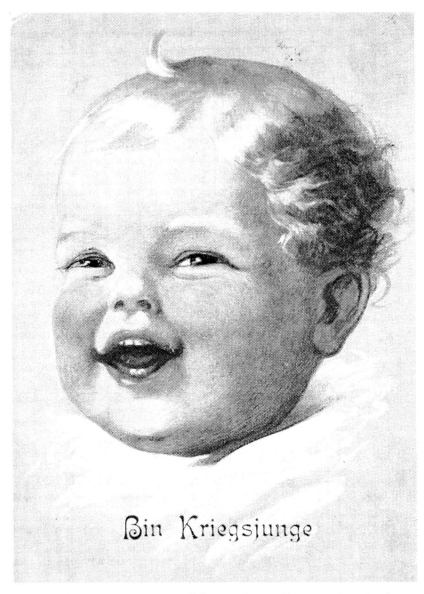

Plate 5.6. "I'm a war boy!" Source: Postcard in possession of author.

Table 5.1 *Deaths of school-aged children
in Vienna*

	6–10-year-olds	11–15-year-olds
1911	612	445
1912	615	455
1913	659	392
1914	646	422
1915	754	469
1916	722	525
1917	729	561
1918	1099	896
1919	801	577

Source: Pirquet, *Volksgesundheit*, I, 172.

During the course of the war, doctors published a stream of articles on the deterioration of children's bodies, brought on by lack of food, medical care and supervision. In the spring of 1918, a study of 56,849 Viennese children revealed that only 4,637 could be classified as completely healthy. Of the children admitted to the Viennese Children's Clinic the same year, 88 percent were underweight, some of them drastically.[130] An epidemic of bedwetting suggested that "an unusually large number of children and youths" were experiencing psychological disturbances.[131] Viennese teacher M. Walter recalled the general appearance of his students: "Pale faces, tired facial expressions, no shine in the eyes, poor postures, these signs indicated deficient nourishment and extreme deprivation."[132]

Over a four-month period in 1915, Viennese police found thirteen baby corpses abandoned in various locations around the city.[133] These discoveries focused attention on children's deaths, and the number of school-aged children dying in Vienna continued to climb during each year of the war. Even discounting the extraordinarily high number of deaths from the influenza epidemic of 1918, children's death rates continued to rise into 1919, as seen in table 5.1.

---

[130] Pirquet, *Volksgesundheit*, I, 157, 154.
[131] ÖStA AdR 1918 "Kind"1001-, carton 1590, #1789–18, Komitee für Jugendgerichtshilfe to MdI, 4 June 1918.
[132] Pirquet, *Volksgesundheit*, I, 152.
[133] AdBDW, Nachlaß Pamer Box 3: Akten. "Uebersicht der Fälle über Kindesmord, Kindesweglegung und Abtreibung der Leibesfrucht." Abortion was illegal in Austria, but Viennese police discovered several abortion rings operating in the city during the war.

Those who survived belonged to a "seriously damaged generation already in the making," according to Otto Glöckel.[134] Coinciding with the sad decline of children's bodies was a perceived radical decline in their behavior. Just as bodies and behavior had been discursively paired at the beginning of the war (healthy, vibrant creatures with sweet, innocent temperaments), the degeneration of children's health was linked to the behavioral plague of the Viennese home front: delinquency.

A delinquency panic ricocheted through the Viennese press in early 1916. From that point on, children were rarely discussed in public without reference to the delinquency buzzwords *Verrohung* or *Verwahrlosung*. Semantically, "children" became more clearly delineated from "youth." In the prewar period, Austrian social reformers had broken young people into four age brackets (0–6, 6–10, 10–14 and 14–18) for statistical purposes. Although "youth" connoted the life phase between fourteen and eighteen, youth welfare (*Jugendfürsorge*) was nearly always discussed in tandem with child protection (*Kinderschutz*).[135] In the wartime delinquency scare, "youth" became equated more closely with corruption, while any lingering fantasies of youthful innocence were reserved for "children." But the differences between the youth and children were not always easy to detect in practice. Stunted growth resulting from malnutrition made it difficult for adults to assess the ages of child offenders. Because Viennese children were "physically stuck" according to Dr. August Bohm of the Municipal Health Department, police doctors were underestimating the ages of delinquents in their care. Twelve- to fourteen-year-olds were mistaken for eight- to ten-year-olds.[136]

Earlier optimism about the regenerative spirit of children and the promise they held for the future dissolved into fears of a coming generation of war-damaged degenerates. Regardless of whose future the children represented, adult commentators predicted a generation of "bad seeds" and lamented a series of missed opportunities. Children who with the "appropriate assistance" could have become "useful ... even distinguished members of the human community and the state" were instead

---

[134] Glöckel, *Selbstbiographie*, 177, reprint of parliamentary speech, 12 July 1917.
[135] See the essays in Joseph M. Baernreither (ed.), *Die Ursachen, Erscheinungsformen und die Ausbreitung der Verwahrlosung von Kindern und Jugendlichen in Österreich*. Schriften des Ersten Österreichischen Kinderschutzkongresses, 2 vols. (Vienna: k.k. Hof- und Staatsdruckerei, 1907). Gustav Schuster v. Bonnott estimated the ratio of delinquency cases in prewar Vienna by ages 6–10, 10–14, 14–18 to be 3:11:15. Bonnott, "Welches sind die Ursachen und Erscheinungsformen der Verwahrlosung von Kindern und Jugendlichen?" in Baernreither, 37–8. For historical background, see Peter Feldbauer, *Kinderelend in Wien: Von der Armenkinderpflege zur Jugendfürsorge, 17.–19. Jahrhundert* (Vienna: Gesellschaftskritik, 1980).
[136] Pirquet, *Volksgesundheit*, I, 153.

developing into "rejects" of society and "enemies" of the state.[137] A journalist wrote caustically, "So much for the 'Century of the Child'... we
are on the verge of raising a stock of moral weaklings, criminals and
idiots!"[138] A fundraising newsletter for a children's home tried to frighten
wealthy donors with fears of lower-class monsters growing in their midst.
In the "social battles" of the future, these "enemies" of society would
become the "dangerous, terrible opponents" of today's children of the
upper classes.[139] In these dire predictions, the child retained great symbolic value, but the thing it symbolized had changed dramatically.

The 1916 delinquency scare in Vienna coincided with similar discussions in Germany. Vienna's was, at least in part, a scare "borrowed" from
the Berlin press, which had been focusing attention on the same issue. The
difference was that the Berliners had statistics upon which to base their
fears; the juvenile courts had compiled frightening accounts of the rise
in youth crime.[140] In Vienna, these same statistics were not available because the juvenile court system was in its infancy when the war broke out,
and Dr. Kesseldorfer, the city's "most experienced and beloved juvenile
jurist," had been conscripted and had "unfortunately been missing in
action for some time."[141] So Viennese journalists borrowed the Berlin
statistics, supplemented them with their own observations from the streets
and launched a public crusade against youth delinquency.

A wide range of actions fell under the rubric of delinquency: stealing,
vandalizing property, smoking, sexual promiscuity, reading "smut" literature, visiting the cinema, loitering, traveling in gangs, playing billiards
and dominoes in cafés, going to the racetrack and wasting money were
some of the most common symptoms of the "new" social malady. If we
look closely at this list, we see that many of the complaints against children centered on their increased *public presence* resulting from wartime
changes in family and school schedules. Initial reports condemned the
growing visibility of co-ed "street gangs that are not always of a harmless
nature." Adults who had once found children "playing war" to be irre-
sistibly sweet now noted the growing recklessness of these child warriors.
A reader wrote to the *Neue Freie Presse* to complain that every day he
could witness from his window in Vienna's XV district "how the youths
amuse themselves with battle games, throwing stones with no concern

[137] ÖStA, AdR 1918 k.k. Min. f. soz. Verwaltung. Jugendfürsorge carton 2472, #170.
[138] WSLB ZAS Jugendfürsorge II, *Österreichische Volkszeitung*, 25 June 1916.
[139] ÖStA, AdR 1918 k.k. Min. f. soz. Verwaltung. Jugendfürsorge carton 2472, #170.
[140] See Ute Daniel, *The War from Within: German Working-Class Women in the First World War*, transl. Margaret Ries (Oxford: Berg, 1997), ch. 4; curiously, Franz Exner's postwar study *Krieg und Kriminalität in Österreich* also refers to German statistics in dis-
cussing Austrian crime rates.
[141] WSLB ZAS Jugendfürsorge I, *Die Zeit*, 20 February 1916.

about whether passers-by will be endangered . . . I was recently witness as a man was struck on the chin by a stone and he vented his indignation at the adolescent boys . . ."[142] Another Viennese resident described the city as a lawless war zone, run by child bandits lacking "morals, ethics and culture." In this Vienna, vandals had destroyed parks by carving up trees, breaking benches and littering. The youths spat, stole signs and painted graffiti wherever they pleased. This writer called for the formation of a citizen militia to combat youth destruction, the "shouting, rough-housing, stone throwing and other incivilities" that took place on the way to and from school.[143] Wartime police reports note countless riots and skirmishes carried out by "Schulpflichtigen" – children not on their way *to* school, but who should have been *in* school at the time they committed their deeds.

At an average school in peacetime, according to socialist school reformer Otto Glöckel, two or three students per year might commit misdemeanors that led to court appearances. By 1917, he estimated the number to be thirty-six. In one school in Vienna's V district, forty students had been arrested, thirty-five of them for stealing.[144] Police noted an increased participation in crimes by children of the middle (*bürgerliche*) classes. In the prewar period, they felt that only "deeply pathological elements" of the middle-classes had engaged in criminal behaviors, whereas the economic hardship of war drove middle-class children without "observable psychic disturbances" into crime.[145]

Wartime public disturbances, or "excesses" in police terminology, almost always included large numbers of children. In April, 1917, "groups of children and women," angry over a butter shortage, swarmed streets in the XVI district. Schoolboys broke the windows of one business and when the owner emerged wielding a broom, they snatched the broom and swung it over their heads as a trophy. At a nearby store, more children broke windows and stole cans of sardines and chocolates from a display case. Three boys and a girl were arrested, along with a female bystander who had praised their work.[146] Wartime police reports record countless incidents of similar street violence involving even hundreds of children at a time. In a typical report, dated July 16, 1917, we read that at 9 o'clock in

---

[142] "Gefährliche Kriegsspiele," *Neue Freie Presse*, 4 November 1915, 1.
[143] Franz Stiedl, *Volkspolizei! Ein Vorschlag für den ethischen, moralischen und kulturellen Wiederaufbau* (Vienna, 1918).
[144] Glöckel, *Selbstbiographie*, 188, reprint of parliamentary education committee report, 8 November 1917.
[145] Pirquet, *Volksgesundheit*, I, 254.
[146] ÖStA, AVA MdI Präs. 22 (1917–1918) carton 2131, #5661. Police chief Gorup to MdI Präs., 4 April 1917.

the evening around 300 school-aged children moved through the streets towards the municipal offices of the working-class XVI district shouting "We are hungry!" On the way they vandalized several bakeries and broke nine windows. No perpetrators were caught and the children scattered when security agents intervened.[147]

Commentators located two roots of wartime delinquency, one predictable, the other perplexing. In the first instance, children were running wild because they had no home supervision. They suffered from the "absent father, weak mother" syndrome of the World War I family. In this situation, even if the mother was present at home, she could not make up for the loss of the conscripted father because women by nature held little disciplinary authority. While fathers could not be blamed for being away at the front, mothers were routinely chastised for "apathy" towards their children: not picking them up from day-care, not setting a curfew and not cooperating with childcare professionals. A director of a Viennese childcare center complained, for instance, that only ten out of 180 parents showed up for parents' night.[148] Gendered notions of parenting were so ingrained that even dedicated mothers could not overcome the authority barrier because "in most cases children obey motherly kindness less than fatherly strictness."[149] Injunctions to children to obey their mothers relied on a father figure in the shadows. Children no longer had to "fear the stronger hand of the father," but they were told to read his authority in the eyes of their mother.[150] Bad behavior was read as a sign of children's unwillingness to *sacrifice*, and thus as a dishonor to soldiers. "The way some children now conduct themselves on the streets is not just inappropriate," scolded one children's author, "it is beneath the dignity of the serious times we are now living through."[151] Children were continually reminded of the Great Reckoning which would follow the Great War: the moment when father returned from the front to inquire, "And how were the children?"

The second most frequently cited cause of child delinquency was popular culture – films and inexpensive editions of "smut literature" in particular. It is paradoxical that in a war that produced mass death and maimed bodies, the latter of which Viennese children could see up close as they performed their "war service" guiding the wounded to hospitals, detective films and romantic comedies were thought to be at the root of moral

---

[147] AdBDW 1917 St./1 #47450.
[148] WSLB ZAS Jugendfürsorge I, *Die Zeit*, 20 February 1916.
[149] WSLB ZAS Jugendfürsorge II, *Österreichische Volkszeitung*, 6 May 1916.
[150] Eckardt, *An das Kind des Kriegers*, 6.
[151] Bernhard Merth, *Ein ernstes Wort an unsere Jugend in der Kriegszeit* (Vienna: Verlag von Heinrich Kirsch, 1916), 5.

decay.[152] Protests against war were illegal in Vienna; protests against the insidious influence of cinema were not. Educators counted up the number of violent or morally dubious actions children viewed at the cinema, and attributed delinquency to this licentiousness in film. Catholic critics thundered in parliament about the continued corruption of young people in venues of popular culture run by "Jews and their press":

> In words and in print, in speeches and in lewd and lascivious performances, from theater with its many frivolous French love and adultery scenes, to the popular music halls, cabarets and cinemas, in the widespread smut literature, to the mass proliferation of erotic pictures, [they] attempt to reach the youth.[153]

Government authorities published a list of 171 banned children's books, and associations tried to convince children to borrow from the more wholesome collections at their libraries.

In the summer of 1916, the Lower Austrian government issued a set of decrees in response to the delinquency scare. Children under sixteen were banned from the following: smoking in public or buying tobacco products; loitering in public places in the evening; visiting coffeehouses, bars or other places of "public amusement"; going to films not approved for children; and playing cards in public places. They were further banned from racing venues of all sorts and from "begging in any form, particularly door-to-door."[154] Officials debated extending the leisure-time prohibitions to include seventeen- and in some cases even eighteen-year-olds.

Despite the hand-wringing and voluminous textual output of adults concerned with declining health and delinquency, and despite the birth in wartime of new local, regional and imperial agencies committed to child and youth welfare,[155] children never regained the position they held in 1914 as symbols of a state that would regenerate itself through war. In fact, the delinquency epidemic, ostensibly a "new" war-related malady, actually marked a return to prewar concerns over children's and

---

[152] See chapter 2 for discussion of how "Kinobesucher" became synonymous with delinquent.

[153] *Stenographische Protokolle.* Haus des Abgeordneten, 64/XXII, 26 February 1918, 2455/I. Anfrage Abgeordneter Wohlmeyer.

[154] NÖLA Präs. 1920, VIIa, XIV-204b, 178. Report of the Ministerium für soziale Fürsorge on youth laws in Austrian crownlands.

[155] During the war, youth welfare organizations were streamlined and centralized, away from the "arbitrariness" of private charities and towards "objective" state agencies. WSLA M. Abt. 207, A 16/11 #2049, Memorandum from Verband für freiwillige Jugendfürsorge. In 1916, the Municipal Youth Office was founded and in 1917, the new Ministry of Health and Social Welfare was founded under the guidance of child advocate Baernreither. See Harald Bachmann, *Joseph Maria Baernreither, 1845–1925: Der Werdegang eines altösterreichischen Minister und Sozialpolitikers* (Neustadt a.d. Aisch: Kommissionsverlag Ph. C. W. Schmidt, 1977).

youth waywardness. Drawing on the premise that life springs from death, Henriette Herzfelder, a familiar figure in the bourgeois women's movement and campaigner for child welfare, had enthusiastically predicted in 1916 that a "new Austria" bearing the face of a child would emerge from the blood and flames of war.[156] Her prediction came true, but not in the way she had anticipated: the war did produce a "new" Austria and it did have a child's face, but this new state was weak and the child was sick.

During the war the malleable image of the child had been pivotal in Austrians' changing evaluations and interpretations of the imperial state and the meaning and effects of war. The symbol of the child was attractive to adults of various political persuasions precisely because the child as a political being did not have an authorized voice. The child was the quintessential *represented* political subject, spoken for but not speaking. It is no wonder, then, that the factor uniting all of the specific behaviors cited in the delinquency scare was children's unruly *public presence*. In food riots and in many other street activities – socializing, loitering, playing, fighting – children's vocal visibility seemed to threaten public order. Without celebrating World War I as a moment at which children "found political voices," we can nonetheless see that their street actions and palpable public presence did challenge adults' employment of idealized, symbolic children for political ends.

Despite recurring, patriotic claims about communal responsibility for Austria's children during the war, the only way to care for Austria's children in the economic chaos of the immediate postwar period was to send them out of Austria. Between 1919 and 1921 a massive foreign rescue mission transported 200,000 Austrian children, or one in three, to foreign countries for "revitalization," rest and medical attention. The most frequent destinations were Switzerland, which took in 58,967 Austrian children, and Holland, which took in 52,661 over three years.[157] Other children received foreign assistance at home: the American Children's Aid Project, the American Red Cross and the Anglo-American Society of Friends organized feeding programs to give Viennese children daily warm meals.[158] Photographs of Viennese children taken by American relief workers document the devastation war had taken on the bodies of the young. (See plate 5.7.) How could these thin, misshapen boys, examples

---

[156] "Die Fürsorge für die weibliche Jugend," *Pädagogisches Jahrbuch* 39 (1916), 90.

[157] Friedrich Reischl, "Die ausländische Kinderhilfe in Wien," in Pirquet (ed.), *Volksgesundheit* I, 365; see also Isabella Matauschek, "Die dänische Kinderhilfsaktion für Wien, 1919–1938" (MA thesis, University of Vienna, 1995).

[158] *Wiens Kinder und Amerika: Die amerikanische Kinderhilfsaktion 1919* (Vienna: Gerlach & Wiedling, 1920), 78.

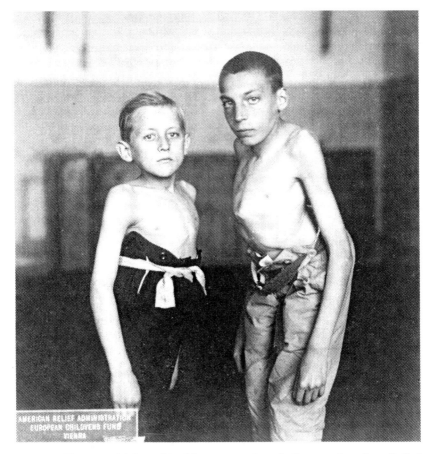

Plate 5.7. Malnourished boys at war's end. Source: American Relief
Administration Collection, Hoover Institution Archives.

of what Vice-Mayor Max Winter feared was a "feeble and decaying generation," replenish Austria's male stock?[159] How could they be counted
on to revive Austria's "painfully maimed *Volkskörper*?"[160]

The dire condition of Austria's children at the time the foreign rescue efforts began is recorded in a 1919 film *The Misery of Children in
Vienna*.[161] Filming in the wake of war and using the motif of the child

---

[159] Hoover Institution Archives, Gilchrist B. Stockton, box 8. America's Relief Work
Action, misc. brochure, 2 June 1919, inauguration of children's kitchen.

[160] Wilhelm Winkler, *Die zukünftige Bevölkerungsentwicklung Deutschösterreichs und der
Anschluss an Deutschland* (Vienna: Hölder, 1919), 3.

[161] Österreichisches Filmarchiv, *Alltag in der öst.-ung. Monarchie* series, roll 6, *Das Kinderelend in Wien*, I (1919).

to depict the unhappy fate of Austria, the filmmakers use before-and-after shots to construct a historical arc of the preceding five years. They register the devastation of war in the bodies of children at a Viennese primary school. In 1914 we see robust, smiling children, in clean uniforms, performing calisthenics for the camera. With no footage from the war years, we return to the children in 1919. Barefoot, heads hung low, wearing tattered rags, they shuffle past in rows, their destination unclear. They use crutches and some appear to be missing limbs.[162] Even more desperate was the situation for children born during the war; the film-makers move on to a children's clinic, where sickly newborns and grossly deformed toddlers are held up for the camera. Their exhaustion mirrors Austria's. Postwar writers continued to employ organic metaphors of the state, describing the events of 1918 not as Austria's defeat, but as its exhaustion (*Erschöpfung*). The message of the film is two-fold: first, the war had taken a heavy toll on children's bodies and minds, and second, the future of Austria, as represented in its youth, did not look promising.

---

[162] See Seth Koven, "Remembering and Dismemberment: Crippled Children, Wounded Soldiers, and the Great War in Britain," *AHR* 99, no. 4 (October 1994), 1,167–202, for the symbol of the crippled child and national recovery.

6   The "fatherless society": home-front men and imperial paternalism

In assessing the breakdown of Vienna in 1918, some residents attributed the palpable social decomposition of the city to a corresponding familial decomposition. Franz Stiedl, for one, described the city as an ethical, moral and cultural wasteland. According to Stiedl, a political unknown, Vienna faced a crisis of authority, the consequences of which threatened its physical infrastructure and the well-being of its future generations. He wrote a detailed plan for saving the city and sent it to dozens of imperial, regional and local government officials. Summing up the features of Vienna's decline, Stiedl sounded the alarm of youth delinquency familiar to us from the previous chapter. He wrote, "Our youth have become savage, corrupted morally, mentally and physically... Petty crimes and felonies have increased so greatly that the police and courts are overloaded, the detention and so-called reform facilities are overfilled." As an order-loving, law-abiding citizen, he found the lawlessness of late-war Vienna intolerable and spewed pages of complaints about the decay of public life in the capital: people loitering, stealing, vandalizing park benches, destroying public signs, joy riding on car fenders, spitting, hanging out the windows on trams, throwing stones, painting graffiti, hanging unauthorized posters, littering and generally making noise. Vienna had become a city of disorder and insecurity, where dead dogs lay in the streets and good citizens could no longer go to the park. For Stiedl, a self-proclaimed "practical family father," loss of *authority* was coterminous with the fall of Vienna. War seemed to have robbed men of the prewar powers they had wielded as fathers, city administrators and civil servants, and Stiedl proposed creating a citizen militia to recover this lost authority.[1]

Stiedl, whose assessment drew on wartime debates about manhood, authority and paternalism in Vienna, was not alone in believing that something very important had been lost over the course of the war. While

---

[1] Franz Stiedl, *Volkspolizei! Ein Vorschlag für den ethischen, moralischen und kulturellen Wiederaufbau* (Vienna, 1918), 3–20.

his unconventional proposal to create a citizen militia to restore "order" was never enacted, the loss of authority it addressed was nevertheless a central concern for police, family experts and many ordinary residents. The public discourse of wartime Vienna was full of references to missing fathers: pamphlets warned children to behave while their fathers were away; women were urged to cope as best they could without male authority in the household; educators discussed the damage boys in lower grades might suffer with the introduction of female teachers. The motif of the "lost father" operated at different levels. In concrete terms, many actual Viennese fathers had become war casualties; of the 25,616 Viennese men who died in service between 1914 and 1918, about 70 percent were married and many had left behind orphans.[2] In a more general sense, the dissolution of social order in the city that we have seen in previous chapters – food riots, youth delinquency and a marked decline of civility – aroused fears that traditional male authority had become a casualty of war, and that Vienna had become, in the words of contemporary psychoanalyst Paul Federn, a "fatherless society."[3]

Two separate but related developments contributed to contemporary fears about the "fatherless society." In prewar society, one of the defining attributes of a man had been the possession of authority, defined as the (perceived) power to make and enforce rules. Within families, this enforcer had been the father; within society at large it had been city fathers, policemen, military and civil servants, topped by the paternal figure of the Emperor. Max Weber's traditional, but still useful definition of "patriarchalism" held that the authority of "the father, the husband, the senior of the house" over wife and children resembled the authority of the "prince (*Landesvater*) over the 'subjects.'"[4] During the war, ordinary men and emperors, once united in their status as *paterfamilias*, saw their authority decline. For ordinary men, a new definition of manliness – a martial masculinity – replaced older definitions of civilian manhood in which patriarchal authority had been an important component. Martial masculinity combined a number of attributes (bodily strength, courage, loyalty, comradeship) but paternal authority was not among

[2] Wilhelm Winkler, *Die Totenverluste der öst.-ung. Monarchie nach Nationalitäten* (Vienna: L. W. Seidl & Sohn, 1919), 19. This death figure is from December, 1917. See also Reinhard J. Sieder, "Behind the Lines: Working-Class Family Life in Wartime Vienna," in Richard Wall and Jay Winter, eds. *The Upheaval of War: Family, Work and Welfare in Europe, 1914–1918* (Cambridge: Cambridge University Press, 1988), 109–38, 131.

[3] Paul Federn, *Die Vaterlose Gesellschaft: Zur Psychologie der Revolution* (Leipzig and Vienna: Anzengruber-Verlag Brüder Suschitzky, 1919).

[4] Max Weber, *From Max Weber: Essays in Sociology*, ed. and transl. H. H. Gerth and C. Wright Mills (New York: Galaxy, 1958), 296.

them.[5] As society's new holder of authority, the fighter replaced the father.

A different expectation undermined the authority of the *Landesvater*. Although both wartime Emperors were soldiers, and, as heads of the Habsburg armed forces, could arguably have met a standard of martial manliness (albeit of a heavily costumed sort), it was their fatherly authority that was most in demand by ordinary people. As Viennese perceived a breakdown of order in the city – evidenced by rampant rule-breaking and ineffective rule-making – and experienced declining material conditions within their own families, they looked increasingly to the Emperors for concrete fatherly assistance. The inability of the Emperors, who were, after all, *symbolic* father figures, to offer real assistance to the "state family" undermined the image of the good father that had long been a staple of Habsburg legitimacy.

Changing perceptions of authority on the home front offer a new angle for the study of manhood in World War I. Historians of World War I have described in various ways a general collapse of patriarchal order that accompanied defeat in Germany and Austria. On an individual level, a crisis of masculinity developed when soldiering men returned to their families. Reinhard Sieder describes demobilization as "the return of the wounded patriarchs." Men were wounded psychically, like Klaus Theweleit's angry Freikorps members, or physically, like Robert Whalen's invalid veterans. Helga Embacher describes emasculated soldiers, "who had to return as losers, hungry, louse-ridden or even as invalids." Elisabeth Domansky paints a similar picture, stating, "On the one hand, there was a large number of fatherless families; and on the other, fatherly authority seems to have changed in those families to which men returned." At the societal level, the collapse of empires, abdication of emperors, demise of prewar military and bureaucratic structures, and rising revolutionary spirit in central Europe entailed a patriarchal crisis for society as a whole. "[T]he collapse of the Austro-Hungarian Monarchy," Sieder suggests, "was in fact the collapse of a male society . . ."[6] In these accounts, historians have

---

[5] See Ernst Hanisch, "Die Männlichkeit des Kriegers: Das österreichische Militärstrafrecht im Ersten Weltkrieg," in Thomas Angerer *et al.* (eds.), *Geschichte und Recht: Festschrift für Gerald Stourzh zum 70. Geburtstag* (Vienna: Böhlau, 1999), 313–38. Hanisch sees the new manliness – "Nur der wehrhafte Mann ist wahrhaft männlich" – as a nineteenth-century development, 316. I argue that the ramifications of the new manliness for male authority within the civilian realm first became manifest during World War I.

[6] See Klaus Theweleit, *Male Fantasies*, 2 vols., transl. Stephen Conway (Minneapolis: University of Minnesota Press, 1987); Robert Weldon Whalen, *Bitter Wounds: German Victims of the Great War, 1914–1939* (Ithaca: Cornell University Press, 1984); on the return and reintegration of war invalids see also Seth Koven, "Remembering and Dismemberment: Crippled Children, Wounded Soldiers and the Great War in Great Britain," *AHR* 99,

usefully delineated a crisis of masculinity or collapse of patriarchal order that occurred on two levels: it happened to actual men within their real families, and it happened to the family writ large as the paternal pillars of prewar society crumbled.

These accounts are limited, however, by a narrow focus on soldiers. The crises they describe stem either from combat itself or from the trauma of demobilization. Historians of different European countries using various methodologies have agreed that the way to approach men's experiences during this war is to look at soldiers, and more specifically, at the front experience.[7] Elisabeth Domansky makes explicit an assumption that is implicit in many other works; namely, that World War I breaks down into a neatly gendered division between front and home front. She writes, "While it is true that not every man went to the front, men did leave in sufficient numbers to make the home front seem to be women's territory." Domansky adds that the war offers us a "separation between the male combat zone of the battlefield and the female noncombat zone of producing and reproducing the means of destruction."[8] Others have asserted that the trouble with the divided spheres of war began when soldiers had to re-enter the feminized zone. Klaus Theweleit explores soldiers' multi-layered interpretations of "the rear" as the polluted realm of women and "the shirkers, the dodgers, the ones who hid in the latrines while the men at the front risked their necks."[9] According to Thomas Kühne and Jürgen Reulecke, the transition from front to home front (in essence, the transition from war to peace) entailed leaving behind the all-male society of the front and led to a postwar nostalgia for comradeship.[10] If we look at these studies together, we see that historians have focused

no. 4 (October 1994): 1,167–202; Helga Embacher, "Der Krieg hat die 'göttliche Ordnung' zerstört! Konzepte und Familienmodelle zur Lösung von Alltagsproblemen, Versuche zur Rettung der Moral, Familie und patriarchalen Gesellschaft nach dem Ersten Weltkrieg," *Zeitgeschichte* 15, no. 9/10 (June/July1988), 347–63, 350; Elisabeth Domansky, "Militarization and Reproduction in World War I Germany," in Geoff Eley (ed.), *Society, Culture and the State in Germany, 1870–1930* (Ann Arbor: University of Michigan Press, 1996), 427–63, 459; Sieder, "Behind the Lines," 109.

[7] Two particularly good studies of the front experience are Leonard V. Smith, *Between Mutiny and Obedience: The Case of the French Fifth Infantry Division During World War I* (Princeton: Princeton University Press, 1993); and Stéphane Audoin-Rouzeau, *Men at War 1914–1918: National Sentiment and Trench Journalism in France during the First World War* (Providence/Oxford: Berg, 1992). In her study of World War I Britain, Joanna Bourke moves beyond the front experience by studying not only men, but male bodies, wherever they be found. Joanna Bourke, *Dismembering the Male: Men's Bodies, Britain and the Great War* (Chicago: University of Chicago Press, 1996).

[8] Domansky, "Militarization and Reproduction," 442, 437.

[9] Theweleit, *Male Fantasies*, I, 396.

[10] See Thomas Kühne, "'…aus diesem Krieg werden nicht nur harte Männer heimkehren,' Kriegskameradschaft und Männlichkeit im 20. Jahrhundert," in Kühne (ed.), *Männergeschichte–Geschlechtergeschichte: Männlichkeit im Wandel der Moderne*

on the political and cultural effects of the front experience and have (perhaps unconsciously) equated the male only with the soldier. In this sense, historians have replicated what George Mosse calls the "Myth of the War Experience," a myth created in the 1920s by a small, elite group of writers who sacralized the combat experience.[11] Making sense of the widespread concern in Vienna about the loss of paternal authority requires that we look beyond soldiers to other sorts of men and other sources of male authority.

Home-front men

We begin with the paradoxical situation of ordinary men on the home front. Contemporaries often asserted that men, and the paternal authority they wielded, were "away at the front" when, in fact, hundreds of thousands of men spent all or part of the war on the home front. Men who before the war had been holders of authority, as real or potential family fathers, civil servants, respectable workers and voters, were now subjected to new, martial standards. Medical experts questioned their genetic fitness for fatherhood, and fellow citizens, in a relentless hunt for shirkers, scrutinized their physiques and devalued their labor. The grueling work men performed at the front (fighting, killing, attacking, defending) changed cultural perceptions of labor in Vienna in ways that devalued home-front male contributions to the economy and society. As we saw in chapter 1, a demonstrated "willingness to sacrifice" (*Opferwilligkeit*) was a key determinant of who was included in – and excluded from – the home-front community at any given moment. For men on the home front, establishing a credible claim to sacrifice was considerably more difficult than it was for women or children because the traditional notion of male sacrifice – offering one's life in battle – dwarfed what any man could offer in the city.[12] This was true even for such traditional figures of authority as Catholic priests, who were assailed for not displaying martial sacrifice. Vienna's Cardinal Piffl complained in the fall of 1914 that clergy on the home front were being systematically "slandered in the

(Frankfurt/New York: Campus, 1996), 174–92; Jürgen Reulecke, "Männerbund Versus the Family: Middle-class Youth Movements and the Family in Germany in the Period of the First World War," in Wall and Winter, *The Upheaval of War*, 439–52, 444.

[11] George L. Mosse, *Fallen Soldiers: Reshaping the Memory of the World Wars* (New York/Oxford: Oxford University Press, 1990), 7.

[12] On soldiering and modern masculinity, see Michael Geyer, "War and the Context of General History in an Age of Total War: Comment on Peter Paret, 'Justifying the Obligation of Military Service,' and Michael Howard, 'World War One: The Crisis in European History,'" *Journal of Military History* 57 (October 1993), 145–63, 153–5.

ugliest terms" for allegedly lacking a "spirit of sacrifice" (*Opfersinn*).[13] A rough definition of a true man emerged from Viennese residents' incessant application of a front standard to the men in their midst: First, a true man had to be a soldier; and second, as a soldier he had to be *at the front*. Performing non-soldiering sorts of labor or residing in the non-soldiering realm of the city stripped a man of masculinity. Authority, the vaguely defined but highly prized social glue missing from Franz Stiedl's Vienna, had long been established in Austrian family law as a *male* attribute, but the war taught that not all men possessed it.[14]

Viennese diarist Demophil Frank asked on November 18, 1915, "Is a tried and tested soldier the true ideal of manliness?" He answered emphatically, "I say no! But nowadays it has been suggested to mankind that only a soldier is a true man." Thirty-three-year-old Frank spent World War I on the Viennese home front. As a member of Austria's draftable population, which included all males between the ages of eighteen and fifty (later fifty-two), he was called before the draft board numerous times and was excused from military service on account of "nerves." His first appearance before the board led to a ten-day stint in a mental ward. When called up for the second time in September, 1915, he experienced a panic attack. "In terror I suffered a nervous shock [and] tossed the whole night with nervous cramps." After a third diagnosis of "unfit," in January, 1916, he wrote, "Certainly my fear of and aversion to the military life are somewhat pathological, but what can I do about it?" Although Frank was deemed unfit for *combat*, this did not excuse him from *service*, and he spent the war in an auxiliary support position (*Hilfsdienst*) in Vienna.[15]

According to Austria's 1912 War Service Law, which established the state's claim to men's labor in wartime, service could mean many things besides combat.[16] As the following figures make clear, a significant number of men who served Austria in World War I were not front soldiers.

---

[13] Martin Krexner, *Hirte an der Zeitenwende: Kardinal Friedrich Gustav Piffl und seine Zeit* (Vienna: Dom-Verlag, 1988), 118.

[14] For the subordination of women and children to men in Austrian family law, see Oskar Lehner, *Familie–Recht–Politik: Die Entwicklung des österreichischen Familienrechte im 19. und 20. Jahrhundert* (Vienna: Springer Verlag, 1987).

[15] Demophil Frank [pseud.], *Wien...Taumel–Qual–Erlösung, 1914–1918* (Vienna: Anzengruber Verlag, 1928), 78, 59, 83. Like many of the diarists publishing in the 1920s who claimed to provide readers with an "authentic" memoir of the war years, Frank appears to have written at least some of the material (republican rhetoric and praise for the socialist program) after the war.

[16] RGBl Nr. 236, 26 December 1912. The *Kriegsleistungsgesetz* stated that entire branches of industry could be placed under military supervision. In addition to the requisition of trains, cars, horses and telephone and telegraph lines for military purposes, the law laid claim to the "persönliche Dienstleistungen" of civilian men, curtailing their employment mobility in wartime.

More than 70 percent of men of draftable age were called up for service. Although this is a remarkable number, and the mobilization of so many men deeply affected the lives of almost every member of the society in some way, 30 percent of men remain statistically unaccounted for in the military record. Of the 8,420,000 men who had been drafted by the end of 1917, 4,010,000 had "left the armed services" for the following reasons:

780,000	died (*gestorben*) or died in battle (*gefallen*)
1,600,000	taken prisoner of war
500,000	became invalid
130,000	passed out of the upper age bracket for service
400,000	routed to munitions industries
600,000	exempted (*enthoben*) for a variety of reasons

That left 4,410,000 men still "in service" at the beginning of 1918, of whom 2,850,000 were with the army in the field (some in support positions) and 1,560,000 were behind the lines with domestic security units and military operations such as offices and depots.[17] With the exception of those who actually died in battle and most of those who became invalids, we cannot know for certain how many of these men could count *combat experience* as part of their *war experience*. Certainly, for Demophil Frank and countless others, the two were not synonymous.

Men on the home front fell into one of five general categories. First, age-exempt males younger than eighteen, called "youths" (*Jugendliche*) and older than fifty-two, often called "old men" (*Greise*), were left in the city. Those of draftable age might be in Vienna for a variety of reasons. Like Frank, men in the second category had been found unfit for military service and were assigned civilian positions. Third, a significant number of men who were found fit for service were nonetheless assigned to positions in industry, transportation and services on the home front. They were exempted on grounds that they possessed a special skill that made them indispensable for the functioning of the war economy. Fourth were soldiers and officers on leave or convalescing in one of Vienna's 306 makeshift hospitals. By March, 1915, 260,000 wounded soldiers had arrived in the city for medical care.[18] Fifth were the approximately 7,000 enemy

---

[17] Edmund von Glaise-Horstenau *et al.* (eds.), *Österreich-Ungarns letzter Krieg*, 7 vols. (Vienna: Verlag der Militärwissenschaftlichen Mitteilungen, 1930–38), VII, 41–2.
[18] AdBDW 1915 V/23 #7535. Report from Polizei-Präs. to MdI, 5 March 1915, "Die Wirkungen des Krieges in Wien." See chapter 5 on hospital accommodations in Vienna.

prisoners of war who were sent to Vienna to perform labor, who lived and worked among the native population, and who were often accorded better treatment than Austrian men in the city.

Although Vienna never became a site of military battles during the war, some home-front men performed "combat" in workplace and bar-room brawls against the "internal enemy." Fights between German- and Czech-speaking men, not uncommon before the war, took on added significance in wartime because these men were supposed to be allied as comrades against external foes. In October, 1915, three factory workers at the Viennese firm of Wagner, Biro & Kurz wrote to police pleading for physical protection from their German-speaking colleagues. On behalf of the Czech-speaking contingent at the factory, they wrote, "Until now all the nations tolerated each other, [but] since the beginning of the week we have been persecuted (*angefeindet*) by the German workers."[19] Exiting the factory one evening, they were ambushed by fifty Germans who shouted "*Da kommen schon die Böhm'!*" ("Here come the Czechs!" – *Böhm'* was derogatory slang for Czech). The Czech workers were insulted, punched and some suffered knife wounds. Fearing for their lives, they could not freely change jobs because their factory was part of the war industry and had consequently been placed under military supervision. Although the German-speaking workers at Wagner, Biro & Kurz were "exempted" from front service, this did not prevent them from engaging in "combat" against internal enemies.

Similar violence erupted in home-front pubs. Neighborhood pubs in Vienna attracted a male clientele that tended to speak the same language, work similar jobs and share a common worldview. Although the pub was technically a *public* place, many pubs in mixed-language, working-class districts had distinctly national reputations. Consequently, Czech-identified pubs served as magnets for German-speakers looking to express their own patriotism by ferreting out traitors. In a typical case from 1915, several German-speaking neighbors reported hearing anti-Austrian singing coming from a Czech tavern in the working-class XV district. They noted that the singing was more frequent and joyous when the Austrian armies had suffered a defeat. But what were the Czechs singing about? Police agents could not investigate the charges of anti-state behavior because the officers "[didn't] know the Czech language."[20] This was a common obstacle for vigilantly patriotic German-speakers, who ran up against their own ignorance of the "enemy" language.

[19] NÖLA Präs. "P" VIb, 6739. Letter sent to k.k. Bezirkspolizei-Kommissariat Innere Stadt, 8 October 1915.
[20] NÖLA Präs. "P" 1918, XVa, 3334. Mayor Weiskirchner to k.k. Polizei-Präs., 16 June 1915.

For German- and Czech-speaking men of higher social circles, shar-
ing restaurant space had become equally tendentious. Late in the war,
Germans in the dining room of the Wiener Rathauskeller complained
that fellow guests, including members of the newly reopened parliament,
were conversing "loudly in the Czech language," which they deemed a
"gross provocation." Alcohol may have contributed to rising tempers,
and in an ensuing scuffle, gentlemen exchanged insults and threatened
each other with walking sticks. The Czech party was eventually chased
from the room and German patrons "cleansed" the restaurant of enemy sentiment by singing a hearty round of the "Wacht am Rhein."[21] In
both the pub and the restaurant, we see that the mere sound of Czech
voices, singing or speaking, offended German men's patriotic sensibilities, even if German-speakers rarely knew what the enemy was actually
saying. Vienna might not be the eastern front, and such defense of the
realm (dining room) might not constitute heroism, but we see that some
home-front men sought opportunities for "combat" nonetheless.

The wartime fates of Viennese men were initially determined at the
Musterung, the required appearance before a medical inspection board.
The stereotype that those who did not pass muster were weak and inferior
creatures was perpetuated in jokes and in popular culture.[22] Inspection
scenes from the popular 1916 film *Wien im Kriege* depict the separation
of the "strong" men from the "weak." In the course of just five seconds,
a brusque doctor examines the eyes, teeth, hands and heart of older recruits. As one muscle-bound recruit with a rippling torso flexes his biceps
for the camera, the doctor and his assistants look on in admiration and the
words "Dear Fatherland, rest assured!" flash on the screen. In another
scene, a feeble man shuffles out of the examination room, dejected after
being found unfit.[23]

Social hygienists and population experts warned that physical weakness of unfit men was a manifestation of more serious genetic inferiority.
Besides a decrease in the *quantity* of Austrian babies (due to the declining birth rate in wartime) they predicted a simultaneous drop in *quality*,
as women on the home front mated with the inferior specimens in their
midst. Clemens von Pirquet, head of Vienna's renowned children's clinic,
wrote that war had removed the strongest and healthiest men from the
marriage pool, leaving the "left-behind weak and sick people" to marry

---

[21] NÖLA Präs. "P" 1918, XIX, 2006. Pol. Dir. Wien report to Statthalterei, 8 May 1918.

[22] See, for example, *Fideles aus dem Hinterland* (Vienna: Verlag Karl Harbauer, 1918). In
"Die Kennerin," a woman who "knows" two men jokes, "Den Pepi ham's b'halten, den
Franzl net; de verstengan aa viel bei der Musterungskommission," 105.

[23] Österreichisches Filmarchiv, *Alltag in der öst.-ung. Monarchie*, roll 4, *Wien im Kriege*
(1916), *Spielfilmfragmente*.

and procreate. The "offspring of inferior fathers" would affect Austria's genetic stock for decades to come.[24] Doctor Julius Tandler seconded this opinion, explaining in the *Wiener Medizinische Wochenschrift* that "the selection of individuals for war proves advantageous for the transmission of physical weaknesses [among] those left behind, meaning those persons found unfit for military service. Among them one finds persons with sensory irregularities and constitutional anomalies which are very often inherited. That results in further damage in the next generation."[25] Besides being based on eugenic speculation, these arguments crumble when we consider that "unfitness" was only one of many reasons a man might be on the home front.

When passing a man on the street in Vienna, it was not always easy to discern which of the above five categories he fell into. Youths, old men, the unfit and most of the exempted workers did not wear the uniform of a soldier, while soldiers and officers on leave or in convalescence and enemy prisoners of war might wear all or part of a uniform, depending on how late in the war it was and how many pieces of their original uniform were still intact. In the absence of a uniform or obvious war-induced physical deformity, it was impossible to "read" from a man's exterior his military history, his reason for exemption, his patriotic sentiment or his age. And yet meticulous scrutiny of men's exteriors was a popular and often malicious pastime in wartime Vienna. As Demophil Frank explained in a diary entry from September, 1915, men on the home front were the frequent targets of denunciation: "Denunciation is exceedingly common. When a man who's been found unfit (*ein Ungeeigneter*) dares to walk around with working limbs and looking healthy, he is immediately reported as a shirker." Frank had to give up his hobby of playing billiards because "especially scrupulous denouncers immediately assess the leg and arm muscles of every billiard player . . . These gentlemen are even tougher than our own . . . legitimate draft commissions."[26] While gentlemen were not the sole practitioners of denunciation (women, too, were avid scrutinizers of the male physique) Frank introduces here two of the main features of the discourse of home-front masculinity: the broad category of the shirker and the widespread use of denunciation to report "suspects" to the authorities.

Contrary to medical experts such as Pirquet and Tandler who described home-front men as genetically "weak," popular opinion detected in them

---

[24] Clemens von Pirquet (ed.), *Volksgesundheit im Krieg* 2 vols., Carnegie Endowment for International Peace series (Vienna: Hölder-Pichler-Tempsky, 1926), I, 18.
[25] WSLB 145654B #108 (Börner pamphlet collection), Julius Tandler, "Krieg und Bevölkerung," *Wiener Medizinische Wochenschrift* 15 (1916), 590–94.
[26] Frank, *Wien*, 60.

hidden strength. Shirker (*Drückeberger*) was an elastic label applied to men accused of being "strong" but feigning weakness. A shirker might be a man who fooled the military doctors with a bogus ailment, who secured a comfortable office job through "connections" and "protection" or who slipped through the cracks of military administration and had never been called for service at all.[27] In the popular imagination, unfitness (*Untauglichkeit*) was often a self-induced state, a ruse used by perfectly healthy men to avoid military service. By the unyielding standards of public opinion, no ailment was deemed legitimate enough, no task worthy enough to warrant exemption from front service. The shirker did not lack physical prowess, but lacked moral qualities of a "true" man – honor, bravery and a willingness to sacrifice. Operating with a highly gendered, location-specific understanding of sacrifice, many Viennese found it impossible to conceive of men sacrificing anywhere but at the front.

Viennese authorities received from citizens countless denunciations detailing the tricks of the shirker. One woman wrote indignantly to the War Ministry that soldiers on leave told her daughter they "rubbed the male organ with salt and pepper so that they wouldn't have to return to the field."[28] Prostitutes were said to entice customers with the promise of venereal disease: "Come on, you'll get infected and won't need to go to the field."[29] Franziska Malik, a 35-year-old Viennese woman in an unhappy marriage, denounced her own husband for deceiving the military doctors who examined him: "My husband Franz Malik has never been in the military. [O]n April 26, 1915 he went for inspection, where he was found unfit. Before the examination he didn't eat anything, smoked very heavily and came home late so that he wouldn't be declared fit."[30] Others could not identify precisely *how* a man had tricked the draft commission, but urged authorities to reconsider a finding of unfit. "A Coffeehouse Observer," baffled by the unfit status of student Anton Glavina, sent a letter of denunciation to the War Ministry: "*He is healthy* and for some inexplicable reason has so far not been drafted into the military. He has a figure like Hercules..."[31] Forty-seven-year-old coach driver Johann Hanselmann

[27] In *Dismembering the Male*, Joanna Bourke offers an extended discussion of the British shirker, and his counterpart, the malingerer, 76–123. She defines malingering as a particular form of shirking: the shirker avoided work and removed himself from service, while the malingerer accomplished this specifically by mutilating his own body. "[T]he malingerer's protest *centered* on his body: often, it was the last remaining thing he could claim as his own," 81.
[28] ÖStA, KA, k.u.k. Militärkommando Wien, Präs. 1915 19-7/67 #12,741, 15,512.
[29] AdBDW, "Beilage zum Stimmungsbericht," 9 March 1916.
[30] AdBDW 1915 St./13 #15692. Malik file.   [31] AdBDW 1916 St./9 #27855.

was similarly denounced by a neighbor who could not fathom why a man who was "fit as a fiddle (*kerngesund*), tall and strong" should be permitted to roam the streets and pubs of Vienna insulting the Emperor and the Austrian war effort. "He has not been a soldier, therefore he doesn't know what it means to be a soldier, to fight for the fatherland, to become a cripple for the fatherland..."[32] These reports from ordinary Viennese show that the *Musterung* was only the beginning of inspection for men on the home front, who remained under the silent, continuous surveillance of fellow citizens.

Some denouncers marshaled their nationalist or anti-Semitic stereotypes, "seeing" in men's bodies or behavior confirmations of these stereotypes. "Ernestine S." denounced an "Italian" living in Vienna for taking scarce bread away from good Germans. "It might be best to investigate," she advised police, "whether this man has been to *Musterung*, because he is healthy, young and strong."[33] Another woman seeking "to fulfill [her] duty as a patriot" expressed a view common among German-speakers that Czech men were inherently disloyal and that those on the home front were conspiring against the state. She denounced a "Slavic-looking" man to the War Ministry: "The man is, by all appearances, a fanatical Czech... [He is] Serb-friendly and also has a very striking appearance of a truly Slavic type – small, with a face like a shriveled potato."[34] For this woman, an individual man (shirker) embodied her suspicions about a broad category of people (Slavs). Thus, the hunt for shirkers did not necessarily create new hostilities, in this case among people of different nationalities, but provided a new context for the expression of already existing ones.

Suspected Jewish shirkers were often identified not by their bodily exteriors but by the locales they frequented. In some circles, *coffeehouse* was a codeword for Jewish men hiding on the home front. The coffeehouse figured symbolically in the distinction between home front and front; to sit in a coffeehouse during war, the most pleasant, urbane and civilized of settings, was to be as far from the trench as a man could be. A group of women identifying themselves as "We Viennese Christian Business-wives" wrote to Mayor Weiskirchner demanding to know why fifty-year-old men were serving as cannon fodder while "all these young people and Jews... loiter at night in the coffeehouses."[35] The Mayor himself publicly conjured up images of Jewish swindlers passing their days

[32] AdBDW 1915 St./15 #21099.
[33] AdBDW 1917 St./27 (no document #). Letter dated 19 October 1917.
[34] AdBDW 1915 St./13 #12549. Letter to KM, 12 June 1915.
[35] AdBDW 1916 St./13 #21202.

in leisure at coffeehouses.[36] "Several good citizens" launched a smear campaign against railway employee Karl Töllsner, informing authorities that he had avoided the draft through "connections" and "protection" and that he could be found days and evenings in a coffeehouse.[37] The coffeehouse shirker committed a double crime: he was avoiding service and at the same time living a parasitic life of luxury, consuming scarce goods such as coffee, tea, milk and sugar. The coffeehouse, which, if we recall from chapter one, also "housed" the profiteer, allowed Viennese anti-Semites to imagine a continuum of Jewish shirkers and profiteers united in their deplorable unwillingness to sacrifice.

A common feature in these shirker accusations was the devaluation of whatever labor the alleged shirker performed. When compared to the work of a soldier, many kinds of traditionally male work appeared secondary, superfluous and decidedly unheroic. If a man was fit to perform demanding tasks on the home front, why had he not been drafted? This was a particular problem for men who were found fit but had exempt status based on occupational indispensability. The Viennese police force was a case in point. At the end of 1914, the force employed 5,792 men,[38] the vast majority of whom were patrolmen stationed around the city, responsible for watching over war-sensitive sites such as factories, bridges and government buildings and maintaining order at the markets and in the streets, where by 1915, spontaneous demonstrations were commonplace. The force needed to project an image of strength and competence to maintain public order and control unruly street crowds. But strong, fit men provoked suspicion and resentment among the population they watched over. In an altercation in 1917, one Viennese woman expressed common contempt for policemen, concluding that they should be sent to the front, "so that they also contribute something – rather than just lying around here." She challenged a policeman: she had had to give her husband up for the war, so why shouldn't he have to go too?[39] On other occasions civilians pelted patrolmen with stones, taunted them, and caused them to draw their weapons.[40] The policeman, certainly an authority figure before the war, saw his authority greatly diminished in wartime by the existence of the front, where "true" men performed sacrifice. Although home-front residents could see policemen in action – controlling crowds,

[36] WSLB Kriegssammlung C67052, Konvolut 2, "Zweite Vollversammlung der christsozialen Mandatare Wiens," 9 October 1916.
[37] AdBDW 1916 St./9 #29279 and 30823. Series of denunciations sent to k.k. Staatsanwalt.
[38] *Statistisches Jahrbuch der Stadt Wien 1914* (Vienna: Wiener Magistrat, 1918), 326.
[39] AdBDW 1917 St./20 #44391.
[40] NÖLA Pras. "P" 1917 XIX, 2554; AdBDW 1917 V/9 #46735.

breaking up fights, conducting searches for contraband materials – the work they performed did not meet the front service standard.

Other sorts of taxing manual labor were similarly devalued by the front comparison. Twenty-three-year-old Karl Kafka was denounced by a butcher who had seen him lifting pieces of meat weighing 100 kilos. "It is incomprehensible to me that a person who can perform such hard labor as a civilian should be found unfit for military service."[41] Still others had special skills that fellow citizens imagined might be put to better use in the field. "A Good Patriot" was convinced that 34-year-old locksmith Johann Geisler would be of more use at the front, writing, "Surely a place can be found for a locksmith!... There are so many many in the line of fire and this man should also find a spot at the front..."[42] Another writer was convinced he was surrounded by 100,000 fit men – tailors, shoe-makers and ironsmiths – cleverly hiding from the authorities. He urged officials at the War Ministry to check the jails, juvenile homes and offices in the city, and to catch up with "the thousands of men registered under false names." Authorities would "be surprised at the handsome men" they would find.[43]

Another keyword in the discourse on shirking was *desk*. Men who spent the war performing office work fueled conspiracy theories about "protection" and "connections." Many municipal, regional and imperial officials had exempt status, and in the eyes of a suspicious public, the comfort of an office position invalidated whatever useful war service a man might perform in his bureaucratic capacity. In 1914, Hans Loewenfeld-Russ, who would later head the Imperial Food Office, wrote to his wife of his misgivings at "serving" from a desk: "If I didn't have to think of you and the children, I don't know if being drafted wouldn't be preferable to this unworthy business at a desk." In Austria, with a long-established tradition of civil service, war had rendered desk work "unworthy." Loewenfeld-Russ reconsidered his predicament a few weeks later and came to a more measured conclusion:

[O]n the other hand, the serious work in the hinterland shouldn't be looked down upon and subordinated to front service... [A]dmittedly, one doesn't risk one's life working behind a desk, but thousands of lives are dependent on the responsible actions of a leading man in the hinterland.[44]

---

[41] AdBDW 1917 St./27 #49320.
[42] AdBDW 1915 St./15 #4267. Letter to KM, 27 December 1914.
[43] KA, KüA, 1916 #61577. Letter to KM, 3 March 1916.
[44] Hans Loewenfeld-Russ, *Im Kampf gegen den Hunger. Aus den Erinnerungen des Staatssekretärs für Volksernährung, 1918–1920* (Vienna: Verlag für Geschichte und Politik, 1986) 8, 19.

Unfortunately for Loewenfeld-Russ and his fellow bureaucrats, many Viennese were not nearly as generous in their evaluation of office work. Police reports show that male office workers were sometimes subjected to verbal abuse, and that their manhood was an easy target for frustrated or resentful clients. Along with the coffeehouse, the office was now considered a hideout for shirkers and the work performed behind desks unworthy of true men.

As has been noted, the kind of labor a man performed was frequently mentioned in shirking charges. In existing accounts of the "crisis of masculinity" that struck Austrian and German societies at the end of World War I, historians have identified *female* labor as a key component of the crisis. That is, soldiers and prisoners of war returned home, angry to find "emancipated" women working in traditionally male roles. As historians Sigrid Augeneder and Gabriella Hauch explain, legally removing women from traditionally male jobs constituted one facet of the return to a "healthy order" (*gesunde Ordnung*) in the postwar period.[45] A 1919 law required women to leave certain jobs in order to make room for the returning men. But removing women would not reverse the other, more subtle gender shift described here, whereby the masculinity of a policeman, a bureaucrat, a butcher, a railroad worker – precisely the jobs that soldiers would return to after the war – was compromised by the wartime elevation of soldiering as the only pursuit of a true man.

There were, no doubt, men hiding on the home front in a variety of capacities just as their denouncers suspected. That is, shirking was not purely a phenomenon of the imagination. But to be simultaneously a civilian and a "man" had also become something of a conceptual impossibility in wartime. As one Viennese man noted to friends in a pub in 1916, "Whoever doesn't wear a uniform these days isn't a complete man."[46] Far from providing male authority, the legions of suspected shirkers represented yet another social problem plaguing the authority-hungry city.

And yet, if we look at the experiences of *soldiers* in the city, we see that even a uniform did not confer authority upon its wearer. The virility of soldiers was a familiar motif in the heavily censored Viennese press. Throughout World War I, civilians in Vienna were fed a steady stream of propaganda about the heroic exploits of Habsburg soldiers on several

[45] Sigrid Augeneder, *Arbeiterinnen im Ersten Weltkrieg: Lebens- und Arbeitsbedingungen proletarischer Frauen in Österreich* (Vienna: Europaverlag, 1987), 215; Gabriella Hauch, *Vom Frauenstandpunkt aus: Frauen im Parlament 1919–1933* (Vienna: Verlag für Gesellschaftskritik, 1995), 27. Hauch discusses the somewhat comical League for Men's Rights founded in the 1920s to "protect the endangered existence of men," 11–14.
[46] AdBDW, 1916 St./9 #24794.

fronts. Their warriors were triumphing against the formidable Russian foe in the north-east, gallantly avenging the Serbs in the south-east, and bravely fighting the Italians and the forces of nature in Tyrolean mountain battles. The press projected an image of the hardened, hyper-masculine World War I front soldier, a type later memorialized by writers such as Ernst Jünger. But as noted above, many "fit" soldiers and officers spent all or part of the war on the home front, exempted as essential workers, on leave or recovering from wounds or illnesses in city hospitals. Once removed from the battlefield the warrior lost his mystique. Soldiers' acrimonious interactions with civilians suggest that contemporaries' "true ideal of manliness" (in Frank's words) was geographically bounded. In other words, a soldier was only a soldier in the field. In the city, a uniformed man was as greatly resented and as little respected as any other home-front man.

Already in the autumn of 1914 residents encountered soldiers in Vienna behaving unheroically. In October, police reported public disapproval of soldiers' state of dress and frequent inebriation:

Drunken and begging soldiers are still being arrested, but the nuisance of wandering convalescent soldiers is not as noticeable as earlier...

It has been noted that these [soldiers] often walk around in defective, shabby clothing which elicits disparaging remarks from among the population...[47]

Two months later the soldiers continued to make unfavorable impressions on the civilian population:

The loitering of soldiers has not let up and evokes very critical comments from the population; trafficking with prostitutes is particularly on the rise...[48]

Soldiers were accused of defacing cemeteries in the city, committing such excesses there as drinking, toppling gravestones and frolicking at night with prostitutes.[49] They were also seen as corrupters of innocent Viennese girls. In 1915, an irate mother wrote to the War Ministry that soldiers stationed in the Prater had violated her sixteen-year-old daughter:

In outrage I am forced to write a short description of the horrible behavior of the Deutschmeister who are housed...in the Prater...[This past] Sunday my daughter spent the whole night with the military. [A]s I interrogated my child she explained that she wasn't alone...10–12 girls, including married women, slept there too...As a mother I am ashamed...[T]his has gone too far...this has gone too far.[50]

[47] AdBDW, Stimmungsberichte, 8 and 15 October 1914.
[48] AdBDW, Stimmungsbericht, 19 December 1914.
[49] ÖStA, KA, Militärkommando Wien 1915 Präs. 19-7/53, #9582. Letter, 14 July 1915.
[50] ÖStA, KA, Militärkommando Wien 1915 Präs. 19-7/67, #12741. Letter, 1 September 1915.

These kinds of experiences with uniformed men in the city make clear why residents did not look to them as figures of authority, and instead imagined that the real men, those truly able to make and enforce rules, were away at the front.[51]

Although front soldiers coveted leave in the hinterland, they had to adjust to different codes of behavior in the city. Despite being in the civilian realm, they were still in service and subject to military discipline. Viennese resident Anton Sedlacek, serving in a field howitzer unit, was on leave in Vienna when he encountered the spite of a home-front officer:

In April, 1915, at the age of $18\frac{1}{2}$, I enlisted. After 17 months I received my first leave. On the last day before my return to the field I was walking through the Hofburg; lost in thoughts, I passed by a flag and didn't salute it. A first lieutenant from the civil guard sent two infantrymen after me, with the order that they carry out salutation exercises with me. I answered that I had to leave for the field in three hours. He gave me a shove and led me to the Roßauer barracks where I was locked up for two days. Then I went to the front.[52]

Sedlacek's experience reminds us that for individual men, the journey between front and home front was fraught with difficulties. While some soldiers on leave made themselves unwelcome by behaving dishonorably in the city, the city could be an unwelcome place in return.

Labeled *Hinterländer*, men of the hinterland, officers were more despised by civilians than were ordinary soldiers. Whatever their actual reason for being in the city, their presence there was considered to be at the expense of other men. "Several fathers report," we read in one letter of complaint sent to the Emperor, "that many reserve officers have been in various comfortable assignments in the hinterland since the beginning of the war, while others have had to serve the whole time in dangerous front duty. It is also said that a large number of officers spend extra long periods in hospitals thanks to help from friendly doctors."[53] Convalescing officers indulging in too much amusement offended a public that believed immodest amusement was disrespectful of front sacrifice. In 1916, police had to intervene when loud, intoxicated, singing officers and their "female company" returned from the wine cellars of Grinzing,

---

[51] The notion of "the front" retained a powerful hold on the civilian imagination, even though "by 1918 the vast majority of Austro-Hungarian soldiers were no longer involved in fighting: they were either at home or, if with the field armies, far from the combat lines." István Deák, "The Habsburg Army in the First and Last Days of World War I: A Comparative Analysis," in B. K. Király and N. F. Dreisiger (eds.), *East Central European Society in World War I* (New York: East European Monographs, 1985), 301–12, 310.

[52] *Ein Volk klagt an! Fünfzig Briefe über den Krieg* (Vienna: Hess & Co. Verlag, 1931), 40–41.

[53] ÖStA, KA, MKSM 1915 10-1/22. Letter to Emperor, no date.

irritating other tram passengers and nearby residents.[54] Class tensions may have fueled incidents such as this, as family members of enlisted men saw officers behaving frivolously or recklessly while their loved ones were far away and in danger. Whatever officers had (or had not) accomplished in the field made little difference to watchful critics. In a 1916 incident that attracted wide attention, Lieutenant Fritz Hoffmann had stabbed and killed a civilian employee of the city gasworks after the man called him a "louse." Viennese resident Karla Zerzan recited the story to a friend: "On Saturday afternoon a lieutenant stationed in the hinterland stabbed a civilian in the Praterstrasse and ran away like a coward, just like a *Hinterländer*."[55] A killer might earn accolades in the field for bravery or determination, but these accolades were not transferable to the home front, where, of course, the killing-work of a soldier was illegal. Whatever Lieutenant Hoffmann might have accomplished in battle, in Vienna his "cowardly" actions stripped him of authority.

Criticism of officers was especially sharp when it came from other men. Occasionally an everyday squabble, which on the surface had little to do with honor or service at all, could flare into a conflict in which manhood was at stake. Such an incident, between General Staff Officer Emil Stettner and an "older gentleman" in a tram, demonstrates that even men who were far from the front used it as a standard by which to assert their manhood and denigrate that of another. Colonel Stettner had urged passengers on a crowded tram to leave the exits open, claiming he was helping to "maintain public order." But in a "disrespectful" tone, and in the presence of military personnel of lower rank, a civilian questioned Stettner's place of authority on the tram. In the ensuing altercation, both men based their authority to speak on a relation to the front, Stettner asserting that he had served for two years at the front and was presently garrisoned in Vienna, and the older gentleman countering that he had two sons at the front who could "stand in for him."[56] During war, the authority to speak, a quintessentially male attribute by the cultural standards of the time, derived from front service.[57]

By 1918, the military personnel on the home front had begun to inspire not only contempt, but fear among the civilian population. Officials

[54] AdBDW St./16 (no document #). Police report, 21 September 1916.
[55] NÖLA Präs. "P" 1916 XIX, 3824. Police to Statthalterei, 27 May 1916. Zerzan was arrested because the statement was considered an insult to an officer and the army generally.
[56] AdBDW 1917 St./27 #42712. Letter to police from Emil Stettner, 12 April 1917.
[57] The link between speaking and voting (a hallmark of political citizenship) is evident in the word *Stimme*, which means both voice and vote. *Stimmrecht*, the franchise, was expanded in Austria in 1907 to include all adult men.

who had promoted (with only limited success) the image of the warrior hero now worried about the droves of wandering men known as the
Heimkehrer (the returnees) coming back from the Russian front and from
prisoner camps in the east.[58] Censors summarized the complaints about
the returnees they found in citizens' letters: "The nuisance of begging is
frequently felt to be a true plague of the land. Soldiers and prisoners of
war are said to make up the main contingent here."[59] A woman warned
a returning family member, "Here you are considered Bolshevik poison
that people want to stamp out with drills and [discipline]."[60] Medical
authorities in the east warned government officials in Vienna that the
returnees included a sizable contingent of "psychopaths" – men suffering from "oversensitivity, excitability, impulsiveness, alcoholism, lack of
ethical feelings, mendacity, hallucinations, violent and criminal tendencies [and] sexual aberrations." War had not caused, but triggered, these
"inborn" tendencies in men who now threatened the general public and
posed "a great danger for the state."[61] Far from being seen as figures of
authority, who, upon return, might replenish the paternal ranks in the
city that Franz Stiedl described as being in a cultural, moral and ethical
freefall, the returnees were considered social pathogens.

Ironically, while the returning Austrian soldiers were considered
"Bolshevik poison," another group of similarly disheveled soldiers elicited
a great deal of sympathy from local residents. The stationing in the capital city of nearly 7,000 enemy prisoners, mostly Russians and Italians,
was the result of government policies designed to fill labor shortages and
ease the economic burden on the state.[62] The state began to "lease"
prisoners to municipalities and private firms in return for a deposit
and the assurance that the employer would provide food and lodging.
The city of Vienna used prisoners to fill in for some of its 14,000 employees who had been called for war service; the "Moskalis," as the
Russians were called, worked in the gas and electrical works, cleaned
streets, cared for horses and loaded coal.[63] Factories, bakeries, butcher-
shops, nurseries, dairies and carpentry shops also employed prisoners.

For the predicament of the returnees, see Richard Plaschka *et al.* (eds.), *Innere Front:
Militärassistenz, Widerstand und Umsturz in der Donaumonarchie 1918*, 2 vols. (Munich:
R. Oldenbourg Verlag, 1974), I, 283.
[59] ÖStA, KA, AOK GZNB 1918, 3759 #5123. Censor's report, May 1918.
[60] ÖStA, KA, AOK GZNB 1918, 3758 #5054. Censor's report, April 1918.
[61] ÖStA, AdR, k.k. Min. u. St.A. f. soz. Verwaltung, Volksgesundheit 1918, 1592, #287.
Letter from medical faculty in Krakow to Min. f. soz. Verwaltung, 7 May 1918.
[62] In December 1917, 6,767 POWs worked in the city. AdBDW 1917 St./11 (no document #), "Nachweisung über die im Wiener Polizeirayon auf Arbeit befindlichen Kriegsgefangenen."
[63] WSLB ZAS Kriegsgefangene II, *Reichspost*, 1 July 1916.

Many women running small firms applied for one or two prisoners to fill in for their missing male family members, while the state tried unsuccessfully to prevent "too active a contact between the civilian population and the prisoners of war (fraternization)." Despite the screening process and the fine an employer faced if his or her prisoners got loose, wandering Russians seem to have been a fairly common sight in Vienna during the second half of the war. Eighteen Russian prisoners working at the city transportation depot in the XVI district were regularly seen lingering on sidewalks, chatting with "civilians of Czech nationality," and strolling through the streets in civilian clothing.[64] Over four days in January, 1918, patrolmen in the XI district received sixteen complaints of Russians on the loose, and concluded that "recently, the supervision of the prisoners of war at the Simmering gasworks has become so inadequate that by day the prisoners can leave the gasworks unnoticed and unhindered to carry on their begging and stealing in the surrounding area."[65] The "total freedom of movement" of some prisoners led to sexual intrigue. For example, Viennese maid servant Anna Fuchs conducted an eighteen-month-long relationship with prisoner Iwan Sytkin, by whom she became pregnant.[66] Censors warned, "The long-standing complaints about the immoral behavior of certain women with the prisoners of war have not ceased... More seriously, the repeated news must be confirmed that many women and girls have become pregnant by Russians."[67] The perceived virility of the prisoners contrasted sharply with official fears about the physical weakness or genetic inferiority of Austrian home-front men.

In contrast to the animosity and open hostility that Austrian men on the home front faced, civilians displayed what the police termed "alarming" acts of compassion towards the enemy prisoners. Viennese police noted in February, 1916,

In numerous cases it has come to pass that the civilian population has tried to come into closer communication... with the prisoners, bestowing upon them food-stuffs, tobacco and the like. Such communication is not only unpatriotic and meant to stir up public nuisance, but is also completely forbidden for state and military reasons.[68]

In an incident a year later, a group of a hundred Russian prisoners being escorted through the XII district to their place of work aroused

---

[64] AdBDW 1917 St./11 #48659/1.   [65] AdBDW 1917 (misfiled) St./6 #52118.
[66] NÖLA Präs. "P" 1918 IV, 752, Bd. I.
[67] ÖStA, KA, GZNB 1917, 3751 #4647. "Stimmung und wirtschaftliche Lage der österr. Bevölkerung im Hinterland," May 1917.
[68] Cited in C. Beck (ed.), *Die Frau und die Kriegsgefangenen* (Nürnberg: Döllinger, 1919), 28.

the sympathies of 300 whistling women and children who shouted at the Austrian escorts, "Pfui! Stop the war when there's nothing to eat," and compared the plight of the Russians to their own absent men: "[T]hat's how our poor devils are also doing in prison."[69] According to authorities, the prisoners had provoked the incident with their attention-grabbing antics, kneeling down before residents begging for bread, cigarettes and money. Some Viennese went so far as to invite the enemy prisoners into their homes as friends. Fifty-seven-year-old widow Theresia Müller and her daughter Leopoldine had Russians over for "frequent" games of cards and served the prisoners wine. The guard in charge of watching over them at the mill where they worked joined in the merriment himself.[70]

Doctors and psychoanalysts who probed this attraction to and sympathy for prisoners cited various psychological and religious explanations for the phenomenon. They contended that the men reminded women on the home front of their own male family members in captivity on the "other side," creating a kind of transferred compassion; hence the above reference to "our poor devils." Although aiding and abetting an enemy to escape constituted a crime against the state punishable by death, various male commentators claimed that women were drawn to the "exotic" men by curiosity, "sexual hunger," or their feminine inclinations to follow the Christian tenet, "Love thy enemies."[71] More plausibly, friendliness towards Russian prisoners signaled a divide between official and popular notions of who constituted the "enemy." As noted in chapter 1, definitions of community on the home front often hinged on levels of perceived suffering. Those who suffered stood in solidarity (however fleetingly) against those who profited. Hardly menacing figures (see plate 6.1), the Russians' tattered clothes and disheveled appearance may have endeared them to civilians who recognized in them fellow sufferers.

For Franz Stiedl, the "practical family father," these civilian relations with "enemies" would have been one more sign of the decaying moral fabric in the city, of people's inability to distinguish right from wrong, and of a lack of (Austrian) male authority. As we have seen, the myriad social problems and epidemic of rule-breaking on the home front, ostensibly caused by the absence of male authority, actually developed in a city populated with hundreds of thousands of men. But when residents looked

[69] AdBDW St./12 #44401. Protokoll Bezirkspolizeikommissariat Meidling, 19 May 1917.
[70] AdBDW 1917 St./20 #12887. Memo from Sicherheits-Abteilung Simmering, 10 March 1917.
[71] WSLB ZAS Kriegsgefangene I, *Neues Wiener Tagblatt*, 11 March 1916, "Warnung vor Begünstigung von Kriegsgefangenen;" A. Th. Sonnleitner, "Suggestion des Fremdartigen," in Beck (ed.), *Die Frau und die Kriegsgefangenen*, 25–31.

Plate 6.1. Russian prisoners of war working as horse stall hands in Vienna. Source: AdBDW Nachlaß Pamer, carton 2, photos.

around for "men" to discipline the children, guide the women and impose order in public life, they did not see the men in their midst, because these men had ceased to *be* men by the standards of wartime culture. They saw genetic misfits, shirkers and uniformed men living parasitically off the sacrifices of others. While authority was a male attribute (men were legally heads of household and occupied, without exception, all positions of government, civic and religious authority in the prewar society), the war changed people's perceptions of where authority lay and who possessed it. When demobilized soldiers returned to their families at war's end (Sieder's "wounded patriarchs"), they faced the same predicament that home-front men had faced all along: over the course of the war, authority had been projected outward, away from the city and away from the civilian realm where the "fatherless" families lived.

Imperial paternalism

Behind the discourse of missing fathers and lost authority on the home front, there existed a familial model that long predated the war and had served as the bedrock of dynastic rule: imperial paternalism. The story of the imperial father in World War I is the story of the demise of a symbol, a demise caused by the great material distress of ordinary people. Many Viennese who were without fatherly support or protection in their real families sought paternal guidance and assistance from the Emperor, who had traditionally been cast in Habsburg parlance as the "father of his peoples." This phrase was usually taken to mean that the Emperor watched over the all the nationalities (or peoples, *Völker*) of the Empire with a judicious and even hand. We will explore here a facet of imperial paternalism more directly related to individuals, many of them the sorts of "little people" whom we have encountered above. This approach differs from that of most historians, who, if they consider the imperial family at all, look at which national and class interest groups (camps or *Lager*) supported or undermined dynastic interests. Rather than measuring the strength or weakness of the dynasty in this structural way, we will assess how ordinary people in the capital conceived of the Emperor, what they expected of him, and how their conceptions changed in wartime. Unlike ordinary men, who failed to meet standards of martial masculinity, the Emperors, top soldiers of the realm, failed as fathers to provide for the state family.

Political histories of the Habsburg Empire depict the elderly Franz Joseph as the venerable "father of his peoples" but do not seriously consider the meaning or significance of dynastic paternal authority in a city in which many actual family fathers had been sent to the field. Karl, in turn, is depicted as weak, inept, too young or naive for the job, and lacking the respect of military leaders and his German allies.[72] These assessments fail to consider the extraordinarily rich and diverse correspondence that ordinary citizens conducted with the Emperors during the war, the emotionally charged encounters that residents (mostly women) tried to arrange with them in public places, and the extremely personal, intimate nature of the information subjects divulged to them. In her study of revolutionary politics in France, Lynn Hunt offers a way to discuss the metaphorical importance of family in the collective political imagination. Referring to the *family romance* in the title of her book, she writes, "I mean the collective, unconscious images of the familial order that underlie revolutionary politics."[73] If we allow that collectively imagined paternal authority is

---

[72] For a standard account of Franz Joseph's and Karl's accomplishments and failures, see Robert A. Kann, *The Multinational Empire: Nationalism and National Reform in the Habsburg Monarchy 1848–1918*, 2 vols. (New York: Columbia, 1950) II, 231–9; for a more recent overview of Franz Joseph's rule and his relations with subjects, see Ernst Hanisch, *Der lange Schatten des Staates: Österreichische Gesellschaftsgeschichte im 20. Jahrhundert* (Vienna: Ueberreuter, 1994), 209–31, especially 212–14; for Karl, see Gordon Brook-Shepherd, *The Last Habsburg* (New York: Viking, 1968).

[73] Lynn Hunt, *The Family Romance of the French Revolution* (Berkeley and Los Angeles: University of California Press, 1992), xiii. For a further exploration of family metaphors

part of people's political reality, we can see that the Emperors were significant figures on the Viennese home front. While denigrating the ordinary men in their midst, "the people" placed great hope in the beneficence of paternal leaders. Dynastic paternalism was nothing new, but it took on a new urgency in wartime as many ordinary Viennese looked to the last two Habsburg Emperors to mitigate their war-induced financial and emotional pains. But in the end, the severe shortages of food, heating supplies, clothing, shoes and medicine that the Viennese suffered (especially in 1917 and 1918) stripped the throne of its potency. The symbolic paternalism of the Emperors had consisted of a projected image of a caring father figure, but when actually tested, the image was exposed as illusion. As the Viennese demanded the material support that a modern social welfare system – but not an imperial family – could provide for a hungry city of two million, the dynastic image of the "good father" was rendered obsolete.

When he died in November, 1916, Emperor Franz Joseph had ruled Austria for sixty-eight years. Despite the development of modified constitutional rule in the second half of the nineteenth century, the Emperor remained a personal, highly visible head of state whose birthdays were celebrated as holidays and whose sixtieth year in power was marked by a grand jubilee in 1908.[74] Indeed, Franz Joseph's tenure as Emperor of Austria and King of Hungary was so long that he had developed into a grandfatherly figure. When he announced Austria's declaration of war on Serbia in 1914, he addressed his subjects as he always had – as the father of his peoples: "I put faith in my peoples, who have always gathered round my Throne, in unity and loyalty, through every tempest, who have always been ready for the heaviest sacrifices for the honour, the majesty, the power of the Fatherland."[75] Throughout the

in politics, see Victoria de Grazia, *How Fascism Ruled Women: Italy, 1922–1945* (Berkeley and Los Angeles: University of California Press, 1992). Austrian family history is oriented towards demographics and long-term structural change. It does not generally consider the wider possibilities of family as a political metaphor. See Michael Mitterauer, *Historisch-anthropologische Familienforschung: Fragestellungen und Zugangsweisen* (Vienna: Böhlau, 1990); and Josef Ehmer, "Die Entstehung der 'modernen Familie' in Wien (1780–1930)," in Laszlo Cseh-Szombathy and Rudolf Richter (eds.), *Familien in Wien und Budapest* (Vienna: Böhlau, 1993), 9–34.

[74] See Daniel Unowsky, "The Pomp and Politics of Patriotism: Imperial Celebrations in Habsburg Austria, 1848–1916," Ph.D. diss., Columbia University, 2000. See also John W. Boyer's discussion of prewar Viennese Mayor Karl Lueger's attempt to fashion himself similarly as a municipal father figure, following an imperial model of public birthday celebrations, commemorative medallions and pamphlets for schoolchildren. *Culture and Political Crisis in Vienna: Christian Socialism in Power, 1897–1918* (Chicago: University of Chicago Press, 1995), 55–6.

[75] *Wiener Zeitung*, 29 July 1914, cited in Edward Crankshaw, *The Fall of the House of Habsburg* (New York: Viking, 1963), 406.

first two years of war he spoke as a caring father, consoling his subjects for their wartime suffering in imperial notices that appeared in news-papers and on posters around the city of Vienna. In July 1916, one such poster stated, "My heart shares, with fatherly grief, in the con-cerns of every one of my loyal subjects, the concerns that burden them and that they have so resolutely endured, the sorrows over the dead, the fear about loved ones in the field, the disruption of peaceful work, the acute difficulties in all realms of life."[76] Part of Franz Joseph's pater-nal credibility lay in his subjects' knowledge of his own great personal losses over the years (his son had committed suicide in 1889 and his wife had been assassinated in 1898), which humanized him and elicited their sympathies.

Historians have frequently asserted that Franz Joseph's death was tan-tamount to the death of the empire he ruled. Karl, his grand-nephew and successor, was only twenty-nine years old and ruled for only two years. Joseph Redlich writes, "In Francis Joseph the last real Emperor of Aus-tria Hungary was entombed." Alan Sked agrees, noting, "Franz Joseph had died (21 Nov 1916) and, although his successor was well-liked, the old Monarchy seemed to have died with the old Emperor."[77] Based on these accounts it would seem fruitless to pursue the theme of imperial paternalism beyond the death of Franz Joseph because the father had died. And yet, if we consider the number of letters and petitions ordinary people wrote to the Emperors during World War I, we see that it actu-ally *increased* during the reign of Karl. Imperial advisers processed the following number of petitions during the war:

1914   19,039
1915   16,071
1916   19,308
1917   30,273
1918   21,056[78]

[76] ÖStA, KA, MS/1. Weltkrieg Flugschriftensammlung Karton 19.
[77] Joseph Redlich, *Emperor Francis Joseph of Austria: A Biography* (New York: Macmillan, 1929), 534; Alan Sked, *The Decline and Fall of the Habsburg Empire, 1815–1918* (London: Longman, 1989), 260. Barbara Jelavich's assessment of Karl is fairly standard: "Weak but well-meaning, the twenty-nine-year-old emperor had neither the training nor the temper-ament for the position." *Modern Austria: Empire and Republic, 1815–1986* (Cambridge: Cambridge University Press, 1987), 137.
[78] Figures from the HHStA *Protokollbände*, 1914–1918. These figures do not include second-tier letters (i.e. those from subjects with no documented service to the state) that were sent directly to the police. Several thousand original letters are still on file in the collection of *Bittschriften* at the HHStA, but the vast majority were forwarded to the relevant ministries for handling.

This increase suggests that ordinary people had a different conception of paternal rule than did political elites, who could write confidently that the dynasty had been defunct even before the war started. "The reputation of the old dynasty had long since dwindled," wrote socialist Otto Glöckel, "The old emperor had become... a living mummy."[79] The figures above show that the "mummy" and his supposedly negligible successor continued to receive a great deal of mail from their subjects.

Based on the rich, intimate correspondence ordinary Viennese conducted with their Emperors during the war, we see that many people who were missing fathers or father figures in their real families turned to the imperial one. My reading of the imperial mail shows that the loss of paternal authority, which, as we have seen, stemmed in part from the dismissive treatment of ordinary men on the home front, placed increasing burden on the "state family," the imperial father and his peoples. The "loss" at the symbolic level was not simply a matter of the old venerable father dying and being replaced by a young, less convincing father. Rather, the dire material misery that caused so many people to write the Emperors in the first place could no longer be alleviated by imperial beneficence. The "fathers of the people" did not have the means to combat mass suffering in wartime. The Emperors were besieged by requests for concrete assistance, which revealed the limits of symbolic paternalism, exposing imperial image as illusion.

Before analyzing the content of letters ordinary people wrote to the Emperors between 1914 and 1918, a bit of background on the practice of letter-writing is in order, because this was not a new phenomenon in wartime. Letters to the imperial family were classified by advisers (and hence are now classified in archives) as *Bittgesuche* (petitions) or *Bittschriften* (begging letters) because nearly all letters to the Emperor included a request of some sort, usually for money, but also for help in resolving a court case or family matter. We know that by 1840 imperial advisers had begun dividing subjects' letters to the Emperor into two categories: those that were pure requests for support and those that dealt with other matters. By the end of the 1870s the Emperor was receiving approximately 30,000 letters yearly. Due to this large volume, and the burden it placed on the staff of his cabinet, imperial advisers implemented a system of two-tiered access to the Emperor. Starting in 1880, only letters from "needy active or pensioned civil servants, as well as servants of the court and the widows and orphans of the above; and further, members of

---

[79] Otto Glöckel, *Selbstbiographie: Aus dem Leben eines großen Schulmannes* (Zurich: Verlag Genossenschaftsdruckerei, 1939), 55.

the better classes" would be handled by the Emperor's aides.[80] In other words, men who had served the state in some way, their dependents, and a vaguely defined set of people from the upper classes had access to the Emperor. All other letters would be forwarded directly to the police for handling at the local level. It is highly unlikely that ordinary letter writers knew of this two-tiered system, as most supplicants wrote as if the Emperor himself were reading their words. Because of this division, it is impossible to know how many total letters were sent to the Emperor; in 1909, imperial advisers stopped cataloging the letters they forwarded to police. The sample of letters examined here comes from both tiers, that is, from the imperial and police archives. Besides shedding light on the everyday living conditions in wartime Vienna, the letters reveal the increasingly real demands placed on the symbolic father, and the shift in the projection and perceptions of paternal authority that accompanied the regime change in 1916.

One type of correspondence consisted of warning letters; demonstrating a protective impulse towards their Emperor, subjects wrote to warn him of impending danger. One man informed police in 1917 that he had overheard assassination plans while pretending to be asleep in a train compartment. "It would be urgently necessary to imprison the traitors and to cancel the Emperor's trip [to the east] because he stands in very serious danger."[81] In 1918, Leopoldine Isakovic requested an audience with the Emperor, claiming she had heard of a planned assassination of Emperor Karl and his wife: "Please [make sure] that our beloved imperial pair is guarded by committed, dependable people, because people want to do [them] in – to unseat the Emperor from the throne, and the Empress, I can't even write the words…"[82] A second type of letter saw subjects offering the Emperor policy advice, bypassing local or regional officials (the "government") about whom they had complaints. (Both Emperors were spared the insults and name-calling – bum, scoundrel, rogue, criminal – that wartime letter writers heaped on government officials at all levels. The Viennese police noted that Mayor Weiskirchner received the highest number of slanderous and threatening letters (*Schmäh- und Drohbriefe*) followed by the prime minister and the governor of Lower Austria.[83] Prime Minister Stürgkh continued to receive hate mail even after he had

[80] *5. Gesammtinventar des Wiener Haus-, Hof- und Staatsarchiv* (Vienna: Verlag Adolf Holzhausens Nachfolger, 1937), 2, 176. This source does not specifically mention whether military personnel were in the group with privileged access to the Emperor, but I assume they were.

[81] AdBDW 1917 St./20 #42854. Aron Schreiner to Pol. Dir. Wien.

[82] AdBDW 1918 St./17 #58154. Leopoldine Isakovic to Ministerpresident.

[83] AdBDW 1917 St./20 #38378. Police report, "Anonyme Schmäh- und Drohbriefe," 25 January 1917.

been assassinated. One anonymous writer penned a complaint, full of indignation and spelling errors, that the Emperor had been duped by his advisers. "His Majesty has no idea about the hunger raging among the working people because...he hasn't been asked by the statesmen who are running the whole thing. Who but the statesmen, governor...and Viennese Mayor Weiskirchner are responsible for this despair?" The writer concluded, "I have only written here in order to open the eyes of His Majesty to the terrible conditions...and before it comes to deadly excesses among the people."[84] A fellow anonymous writer urged that His Majesty "must come unexpectedly and unannounced and talk with the little people, then he'll find out the truth..."[85] These letters allow us a glimpse of the political landscape from the perspective of non-elites. The writers believed (even as late as 1918) in a paternal Emperor who would serve their interests if only he were not being misled by layers of malevolent bureaucrats.[86]

The vast majority of letters to the Emperors contained neither warnings nor advice, but rather appeals for financial assistance, in which writers invariably mentioned the war as the source of their financial hardships. Many of these were from elderly persons or their dependents, who already received a pension but who could not cope with the rampant inflation, which had soared to 200 percent by 1917. They also included a new group of supplicants who gained privileged access to the Emperor in wartime: mothers and fathers of "child-rich" families with many sons in service. We see from the "child-rich" cases, however, that even many first-tier letters circulated to the police for verification. For example, Norbert Maurer, a 69-year-old widowed weaver's assistant from Vienna's XIV district who had eight sons in service, wrote to the Emperor for financial assistance in 1917. He pleaded that his sons' conscription had left him destitute. But police undermined his petition, writing, "The petitioner appears unobjectionable; his sons, in contrast, are known here to be violent, thieving street gang members who heretofore have not supported their father in any way."[87] Karl Paschkusz, a Viennese father with six sons in service, similarly wrote for financial assistance, emphasizing the sacrifices his sons had made for the state, including one who had "lost his right leg below the thigh" in battle. But like Maurer, the long list of

[84] AdBDW 1917 St./27 #38978. Anon. letter to MKSM.
[85] AdBDW 1918 St./16 #55053. Anon. letter to Emperor Karl.
[86] Scholars have written about the importance of the person of the monarch in the lives of people who had no access to other political forums. See, for example, John-Paul Himka, "Hope in the Tsar: Displaced Naive Monarchism Among the Ukrainian Peasants of the Habsburg Empire," *Russian History/Histoire Russe* 7 (1980), 125–38.
[87] HHStA 1917 Kabinettskanzlei Bittschriften #8832. Petition of Norbert Maurer.

petty crimes committed by the Paschkusz boys seems to have disqualified their father from access to the imperial coffers.[88] In these cases, we see that the police served as a filter, mediating the relationship of sovereign and subject and occasionally undermining the self-representation of the latter.

Letters to the Emperor varied in style and tone, but followed a recognizable pattern.[89] Those that made it to imperial advisers were usually written by a scribe; the elegant handwriting differs from the shaky, unsure penmanship of the supplicant's signature. In contrast, second-tier letters forwarded to the police are sometimes written on ordinary notebook paper in the supplicant's own hand. Some writers acknowledged that they did not know the protocol for writing to the Emperor. "I don't know how one should write to His Majesty's throne," one woman confided in a letter to his advisers.[90] All letters appeal in some way to the fatherly authority and magnanimity of the Emperor; a typical salutation has the supplicant throwing himself or herself at the Emperor's feet. Theresia Kreiper began, "For the first time in my life, I venture to approach the illustrious throne of Your Imperial and Royal Apostolic Majesty, and to seek mercy there, where no one has yet gone unheard..."[91] After hailing the kindness and generosity of the Emperor, and begging forgiveness for the imposition, letter writers go on to document their relation to the state (father's civil service, son's military service, etc.) and then the ailments, operations, nervous disorders, lame limbs, inability to work, and family deaths that had brought them to his throne.

Confident that he really was the caring, paternal figure projected in public announcements, Viennese residents confided in the Emperor about matters of everyday concern. To say that he was a father "figure" elides, in some ways, the extent to which people relied on him for *practical* fatherly assistance. In 1918, Paula Neuwirth, a woman from the VIII district who already received a small pension, wrote a typical appeal:

Your Majesty!
The undersigned most humble subject... asks for assistance. The most humble petitioner, as the orphan of a chancery clerk, receives through Your Majesty's munificence a monthly allowance (*Gnadengabe*) of 13Kr 33hl. [I am] suffering from

---

[88] HHStA 1917 Kabinettskanzlei Bittschriften #4734. Petition of Karl Paschkusz.

[89] My attention to the style and tone of the letters, and to the importance of self-representation in "official" correspondence is informed by Sheila Fitzpatrick, "Supplicants and Citizens: Public Letter-Writing in Soviet Russia in the 1930s," *Slavic Review* 55, no. 1 (Spring 1996), 78–105; and Natalie Zemon Davis, *Fiction in the Archives: Pardon Tales and their Tellers in Sixteenth-Century France* (Stanford: Stanford University Press, 1987).

[90] ÖStA, KA, MKSM 1915 44-1/#111. Letter from Maria Sophie Lechner to MKSM, 17 February 1915.

[91] HHStA 1917 Kabinettskanzlei Bittschriften, #4076. Petition of Theresia Kreiper.

heart and nerve troubles, waging today's terrible battle for life; due to shortage of materials, the rent and little bit of needlework don't suffice to keep a meager life going. I would gladly do the most menial work but many get hung up on [my] age, 57, and many believe [I] can't work. The war has made me directly into a beggar because I can't rely on support from any source . . . so that my last [belongings] have gone to the pawn shop, [I hawked] my sewing machine in order to pay taxes . . . I can't afford to buy warm shoes or underwear because of this horrible inflation . . .[92]

Neuwirth was granted a one-time payment of 30 crowns. The fact that she was fifty-seven years old and still referring to herself as an "orphan" reflected the custom of unmarried women retaining familial status via their late fathers. For this helpless, grown "orphan," the Emperor was next in line after her real father had died. When Olga Hubaczek, a 69-year-old "orphan" and Galician refugee who spent the war in Vienna was turned out by her real family – "[They] told me I should leave them, that the times were so difficult and they couldn't put me up any longer" – she turned to the Emperor as a last resort.[93] Similarly, Marie Burggraf, a 21-year-old Viennese maidservant who received no support from her actual father, wanted to enter nursing school and appealed in 1917 to the Emperor for help buying the required uniform.[94] Others requested (and frequently received) imperial assistance for rent, heating, food and shoes. In these instances the Emperor came to figure in the everyday lives of his subjects, providing support that might otherwise come from a real father.

In contrast to the grown orphans who wrote the Emperor as dependent daughters, a man might choose to approach His Majesty as a fellow father, albeit of a smaller family. A brochure written in 1914 entitled "For the Fathers of Warriors" advised older men to remember their paternal links to the state: "In younger years you would surely have gone into the field without question to help the Emperor . . . In your sons you have now sent a representative."[95] Letters from fathers with sons in service reveal that the boundary separating real families from the symbolic one of the sovereign and his subjects was disappearing in wartime. As if in a paternal chain, ordinary fathers with authority within the domain of their own families in turn became the dependents when appealing to the imperial father above. But they established their own fatherly credentials before asking for money. "A master craftsman for thirty years, I have always fulfilled my duties to the state and my fellow citizens," wrote Joseph Palkowitsch from Vienna's XVI district, "I have raised my daughter and six sons to be

[92] HHStA 1918 Kabinettskanzlei Bittschriften, #1981. Petition of Paula Neuwirth.
[93] HHStA 1918 Kabinettskanzlei Bittschriften, #2483. Petitition of Olga Hubaczek.
[94] HHStA 1917 Kabinettskanzlei Bittschriften, #7163. Police report on petition from Marie Burggraf.
[95] Ignaz Seipel, *Kriegsbriefe: An den Vater des Kriegers* (Salzburg: Georg Lorenz, 1914), 8.

useful members of society." But the war had left him with no workers and no wood for his workshop.[96] A popular human interest genre, newspaper articles on "child-rich" families with many sons in service depicted the home-front fathers as stoic patriarchs, suffering in the absence of their sons, but proud of their sacrifices made "in the service of the Emperor." In 1917, the *Illustrierte Kronenzeitung* featured 68-year-old Karl Haider along with his six sons in service (see plate 6.2). This would have been a typical "child-rich" feature, except that the working-class Haider took the unusual step of clipping the article and sending it on to the Emperor, in an appeal for financial assistance.

As the father of six enlisted sons who were meant to provide support for me, a 68-year-old man, I have been left in great distress and I make a bare living by shoveling snow, which I do very gladly in the service of my beloved fatherland until a victorious peace comes about.[97]

Haider's self-representation is complex. On the one hand, he wanted the Emperor to see him pictured as head of his own large and patriotic family. But as an elderly man shoveling snow for the fatherland, the destitute Haider was reduced to "asking His Majesty to grant merciful assistance." He, Palkowitsch, and other needy fathers were able to do so in part because of their dual position on the paternal chain: their own familial authority granted them the right to seek the paternal beneficence of the sovereign.

Still other supplicants sought paternal aid from the sovereign in the form of imperial guardianship (*Patenschaft*) for their children. For ordinary people, guardianship from any member of the imperial family was highly prized because a guardian took on a lasting financial commitment to a child, something like a beneficent godfather or godmother. Guardianships were often based on some sort of symbolic coincidence that linked ordinary families to the imperial family.[98] In 1915, Joseph and Anna Sanda requested guardianship for their newborn triplets, whom they named Franz, Joseph and Karl. Similarly, Ottakar and Mathilde Spitzer, war refugees in Vienna, requested imperial guardianship for their son, who was born on August 17, 1917, Karl's first birthday as Emperor. A Hungarian couple requested guardianship for their twins, whom they

[96] HHStA 1917 Kabinettskanzlei, Bittschriften, #5440. Petition of Josef Palkowitsch.
[97] HHStA 1917 Kabinettskanzlei, Bittschriften, #4130. Karl Haider to Emperor Karl, 28 January 1917. I do not know the outcome of Haider's petition.
[98] Imperial guardianships (and one-time gifts for children denied guardianship) were paid from a fund abbreviated as the Gen. Dir. d. Ah. Privat- u. Familienf. A famous fictional guardianship was granted in Josef Roth's 1932 novel, *The Radetzky March*, to the descendants of infantry lieutenant Trotta after he took a bullet intended for the Emperor at the Battle of Solferino.

Plate 6.2. "Family father" Karl Haider petitions the Emperor with a newspaper article on his many sons in service. Source: *Illustrierte Kronenzeitung*, 1917.

named Karl and Zita, born on "the very day" the royal couple had arrived in Budapest.[99]

The institution of guardianship, which predated the war, was not designed as a program of social welfare; rather, it was intended as a kind of one-in-a-million stroke of good fortune for the ordinary subjects on whom it was bestowed.[100] By 1917, however, imperial advisers noted that requests for guardianship had begun to spiral out of control. The tradition of linking ordinary families to the imperial family through names, birthdays or other significant dates or coincidences had instead become a way for desperate parents to combat the financial misery of the wartime economy. "The requests for guardianship have increased so dramatically of late," advisers noted, "that, apart from the financial burden, the danger exists that through frequent granting of guardianship by His Majesty, this especially revered act of mercy might lose its value."[101] Under new wartime guidelines, guardianship was to be granted "only in very special, exceptional cases" – brave action by the father in combat was an important consideration – and rejected applicants were given a small, one-time payment or bracelet with the Emperor's initials. The increase in guardianship requests signals one of the changing demands on paternal authority during the war: needy families were turning to the symbolic father for the kind of real material support that a social welfare system, but not an imperial family, could provide. Imperial gifts were small and distributed according to the whim of advisers. As with traditional forms of charity in which the moral character of applicants was a prime consideration, the "worthiness" of the imperial supplicants mattered more than their actual need. No matter how beneficent, imperial gift-giving was not designed to support financially the residents of a modern city, even one populated by newborn Franzs, Josephs, Karls and Zitas.

A similar surge in petitions for financial support came from within the military itself. As loyal servants of the Emperor, officers of the Habsburg armed forces had traditionally enjoyed imperial patronage, petitioning in situations of career or family misfortunes.[102] The patronage rested in

---

[99] HHStA 1916 Kabinettskanzlei Bittschriften, #1-11,000; ÖStA KA, MKSM 1917 carton 1317, #68-2/14; #68-2/11.

[100] I have been unable to determine the legal origin of these "good fortune guardianships." They are not mentioned in regulations on imperial pensions for widows and orphans of military and civil servants. *Nachschlage-Register zu den österr. Reichsgesetzen, Landesgesetzen und Verordnungen* (Vienna, 1908), 676–81.

[101] ÖStA KA, MKSM 1917 carton 1317, #68-2/8.

[102] On pensioners, widows and orphans of the Habsburg officer corps, see István Deák, *Beyond Nationalism: A Social and Political History of the Habsburg Officer Corps, 1848–1918* (New York: Oxford University Press, 1992), ch. 8.

part in the belief that officers needed to maintain their *Stand* and that this maintenance was in the interest of the state. In 1918, however, the War Minister issued an unusual warning to officers to stop pestering the Emperor. Officers, it seemed, had begun to circumvent the normal channels of administrative appeal and were approaching the Emperor in person and in writing in ever-increasing numbers with trivial matters of "pure personal interest." "While every man's path to His Majesty the commander should remain open, now as before, for <u>important</u> matters, and while nothing is further from my intention than the wish to erect certain barriers to this," wrote the War Minister, "I am nevertheless duty-bound to point out most emphatically that I find it thoroughly inappropriate" to disturb the Emperor with petty, personal matters. He appealed to the officers as *men*. Trivial or unnecessary petitions were incompatible with military discipline and "are evidence of a low degree of soldierly, manly sensibility."[103] He does not speculate on the cause of this troubling and unmanly increase in personal, direct appeals the Emperor, but we can surmise that it did not differ terribly from the causes behind imperial petitioning more generally: hunger, material shortages and inflation led people to the Emperor after they had presumably failed to find assistance through other channels.

A number of street incidents during the second half of the war suggest that certain segments of the Viennese population had abandoned the letter-writing route altogether and had resolved to encounter the Emperor personally. Here, the notion that the Emperor was a symbolic father gave way to the belief (or hope) that he was an approachable, kindly man, ready and willing to help those in need. We might think of these incidents as small punctures in the imperial aura that cumulatively signaled a weakening of symbolic power. In the early summer of 1917, police became alarmed about the repeated incidents in which subjects (usually women) flagged down the Emperor's motorcade or approached him directly in public with appeals for financial help or legal leniency. Unbeknownst to most of the offenders, who had apparently taken the paternal projection of the Emperor to heart as "real," it was illegal to disturb (*behelligen*) the sovereign. They would not have known this from reading official literature, in which the Emperor was depicted as a down-to-earth man of the people. In a typical passage from a schoolbook, Emperor Karl stops his motorcade at an outdoor snack bar at lunchtime:

Soon countless children and a few grown-ups from the village gathered around the automobile. His Majesty then distributed his food to the children and gave

---

[103] ÖStA, KA, MKSM 1918 30-2/1-2. Memo (no date) from KM to various military Kommandos.

drinks to the adults. The generosity of the Monarch was received with wild cheers from the population.[104]

Supplicants in Vienna who sought to experience this generosity first hand, however, were arrested and charged with violating an 1854 law that only indirectly related to the Emperor. The law spelled out punishments for "any unauthorized behavior" committed in public places, including "any demonstrative action, in which criticism of the government or contempt of its decrees should be expressed . . ."[105] The vagueness of this law reveals a contradiction at the heart of imperial paternalism. A clear law prohibiting personal contact with the Emperor would have run contrary to the paternal image projected in official literature. Local police were therefore charged with enforcing a vaguely worded decree that took many supplicants by surprise. In a memo to local district heads, Lower Austrian Governor Bleyleben voiced concern over the street incidents, writing, "Because these actions are an annoyance for his Majesty's person [you] are instructed to keep the nuisance . . . in check using appropriate means." He continued, "Issuing a general ban and inserting a corresponding notice in the official newspaper or in the daily newspapers is obviously to be avoided."[106] In other words, subjects were prohibited by local authorities from approaching the Emperor, but they could not be *told* of this prohibition because it would shatter his paternal image.

In twenty-three recorded cases of "disturbing the court" (*Hofbehelligung*) that took place between mid-1917 and early 1918, subjects were arrested for approaching the Emperor they had been led to believe cared deeply about their problems. Theresia Samm and her twelve-year-old daughter Maria stopped Emperor Karl's motorcade along a road outside Vienna and passed a letter requesting the release of husband Joseph from military service because the family was in "extreme need." Karl Mihokovic stopped the Emperor on Favoritenstraße to request a pension; the same day, twenty-year-old clerk Marta Zeisberg sprung from the crowd during an imperial procession on the Burgplatz, landed on her knee in front of the Emperor and tried to pass a note requesting help for her fiancé; a policeman from Vienna's VI district reported hearing rumors that shop owners were planning to stop the imperial motorcade to inform His Majesty about butter shortages; Barbara Plihal, Maria Hbozanek and Sofie Lang, who were called to the police station for "suspicious loitering"

[104] *Kaiser Karl I. und Kaiserin Zita: Lebensbild für Jugend und Volk* (Linz: Verlag des kathol. Preßvereines, 1917), "recommended" by the k.k. Landesschulrate, 41–2.
[105] Kaiserliche Verordnung vom 20. April 1854, §11.
[106] ÖStA, AVA MdI Präs 22 (1917–1918) box 2131, #11763. Memo to Bezirkshauptmannschaften.

in the X district, admitted, after "repeated lies," that they were waiting for the Emperor "in order to inform him personally of the rampant abuses at the local markets"; Leopoldine Ramberger from the VIII district passed a note to the Emperor as he was on his way to church, pleading for a pardon in an abortion case; Marie Fraisl tried to pass the following note to the Emperor as he passed through the XX district: "I beg you, my children have tuberculosis and are dying in misery because I have <u>no</u> food. [T]hey will have to starve if help doesn't come..."[107] The incidents were handled in such a way as to preserve the appearance of imperial concern but to discourage repeat offenses. When the Emperor noticed a supplicant, he appeared concerned and graciously took the note; only after he had passed were the subjects arrested by local policemen.

Individual acts of disturbing the court were easier for authorities to prevent than the large-scale demonstration marches that began taking place in April, 1917. In these incidents, hundreds of women working in shoe, cork, paper and recycling factories outside Vienna banded together to march to Karl's castle in the nearby village of Laxenburg. Reminiscent of French women's march to Versailles in 1789, the women marching to Laxenburg demanded flour, bread, potatoes, lard and sugar, and intended to take their case "to the top."[108] Authorities reported hearing from several parties the defiant declaration, "Then I'll go to the Emperor myself." The women, who explained "that it was not their intention to disturb the Majesties on the street," were warned about the illegality of their actions. In one march, a small group of women representing a crowd of about 1,000 met with local police authorities who promised to pass their requests on to imperial aides.[109] Although the women apparently failed to secure an imperial audience, these marches spell out for us some common people's perceptions of authority. The statement "Then I'll go to the Emperor myself," likely voiced in exasperation, combines self-assertion, defiance of local authorities and a confidence that one man at the top still had the power to alleviate suffering.

The increase in "disturbing the court" that seems to have taken place at all levels of society, from elderly parents to military officers to working-class women, might initially suggest an increase in the faith in the paternal

---

[107] ÖStA, AVA MdI Präs. carton 2131/22 #11263; NÖLA Präs. "P" 1918, Ib, 601; AdBDW 1917 V/9 #47642, 1918 St./16 #54978 and 59998.

[108] For the women's march on Versailles, see Darline Gay Levy and Harriet B. Applewhite, "Women and Militant Citizenship in Revolutionary Paris," in Sara E. Melzer and Leslie W. Rabine (eds.), *Rebel Daughters: Women and the French Revolution* (New York: Oxford University Press, 1992), 79–101. Unlike the French women, the Austrian women were not armed.

[109] At least two marches took place, one on 10 April and the second on 18 April 1917. ÖStA, AVA MdI Präs. 22 (1917–18) carton 2131, #5995 and 6608.

authority of the Emperor. What I believe the phenomenon instead indicates is that the wartime conditions began to overtax the Emperor's symbolic powers. If we compare inflationary prices of basic goods with a typical one-time payment a supplicant might receive as a "mercy gift," we see that neither Franz Joseph nor Karl could alleviate the suffering of the many Viennese residents who appealed to them for paternal assistance. An imperial gift typically ranged from nothing (for rejected petitions) to 100 crowns for exceptionally worthy cases. The average successful applicant received 30 or 50 crowns. In July, 1917, the black market price for a liter of milk was 6 crowns and a kilogram of flour was 22 crowns.[110] As a stop-gap measure, a successful petition might buy a little extra food, but it could not provide a long-term solution to the economic misery of the petitioner.

The worsening material circumstances that led increasing numbers of subjects to make direct, sometimes desperate, appeals to the Emperor, also took place against the backdrop of a regime change. The old Emperor had been replaced in 1916, and the rash of incidents above involving the imperial motorcade, women's marches to the palace at Laxenburg and the increasing appeals from officers date from 1917 and 1918, during the reign of Karl. The regime change necessitated a repackaging of imperial paternalism – a new image would have to be crafted for the young Emperor – at a time when petitions were on the rise.

The project of creating new paternal symbols began at the funeral of Franz Joseph. Not surprisingly, public notices of Franz Joseph's death announced the passing of a father. Karl published a statement to soldiers:

Soldiers! Your highest commander [the] illustrious Emperor and King Franz Joseph I, who through almost seven decades has led you, your grandfathers and fathers with love and care, who has looked after you like a father, has gone home to God.[111]

For all of the men who died anonymously in battle, and for all of their Viennese family members who had no chance to mourn them publicly or pay respects at a funeral, Franz Joseph's funeral procession offered an opportunity for vicarious, communal grieving. Attracting hundreds of thousands of bystanders, the funeral procession wound around the Ringstrasse and reached an even greater audience when it was filmed and later shown to cinema audiences. Press reports focused on the massive

---

[110] Wilhelm Winkler, *Die Einkommensverschiebungen in Österreich während des Weltkrieges*, Carnegie Endowment for International Peace series (Vienna: Hölder-Pichler-Tempsky, 1930), 125.
[111] ÖStA KA, MS/1. Weltkrieg Flugschriftensammlung carton 19. Wien: Stellungskundmachung.

turnout and police took great pains with security. The procession also marked the public debut of the new imperial family. What would in peacetime have been a ceremonial opportunity to display the paternal qualities of the new Emperor was clouded, however, by subjects' concerns about food. Despite the cathartic potential of this grand, public funeral in wartime, the mood of the Viennese population appears to have been one of apathy. A witness to the event, Joseph Redlich, reported that despite the large crowds, "Genuine popular sorrow was not called out in Vienna by the death of Francis Joseph: frightful losses in the war, which still raged, suffering and the permanent under-feeding of millions in the capital had produced a sort of apathy there."[112] Viennese police reported that the death and funeral procession had "to a certain extent turned the thoughts of the population away from food concerns, but had not influenced the general mood of the people."[113] Inheriting the Habsburg throne in late 1916 meant inheriting what had become intractable material shortages in Vienna.

The new Emperor, together with his wife, Zita, and young son and heir, Otto, was displayed at the funeral as a family man, head of his own young family and of the peoples of the Empire. A book published for primary school pupils in 1918 recounted the debut of the new imperial trio at Franz Joseph's funeral:

The illustrious parental couple arranged it that their first-born child was introduced at the hand of his mother. From this picture arose quite magically a bond of understanding between the ruling pair and the people: the tender gesture of the mother captivated the empire![114]

Imperial advisers made a concerted effort to construct and project a paternal image for Karl. By February, 1917, Professor Rudolf Peerz had been commissioned to write an official booklet entitled *Emperor Karl and His House*. "This undertaking," wrote the War Aid Bureau, "stems from the general need of the population to learn as quickly as possible more about the lives of His Majesty and the imperial family," in order to "fuse" the pre-existing attachment to the ruling house with the persons of Karl, Zita and their children. Karl also quickly instituted the new imperial birthdays and name days as school holidays, marking the Empress's birthday as "Zita Day" and November 21 as commemoration of Franz Joseph's death and Karl's ascension to the throne.[115] Karl was presented as a loving

---

[112] Redlich, *Emperor Francis Joseph*, 533.
[113] AdBDW, Stimmungsbericht 7 December 1916.
[114] *Unser Kaiserpaar*, Donauland Bücherei I (Vienna: Verlag J. Roller, 1918), 304.
[115] ÖStA AVA, MdI Präs. 1915–1918, 38, carton 2294, #3678. Memo from Ministerium für Kultus und Unterricht to MdI Präs, 12 March 1917.

father and husband. One schoolbook explained, "Love for the children binds Emperor Karl with an inner love for his wife. He is an exceedingly attentive husband."[116] In addition, Karl tried to link his roles as real family father and "father of his peoples" in a series of imperial amnesties granted to civilians and military personnel charged with a variety of political crimes. He announced an amnesty on March 12, 1918, which was opposed by military leaders, but which coincided with the birth of his son. The happiness that the amnesty would bring to prisoners and their families would mirror the "joyous event of the delivery by my wife the Empress and Queen," momentarily aligning all families that made up the family of the state.[117] In the Empress, it seemed that Karl even had a symbolic advantage over Franz Joseph because his imperial paternalism could be paired with her imperial maternalism for a more complete and convincing familial package.

Many official publications heralded the maternal virtues of Empress Zita. A 1917 schoolbook noted, "This word 'Empress' has a very special ring for our ears. How many years have passed in which the Kaiserburg in Vienna was without an Empress!"[118] In her new role as "mother of the land" (*Landesmutter*) Zita became the titular head of organizations considered appropriate to her gender: children's welfare societies and women's volunteer groups. A member of the Christian Women's League of Austria who met with Zita in 1917 recalled a down-to-earth feminine goodness in the Empress: "I didn't have the feeling I was talking to the highest-ranking woman in the Monarchy, but rather with a personality whose thoughts and aspirations are completely devoted to the well-being of her fellow man. With every word the Empress spoke, one noticed that it came from the heart."[119] In a public letter to his wife, Karl hailed her as a "real soldier's wife" (*echte Soldatenfrau*) who could serve as a model for other women in distress.[120] Petitions sent to the Empress most often concerned family themes, and some were written in a mother-to-mother tone. Marie Toman, a coach driver's wife from Vienna, wrote the Empress seeking medical attention for her sick daughter; another petitioner sought the Empress's assistance for treatment for a child with a stutter; Rosa Püttner of Vienna wrote to ask Zita's help in finding a place at a spa for her seriously ill mother. Imperial image makers – those who wrote and published books and pamphlets for popular consumption – must be credited with successfully projecting a maternal, wifely, solidly

---

[116] *Kaiser Karl I. und Kaiserin Zita*, 22.   [117] ÖStA, KA, MKSM 1918 85-4/1.
[118] *Kaiser Karl I. und Kaiserin Zita*, 38.
[119] "Audienz bei der Kaiserin," *Oesterreichische Frauen-Zeitung* 1, no. 1 (1917), 3.
[120] *Unser Kaiserpaar*, 319.

"feminine" image of Zita that found a receptive audience at least among some (mostly female) petitioners.[121]

Despite this carefully crafted media effort, which focused heavily on familial themes, Emperor Karl's rule presents us with a paradox. In symbolic terms, it would seem that the young ruling pair were at least a plausible replacement for the elderly, paternal Franz Joseph. In them, the dynasty had a dynamic couple (a caring father and husband and his good-hearted wife) who, along with their rosy-cheeked children, might have signaled a Habsburg revitalization, a biological, spiritual and generational rebirth that would mollify contemporary fears about population decline and degeneration. Why, then, did contemporary elites write Karl off as a father figure? Psychoanalyst Paul Federn, who offered the term "fatherless society" to describe Austria wrote, "The collapse of the patriarchy (*Vatertum*) among people loyal to the Emperor was...facilitated by the personality of the young Emperor, [who was] little suited as a father figure." He noted that "defaming rumors" spread by anti-dynastic movements in the wake of the Sixtus Affair had undermined the support of many loyal subjects.[122] As an alternative explanation for Karl's failure to establish himself as a symbolic father, we should consider evidence from the petitions and cases of "disturbing the court" that the Viennese populace was in need of something more than symbolic care. Symbolic paternalism rested on a certain degree of detachment from the everyday and the mundane; the image of the Emperor was not meant to be tested by real-life circumstances. By 1917, however, the relationship of the sovereign and subjects was mired in the everyday; it was about money, food, shoes and the inability of the government to provide these things to the people.

One angry letter-writer posed the rhetorical question in 1918: "Do we have an Emperor or not?" The writer presented a laundry list of complaints about food, heating supplies, inflation and government corruption, before striking at the heart of imperial paternalism: "In circumstances like these in which one has to fight to live in Austria, one has lost heart and soul for the Emperor and the Empire and can only

---

[121] ÖStA AVA, MdI "S" carton 53, #2819; carton 44 #2157; HHStA 1917 Kabinettskanzlei Bittschriften #7694. Letters to Zita are scattered in several archives. I have been unable to locate the records of the Obersthofmeister-Amt Ihrer Majestät der Kaiserin und Königin, the office that handled petitions to Zita, although I know she received at least fifty-nine such petitions in 1917.

[122] In this diplomatic scandal, Karl was seen by German nationalists to have "betrayed" Germans after entering into secret negotiations on a separate peace with the French, via Zita's brother, Prince Sixtus; see chapter 4 for rumors in the wake of the scandal that Zita was an "Italian" and thus an enemy of Austria.

count the hours until the state of Austria collapses."[123] We can imagine
from this passage that the letter-writer had been a one-time believer in
the Emperor, before wartime "circumstances" eroded confidence in the
Emperor's power to care for his peoples, which had been a central tenet
of dynasticism.

Political histories of the fall of the Habsburg Empire, which, as noted
above, focus on the structural arrangements of pro- and anti-dynastic interest groups, have had little use for ordinary individuals' changing perceptions of imperial rule. If mentioned at all, paternalism is presented as a
legitimating rhetorical device used by the ruling house, but it is not taken
seriously as something that subjects might have believed in, and in times
of distress actually *relied on*, in their everyday lives. As the letters, petitions
and personal encounters cited here demonstrate, needy people tested the
symbolic father, hoping he was real. Letters from subjects behind on their
current events continued to arrive for Karl in December, 1918, after he
had stepped down and a republic had been declared. The strongly paternalistic tone of socialist leaders in "Red Vienna" of the 1920s must
be understood against the backdrop of the paternalistic expectations and
fantasies of ordinary Viennese during wartime.[124]

What Franz Stiedl and many other Viennese interpreted as a loss of
authority and an absence of fathers in the city was due in part to the
large numbers of Viennese men conscripted into the military. But with
hundreds of thousands of men still in Vienna, conscription cannot fully
explain the widespread conviction that fathers were missing. Rather, as
has been argued in this chapter, fatherly authority had ceased in wartime
to be one of the defining attributes of manhood for ordinary men, and
symbolic imperial paternalism had collapsed under the weight of subjects'
concrete material needs. Combined, these developments constituted the
discourse on the fatherless society. Putting society back together again
after the war would require putting families back together; to do this,
a civilian, urban alternative to the new martial masculinity would have
to become available to ordinary men. This was a challenge not only for

---

[123] AdBDW 1918 St./16 #55053. Anon. letter to Emperor, April 1918.
[124] In his study of inter-war Vienna, Helmut Gruber is critical of the Social Democratic
leadership for its paternalistic attitude towards workers. He writes, "The socialist leaders
appeared as authority figures in the workers' world in two related guises: as city fathers
and as oligarchs of the SDAP. Furthermore, their cultural program was paternalistic,
especially in its demands for discipline both in the organizations themselves and on
the part of the workers undergoing 'civilization.'" *Red Vienna: Experiment in Working-
Class Culture, 1919–1934* (New York and Oxford: Oxford University Press, 1991),
185.

men who fought,[125] but for men who experienced the changing definition of manhood from the home front. Defining new roles for men (or re-establishing old ones) was a cultural project of the postwar decade. Discussion during the late 1920s of a continuing "crisis of fatherhood"[126] suggests that prewar models of paternal authority in families and in society at large were not easily resurrected.

---

[125] See Peter Melichar, "Die Kämpfe merkwürdig Untoter: K.u.k. Offiziere in der Ersten Republik," *Österreichische Zeitschrift für Geschichte* 9, no. 1 (1998), 51–84.

[126] See Rosa Mayreder, *Krise der Väterlichkeit* (Vienna: Anzengruber Verlag, 1928).

Conclusion

World War I was a watershed moment for the idea of the home front. Never before had civilians been mobilized so completely in the service of the state and in the business of war-making, and never again would it be assumed that civilian society was immune from the violence of war. World War I marks the beginning of a trend in twentieth-century warfare, in which distinctions between civilian and military realms have gradually been eroded. The case of Vienna starkly contrasts the home front of the 1914 imagination with the reality of the home front as it evolved over four and a half years. In its ideal form, the home front was meant to be a preserve; it was the realm of women, children and family to which soldiers who had been away on uncivilized business could return. The existence of such a home front promised that society at war could eventually return to the normal, that it could revert back to society not at war. But wartime Vienna was not a place inhabited by nurturing women and innocent children holding out in good spirits for the return of their loved ones. Rather, residents waged an internecine war against one another; scarcity and psychological insecurity ignited pre-existing tensions about belonging and community, and turned everyday life into a series of minor battlefields.

The preceding chapters have traced the slow collapse of the home front, focusing on moments at which Viennese residents lost confidence in the mission of the Habsburg state and the war it was waging. This study adds a new dimension to the long-standing historical thesis that the Habsburg state collapsed for "internal" rather than "external" reasons: the collapse was even more deeply internal than previously imagined. The state was discredited not only in the eyes of national minorities in other parts of Austria or in the minds of weary troops at the front, as other histories have shown, but also in the markets, apartment houses, schoolyards, streets and pubs of its own imperial capital.

This study has found the roots of the collapse of the Habsburg state in the mundane and the everyday. Nowhere did the mundane more clearly constitute a "matter of state" during World War I than in the realm of

food. Despite some ambitious propaganda efforts – most notably at the
Vienna War Exhibition – state authorities never succeeded in painting the
external enemy as the true victimizer of the Austrian people. As seen in
chapter 1, the "starvation war" or the "hunger blockade" waged by the
Allies paled next to the perceived food abuses committed by Hungarians,
local Austrian farmers and, most devastating for home front unity, merchants and fellow consumers. The food crisis was divisive at the level of
high politics, where the military high command competed against civilian authorities for supplies, Austrian and Hungarian state officials traded
insults and accusations of hoarding, and the Viennese municipal government accused the Austrian state of betraying the capital city. It was
similarly divisive at the level of everyday life, where buttered bread, coffee with milk, or the price of an egg spawned denunciations, verbal and
physical scuffles between merchants and customers and the daily unrest, "excesses," altercations and full-blown food riots that characterized
life on the Viennese home front. Pre-existing national and ethnic hatreds shaped Viennese reactions to material shortage; the much-abused
"profiteering Jews" or "russophile Czechs" were often blamed for others'
hunger. From citizens' letters, newspaper accounts and police reports,
we have seen that German-speaking, Christian Viennese assailed Slavs
and Jews (Austrian citizens one and all) as outsiders or parasites whose
interests were at odds with those of the "community" or "the people."
Class-based mobilization of the "poor" against the "rich" was muddied
by the fact that many of the "poor" – Jewish refugees and Slavic immigrants in Vienna's working-class neighborhoods – were excluded on
national grounds from the rhetorical "community of sufferers."

State authorities tried to redirect Viennese attention away from these
internal divisions and refocus them on "the war." We saw in chapter 2
that their greatest effort came mid-way through the war with the opening
of the Vienna War Exhibition, a massive entertainment and propaganda
complex that had aimed to reinforce civilian duties of *Opferwilligkeit* and
Durchhalten. In the summer of 1916, the Exhibition tried to resurrect the
1914 dream of a dedicated home front working in unity with a heroic
front. The show represented a total war as it *ought* to be fought, rather
than the Habsburg war effort as it was actually unfolding. The War Exhibition was the crown jewel in a state propaganda effort otherwise lacking
luster. Chapter 3 examined this propaganda effort and the state's struggle
to control the flow of information on the home front. While the Catholic
Church and wide segments of the German-language Viennese press made
up for the state's weak official propaganda program by actively promoting the virtues of Austria and regularly professing support for the imperial family, state authorities focused more on censorship, the negative

component of information management. But the censors' work left traces that undermined Viennese confidence in the "truth" of official accounts of the war. When confronted with censored mail or white spaces in the newspapers, citizens were left to fill in missing pieces of information with unofficial "truths" in circulation. Rumor-spreading was deemed an epidemic in Vienna, and police struggled to catch and suppress these fleeting bugs. In the process, they left for the historian useful records of the stories Viennese were telling about the war, but they also left the distinct impression that the state was not winning the battle to control civilian perceptions of it. Neither the propaganda campaigns nor the censorship apparatus of the Habsburg state were comparable to the information management techniques of later twentieth-century dictatorial regimes.

Absent a formal institution for recruiting and mobilizing civilians for war, the state had relied heavily on the family. No other institution played as central – or as contradictory – a role in home-front mobilization. The state had attempted to mobilize civilians in their familial capacities, turning the family inside out and realigning women and children to the state in new ways. Women's voluntary service to the state, for example, was promoted as an act of sisterhood rather than citizenship. Children were told that collecting metal scraps door-to-door for the war munitions industries would earn them membership in the "state family." Their deeds would honor the fathers in the field. And yet this mobilization came at a cost. Unruly crowds of women waging battle for food and a generation of children slipping into delinquency, neither subject to proper "authority," were read as signs both of the deterioration of the family and of the unraveling of society more generally. Add to this the fact that the crumbling state itself had relied on family metaphors for its legitimacy, and residents experienced the fall of Vienna as the undifferentiated, simultaneous collapse of state, society and family.

Although they were not yet full political citizens, women's conceptions of the state had been crucial to the project of mobilizing civilians for war. As argued in chapter 4, the organized women's groups of the Frauenhilfsaktion Wien had performed valuable services to the state and social services on the home front, but their dream of a unified Austrian sisterhood was marred by class and confessional differences. Once mobilized, Viennese women were also politicized. Women practiced politics in venues not normally considered by historians to be political, and their actions refute the notion that politics were "shut down" for the duration that the parliament was suspended. Who needed the defunct parliament, when Vienna had consumers like Frau Ungar to expose the vices and identify the villains of wartime governance? Frau Ungar, a known agitator in the food lines of the III district, summarily vilified "quite openly the mayor, the police chief, the minister" and, according to her denouncers, even slandered "the Empress, our angel." She "has said several times that *our Emperor and the German should be whacked* because they carry on the war."[1] Male parliamentarians might later adopt, but did not invent, such platforms of discontent. Denunciation itself was clearly political, and offered denouncers, many of whom were women, the chance to articulate their own positions *vis-à-vis* the state.

Although the war had not led to the anticipated sisterhood of all women, it had brought women into unprecedented contact with the state. These contacts came in legal disputes over marriage to foreigners, in payments of state support subsidies to female family members of men in service, in court cases of women accused of making "anti-state comments," and in women's service in Auxiliary units behind the lines. Female citizenship had evolved during the war, but in all of these instances women's "Austrianness" was tied closely to their capacities as mothers, sisters or daughters. In this sense, traditional familial notions of feminine "nature" promoted by the Frauenhilfsaktion survived the war intact, despite the fact that "womenfolk" and "female-persons" were brawling in the streets.

Chapter 5 revealed that a similar dichotomy between the ideal and the real developed when children were mobilized for war. In various images produced by the state and the Viennese press between 1914 and 1916, idealized children held great symbolic promise. The Austrian child, as embodied in the imperial orphans or Rosa Zenoch, the heroic girl from Rawa Ruska, had promised to transcend the chronic fragmentation that had bedeviled Austrian politics in the decades before the war. The symbolic Austrian child was above politics. Robust and healthy, the child also came to symbolize in Austria, as elsewhere in Europe, the regenerative powers of war. Taken from the lexicon of turn-of-the-century population politics, tributes to "tomorrow's healthy stock," "the seeds of a new generation," and "the blossom of youth" helped to obscure the fact that the stock of the present was being slaughtered in unprecedented industrial warfare. The idealized child helped make sense out of senselessness by providing the "face of the future" in whose name the war was being waged.

For real children in Vienna, four and a half years of war could not have yielded a bleaker future. Two forces combined to undermine the symbolic "Austrian child." It turned out, of course, that children were not a political *tabula rasa* on whom a united Austrian future could be written. Rather, they had already been implicated in the national and class

---

[1] AdBDW 1917 St./27 #49168. Denunciation from Frau Heinerle, Hausmeisterin, geschrieben von Antonie Milhbauer in Wien, 3. Bezirk.

fragmentation of prewar Vienna, and their participation in *parteiliche* actions continued unabated. For children defending their turf in the streets and schoolyards, war offered new opportunities for neighborhood "heroism." German-speaking children aped the anti-Slavic attitudes of their parents and teachers, and native Viennese children behaved towards the war refugees, fellow Austrians, the same way their parents did, with suspicion and resentment. As political creatures, children proved "particular" rather than "universal." Second, state policies towards children during the war greatly harmed their mental and physical development. Austrian authorities initially saw schools as an effective institution for mobilizing children for war, but then enacted policies that undermined this very institution. Male teachers were conscripted; the school curriculum was altered to allow schoolchildren to perform thousands of hours of war service for the state; and countless school buildings in Vienna were converted into military hospitals. With the education system effectively gutted, a new rhetoric circulated: war itself was the new teacher, the great *Lehrmeister*, from whom children would learn – if not reading and writing – then character, courage and the virtue of sacrifice. Viennese children's health was similarly sacrificed to the war. At the very highest levels of state, Habsburg military authorities had always ensured that the front had priority over the home front in food allocation. In this calculation, the soldiers of today had to be fed before the soldiers of tomorrow. When we think of the damage World War I inflicted on the human body, Otto Dix's postwar paintings of broken, hobbling veterans, men pieced together with various prosthetic devices come to mind. Images of postwar Austrian children who survived the conditions of near-starvation at home leave a similar impression; in them, we see the loss of a world war registered in individual bodies.

The body also provides one angle from which to understand the experiences and paradoxes of adult men on the home front. Chapter 6 challenged the assumption – promoted by contemporaries and adopted by historians – that front and home front in total war broke down neatly along gender lines, and that the latter was occupied only by women and children. As male diarists and authors explained, the hundreds of thousands of men who spent all or part of the war in Vienna suffered daily scrutiny of their bodies by suspicious neighbors, co-workers and strangers. To be a man in the city was a paradox because the attributes of the new, martial manliness could only be acquired at the front. Although women and children could, and were encouraged to, display sacrifice in the city, for a man to do the same had become something of a conceptual impossibility. One noted prewar attribute of manliness, paternal authority, seemed to evaporate on the home front when the soldiers rolled out to battle.

Viennese journalists and commentators blamed a host of wartime social
maladies – including youth delinquency, theft, vandalism, prostitution
and all manner of "moral decay" – on the absence of "fathers," despite
the presence of "men."

Like average home-front men, the two wartime Emperors had also
faced a crisis of paternal authority. The symbolic imperial paternalism
that had long been a pillar of Habsburg rule was placed under enormous
material stress during the war. The Viennese had penned thousands of
heart-felt petitions to their Emperors, asking for money, guardianships,
medicine, heating supplies and food. Women had leapt out of crowds to
deliver letters to the Emperor's feet; military officers had sent unusual appeals asking for help with family matters. From all directions, the symbolic
father was being asked to provide real material support. Daily encounters with desperate subjects cumulatively diminished the aura of imperial
rule. The unraveling of Habsburg rule can be understood, in part, as the
slow realization among the people that the Emperor could not, in reality,
"provide" for the state family.

By the final year of the war, the duties of *Opferwilligkeit* and *Durchhalten*,
impressed upon civilians since 1914, were thoroughly bankrupt concepts.
The tables had turned, and wide segments of the population came to
fault the state for failing to carry out *its* duties. In the week of June 15,
1918, when the weekly potato ration stood at only $\frac{1}{2}$ kg. per person and
the Austrian Food Office was threatening a further cut in bread rations,
Social Democrat Jakob Reumann blasted the "negligence" of the state,
and insisted that the people had not failed in their duty to hold out.
Rather, the state had taken no precautions to make their *Durchhalten* possible.[2] He made these comments at a council meeting at which municipal
representatives of other political parties similarly held the *Regierung*, by
which they meant the Austrian state, responsible for the "catastrophe" in
Vienna. Councilor Leopold Kunschak likened the proposed cut in bread
rations to an "assassination attempt on the health of the people."[3] For
Kunschak and other members of Mayor Weiskirchner's ruling Christian
Social party, attacks on the Austrian *Regierung* served to deflect blame
for wartime suffering away from the Viennese municipal government.
While we have seen that ordinary letter-writers were not always cognizant
of the distinct layers – neighborhood, municipal, provincial, state and
imperial – that constituted "the government," politicians in the capital

---

[2] Report from Pol. Dir. Wien to MdI, 19 June 1918, on "Gemeinderatsbeschluß zur
Kürzung der Brotration," in Rudolf Neck, *Arbeiterschaft und Staat im Ersten Weltkrieg,
1914–1918*, 2 vols. (Vienna: Europa-Verlag, 1964–68), II, 616.
[3] *Ibid.*, II, 619.

were adamant that Vienna had been betrayed by the Austrian state. Mayor Weiskirchner acknowledged that *Opferwilligkeit* ought still to be emphasized, but noted "there comes a psychological moment at which the carrying capacity of the population is at its end and *Durchhalten* has reached its limit."[4] In the capital, this moment came in mid-June, 1918.

This moment of definitive home-front exhaustion coincided with Austria's collapse on the battlefield. The very same week the bread rationing crisis unfolded in Vienna, the Habsburg Army launched its last offensive at the Piave River on the Italian front. The troops were "undernourished and insufficiently equipped for a major onslaught," and deadly mayhem ensued.[5] At the Piave, the army lost 142,000 men in nine days; this included 11,643 dead and 24,474 prisoners of war.[6] While heavy rains swept away bridges and military equipment on the Piave, tens of thousands of civilians had taken to the streets in Vienna and were plundering the potato fields around the city. Nearly 47,000 male and female workers were on strike, and police contemplated the eventual summons of military assistance. Thus, we see a "convergence of collapse" in both realms of the total war. If we recall the picture postcards from the early war years, depicting soldiers and civilians in harmonious, mutual sacrifice (see plate 1, introduction) the irony of this convergence becomes clear. The split-image postcard from the summer of 1918 would show corpses in the Italian mud, paired with marauding women and youths hauling contraband potatoes.

The deterioration of social relations in Vienna was well advanced, and the governability of the city severely compromised, by the time the Austrian state structure collapsed in the fall. At the level of high politics, the fall of 1918 is remembered for a series of dramatic gestures. Emperor Karl made a last-ditch effort to save his realm, proposing to restructure it as a federal state; ignoring this proposal, national councils were breaking away to declare independence; and German-speaking politicians convened in Vienna to explore the prospects for post-imperial Austria. In the streets of the capital, however, these machinations of high politics failed to attract the attention of the populace. Of the Emperor's manifesto, the Viennese police noted dryly that it had failed to garner interest "among the wide masses of the population." They maintained, by way of explanation, that the people were "only interested in the food situation, and they

---

[4] *Ibid.*, II, 616.
[5] Mark Cornwall, *The Undermining of Austria-Hungary: The Battle for Hearts and Minds* (New York: St. Martin's Press, 2000), 302–3.
[6] Holger Herwig, *The First World War: Germany and Austria-Hungary, 1914–1918* (London: Arnold, 1997), 371.

stand rather indifferent before political events."[7] Of course, indifference on the part of a population to the crumbling of its state was of political significance in its own right.

Of greater immediate interest to many residents in this city preoccupied with "internal enemies" was a new, invisible foe: Spanish influenza. Sporadic cases of the flu had been reported in Vienna in the spring and summer of 1918. The first recorded case of the autumn epidemic was a 25-year-old pregnant woman admitted to Vienna's Allgemeines Krankenhaus on September 8, where she was placed in an overcrowded room and died six days later. In the meantime, seven other women in the room had been infected, including a nurse. Although doctors knew they needed to isolate influenza patients, it took a full month "on account of the given difficulties" before special isolation wards were established.[8] The difficulties included shortages of doctors, wagons to transport the ill, and hospital beds for civilians. The influenza epidemic overburdened the medical infrastructure of the city, which was already under great stress from a near doubling of deaths from tuberculosis between 1914 and 1918.[9] With the outbreak of another communicable disease, panic spread through the population. People were distressed "not only by the danger of the disease itself, but especially on account of the fact that in case of infection, timely medical treatment and necessary care [were] not available."[10] Despite public health measures intended to limit people from congregating in public spaces, 3,927 Viennese died of Spanish influenza in the fall of 1918 and thousands of others fell ill.[11] Thus, many Viennese spent their last few weeks as Habsburg subjects not contemplating lofty questions about the Austrian Staatsidee or the future of the Empire, but combating the flu.

As a political narrative, the civic disintegration of Vienna during World War I ends with a fizzle rather than an explosion. Historians have disagreed about whether a "revolution" took place in Vienna in 1918.[12] The

[7] Memo Pol. Dir. Wien to MdI, 18 October 1918. In Neck, *Arbeiterschaft und Staat*, II, 707.
[8] J. Pal, "Über Grippe," *Wiener medizinische Wochenschrift* 69, no. 2 (1919), 1.
[9] Whereas 6,223 Viennese died of tuberculosis in 1914, the disease claimed 11,741 and 11,581 Viennese lives in 1917 and 1918 respectively. *Die Gemeindeverwaltung der Bundeshauptstadt Wien in der Zeit 1. Juli 1919 bis 31. Dezember 1922 unter dem Bürgermeister Jakob Reumann* (Vienna: Magistrat der Stadt Wien, 1927), 371.
[10] *Amtsblatt der k.k. Reichshaupt- und Residenzstadt Wien* 85 (22 October 1918), 2,066. Report of Gemeinderats-Sitzung of 15 October 1918, Anfrage Angermayer.
[11] Siegfried Rosenfeld, *Die Grippeepidemie des Jahres 1918 in Österreich* (Vienna: Franz Deuticke, 1921), 12.
[12] For thorough review of the historiography on the Austrian revolution, see the Eighteenth Annual Robert A. Kann Memorial Lecture by John W. Boyer, "Silent War and Bitter Peace: The Revolution of 1918 in Austria," *Austrian History Yearbook* 34 (2003), 1–56.

political actors in this study – the women, children and "left at home" men of Vienna – did not rise in revolt to oust their Emperor and declare themselves sovereign. Heads did not roll. At most, a few imperial insignia were torn from officers' uniforms. They did not declare themselves a nation, as French revolutionaries had done, nor did they seize the state in the name of a particular class, as had happened the previous year in Russia. Not even the relatively mild revolution in Berlin in 1918 resembled the situation in Vienna. In Berlin, the class interests of the socialist government that took power corresponded to class-specific consumer protest on the home front that had helped to undermine the legitimacy of the old state. As historian Belinda Davis describes it, a socialist government took power and aimed to provide the "just distribution of material goods and of political power" that "women of lesser means" had been demanding throughout the war.[13] Unlike in Germany, the "revolutionary" government that came to power in Austria transcended class lines; it was a multi-party coalition of socialists, Catholics and German nationalists. Such a coalition reflected the vulnerability felt by German-speaking Austrians at the moment of Habsburg collapse. Even socialists were deeply concerned about the "national" future of Austria and set aside ideological differences in order to "preserve the sinking ship of our common social life."[14] In what might be a revolutionary first, the representatives of German-Austria did not declare themselves a nation, but declared themselves a *part of* another nation.[15]

Regardless of whether we call the transfer of power a revolution, this study has argued throughout that matters of state are not merely proclaimed, they are also *lived*. From the perspective of everyday life in Vienna, the transition in November 1918 from Empire to the Republic of German-Austria was marked by continuity. Where political history records a significant rupture in 1918, the history of everyday life does not. That is to say, life looked much the same after the war ended as before. The food supply to Vienna deteriorated even further after November. In November, German-Austrian authorities had concluded a treaty with Poland that should have provided considerable quantities of potatoes, eggs and meat, "[y]et by December 4, no more than one cartload of eggs had appeared at the frontier."[16] Food deliveries from Hungary were

---

[13] Belinda J. Davis, *Home Fires Burning: Food, Politics, and Everyday Life in World War I Berlin* (Chapel Hill: University of North Carolina Press, 2000), 236.

[14] Socialist Karl Renner quoted in Boyer, "Silent War and Bitter Peace," 25.

[15] The provisional national assembly proclaimed German-Austria a constituent part – *Bestandteil* – of Germany. See S. W. Gould, "Austrian Attitudes Toward Anschluss, October 1918–September 1919," *JMH* 22, no. 3 (1950), 220–31.

[16] David Strong, *Austria (October 1918–March 1919): Transition from Empire to Republic* (New York: Columbia University Press, 1939), 163.

sporadic, and on December 20, 1918, "notice was given that there would be no more supplies forthcoming from Hungary for an indefinite period."[17] It was two years after the war's end before the state began to rescind wartime rationing measures. Bread, milk, lard, potatoes, soap and coal were rationed into the 1920s.[18] Denunciations over food, couched in patriotic language, continued to arrive from "true citizens" and "good Austrians," even though Austria had transformed into a different state. Viennese residents continued the wartime practice of ferreting out "internal enemies," blaming them for the city's social and economic woes. The War Profiteering Office continued operations until 1923.

To claim that the war in Vienna ended with a fizzle rather than an explosion is not to say that the civic disintegration lacked political consequences. Rather, many of Vienna's wartime conflicts were woven, unresolved, into the fabric of political life in the postwar period. For this reason, we might rethink the place of the years 1914–18 in the periodization of Austrian history. Typically, as in this study, the war years are written as the book end of the imperial era. But the acrimony generated during the war also set the tone for bitter struggles over both family "reconstruction" and ethnic community boundaries that were hallmarks of the inter-war period.

Since 1916, when the delinquency scare first broke in the press, Viennese had been deeply convinced that disorder within families was the germ for disorder within society. Restoring "order" – a broad concept encompassing not only familial and social, but also political and economic stability – was the overarching concern of postwar government.[19] Austrians were not alone in the search for order. Other historians have described metaphoric "reconstruction" projects underway across Europe after World War I. These efforts invariably focused on gender: restoring relations between men and women, grappling with women's new public visibility, and mending the bodies and minds of broken men were seen as fundamental to the restoration of order – even civilization – in postwar Europe.[20] In Austrian proposals for "restoring" the family, we see longing for a return to an idealized past, a resurrection of a prewar model of family that entailed putting the sexes back in their proper places. The

---

[17] Strong, *Austria*, 160.   [18] *Die Gemeindeverwaltung der Bundeshauptstadt Wien*, 523–5.
[19] See Helga Embacher, "Der Krieg hat die 'göttliche Ordnung' zerstört! Konzepte und Familienmodelle zur Lösung von Alltagsproblemen, Versuche zur Rettung der Moral, Familie und patriarchalen Gesellschaft nach dem Ersten Weltkrieg," *Zeitgeschichte* 15, no. 9/10 (June/July 1988), 347–63.
[20] See Susan Kingsley Kent, *Making Peace: The Reconstruction of Gender in Interwar Britain* (Princeton: Princeton University Press, 1993); Mary Louise Roberts, *Civilization Without Sexes: Reconstructing Gender in Postwar France, 1917–1927* (Chicago: University of Chicago Press, 1994).

family, the institution just mobilized for war, became the institution from which peacetime rebuilding would originate. As would happen again after the Second World War, "the family not only remained the norm after the war; more than ever it constituted the ideal."[21] While Austria's political parties in 1918 had very different conceptions of what a postwar family would look like, and how its individual members would contribute to the building of a new state, they were in agreement that restored families were the cornerstone of the new Austria.

Traditional family themes emerged most clearly in postwar electoral politics. When Austrian women achieved suffrage in November, 1918, the new political citizens were immediately conceived as citizen-wives and citizen-mothers, and election materials put heavy emphasis on feminine themes. In ways that corresponded to the theoretical sisterhood of the Frauenhilfsaktion Wien, the political parties appealed to Austria's female citizens in their familial capacities as mothers and wives. "Vote well!" the Christian Socials advised women, "It's for you and your children!" The Social Democrats urged, "Mothers!! Think of your dead sons."[22] While much of the immediate postwar family discourse centered on women, commentators also expressed optimism that returning soldiers would restore paternal authority once they integrated back into family life. Down with the shirkers, cowards and genetically unfit men who had haunted the home front; the real men were coming home!

Political and religious tracts instructed returning soldiers that becoming a *civilian* was synonymous with becoming a *family man* again. A socialist pamphlet described for returning POWs the important place they would occupy in family and society: "Your return from the lonely prison of captivity signals a turning point in your lives. You have been granted freedom . . . and with that the energy to be active and to produce for yourselves, for your families, for your class, for the living generation."[23] In 1919, a pastoral letter read aloud in Catholic churches across German-Austria similarly addressed itself to the *Heimkehrer* (homecomers). It admonished them not to despair over the defeat because they had new, pressing duties to fulfill:

[Don't ask:]'What was the point of our heroic battles through five years, of our colossal sacrifices, our loyalty, our persistence; everything was lost, it all collapsed,

---

[21] Irene Bandhauer-Schöffmann and Ela Hornung, "War and Gender Identity: The Experience of Austrian Women, 1945–1950," in David F. Good *et al.* (eds.), *Austrian Women in the Nineteenth and Twentieth Centuries* (Providence/Oxford: Berghahn Books, 1996), 213–33, 229.

[22] Bernhard Denscher (ed.), *Wahljahr 1919* (Vienna: Wiener Stadt- und Landesbibliothek, 1989), 19, 27.

[23] *An die Heimkehrer und Soldaten* (Vienna: Wiener Volksbuchhandlung, 1919), 2.

it was all for nothing!'... You, dear homecomers, are to begin again the sacred, serious duties within the family, of which you are the head. The children, who for too long have been deprived of the strong hand of the father in their upbringing, must again be strictly disciplined. We ask you to lead a true, Christian family life and your home will become paradise.[24]

In these scenarios, the Austrian man was to undergo a transition from soldier back to family man. But for the transition to succeed, for the man to become a "provider" and reassert authority, a certain number of material conditions would have to be in place, and in postwar Vienna, they were not. 1919 and 1920 were years of high unemployment, inflation, food shortage, housing shortage and rising crime, including violent crime committed with weapons brought back from the front. Disorder multiplied and contributed to the very widespread, pessimistic sentiment that the new Austria of six million people, one-third of whom lived in the capital, lacked *Lebensfähigkeit*, or the ability to sustain life.

We have seen that one of the most divisive issues during the war had been the delineation of community boundaries. As the imperial capital of Austria, Vienna had been a cosmopolitan crossroads for locals, Austrian citizens from distant provinces and foreigners. But residents' provincial or local conceptions of "belonging" in Vienna had sometimes conflicted with Vienna's position as imperial capital. That fellow Austrian citizens – Jews, "Czechs" (a term sometimes used to connote all Slavs), Poles and Italians – were branded as outsiders or even enemies in the capital spoke to Vienna's metropolitan provinciality to be sure, but also to the weakness of the Austrian *Staatsidee*. Austria had not generated a patriotism that allowed fellow citizens to feel a connectedness among themselves. Supranational Austria had failed as an "imagined community."

What it generated instead were "expulsion fantasies." In wartime denunciation letters from Vienna, the proposed solution for dealing with a variety of unwanted persons – "foreigners," refugees, shirkers, people with questionable *Gesinnung* – was to physically expel them from the community. In 1914, a writer suggested that the proper treatment for a couple overheard speaking English in public would be a removal to a "concentration camp." Another writer concluded about a Herr Scheitling, a Viennese businessman who was "born Swiss," and had "no religion": "He should not be tolerated in Austria." Of another "alien" – "a gentleman with the name Kudnitsch or Cudnic or something like that" – a writer proposed "expulsion or at least internment." Such dark sentiments continued to surface throughout the war. "Wouldn't it be best," one writer asked in 1916 in reference to an "alleged Romanian," if the

---

[24] "Hirtenbrief," *Wiener Diözesanblatt* 57, no. 21/22 (24 November 1919), 65–9, 66–7.

police "freed Vienna of such a dark existence?" Two years later, a "true patriot" demanded the "removal from Vienna" of Ernst Stein, a "traitor and spy" who should be sent "where he belongs – at the front..., on the gallows, or at least in prison." Women, too, policed the boundaries of community. During the war Christian consumers at the markets had "repeatedly pointed to the need to remove (*abzutransportieren*) the Jewish refugees."[25] These expulsion fantasies reflected residents' deep convictions that some Austrians "belonged" in Vienna and others did not.

The expulsion fantasies of the war years found expression in citizenship laws in the new Republic of German-Austria. Reviewing postwar parliamentary debates on citizenship, historian Margarete Grandner explains that a concerted effort was made (with the agreement of all major parties) that "provisions would have to be made that would make citizenship (*Einbürgerung*) impossible for Jewish refugees in German-Austria."[26] War refugees from Dalmatia, Istria, Galicia and Bukowina would be denied *Heimatberechtigung* (legal domicile) in a local municipality and would have to leave the territory of German-Austria. On September 9, 1919, the Lower Austrian regional government served notice ordering persons without legal domicile to leave the territory of German-Austria within eleven days:

> The exceedingly difficult overall economic condition of German-Austria makes it absolutely necessary to remove those persons from the territory who do not have domicile.
>
> The foodstuffs available to German-Austria for provisioning its own population are completely inadequate...
>
> ... [A]ll one-time subjects (*Angehörigen*) of the Austro-Hungarian Monarchy who do not have domicile in a municipality within German-Austria, who have not been in permanent residence since before August 1, 1914 or who have not since acquired German-Austrian citizenship are required to leave German-Austrian territory by September 20, 1919.
>
> Persons who have not left voluntarily by this date will be summarily... deported.[27]

With this decree, expulsion fantasies became law. Many of those expelled were the sorts of people that had been targeted during the war: refugees, recent immigrants, "Austrians," who in the *einheimische* view had no right to be in Vienna. The decree justified expulsion on the basis of shortages of

[25] AdBDW 1914 St./8 #3471; 1916 St./9 #15745; 1915 St./13 #20,437; St./16 #30,921; 1918 St./18 #54184. Letters to Viennese police. Also Stimmungsbericht, 27 April 1916.

[26] Margarete Grandner, "Staatsbürger und Ausländer: Zum Umgang Österreichs mit den jüdischen Flüchtlingen nach 1918," in Gernot Heiss and Oliver Rathkolb (eds.), *Asyl und Wider Willen: Flüchtlinge in Österreich im europäischen Kontext seit 1914* (Vienna: Ludwig-Boltzmann-Institut, 1995), 60–85, 63.

[27] "Sever-Erlaß" cited in Grandner, "Staatsbürger und Ausländer," 72.

food and other material resources, reflecting the food-centered notions of community that had developed over the preceding five years. Law-enforcement officials had help enforcing this decree from anti-Czech and anti-Semitic street gangs who policed the boundaries of their "German, Christian" community.

The everyday ways in which postwar Vienna was "crippled," to use a metaphor favored by contemporaries, by these legacies inherited from the war years deserves further study. When historians account for the violent, unstable atmosphere in Austria in the 1920s – characterized by riots, street fighting, assassinations, putsches, arson fires and the like – they understandably look back to wartime violence.[28] It is now a common assumption that the political violence of the inter-war years is attributable partly to the *Frontgeist* – the spirit of the front; soldiers who never experienced a "demobilization of the mind" are said to have carried their violent tendencies back into civilian life. To account for the violent political culture of inter-war Central Europe, however, we must also take into consideration the home-front-*geist* – the material desperation, low-level violence, incivility, insults, intolerance, feelings of victimization and willingness to draw quick, arbitrary judgments of who is included in, and excluded from, the "community" (however defined at a particular moment) that characterized World War I Vienna. At the end of World War I, there was no official demobilization for civilians. It is one of the paradoxes of total war that there was no opportunity for civilians to change uniforms and return to "normal life," because they were presumed to have been living normal life all along.

---

[28] Gerhard Botz, *Gewalt in der Politik: Attentate, Zusammenstösse, Putschversuche, Unruhen in Österreich 1918 bis 1938* (Munich: Wilhelm Fink Verlag, 1983), 304, counts 215 deaths and 640 seriously wounded from "political violence" between 1918 and 1933.

Bibliography

ARCHIVAL SOURCES

ARCHIV DER BUNDESPOLIZEI-DIREKTION WIEN (ADBDW)

"St." and "V" files, 1914–1918
Stimmungsberichte
Nachlaß Pamer

ÖSTERREICHISCHES STAATSARCHIV (ÖSTA)

Kriegsarchiv (KA), various
    MKSM Militärkanzlei Seiner Majestät
    MS/I. Weltkrieg Flugschriftensammlung
    KÜ Kriegsüberwachungsamt
    MK/KM Ministerialkommission im Kriegsministerium
    AOK GZNB Armeeoberkommando-Gemeinsames Zentralnachweisbüro
    Mil Kommando Wien
Allgemeine Verwaltungsarchiv (AVA), various
    Ministerium des Innern (MdI) Präsidialakten (Präs.) and "S" series
Archiv der Republik (AdR), various
    k.k. Ministerium für soziale Verwaltung und Volksgesundheit
    Nachlaß Loewenfeld-Russ

NIEDERÖSTERREICHISCHES LANDESARCHIV (NÖLA)

Präsidialakten (Präs.)

HAUS-, HOF-, UND STAATSARCHIV (HHSTA)

Kabinettskanzlei Bittschriften

WIENER STADT- UND LANDESARCHIV (WSLA)

Gemeinderats-Protokolle der Obmänner-Konferenz
Landesgericht Strafsachen

ÖSTERREICHISCHES FILMARCHIV
Alltag in der öst.-ung. Monarchie, rolls 1–6

HOOVER INSTITUTION ARCHIVES
American Relief Administration Collection

NEWSPAPERS

Wiener Stadt- und Landesbibliothek, Zeitungsausschnitt-Sammlung (WSLB
  ZAS)
Amtsblatt der Stadt Wien
Arbeiterinnenblatt
Arbeiterinnen-Zeitung
Arbeiterzeitung
Česká Vídeň
Der Bund
Dělnické Listy
Fremdenblatt
Illustrierte Kronenzeitung
Illustriertes Wiener Extrablatt
Das Interessante Blatt
Kinematographische Rundschau
Der Kinobesitzer
Neue Freie Presse
Neues Frauenleben
Neues Wiener Tagblatt
Oesterreichische Frauen-Zeitung
Österreichischer Komet. Fachblatt für Kinematographie
Pädagogisches Jahrbuch
Reichspost
Verordnungsblatt für den Dienstbereich des k.k. nö. Landesschulrates
Vídeňský Denník
Wiener Diözesanblatt
Wiener Hauswirtschaftliche Rundschau
Wiener Medizinische Wochenschrift

PRIMARY PUBLISHED SOURCES

Almanach des Kriegsjahres 1914–15 der patriotischen Frauen Österreichs. Herausgegeben zu Gunsten des Witwen- und Waisenhilfsfond für die gesamte bewaffnete Macht. Vienna, n.d.
Altmann, Ludwig and Karl Warhanek (eds.), *Das Strafgesetz und die Strafprozeßordnung.* Vienna, 1911.
Amtsblatt der k.k. Reichshaupt- und Residenzstadt Wien, 1914–18.

An die Heimkehrer und Soldaten. Vienna, 1919.

Aus großer Zeit (1914–1916): Ein Kriegs-Lesebüchlein für die Jugend und das Volk. Vienna, 1918.

Baernreither, Joseph M. (ed.), *Die Ursachen, Erscheinungsformen und die Ausbreitung der Verwahrlosung von Kindern und Jugendlichen in Österreich.* Schriften des Ersten Österreichischen Kinderschutzkongresses. 2 vols. Vienna, 1907.

Beck, C. (ed.), *Die Frau und die Kriegsgefangenen.* Nürnberg, 1919.

Bericht über die Tätigkeit des Kriegsfürsorgeamtes während der Zeit von seiner Errichtung bis zum 31. März 1917. Vienna, 1917.

Blasel, Leopold. *Wien. Zum Tode Verurteilt: Eine aktuelle Studie zu den Wahlen in die Konstituante.* Vienna, 1918.

Der Brief Sr. Majestät unseres allergnädigsten Kaisers Franz Joseph I. an die Kinder im Weltkriege. Vienna, 1914–15.

Denkschrift über die von der k.k. Regierung aus Anlaß des Krieges getroffenen Maßnahmen. 4 vols. Vienna, 1918.

Dreizehnter Jahresbericht über die k.k. Staatsrealschule im X. Bezirk in Wien. Vienna, 1915.

Eckardt, Johannes (ed.), *An das Kind des Kriegers: Kriegsbriefe V.* Salzburg, 1914.

Ein Volk klagt an! Fünfzig Briefe über den Krieg. Vienna, 1931.

Ergebnisse der Volkszählung vom 31. Dezember 1910 in der k.k. Reichs-Residenzstadt Wien. Vienna, n.d.

Federn, Paul. *Die Vaterlose Gesellschaft: Zur Psychologie der Revolution.* Leipzig and Vienna, 1919.

Fideles aus dem Hinterland. Vienna, 1918.

Foerster, F. W. *Das österreichische Problem: Vom ethischen und staatspädagogischen Standpunkte.* Vienna, 1916.

Frank, Demophil [pseud.]. *Wien... Taumel–Qual–Erlösung, 1914–1918.* Vienna, 1928.

Die Frauen-Hilfsaktion Wien. Vienna, n.d.

Frauenkriegskalender 1915. Herausgegeben vom Bund österreichischer Frauenvereine. Vienna, 1915.

Fraungruber, Hans. *Aus dem Weltkriege: Ernste und heitere Berichte.* Vienna and Prague, 1916.

Freundlich, Emmy. *Die Industrielle Arbeit der Frau im Kriege.* Vienna, 1918.

Geller, Leo. *Allgemeines bürgerliches Gesetzbuch summt einschlägigen Novellen.* Vienna, 1892.

Die Gemeinde Wien während der ersten Kriegswochen. 1. August bis 22. September 1914. Nach dem vom Bürgermeister Dr. Richard Weiskirchner dem Wiener Gemeinderate erstatteten Bericht zusammengestellt vom Sekretariate der Wiener christsozialen Parteileitung. Vienna, 1914.

Die Gemeindeverwaltung der Bundeshauptstadt Wien in der Zeit 1. Juli 1919 bis 31.Dezember 1922 unter dem Bürgermeister Jakob Reumann. Vienna, 1927.

Göri, Josef and Leo Tumlirz (eds.), *Österreich-ungarisches Kriegslesebuch 1914/17. Als Vorlesebuch für den Schulgebrauch.* Leipzig, 1917.

Golias, Eduard. *Die Kinder und der Krieg. Ernstes und Heiteres aus der Welt der Kleinen.* Vienna, 1915.

Granitsch, Helene. *Kriegsdienstleistung der Frauen.* Vienna, 1915.

Große Kommission des Kaiser-Jubiläumsfondes für Kinderschutz und Jugendfürsorge. Tätigkeitsbericht des Erziehungsrates. Vienna, 1915.

Guttmann, Richard. *Die Kinomenschheit: Versuch einer prinzipiellen Analyse.* Vienna, 1916.

Jahresbericht der Kriegspatenschaft 1917. Vienna, 1918.

Joachim, Johann. *Österreichs Volksernährung im Kriege.* Vienna, 1915.

Jugend- und Kriegerwaisen-Fürsorge. Drei Vorträge gehalten in der Wiener Urania. Vienna, 1917.

Kaiser Karl I. und Kaiserin Zita: Lebensbild für Jugend und Volk. Linz, 1917.

Key, Ellen. *A Century of the Child.* New York, 1909.

Knoll, August M. (ed.), *Kardinal Fr. G. Piffl und der österreichische Episkopat zu sozialen und kulturellen Fragen, 1913–1932.* Vienna, 1932.

Der Krieg und die Frau. Vortrag gehalten von Pfarrer Erich Stöckl in der evang. Stadtkirche A. B. zu Wien am 3. Dezember 1914. Vienna, 1914.

Kriegsarbeit des Vereines "Soziale Fürsorge für erwerblose Frauen und Mädchen unter dem hohen Protektorat der Frau Erzherzogin Marie Valerie" 1914–1916. Vienna, 1916.

Kriegsausstellung Wien 1917. Vienna, 1917.

Kriegszustand. Instruktionen für Polizeiorgane. Vienna, 1914.

Langer, U. *Kettenhandel und preistreiberische Machenschaften.* Vienna, 1917.

Liechtenstein, Eduard von und zu and Rudolf Peerz. *Die Sorge um das kommende Geschlecht: Entwicklungsgedanken über Jugendschutz und Kriegerwaisenfürsorge in Österreich.* Vienna, 1916.

Liszt, Eduard Ritter von. *Der Einfluss des Krieges auf die soziale Schichtung der Wiener Bevölkerung.* Vienna and Leipzig, 1919.

Lowenstein, Heinrich. *Meine Tätigkeit als Gemeinderat 1914–1918.* Vienna, 1919.

Machar, J. S. *The Jail Experiences in 1916.* Translated by P. Selver. Oxford, 1921 (orig. 1919).

Mayreder, Rosa. *Krise der Väterlichkeit.* Vienna, 1928.

Mein Haushalt: Offizielles Organ des Ersten Wiener Consum-Vereines. Vienna, 1914.

Merth, Bernhard. *Ein ernstes Wort an unsere Jugend in der Kriegszeit.* Vienna, 1916.

Mitteilungen der statistischen Abteilung des Wiener Magistrates. Monatsberichte, 1914–1919.

Mitton, G. E. *Austria-Hungary.* London, 1914.

Müller, Anitta. *Ein Jahr Flüchtlingsfürsorge, 1914–15.* Vienna, 1916.

Müller-Guttenbrunn, Adam. *Völkerkrieg! Österreichische Eindrücke und Stimmungen.* Graz, 1915.

———. *Kriegstagebuch eines Daheimgebliebenen: Eindrücke und Stimmungen aus Österreich-Ungarn.* Graz, 1916.

Nordeck zur Rabenau, Ludwig von. *Die Ernährungswirtschaft in Oesterreich.* Berlin, 1918.

Offizieller Katalog der Kriegsausstellung. Vienna, 1916.

Pal, J. "Über Grippe." *Wiener medizinische Wochenschrift* 69, no. 2 (4 January 1919).

Polgar, Alfred. *Hinterland.* Berlin, 1929.

Rosenfeld, Siegfried. *Die Wirkung des Krieges auf die Sterblichkeit in Wien.* Vienna, 1920.

———. *Die Grippeepidemie des Jahres 1918 in Österreich.* Vienna, 1921.

Rothe, Richard. *Die Kinder und der Krieg: Beitrag zur grundlegenden Gestaltung der Ausdruckskultur.* Prague, Vienna, Leipzig, 1915.

Die Schulen Niederösterreichs und die dritte österreichische Kriegsanleihe. Bericht der Anglo-Österreichischen Bank. Vienna, n.d.

Seipel, Ignaz. *Kriegsbriefe: An den Vater des Kriegers.* Salzburg, 1914.

Soldatengrüße aus dem Felde: Feldpostkarten und Briefe unserer Vaterlandsverteidiger an die Illustrierte Kronen-Zeitung. Vienna, 1915.

Staatliche Flüchtlingsfürsorge im Kriege 1914/15. Vienna, 1915.

Statistische Jahrbücher der Stadt Wien. Vienna, 1912, 1918.

Statistische Monatsberichte der Stadt Wien. Vienna, 1914–18.

Staudigl, Oskar (ed.), *Aus grosser Zeit (1914–1916): Ein Kriegs-Lesebüchlein für die Jugend und das Volk.* Vienna, 1918.

Stenographische Protokolle über die Sitzungen des Hauses der Abgeordneten. Vienna, 1917–18.

Stiedl, Franz. *Volkspolizei! Ein Vorschlag für den ethischen, moralischen und kulturellen Wiederaufbau.* Vienna, 1918.

Sulík, Josef. *Proč máme vychováti své děti v českých školách?* Vienna, 1914.

Unser Kaiserpaar. Vienna, 1918.

Urban, Gisela. *Österreichisches Kriegs-Kochbuch vom k.k. Ministerium des Inneren überprüft und genehmigt.* Vienna, 1915.

Das Verhalten der Tschechen im Weltkrieg. Die Anfrage der Abg. Schürff, et al. Vienna, 1918.

Volksernährung in Kriegszeiten. Merkblatt, herausgegeben vom k.k. Ministerium des Innern. Vienna, 1915.

Wiens Kinder und Amerika: Die amerikanische Kinderhilfsaktion 1919. Vienna, 1920.

Winkler, Wilhelm. *Die Totenverluste der öst.-ung. Monarchie nach Nationalitäten.* Vienna, 1919.

——. *Die Tschechen in Wien.* Vienna, 1919.

——. *Die zukünftige Bevölkerungsentwicklung Deutschösterreichs und der Anschluss an Deutschland.* Vienna, 1919.

Wir spielen Weltkrieg! Vienna, 1915.

SECONDARY SOURCES

Amann, Klaus and Hubert Lengauer (eds.), *Österreich und der große Krieg, 1914–1918.* Vienna, 1989.

Amato, Joseph A. *Victims and Values: A History and Theory of Suffering.* New York, 1990.

Anderson, Harriet. *Utopian Feminism: Women's Movements in Fin-de-siècle Vienna.* New Haven, 1992.

Audoin-Rouzeau, Stéphane. *Men at War 1914–1918: National Sentiment and Trench Journalism in France during the First World War.* Providence/Oxford, 1992.

——. *La Guerre des enfants, 1914–1918: Essai d'histoire culturelle.* Paris, 1993.

Augeneder, Sigrid. *Arbeiterinnen im Ersten Weltkrieg: Lebens- und Arbeitsbedingungen proletärischer Frauen in Österreich.* Vienna, 1987.

Bachmann, Harald. *Joseph Maria Baernreither, 1845–1925: Der Werdegang eines altösterreichischen Minister und Sozialpolitikers.* Neustadt a.d. Aisch, 1977.

Bandhauer-Schöffmann, Irene and Ela Hornung. "War and Gender Identity: The Experience of Austrian Women, 1945–1950." In David F. Good *et al.* (eds.), *Austrian Women in the Nineteenth and Twentieth Centuries.* Providence/Oxford, 1996.

Becker, Jean-Jacques. *The Great War and the French People.* Translated by Arnold Pomerans. New York, 1986.

Beller, Steven. "The Tragic Carnival: Austrian Culture in the First World War." In Aviel Roshwald and Richard Stites (eds.), *European Culture in the Great War: The Arts, Entertainment, and Propaganda, 1914–1918.* Cambridge, 1999.

Bögl, Günther and Harald Seyrl. *Die Wiener Polizei im Spiegel der Zeiten.* Vienna, 1993.

Botz, Gerhard. *Gewalt in der Politik: Attentate, Zusammenstösse, Putschversuche, Unruhen in Österreich 1918 bis 1938.* Munich, 1983.

Bourke, Joanna. *Dismembering the Male: Men's Bodies, Britain and the Great War.* Chicago, 1996.

Boyer, John W. "Freud, Marriage, and Late Viennese Liberalism: A Commentary from 1905." *JMH* 50 (March, 1978): 72–102.

——. *Political Radicalism in Late Imperial Vienna: Origins of the Christian Social Movement, 1848–1897.* Chicago, 1981.

——. *Culture and Political Crisis in Vienna: Christian Socialism in Power, 1897–1918.* Chicago, 1995.

——. "Silent War and Bitter Peace: The Revolution of 1918 in Austria." *Austrian History Yearbook* 34 (2003): 1–56.

Brix, Emil. *Die Umgangssprachen in Altösterreich zwischen Agitation und Assimilation.* Vienna, 1982.

Brook-Shepherd, Gordon. *The Last Empress: The Life and Times of Zita of Austria-Hungary, 1892–1989.* London, 1991.

Brousek, Karl M. *Wien und seine Tschechen.* Vienna, 1980.

Bruckmüller, Ernst. *Sozialgeschichte Österreichs.* Munich, 1985.

Burger, Hannelore. "Zum Begriff der österreichischen Staatsbürgerschaft: Vom Josephinischen Gesetzbuch zum Staatsgrundgesetz über die allgemeinen Rechte der Staatsbürger." In Thomas Angerer *et al.* (eds.), *Geschichte und Recht: Festschrift für Gerald Stourzh zum 70. Geburtstag.* Vienna, 1999.

de Certeau, Michel. *The Practice of Everyday Life.* Translated by Steven Rendall. Berkeley, 1984.

Coffin, Judith. "A 'Standard' of Living? European Perspectives on Class and Consumption in the Early Twentieth Century." *International Labor and Working-Class History* 55 (1999): 6–26.

Cohen, Gary B. "Neither Absolutism nor Anarchy: New Narratives on Society and Government in Late Imperial Austria." *Austrian History Yearbook* 29 (1998): 37–61.

Cornwall, Mark. "News, Rumour and the Control of Information in Austria-Hungary, 1914–1918." *History* 77, no. 249 (1992): 50–64.

——. "Morale and Patriotism in the Austro-Hungarian Army, 1914–1918." In John Horne (ed.), *State, Society and Mobilization in Europe During the First World War.* Cambridge, 1997.

———. *The Undermining of Austria-Hungary: The Battle for Hearts and Minds.* New York, 2000.

Cott, Nancy F. "Marriage and Women's Citizenship in the United States, 1830–1934." *AHR* 103, no. 5 (December 1998): 1,440–74.

Cozine, Alicia K. "A Member of a State: Citizenship Law and Its Application in Czechoslovakia, 1918–1938." Ph.D. diss., University of Chicago, 1996.

Daniel, Ute. "Women's Work in Industry and Family: Germany 1914–18." In Jay Winter and Richard Wall (eds.), *The Upheaval of War: Family, Work, and Welfare in Europe, 1914–1918.* Cambridge, 1988.

———. "Informelle Kommunikationen und Propaganda in der deutschen Kriegsgesellschaft." In Siegfried Quandt (ed.), *Medien, Kommunikation, Geschichte.* Gießen, 1993.

———. *The War from Within: German Working-Class Women in the First World War.* Translated by Margaret Ries. Oxford, 1997.

Daunton, Martin and Matthew Hilton (eds.), *The Politics of Consumption: Material Culture and Citizenship in Europe and America.* New York, 2001.

Davis, Belinda J. *Home Fires Burning: Food, Politics, and Everyday Life in World War I Berlin.* Chapel Hill, 2000.

Deák, István. "The Habsburg Army in the First and Last Days of World War I: A Comparative Analysis." In B. K. Király and N. F. Dreisiger (eds.), *East Central European Society in World War I.* New York, 1985.

———. *Beyond Nationalism: A Social and Political History of the Habsburg Officer Corps, 1848–1918.* New York, 1992.

Denscher, Bernhard (ed.), *Gold gab ich für Eisen: Österreichische Kriegsplakate, 1914–1918.* Vienna, 1987.

———. *Wahljahr 1919.* Vienna, 1989.

Domansky, Elisabeth. "Militarization and Reproduction in World War I Germany." In Geoff Eley (ed.), *Society, Culture and the State in Germany, 1870–1930.* Ann Arbor, 1996.

Drda, Elgin. "Die Entwicklung der Majestätsbeleidigung in der österreichischen Rechtsgeschichte unter besonderer Berücksichtigung der Ära Kaiser Franz Josephs." Ph.D. diss., University of Linz, 1992.

Dröge, Franz. *Der zerredete Widerstand: Soziologie und Publizistik der Gerüchte im 2. Weltkrieg.* Düsseldorf, 1970.

Ehmer, Josef. "Die Entstehung der 'modernen Familie' in Wien (1780–1930)." In Laszlo Cseh-Szombathy and Rudolf Richter (eds.), *Familien in Wien und Budapest.* Vienna, 1993.

Eksteins, Modris. *Rites of Spring: The Great War and the Birth of the Modern Age.* New York, 1989.

Elshtain, Jean Bethke. *Women and War.* New York, 1987.

———. "Commentary: Political Children." *Childhood: A Global Journal of Child Research* 3, no. 1 (February 1996): 11–28.

Embacher, Helga. "Der Krieg hat die 'göttliche Ordnung' zerstört! Konzepte und Familienmodelle zur Lösung von Alltagsproblemen, Versuche zur Rettung der Moral, Familie und patriarchalen Gesellschaft nach dem Ersten Weltkrieg." *Zeitgeschichte* 15, no. 9/10 (June/July 1988): 347–63.

Engel, Barbara Alpern. "Not by Bread Alone: Subsistence Riots in Russia during World War I." *JMH* 69 (December, 1997): 696–721.

Exner, Franz. *Krieg und Kriminalität in Österreich*. New Haven, 1927.

Fava, Andrea. "War, 'National Education' and the Italian Primary School, 1915–1918." In John Horne (ed.), *State, Society and Mobilization in Europe During the First World War*. Cambridge, 1997.

Feigl, Erich. *Kaiserin Zita*. Vienna, 1977.

Feldbauer, Peter. *Kinderelend in Wien: Von der Armenkinderpflege zur Jugendfürsorge, 17.–19. Jahrhundert*. Vienna, 1980.

Ferro, Marc. *The Great War, 1914–1918*. New York, 1973.

Fitzpatrick, Sheila. "Supplicants and Citizens: Public Letter-Writing in Soviet Russia in the 1930's." *Slavic Review* 55, no. 1 (1996): 78–105.

———. "Signals from Below: Soviet Letters of Denunciation of the 1930s." *JMH* 68, no. 4 (December 1996): 831–66.

———. *Everyday Stalinism: Ordinary Life in Extraordinary Times. Soviet Russia in the 1930's*. New York, 1999.

Fitzpatrick, Sheila and Robert Gellately. "Introduction to the Practices of Denunciation in Modern European History." *JMH* 68, no. 4 (December 1996): 747–67.

Fritz, Walter. *Dokumentarfilme aus Österreich, 1909–1914*. Vienna, 1980.

———. *Kino in Österreich, 1896–1930: Der Stummfilm*. Vienna, 1981.

Führ, Christoph. *Das k.u.k. Armeeoberkommando und die Innenpolitik in Österreich, 1914–1917*. Graz, Vienna, Cologne, 1968.

Fussell, Paul. *The Great War and Modern Memory*. New York, 1975.

Galántai, József. *Hungary in the First World War*. Translated by Éva Grusz and Judit Pokoly. Budapest, 1989.

Geyer, Michael. "War and the Context of General History in an Age of Total War: Comment on Peter Paret, 'Justifying the Obligation of Military Service,' and Michael Howard, 'World War One: The Crisis in European History,'" *Journal of Military History* 57 (October 1993): 145–63.

Glaise-Horstenau, Edmund von *et al.* (eds.), *Österreich-Ungarns letzter Krieg*. 7 vols. Vienna, 1930–38.

Glettler, Monika. *Sokol und Arbeitervereine der Wiener Tschechen bis 1914*. Munich and Vienna, 1970.

———. *Die Wiener Tschechen um 1900: Strukturanalyse einer nationalen Minderheit in der Großstadt*. Munich, 1972.

Glöckel, Otto. *Selbstbiographie: Aus dem Leben eines großen Schulmannes*. Zurich, 1939.

Good, David F. *et al.* (eds.), *Austrian Women in the Nineteenth and Twentieth Centuries*. Providence, 1996.

Gould, S. W. "Austrian Attitudes Toward Anschluss, October 1918–September 1919." *JMH* 22, no. 3 (September 1950): 220–31.

Grandner, Margarete. *Kooperative Gewerkschaftspolitik in der Kriegswirtschaft: Die freien Gewerkschaften Österreichs im Ersten Weltkrieg*. Vienna, 1992.

———. "Staatsbürger und Ausländer: Zum Umgang Österreichs mit den jüdischen Flüchtlingen nach 1918." In Gernot Heiss and Oliver Rathkolb (eds.), *Asylland Wider Willen: Flüchtlinge in Österreich im europäischen Kontext seit 1914*. Vienna, 1995.

Gratz, Gustav and Richard Schüller. *Der wirtschaftliche Zusammenbruch Österreich-Ungarns: Die Tragödie der Erschöpfung*. Vienna, 1930.

Grayzel, Susan R. *Women's Identities at War: Gender, Motherhood, and Politics in Britain and France during the First World War.* Chapel Hill, 1999.

de Grazia, Victoria. *How Fascism Ruled Women: Italy, 1922–1945.* Berkeley and Los Angeles, 1992.

Greenhalgh, Paul. *Ephemeral Vistas: The Expositions Universelles, Great Exhibitions and World's Fairs, 1851–1939.* Manchester, 1988.

Gruber, Helmut. *Red Vienna: Experiment in Working-Class Culture, 1919–1934.* New York and Oxford, 1991.

Hacker, Hanna. "Ein Soldat ist meistens keine Frau." *Österreichische Zeitschrift für Soziologie* 20, no. 2 (1995): 45–63.

Halliday, John. "Satirist and Censor: Karl Kraus and the Censorship Authorities during the First World War." In Sigurd Paul Scheichl and Edward Timms (eds.), *Karl Kraus in neuer Sicht.* Munich, 1988.

Hamann, Brigitte. *Hitler's Vienna. A Dictator's Apprenticeship.* Translated by Thomas Thornton. Oxford, 1999.

Hämmerle, Christa. "'Wir strickten und nähten Wäsche für Soldaten...' Von der Militarisierung des Handarbeitens im Ersten Weltkrieg." *L'Homme: Zeitschrift für Geschichte* 3, no. 1 (1992): 89–128.

——, ed. *Kindheit im Ersten Weltkrieg.* Vienna, 1993.

——. "'Zur Liebesarbeit sind wir hier, Soldatenstrümpfe stricken wir...' Zu Formen weiblicher Kriegsfürsorge im Ersten Weltkrieg." Ph.D. diss., University of Vienna, 1996.

——. "'...wirf ihnen alles hin und schau, daß du fort kommst.' Die Feldpost eines Paares in der Geschlechter(un)ordnung des Ersten Weltkrieges." *Historische Anthropologie* 6, no. 3 (1998): 431–58.

Hanák, Péter. "Die Volksmeinung während des letzten Kriegsjahres in Österreich-Ungarn." In Richard Georg Plaschka and Karlheinz Mack (eds.), *Die Auflösung des Habsburgerreiches: Zusammenbruch und Neuorientierung im Donauraum.* Vienna, 1970.

Hanisch, Ernst. *Der lange Schatten des Staates: Österreichische Gesellschaftsgeschichte im 20. Jahrhundert.* Vienna, 1994.

——. "Die Männlichkeit des Kriegers: Das österreichische Militärstrafrecht im Ersten Weltkrieg." In Thomas Angerer et al. (eds.), *Geschichte und Recht: Festschrift für Gerald Stourzh zum 70. Geburtstag.* Vienna, 1999.

Harmat, Ulrike. "Die Auseinandersetzungen um das Ehescheidungsrecht und die sog. 'Sever-Ehen,' 1918–1938." Ph.D. diss., University of Vienna, 1996.

Hauch, Gabriella. *Frau Biedermeier auf den Barrikaden: Frauenleben in der Wiener Revolution 1848.* Vienna, 1990.

——. *Vom Frauenstandpunkt aus: Frauen im Parlament 1919–1933.* Vienna, 1995.

Hautmann, Hans. "Hunger ist ein schlechter Koch: Die Ernährungslage der österreichischen Arbeiter im Ersten Weltkrieg." In Gerhard Botz et al. (eds.), *Bewegung und Klasse: Studien zur österreichischen Arbeitergeschichte.* Vienna, 1978.

Heiss, Gernot and Oliver Rathkolb (eds.), *Asylland Wider Willen: Flüchtlinge in Österreich im europäischen Kontext seit 1914.* Vienna, 1995.

Herwig, Holger. *The First World War: Germany and Austria-Hungary, 1914–1918.* London, 1997.

Higonnet, Margaret Randolph *et al.* (eds.), *Behind the Lines: Gender and the Two World Wars.* New Haven, 1987.

Hilton, Matthew. "The Female Consumer and the Politics of Consumption in Twentieth-Century Britain." *Historical Journal* 45, 1 (2002): 103–28.

Himka, John-Paul. "Hope in the Tsar: Displaced Naive Monarchism Among the Ukrainian Peasants of the Habsburg Empire." *Russian History/Histoire Russe* 7 (1980).

Hirschfeld, Gerhard *et al.* (eds.), *". . . keiner fühlt sich hier als Mensch." Erlebnis und Wirkung des Ersten Weltkriegs.* Essen, 1993.

Hödl, Klaus. *Als Bettler in die Leopoldstadt: Galizische Juden auf dem Weg nach Wien.* Vienna, 1994.

Hoffmann-Holter, Beatrix. *'Abreisendmachung': Jüdische Kriegsflüchtlinge in Wien 1914–1923.* Vienna, 1995.

Holquist, Peter. "'Information is the Alpha and Omega of Our Work': Bolshevik Surveillance in Its Pan-European Context." *JMH* 69 (September 1997): 415–50.

Holzer, Barbara. "Die Politische Erziehung und der vaterländische Unterricht in Österreich zur Zeit des Ersten Weltkrieges." Diplomarbeit, University of Vienna, 1987.

Horne, John (ed.), *State, Society and Mobilization in Europe During the First World War.* Cambridge, 1997.

Hüppauf, Bernd. "Die Stadt als imaginierter Kriegsschauplatz." *Zeitschrift für Germanistik* 5, no. 2 (1995): 317–35.

Hunt, Lynn. *The Family Romance of the French Revolution.* Berkeley/Los Angeles, 1992.

Jahn, Hubertus F. *Patriotic Culture in Russia During World War I.* Ithaca, 1995.

Jászi, Oskar. *The Dissolution of the Habsburg Monarchy.* Chicago, 1929.

Jelavich, Barbara. *Modern Austria: Empire and Republic, 1815–1986.* Cambridge, 1987.

John, Michael. "'Kultur der Armut' in Wien 1890–1923: Zur Bedeutung von Solidarstrukturen, Nachbarschaft und Protest." *Zeitgeschichte* 20, no. 5/6 (May/June 1993): 158–86.

John, Michael and Albert Lichtblau. "*Česká Vídeň*: Von der tschechischen Großstadt zum tschechischen Dorf." *Archiv 1987: Jahrbuch des Vereins für Geschichte der Arbeiterbewegung.* Vienna, 1987.

Jusek, Karin. *Auf der Suche nach der Verlorenen: Die Prostitutionsdebatten im Wien der Jahrhundertwende.* Vienna, 1994.

Kann, Robert A. *The Multinational Empire: Nationalism and National Reform in the Habsburg Monarchy, 1848–1918.* 2 vols. New York, 1950.

Kann, Robert A. *A History of the Habsburg Empire, 1526–1918.* Berkeley, 1974.

Kapferer, Jean-Nöel. *Rumors: Uses, Interpretations and Images.* Translated by Bruce Fink. New Brunswick, NJ, 1990.

Kenez, Peter. *The Birth of the Propaganda State: Soviet Methods of Mass Mobilization, 1917–1929.* Cambridge, 1985.

Kent, Susan Kingsley. *Making Peace: The Reconstruction of Gender in Interwar Britain.* Princeton, 1993.

King, Jeremy. "Loyalty and Polity, Nation and State: A Town in Habsburg Central Europe, 1848–1948." Ph.D. diss., Columbia University, 1998.

Kocka, Jürgen. *Facing Total War: German Society, 1914–1918.* Leamington Spa, 1984.

Koven, Seth. "Remembering and Dismemberment: Crippled Children, Wounded Soldiers and the Great War in Great Britain." *AHR* 99, no. 4 (October 1994): 1,167–202.

Koven, Seth and Sonya Michel (eds.), *Mothers of a New World: Maternalist Politics and the Origins of Welfare States.* New York, 1993.

Kraus, Karl. *The Last Days of Mankind.* Translated by F. Ungar. New York, 1974.

Krexner, Martin. *Hirte an der Zeitenwende: Kardinal Friedrich Gustav Piffl und seine Zeit.* Vienna, 1988.

Kühne, Thomas. "'...aus diesem Krieg werden nicht nur harte Männer heimkehren,' Kriegskameradschaft und Männlichkeit im 20. Jahrhundert." In Kühne (ed.), *Männergeschichte–Geschlechtergeschichte: Männlichkeit im Wandel der Moderne.* Frankfurt/New York, 1996.

Landwehr, General [Ottokar]. *Hunger: Die Erschöpfungsjahre der Mittelmächte 1917–18.* Zurich, 1931.

Leed, Eric. *No Man's Land: Combat and Identity in World War I.* Cambridge, 1979.

Lehner, Oskar. *Familie–Recht–Politik: Die Entwicklung des österreichischen Familienrechte im 19. und 20. Jahrhundert.* Vienna, 1987.

Lindenberger, Thomas. *Strassenpolitik: Zur Sozialgeschichte der öffentlichen Ordnung in Berlin, 1900–1914.* Bonn, 1995.

Loewenfeld-Russ, Hans. *Die Regelung der Volksernährung im Kriege.* Vienna, 1926.

——. *Im Kampf gegen den Hunger: Aus den Erinnerungen des Staatssekretärs für Volksernährung, 1918–1920.* Vienna, 1986.

Lüdtke, Alf (ed.), *Alltagsgeschichte: Zur Rekonstruktion historischer Erfahrungen und Lebensweisen.* Frankfurt, 1984.

Marwick, Arthur (ed.), *Total War and Social Change.* New York, 1988.

Matauschek, Isabella. "Die dänische Kinderhilfsaktion für Wien, 1919–1938." MA thesis, University of Vienna, 1995.

May, Arthur J. *The Passing of the Hapsburg Monarchy, 1914–1918.* 2 vols. Philadelphia, 1966.

Melichar, Peter. "Die Kämpfe merkwürdig Untoter: K.u.k. Offiziere in der Ersten Republik." *Österreichische Zeitschrift für Geschichte* 9, no. 1 (1998).

Mitterauer, Michael. *Historisch-anthropologische Familienforschung: Fragestellungen und Zugangsweisen.* Vienna, 1990.

Mosse, George L. *Fallen Soldiers: Reshaping the Memory of the World Wars.* New York/Oxford, 1990.

Musil, Robert. *The Man Without Qualities.* Translated by Sophie Wilkins. New York, 1994.

Neck, Rudolf. *Arbeiterschaft und Staat im Ersten Weltkrieg, 1914–1918.* 2 vols. Vienna, 1964–68.

—— (ed.). *Österreich im Jahre 1918: Berichte und Dokumente* Munich, 1968.

Nierhaus, Irene. "Die nationalisierte Heimat: Wehrmann und städtische Öffentlichkeit." In Gisela Ecker (ed.), *Kein Land in Sicht: Heimat–weiblich?* Munich, 1997.

Ostler, H. Jürgen. *'Soldatenspielerei'? Vormilitärische Ausbildung bei Jugendlichen in der österreichischen Reichshälfte der Donaumonarchie, 1914–1918.* MA thesis, University of Hamburg, 1990.

Pedersen, Susan. "Gender, Welfare and Citizenship in Britain during the Great War." *AHR* 95, no. 4 (October 1990): 983–1,006.

———. *Family, Dependence and the Origins of the Welfare State in Britain and France, 1914–1945.* Cambridge, 1993.

Pirquet, Clemens von (ed.), *Volksgesundheit im Kriege.* 2 vols. Vienna, 1926.

Plaschka, Richard *et al.* (eds.), *Innere Front: Militärassistenz, Widerstand und Umsturz in der Donaumonarchie 1918.* 2 vols. Munich, 1974.

Rauchensteiner, Manfried. *Der Tod des Doppeladlers: Österreich-Ungarn und der Erste Weltkrieg.* Graz, 1993.

Raulff, Ulrich. "Clio in den Dünsten: Über Geschichte und Gerüchte." In Bedrich Loewenstein (ed.), *Geschichte und Psychologie: Annährungsversuche.* Pfaffenweiler, 1992.

Rearick, Charles. *The French in Love and War: Popular Culture in the Era of the World Wars.* New Haven, 1997.

Rechter, David. "Galicia in Vienna: Jewish Refugees in the First World War." *Austrian History Yearbook* 28 (1997): 113–30.

———. *The Jews of Vienna and the First World War.* London, 2001.

Redlich, Josef. *Österreichische Regierung und Verwaltung im Weltkriege.* Vienna, 1925.

———. *Austrian War Government.* New Haven, 1929.

———. *Emperor Francis Joseph of Austria: A Biography.* New York, 1929.

Riley, Denise. *"Am I That Name?" Feminism and the Category of "Women" in History.* Minneapolis, 1998.

Roberts, Mary Louise. *Civilization Without Sexes: Reconstructing Gender in Postwar France 1917–1927.* Chicago, 1994.

Rosenhaft, Eve. "Women, Gender and the Limits of Political History in the Age of 'Mass' Politics." In Larry Eugene Jones and James Retallack (eds.), *Elections, Mass Politics and Social Change in Modern Germany.* Washington, DC, 1992.

Roshwald, Aviel and Richard Stites (eds.), *European Culture in the Great War: The Arts, Entertainment, and Propaganda, 1914–1918.* Cambridge, 1999.

Rozenblit, Marsha L. *Reconstructing a National Identity: The Jews of Habsburg Austria During World War I.* New York, 2001.

Safrian, Hans and Reinhard Sieder. "Gassenkinder–Straßenkämpfer: Zur politischen Sozialisation einer Arbeitergeneration in Wien, 1900–1938." In Lutz Niethammer and Alexander von Plato (eds.), *"Wir kriegen jetzt andere Zeiten": Auf der Suche nach der Erfahrung des Volkes in nachfaschistischen Ländern.* Berlin, 1985.

Schorske, Carl E. *Fin-de-Siècle Vienna: Politics and Culture.* New York, 1981.

Schulze, Winfried (ed.), *Sozialgeschichte, Alltagsgeschichte, Mikro-Historie.* Göttingen: 1994.

Scott, Joan W. *Gender and the Politics of History.* New York, 1988.

Sieder, Reinhard J. "Behind the Lines: Working-Class Family Life in Wartime Vienna." In Richard Wall and Jay Winter (eds.), *The Upheaval of War: Family, Work and Welfare in Europe, 1914–1918.* Cambridge, 1988.

Sked, Alan. *The Decline and Fall of the Habsburg Empire, 1815–1918.* London, 1989.

Spann, Gustav. "Zensur in Österreich." Ph.D. diss., University of Vienna, 1972.

———."Vom Leben im Krieg: Die Erkundung der Lebensverhältnisse der Bevölkerung Österreich-Ungarns im Ersten Weltkrieg durch die Briefzensur." In Rudolf Ardelt *et al.* (eds.), *Unterdrückung und Emanzipation: Festschrift für Erika Weinzierl zum 60. Geburtstag.* Vienna/Salzburg, 1985.

Stark, Gary D. "All Quiet on the Home Front: Popular Entertainments, Censorship, and Civilian Morale in Germany, 1914–1918." In Frans Coetzee and Marilyn Shevin-Coetzee (eds.), *Authority, Identity and the Social History of the Great War.* Providence, 1995.

Staudinger, Anton. "Die christliche Familie im Krieg." In Klaus Amann and Hubert Lengauer (eds.), *Österreich und der grosse Krieg, 1914–1918.* Vienna, 1989.

Stourzh, Gerald. "Ethnic Attribution in Late Imperial Austria: Good Intentions, Evil Consequences." In Ritchie Robertson and Edward Timms (eds.), *The Habsburg Legacy: National Identity in Historical Perspective.* Edinburgh, 1994.

———. *Die Gleichberechtigung der Nationalitäten in der Verfassung und Verwaltung Österreichs, 1848–1918.* Vienna, 1985.

Strong, David. *Austria (October 1918–March 1919): Transition from Empire to Republic* New York, 1939.

Taylor, A. J. P. *The Habsburg Monarchy, 1809–1918.* New York, 1965.

Taylor, Lynne. "Food Riots Revisited." *Journal of Social History* 30, no. 2 (Winter, 1996): 483–96.

Theweleit, Klaus. *Male Fantasies.* 2 vols. Translated by Stephen Conway. Minneapolis, 1987.

Tichy, Marina. *Alltag und Traum: Leben und Lektüre der Wiener Dienstmädchen um die Jahrhundertwende.* Vienna, 1984.

Timms, Edward. *Karl Kraus, Apocalyptic Satirist: Culture and Catastrophe in Habsburg Vienna.* New Haven, 1986.

Ulrich, Bernd. *Die Augenzeugen: Deutsche Feldpostbriefe in Kriegs- und Nachkriegszeit, 1914–1933.* Essen, 1997.

Unfried, Berthold. "Arbeiterproteste und Arbeiterbewegung in Österreich während des Ersten Weltkrieges." Ph.D. diss., University of Vienna, 1990.

Unowsky, Daniel. "The Pomp and Politics of Patriotism: Imperial Celebrations in Habsburg Austria, 1848–1916." Ph.D. diss., Columbia University, 2000.

Vasari, Emilio. *Zita: Kaiserin und Königin.* Munich/Vienna, 1976.

Verhey, Jeffrey. "Some Lessons of the War: The Discourse on Propaganda and Public Opinion in Germany in the 1920's." In Bernd Hüppauf (ed.), *War, Violence and the Modern Condition.* Berlin/New York, 1997.

Vincent, C. Paul. *The Politics of Hunger: The Allied Blockade of Germany.* Athens, Ohio, 1985.

Vogel, Jacob. "Die Politik des Gerüchts. Soziale Kommunikationen und Herrschaftspraxis in Frühneuzeit und Moderne." *Werkstatt Geschichte* 15 (1996): 3–10

Wall, Richard and Jay Winter (eds.), *The Upheaval of War: Family, Work and Welfare in Europe, 1914–1918.* Cambridge, 1988.

Wank, Solomon. "Some Reflections on the Habsburg Empire and Its Legacy in the Nationalities Question." *Austrian History Yearbook* 28 (1997): 131–46.

——. "The Habsburg Empire." In Karen Barkey and Mark von Hagen (eds.), *After Empire: Multiethnic Societies and Nation-Building. The Soviet Union and the Russian, Ottoman, and Habsburg Empires*. Boulder, 1997.

Wegs, Robert. *Growing Up Working Class: Continuity and Change Among Viennese Youth, 1890–1938*. University Park, PA, 1989.

——. "Youth Delinquency and 'Crime': The Perception and the Reality." *Journal of Social History* 32, no. 3 (Spring 1999): 603–21.

Whalen, Robert Weldon. *Bitter Wounds: German Victims of the Great War, 1914–1939*. Ithaca, 1984.

Winkler, Wilhelm. *Die Einkommensverschiebungen in Österreich während des Weltkrieges*. Vienna, 1930.

Winter, Jay. *Sites of Memory, Sites of Mourning: The Great War in European Cultural History*. Cambridge, 1995.

Winter, Jay and Jean-Louis Robert (eds.), *Capital Cities at War: London, Paris, Berlin 1914–1919*. Cambridge, 1997.

Würgler, Andreas. "Fama und Rumor: Gerücht, Aufruhr und Presse im Ancien Régime." In *Werkstatt Geschichte* 15 (1996): 20–32.

Zaar, Birgitta. "Dem Mann die Politik, der Frau die Familie – die Gegner des politischen Frauenstimmrechtes in Österreich, 1848–1918." *Österreichische Zeitschrift für Politikwissenschaft* 16 (1987): 351–62.

Zöllner, Erich (ed.), *Volk, Land und Staat: Landesbewußtsein, Staatsidee und nationale Fragen in der Geschichte Österreichs*. Vienna, 1984.

Index

Studies in the Social and Cultural History of Modern Warfare

Titles in the series:

1 *Sites of Memory, Sites of Mourning: The Great War in European Cultural History*
Jay Winter
ISBN 0 521 49682 9 (paperback)

2 *Capital Cities at War: Paris, London, Berlin 1914–1919*
Jay Winter and Jean-Louis Robert
ISBN 0 521 57171 5 (hardback) 0 521 66814 X (paperback)

3 *State, Society and Mobilization in Europe during the First World War*
Edited by John Horne
ISBN 0 521 56112 4 (hardback) 0 521 52266 8 (paperback)

4 *A Time of Silence: Civil War and the Culture of Repression in Franco's Spain, 1936–1945*
Michael Richards
ISBN 0 521 59401 4

5 *War and Remembrance in the Twentieth Century*
Edited by Jay Winter and Emmanuel Sivan
ISBN 0 521 64035 0 (hardback) 0 521 79436 6 (paperback)

6 *European Culture in the Great War: The Arts, Entertainment and Propaganda, 1914–1918*
Edited by Aviel Roshwald and Richard Stites
ISBN 0 521 57015 8 (hardback) 0 521 01324 0 (paperback)

7 *The Labour of Loss: Mourning, Memory and Wartime Bereavement in Australia*
Joy Damousi
ISBN 0 521 66004 1 (hardback) 0 521 66974 X (paperback)

8 *The Legacy of Nazi Occupation: Patriotic Memory and National Recovery in Western Europe, 1945–1965*
Pieter Lagrou
ISBN 0 521 65180 8

9 *War Land on the Eastern Front: Culture, National Identity and German Occupation in World War I*
Vejas Gabriel Liulevicius
ISBN 0 521 66157 9

Printed in the United States
101117LV00004B/250-255/A

9 780521 042192